J. César Félix-Brasdefer, Rachel L. Shively (Eds.)
New Directions in Second Language Pragmatics

Trends in Linguistics
Studies and Monographs

Editors
Chiara Gianollo
Daniël Van Olmen

Editorial Board
Walter Bisang
Tine Breban
Volker Gast
Hans Henrich Hock
Karen Lahousse
Natalia Levshina
Caterina Mauri
Heiko Narrog
Salvador Pons
Niina Ning Zhang
Amir Zeldes

Editor responsible for this volume
Chiara Gianollo

Volume 356

New Directions in Second Language Pragmatics

Edited by
J. César Félix-Brasdefer
Rachel L. Shively

ISBN 978-3-11-111644-0
e-ISBN (PDF) 978-3-11-072177-5
e-ISBN (EPUB) 978-3-11-072187-4

Library of Congress Control Number: 2020948391

Bibliographic information published by the Deutsche Nationalbibliothek
The Deutsche Nationalbibliothek lists this publication in the Deutsche Nationalbibliografie; detailed bibliographic data are available on the Internet at http://dnb.dnb.de.

© 2022 Walter de Gruyter GmbH, Berlin/Boston
This volume is text- and page-identical with the hardback published in 2021.
Typesetting: Integra Software Services Pvt. Ltd.
Printing and binding: CPI books GmbH, Leck

www.degruyter.com

Preface

It is with great pleasure that we have edited this book, *New Directions in Second Language Pragmatics*, in honor of our mentor, Andrew D. Cohen. Both editors have known Andrew Cohen since each of us started our graduate work at the University of Minnesota in the late 1990s, in the case of César, and in the early 2000s, in the case of Rachel. It was Andrew Cohen who introduced both of us to cross-cultural and second language (L2) pragmatics, including the learning, teaching, and assessing of speech acts, and the study of indirect meaning, deictic expressions, discourse markers, and variation in pragmatics. His passion for pragmatics and for the teaching and learning of second languages, more generally, inspired us both and set us on our respective career paths in the field of pragmatics.

Andrew D. Cohen is a preeminent scholar in applied linguistics whose pioneering work in the areas of pragmatics, assessment, and language education goes back more than four decades. Over the course of his career, he has held positions at a variety of institutions across the globe, including Associate Professor at Hebrew University in Jerusalem (Israel) and Professor Emeritus at the University of Minnesota (USA), as well as Fulbright Lecturer and Researcher at the Pontifícia Universidade Católica de São Paulo (Brazil) and Visiting Professor at the University of Auckland (New Zealand). Andrew Cohen has been a frequent presenter and keynote speaker at prestigious conferences such as that of the American Association of Applied Linguistics (AAAL) and the International Association of the Teachers of English to Speakers of Other Languages (TESOL). In 2006, Andrew was recognized for his many contributions to the field by being awarded with AAAL's Distinguished Scholarship and Service Award. Further, from 1996 to 2002, Andrew Cohen served as Secretary General of the International Association of Applied Linguistics (AILA), a position that reflects his leadership internationally in the field. Over the course of his years at the University of Minnesota, Andrew Cohen served as the Director of and led various projects for the Center for Advanced Research on Language Acquisition (CARLA), a national Language Resource Center. His work at CARLA focused on a range topics: researching and creating materials and trainings on language strategy use in various contexts; developing and researching a guidebook for study abroad students; collaborating on research at the Concordia Language Villages; and helping create websites for the teaching and learning of pragmatics in Japanese and Spanish and for the learning of grammar strategies in Spanish. This list is just a sampling of Andrew Cohen's many contributions to scholarship and teaching practice in applied linguistics.

As a multilingual speaker of 13 languages, Andrew Cohen's passion for learning languages and, more specifically, pragmatic aspects of those languages has inspired many students, scholars, and conference participants to research pragmatics in L2 contexts. Consistent with his lifelong journey as a polyglot, he is still to this day learning new languages, which include, in addition to English (his native language) the following: Latin, French, Italian, Spanish, Quechua, Aymara, Portuguese, Hebrew, Arabic, German, and Japanese (Cohen 2001). He is currently learning Chinese as his thirteenth language. As a scholar, Andrew Cohen has focused on studying language use in order to inform L2 learning and teaching, as evident in his numerous publications on the topic (e.g., Bachman and Cohen 1998; Boxer and Cohen 2004; Cohen 2005, 2015, 2018a, 2018b). His multilingual experience has impacted key topics in his work, including his influential research on research methods (e.g., verbal reports) to examine cognitive processes during the production of speech acts (Cohen 1994, 1996, 1998, 2011, 2000, 2014, 2015; Cohen and Macaro 2007). His work on language learner strategies was influenced by his 1998 publication (later published as a second edition in 2011), which focused on strategies in learning and using an L2. And in his 2019a article he offers a comprehensive approach for strategy instruction for learning and performing target language pragmatics.

Andrew Cohen's research has also impacted our understanding about researching instruction in L2 pragmatics. His teaching is informed by his research, as evidenced by his and Noriko Ishihara's outstanding co-authored book entitled *Teaching and Learning Pragmatics: Where Language and Culture Meet*, which has been translated into Arabic, Japanese, and Korean, in addition to the original English version (Ishihara and Cohen 2010). Andrew Cohen's teaching contributions to pragmatics have impacted the research of numerous scholars in second language acquisition, L2 pragmatics, and language teachers in various languages (Cohen 1995, 2002; Félix-Brasdefer and Cohen 2012). And with the need to maximize language teaching and learning through technology, Andrew Cohen and colleagues (Noriko Ishihara and Julie M. Sykes) created websites for the teaching and learning of speech acts in Japanese (http://carla.umn.edu/speechacts/japanese/introtospeechacts/index.htm) and Spanish (https://carla.umn.edu/speechacts/sp_pragmatics/home.html; e.g., Sykes and Cohen 2008). Another example of the integration of research and teaching in Andrew Cohen's work is in the Maximizing Study Abroad project. An initiative that spanned a number of years, Andrew Cohen and his colleagues developed a series of self-access instructional guides for study abroad students, study abroad advisers, and language instructors (e.g., Paige, Cohen, Kappler, Chi, and Lassegard 2006). The guidebooks focus on strategies to enhance language and culture learning and provide activities to assist in that pursuit. Andrew Cohen later co-led empirical research with

R. Michael Paige to examine the extent to which the student guide was effective in helping study abroad students improve their intercultural competence and pragmatic abilities (e.g., Paige, Cohen, and Shively 2004; Cohen and Shively 2007). Not only has the research on this project been insightful for the field of language learning in study abroad, the creation of the guidebooks represents a key contribution.

Another area in which Andrew Cohen's work has been influential is in L2 assessment. His work on L2 testing, language learner strategies, and speech act assessment has had a critical impact in the field. While his work has informed much assessment for research purposes, he has also crucially focused on classroom-based assessment practices, an area that has, to date, not received the attention it merits (e.g., Cohen 2019b; Ishihara and Cohen 2010; Salaberry and Cohen 2006). In a recent publication on the topic (Cohen 2019b), Andrew Cohen provided a historical context for assessment in L2 pragmatics and outlined areas where more work is needed, for example, the need to assess knowledge and ability to use prosodic features (e.g., pitch, tempo, voice quality) to express aspects such as tentativeness, politeness, and level of directness.

The various contributions of this book reflect and expand on three of Andrew Cohen's major research areas: learning, teaching, and assessing L2 pragmatics. But the chapters in this book go a step further by refining research methodologies, problematizing central topics in language learning, examining topics in digital environments, and proposing innovative approaches for researching and teaching pragmatics in foreign language and study abroad contexts. We hope that with this volume, we both honor Andrew Cohen's legacy in applied linguistics, as well as build on his work by showcasing studies and essays by his colleagues, former students, and friends that suggest new directions in the field of L2 pragmatics.

J. César Félix-Brasdefer and Rachel L. Shively

References

Bachman, Lyle F. & Andrew D. Cohen (eds.). 1998. *Interfaces between second language acquisition and language testing research*. Cambridge: Cambridge University Press.
Boxer, Diana & Andrew D. Cohen. 2004. *Studying speaking to inform second language learning*. Clevedon: Multilingual Matters.
Cohen, Andrew D. 1994. Verbal reports on learning strategies. In Alister Cumming (eds.), *Alternatives in TESOL research: Descriptive, interpretive, and ideological orientations*. TESOL Quarterly 28(4). 678–682.

Cohen, Andrew D. 1995. SLA theory and pedagogy: Some research issues. In Fred R. Eckman, Diane Highland, Peter W. Lee, Jean Mileham, & Rita R. Weber (eds.), *Second language acquisition theory and pedagogy*, 219–233. Mahwah, NJ: Lawrence Erlbaum.

Cohen, Andrew D. 1996. Verbal reports as a source of insights into second language learner strategies. *Applied Language Learning* 7(1–2). 5–24.

Cohen, Andrew D. 1998. Strategies and processes in test-taking and SLA. In Lyle F. Bachman & Andrew D. Cohen (eds.), *Interfaces between second language acquisition and language testing research*, 90–111. Cambridge: Cambridge University Press.

Cohen, Andrew D. 2000. Exploring strategies in test-taking: Fine-tuning verbal reports from respondents. In Glayol Ekbatani & Herbert Pierson (eds.), *Learner-directed assessment in ESL*, 127–150. Mahwah, NJ: Lawrence Erlbaum.

Cohen, Andrew D. 2001. From L1 to L12: The confessions of a sometimes frustrated multiliterate. In Diane Belcher & Ulla Connor (eds.), *Reflections on multiliterate lives*, 79–95. Clevedon: UK: Multilingual Matters.

Cohen, Andrew D. 2002. Innovative approaches to language teaching and learning and their impact on the acquisition of Romance languages. In Manel Lacorte & Teresa C. Krastel (eds.), *Romance languages and linguistic communities in the United States*, 59–70. College Park, MD: Latin American Studies Center, University of Maryland.

Cohen, Andrew D. 2005. Strategies for learning and performing L2 speech acts. *Intercultural Pragmatics* 2(3). 275–301.

Cohen, Andrew D. 2011 [1998]. *Strategies in learning and using a second language.* 2nd edn. New York: Pearson/Longman.

Cohen, Andrew D. 2014. Strategies for the super-multilinguals in an increasingly global world. In Bernard Spolsky, Ofra Inbar-Lourie, & Michal Tannenbaum (eds.), *Challenges for language education and policy: Making space for people*, 270–280. New York: Routledge.

Cohen, Andrew D. 2015. Achieving academic control in two Languages: Drawing on the psychology of language learning in considering the past, the present, and prospects for the future. *Studies in Second Language Learning and Teaching* 5(2). 327–345.

Cohen, Andrew D. 2018a. *Learning pragmatics from native and nonnative language teachers.* Bristol: Multilingual Matters.

Cohen, Andrew D. 2018b. Reflections on a career in second language studies: Promising pathways for future research. *L2 Journal* 10(1). 1–19.

Cohen, Andrew D. 2019a. Strategy instruction for learning and performing target language pragmatics. In Anna U. Chamot & Vee Harris (eds.), *Learning strategy instruction in the language classroom: Issues and implementation*, 140–152. Bristol: Multilingual Matters.

Cohen, Andrew D. 2019b. Considerations in assessing pragmatic appropriateness in spoken language. *Language Teaching* 53(2). 183–202.

Cohen A. 1996. Verbal reports as a source of insights into second language learning strategies. *Applied Language Learning* 7(1–2). 5–24.

Cohen, Andrew D. & Ernesto Macaro. (eds.). 2007. *Language learner strategies: Thirty years of research and practices.* Oxford: Oxford University Press.

Cohen, Andrew D. & Rachel Shively. 2007. Acquisition of requests and apologies in Spanish and French: Impact of study abroad and strategy-building intervention. *The Modern Language Journal* 91(2). 189–212.

Félix-Brasdefer, J. César & Andrew D. Cohen. 2012. Teaching pragmatics in the foreign language classroom: Grammar as a Communicative Resource. *Hispania* 95(4). 650–669.

Ishihara, Noriko & Andrew D. Cohen. 2010. *Teaching and learning pragmatics: Where language and culture meet*. Harlow: Pearson.

Paige, R. Michael, Andrew D. Cohen, Barbara Kappler, Julie Chi, & James P. Lassegard.2006. *Maximizing study abroad: A student's guide to strategies for language and culture learning and use* (2nd ed.). Minneapolis: Center for Advanced Research on Language Acquisition, University of Minnesota.

Paige, R. Michael, Andrew D. Cohen, & Rachel Shively. 2004. Assessing the impact of a strategies-based curriculum on language and culture learning abroad. *Frontiers: The Interdisciplinary Journal of Study Abroad* 10. 253–276.

Salaberry, Rafael & Andrew D. Cohen. 2006. Testing Spanish. In Rafael Salaberry & Barbara A. Lafford (eds.), *Spanish second language acquisition: From research findings to teaching applications*, 149–172. Washington, D. C.: Georgetown University Press.

Sykes, Julie M. & Andrew D. Cohen. 2008. L2 pragmatics: Six principles for online materials development and implementation. *Acquisition of Japanese as a Second Language* 11. 81–100.

Tarone, Elaine E., Susan M. Gass, & Andrew D. Cohen. (eds.). 1994. *Research methodology in second language acquisition*. Hillsdale, NJ: Erlbaum.

Acknowledgements

We would like to acknowledge all those who have offered their help in this edited volume. We especially thank all the contributors that made the publication of this volume possible. We would also like to thank the reviewers of the individual chapters for their helpful and constructive comments: Kathleen Bardovi-Harlig, Patricia Bou-Franch, Diana Boxer, Roever Carsten, Lori Czerwionka, Sebastien Dubreil, Marta González-Lloret, Todd Hernández, Tom Holtgraves, Gabriele Kasper, Dale A. Koike, Maria Kogetsidis, Carmen Maíz Arévalo, Troy McConachy, Montserrat Mir, Sabrina Mossman, Mihn Nguyen, Lynn Pearson, María Elena Placencia, Anne Pomerantz, Jon Reinhardt, Steven Ross, Marianna Rychina, Cecilia Sessarego, Rachel Showstack, Yunwen Su, Naoko Taguchi, Xiaofei Tang, Veronika Timpe-Laughlin, Marta Vacas Matos, Soo Jung Youn, and Adam van Compernolle. A special 'thank-you' goes to Chiara Gianollo, Series Editor at Mouton de Gruyter, Barbara Karlson, inhouse-editor, and Suruthi Manogaran, Project Manager, for their advice throughout the publication process and the preparation of this volume. Thanks also to Ivette Dreyer for her careful reading of some chapters of the volume. Last but not least, we thank our families for their patience throughout the conceptualization and realization of this project.

Contents

Preface —— V

Acknowledgements —— XI

List of contributors —— XVII

J. César Félix-Brasdefer and Rachel L. Shively
Introduction —— 1

Part I: Learning and teaching speech acts

J. César Félix-Brasdefer
1   Pragmatic competence and speech-act research in second language pragmatics —— 11

Naoko Taguchi, Loretta Fernández and Yuechun Jiang
2   Systemic functional linguistics applied to analyze L2 speech acts: Analysis of advice-giving in a written text —— 27

Montserrat Mir
3   Learning about L2 Spanish requests abroad through classroom and ethnography-based pragmatics instruction —— 58

Tania Gómez and Luz Ede-Hernandez
4   Effectiveness of a post-study abroad pedagogical intervention in learning compliments and compliment responses in L2 Spanish —— 81

Enrique Rodríguez
5   ¡Madre mía de mi alma!: Pragmalinguistic variation and gender differences in perception of *piropos* in Badajoz, Spain —— 103

Part II: Assessing pragmatic competence

Rachel L. Shively
6   Assessing L2 pragmatic competence —— 131

Carsten Roever and Rod Ellis
7 Testing of L2 pragmatics: The challenge of implicit knowledge —— 142

Nancy Bell, Maria Shardakova and Rachel L. Shively
8 The DCT as a data collection method for L2 humor production —— 156

Steven J. Ross and Qi Zheng
9 Strategic competence and pragmatic proficiency in L2 role plays —— 179

Part III: Analyzing discourses in L2 digital contexts

Julie M. Sykes
10 Researching digital discourse in second language pragmatics —— 197

Megan DiBartolomeo
11 Pragmalinguistic variation in L2 Spanish e-mail requests: Learner strategies and instructor perceptions —— 208

Stephanie W. P. Knight
12 Affordances of game-enhanced learning: A classroom intervention for enhancing concept-based pragmatics instruction —— 236

Part IV: Current issues in L2 pragmatics

Kathleen Bardovi-Harlig
13 Explicit knowledge in L2 pragmatics? —— 255

Diana Boxer and Eleonora Rossi
14 Studying speech acts: An expanded scope and refined methodologies —— 270

Rafael M. Salaberry
15 Converging agendas of rationalist and discursive approaches for the development of a pedagogy of L2 pragmatics —— 286

Noriko Ishihara
16 From a native-nonnative speaker dichotomy to a translingual framework —— 300

Bruce Fraser
17 An introduction to discourse markers —— 314

Elite Olshtain
Epilogue: A personal tribute to Andrew Cohen —— 336

Index —— 339

List of contributors

Kathleen Bardovi-Harlig is Provost Professor of Second Language Studies at Indiana University, USA.

Nancy D. Bell is Associate Professor and ESL Coordinator at Washington State University, USA.

Diana Boxer is Distinguished Teaching Scholar and Professor of Linguistics at the University of Florida, USA.

Megan DiBartolomeo is a doctoral student of Hispanic Linguistics at Indiana University, USA.

Rod Ellis is Research Professor at the School of Education at Curtin University, Australia.

Luz Ede-Hernández is Assistant Professor of Spanish at University of Wisconsin-Whitewater, USA.

Loretta Fernández is Visiting Assistant Professor Foreign Language Education at University of Pittsburgh, USA.

Bruce Fraser is Emeritus Professor of Linguistics and Education at Boston University, USA.

J. César Félix-Brasdefer is Professor of Linguistics and Spanish at Indiana University, USA.

Tania Gómez is Associate Professor of Hispanic Studies at College of Saint Benedict | Saint John's University, USA.

Noriko Ishihara is Professor of Applied Linguistics/EFL at Hosei University, Japan.

Yuechun Jiang is Assistant Professor at Beijing Foreign Studies University, P. R. China.

Stephanie W. P. Knight is Assistant Director at the Center for Applied Second Language Studies, University of Oregon, USA.

Monserrat Mir is Professor of Applied Linguistics and Spanish at Illinois State University, USA.

Elite Olshtain is Emeritus Professor of Language Education at Hebrew University of Jerusalem, Israel.

Enrique Rodríguez is a doctoral student of Hispanic Linguistics at Indiana University, USA.

Carsten Roever is Associate Professor in Applied Linguistics at the University of Melbourne, Australia.

Eleonora Rossi is an Assistant Professor of Linguistics at the University of Florida, USA.

https://doi.org/10.1515/9783110721775-205

Steven Ross is Professor in Second Language Acquisition at the University of Maryland, USA.

Rafael Salaberry is Professor of Spanish Linguistics and Second Language Acquisition at Rice University, USA.

Maria Shardakova is Associate Professor and Russian Language Program Director at Indiana University, USA.

Rachel L. Shively is Associate Professor of Spanish and Applied Linguistics at Illinois State University, USA.

Julie M. Sykes is Associate Professor of Linguistics and Director of the Center for Applied Second Language Studies at the University of Oregon, USA.

Naoko Taguchi is Professor of Applied Linguistics at Northern Arizona University, USA.

Qi Zheng is a doctoral student in Second Language Acquisition at the University of Maryland, USA.

J. César Félix-Brasdefer and Rachel L. Shively

Introduction

1 Learning, teaching, and assessing pragmatics in L2 contexts

Pragmatics is broadly defined as the study of language use in context from the perspective of speakers (users) and the effects language has on the emotions and attitudes of interlocutors. There are numerous definitions of pragmatics that include cognitive and sociocultural perspectives (see Félix-Brasdefer 2017, 2019a; Huang 2014; Levinson 1983; see also Chapter 1, this volume). Researchers in L2 pragmatics often adopt Crystal's (1997: 301) definition of pragmatics because it comprises both the speaker and the interlocutor: "the study of language from the point of view of users, especially of the *choices* they make, the *constraints* they encounter in using language in *social interaction* and the *effects* their use of language has on *other participants* in the *act of communication*." This definition encompasses both the speaker's production of meaning and the hearer's interpretation of that meaning in communicative settings. It includes both the illocutionary force of a speech act as well as the perlocutionary effects of what is said on the feelings, attitudes, and emotions of the interlocutor during the negotiation of meaning in interaction (Félix-Brasdefer 2019b, Kasper 2006; see also Chapter 1, this volume). For a current overview of the field of pragmatics, including the teaching and learning of pragmatics in face-to-face and digital contexts, see Koike and Félix-Brasdefer (2021).

Second language (L2) pragmatics, also known as Interlanguage Pragmatics (ILP), which began with initial studies published in the early 1970s, focuses on how learners produce and comprehend communicative action in different learning contexts, such as foreign language (FL), study abroad, and domestic immersion. Unlike ILP, which focuses on the *use* of the target language by non-native speakers (NNSs), Bardovi-Harlig (2013) proposed the term 'L2 pragmatics' to refer to the *learning* that occurs in the developing system of one or more learners over time, and in different learning environments. More specifically, L2 pragmatics is concerned with how learners of second (third, fourth) languages develop pragmatic competence over time including the ability to produce speech acts (e.g., apologizing, complimenting, complaining, refusing), the understanding of indirect meaning (e.g., implicature), deixis (e.g., vocatives and reference in pronominal selection), and discourse markers (e.g., *well, so, then* [see Chapter 17, this volume]). A great deal of research in L2 pragmatics has been influenced by Andrew Cohen's work, which goes back to the early 1980s, and addresses a range of topics including speech act description, strategy-use, assessment of speech acts, the effects of instruction on the learning of pragmatics, and the instruction of pragmatics by native and nonnative language teachers (Cohen 2018a, 2018b; Ishihara & Cohen 2010). Cohen and Olshtain's seminal work (1981) laid the foundation and set the agenda for examining different aspects of pragmatic knowledge and learning, for refining methodologies and assessment in pragmatics, and for developing pragmatics instruction and pedagogical materials. The various chapters in this volume address and expand on that legacy and on some of these topics.

The chapters in this volume examine current issues and propose future directions related to three key areas in L2 pragmatics: learning, teaching, and assessment. Research on the *learning* of pragmatic competence addresses the learner's ability to understand and produce communicative action over time (longitudinal research) or across proficiency levels (cross-sectional research), and according to the learning context, such as formal (the classroom) or naturalistic (study abroad) (e.g., Bardovi-Harlig, 1999, 2013; Félix-Brasdefer 2017; Kasper and Rose 2002; Pearson and Hasler-Barker 2021; Taguchi 2017). Work on the *teaching* of pragmatics focuses on how instructors can help learners improve their learning of pragmatics through implicit or explicit methods, or a combination of the two (Koike and Pearson 2005; Rose and Kasper 2001; Sessarego 2021). By carrying out pedagogical interventions, we can explore effective ways to assist L2 learners in developing their pragmatic competence, whether that be in the FL classroom or during a study abroad experience (Alcón-Soler 2015; Pérez-Vidal and Shively 2019; Shively 2021). Finally, a third area represented in this volume is the assessment of L2 pragmatic competence (Cohen 2019). By assessing L2 learners, we are able to collect information about what they know about the L2, are able to do with the L2, and have accomplished over a period of time.

This volume brings together varying perspectives in L2 pragmatics to show both historical developments in the field, while also looking towards the future, including theoretical, empirical, and implementation perspectives. Combined, the chapters in this volume focus on various aspects related to the learning, teaching, and assessing of L2 pragmatics and cover a range of learning environments. The authors address current topics in L2 pragmatics such as: speech acts from a discursive perspective; pragmatics instruction in the FL classroom and during study abroad; assessment of pragmatic competence; research methods used to collect pragmatics data; pragmatics in computer-mediated contexts; the role of implicit and explicit knowledge; discourse markers as a resource for interaction; and the framework of translingual practice.

2 Overview of the book

This volume is organized into four sections: Part I, "Learning and teaching speech acts;" Part II, "Assessing pragmatic competence;" Part III, "Analyzing discourses in L2 digital contexts;" and, Part IV, "Current issues in L2 pragmatics." Part I includes five chapters that address various issues related to researching and teaching speech acts. In Chapter 1, "Pragmatic competence and speech-act research in second language pragmatics," Félix-Brasdefer discusses three key topics in the L2 pragmatics literature with regard to speech act production and comprehension: pragmatic competence, speech acts in interaction, and the instruction of speech acts. Using a pragmatic-discursive approach, the author examines the learning and teaching of speech acts at the discourse level in various intercultural contexts. The second chapter in the volume, "Systemic functional linguistics applied to analyze L2 speech acts: Analysis of advice-giving in a written text," explores the application of systemic functional linguistics to the analysis of advice-giving in written texts among Chinese students studying English at a university in Beijing. The learners completed a writing task in which they read a personal problem described by a hypothetical peer and provided advice to the peer in writing. In their analysis of learners' advice-giving texts, Taguchi, Fernandez, and Jiang examine both the use of pragmalinguistic resources as well as how participants discursively constructed their advice, the latter within a systemic functional linguistics framework.

The following two chapters in Part I consider the effects of pedagogical interventions in pragmatics in two different contexts. Chapter 3, "Learning about L2 Spanish requests abroad through classroom and ethnography-based pragmatics instruction," investigates the impact of a pedagogical intervention on the learning of Spanish requests during a short-term study-abroad program. As Mir argues, the results from this study suggest not only that pragmatic development can occur during short stays abroad, but also that discussion about pragmatics with host families and observation of local people outside of class is a key complement to in-class pragmatics instruction. In a second chapter focused on teaching pragmatics (Chapter 4) and entitled "Effectiveness of a post-study abroad pedagogical intervention in learning compliments and compliment responses in L2 Spanish," Gómez and Ede-Hernandez look at the effects of language learning strategy instruction to teach students how to give and receive compliments. Contrasting with the previous chapter, participants in this study had already studied abroad prior to the pragmatics intervention and were continuing language study in their own country. Performance was measured using a pre- and post-written production task and the instructional treatment included awareness-raising pragmatic strategies, modeling, evaluation, and expansion of student self-directed learning.

Finally, in the last chapter of Part I (Chapter 5), "*¡Madre mía de mi alma!:* Pragmalinguistic variation and gender differences in perception of *piropos* in Badajoz, Spain", Rodríguez examines the production and perception of *piropos* (flirtatious remarks) in the region of Badajoz, Spain. The author used a written production task and a Likert-scale to examine production and perception of *piropos*. In addition to the pragmalinguistic and sociopragmatic norms identified, Rodríguez found gender differences in the perception of *piropos*. This chapter ends with pedagogical implications for the teaching of *piropos* in the classroom and in study abroad contexts.

Turning now to Part II, the four chapters in this section highlight new avenues for L2 pragmatics assessment. In the first chapter (Chapter 6), "Assessing L2 pragmatic competence," Shively provides an overview of key issues and debates in the assessment of L2 pragmatics and sheds light on historical developments in assessment methods. In Chapter 7, "Testing of L2 pragmatics: The challenge of implicit knowledge," Roever and Ellis discuss explicit and implicit L2 pragmatic knowledge and how each is represented in testing. They argue that the distinction between explicit and implicit knowledge should receive more attention in discussions about testing in pragmatics and explore this topic further by examining various testing instruments and the type of L2 pragmatic knowledge that they activate. In the third chapter in this section (Chapter 8), "The DCT as a data collection method for L2 humor production," Bell, Shardakova, and Shively offer an innovative approach to researching L2 humor. While previous research has examined humor qualitatively, these authors discuss the development and pilot-testing of a discourse completion task designed to elicit humor, which may allow researchers to analyze L2 humor quantitatively. The benefits of quantitative analysis include the potential to detect patterns in L2 humor use related to L2 proficiency, cultural and linguistic background, and target language. Ross and Zheng, in the final chapter of Part II, "Strategic competence and pragmatic proficiency in L2 role plays" (Chapter 9), analyze role plays designed for oral proficiency interviews (OPIs) and propose adding aspects of strategic competence to the way that role play tasks on OPIs are assessed. The authors further discuss how performances in role play interactions provide evidence for pragmatic competence. Taken together, the chapters in Part II offer new perspectives on assessing role play performances, encourage us to expand on what is assessed in L2 pragmatics by examining communication in a humorous mode, and suggest that we direct our attention to the types of L2 pragmatic knowledge that we are testing.

Part III shifts to the analysis of digital discourses in L2 pragmatics and includes three chapters. In Chapter 10, "Researching digital discourse in second language pragmatics," Sykes explores the role of digital technologies in L2 pragmatics in two areas: (1) extended content and contexts and (2) research capabilities. The author argues that an essential part of learners' multilingual repertoire are the skills to interact in digital spaces. In her chapter, Sykes discusses ways that L2 learners can develop their pragmatic abilities through exploring specific digital practices. While digital technologies provide content and context for L2 learning, they can also enhance, shape, and change L2 pragmatics research, including digital analytics such as eye-tracking and simulation research. A second chapter addressing the topic of digital contexts is Chapter 11, "Pragmalinguistic variation in L2 Spanish e-mail requests: Learner strategies and instructor perceptions." In this chapter, DiBartolomeo focuses on pragmalinguistic variation in the e-mail requests of second-year Spanish L2 learners and recipients' perception of these requests. The author shows that L2 learners primarily used speaker-oriented requests regardless of the language, and that they tended to employ direct requests regardless of degree of imposition or language. Finally, in the last chapter of this section, "Affordances of game-enhanced learning: A classroom intervention for enhancing concept-based pragmatics instruction" (Chapter 12), Knight proposes the use of game-enhanced learning to complement the conceptual explorations inherent in concept-based pragmatics instruction (CBPI). She establishes the need for learner authentication of language learning by examining the reality of attrition in world language education in the United States. She concludes by providing an example of a pedagogical intervention that involves game-based learning within the CBPI approach.

In the final section of the volume, Part IV, "Current issues in L2 pragmatics," we turn our attention to key topics that touch upon themes in Andrew Cohen's work. These topics include the notion of implicit versus explicit pragmatic knowledge, speech acts and refined methodologies, interactional competence, and the native-nonnative speaker dichotomy. Chapter 13 by Bardovi-Harlig, entitled "Explicit knowledge in L2 pragmatics?," explores the concept of explicit knowledge, an issue that has largely been ignored in L2 pragmatics research. Although the contrast of implicit and explicit knowledge is a consideration in the design of tasks for L2 acquisition research (see also Chapter 7, this volume), considerations of authenticity, consequentiality, and modality have heretofore primarily been the focus when evaluating tasks in L2 pragmatics. Bardovi-Harlig argues that pragmatics research design should take explicit knowledge into account in addition to investigating it directly. In the next chapter, "Studying speech acts: An expanded scope and refined methodologies" (Chapter 14), Boxer and Rossi focus on both theoretical and methodological issues regarding speech acts and methods in pragmatics research. The authors examine three key issues: the scope of speech act research, how that scope has changed over time, and the various methods used to carry out such research. This chapter advances our understanding of speech act processing by discussing methods that can examine the workings of the brain when engaged in speech acts and suggesting how qualitative methods can complement experimental approaches.

The final three chapters of the volume discuss current issues related to discursive pragmatics, translingual practice, and discourse markers. First, adopting a pragmatic-discursive approach, in Chapter 15, "Converging agendas of rationalist and discursive approaches for the development of a pedagogy of L2 pragmatics," Salaberry proposes integrating the considerable knowledge base on teaching L2 pragmatics that has been developed using the principles of a rationalist approach to pragmatics with more recent discursive approaches and a focus on interactional competence. The author examines the theoretical distinction between two sub-constructs related to interactional competence: the local and variable co-construction of knowledge during actual interactions versus the generalizable and stable discourse competence that individuals develop. The author argues that the pedagogical techniques developed on the basis of rationalist pragmatics over the past decades can inform the teaching of L2 interactional competence. Ishihara's chapter "From a native-nonnative speaker dichotomy to a translingual framework" (Chapter 16) also takes stock of traditional concepts in L2 pragmatics, by taking a critical look at the dichotomous categories "native" and "nonnative speaker." The author traces the use of this dichotomy in Andrew Cohen's work and builds on that work to offer an alternative framework: translingual practice. In a translingual framework, as Ishihara describes, languages are viewed as interconnected, not as independent systems in the mind of the multilingual speaker. Rather than viewing multilinguals as having a deficit or as experiencing interference, the focus in this framework is complementary meaning-making practices involving all the languages that the individual speaks. Ishihara offers examples of translingual practice specifically focused on pragmatics. In the last chapter of this section, entitled "An introduction to discourse markers" (Chapter 17), Fraser offers a comprehensive overview of discourse markers, and briefly discusses teaching discourse markers in an L2. Fraser points out that while the second language learner may acquire discourse markers late in the acquisition process, they will encounter them early on and can benefit from becoming familiar with them.

Taken together, the chapters in this volume foreground innovations and new directions in the field of L2 pragmatics while, at the same time, ground their work in the existing literature. Consequently, this volume both highlights where the field of L2 pragmatics has been and offers cutting-edge insights into where it is going in the future.

References

Alcón-Soler, Eva. 2015. Pragmatic learning and study abroad: Effects of instruction and length of stay. *System* 48. 62–74.
Bardovi-Harlig, Kathleen. 1999. Exploring the interlanguage of interlanguage pragmatics: A research agenda for acquisitional pragmatics. *Language Learning* 49. 677–713
Bardovi-Harlig, Kathleen. 2013. Developing L2 pragmatics. *Language Learning* 63(1). 68–86.
Cohen, Andrew D. 2018a. *Learning pragmatics from native and nonnative language teachers*. Bristol: Multilingual Matters.
Cohen, Andrew D. 2018b. Reflections on a career in second language studies: Promising pathways for future research. *L2 Journal* 10(1).1–19.
Cohen, Andrew D. 2019. Considerations in assessing pragmatic appropriateness in spoken language. *Language Teaching* 53(2). 183–202.
Cohen, Andrew D. & Elite Olshtain. 1981. Developing a measure of sociolinguistic competence: The case of apology. *Language Learning* 31. 112–134.
Crystal, David. 1997. *The Cambridge encyclopedia of language* (2nd ed.). Cambridge: Cambridge University Press.
Félix-Brasdefer, J. César. 2017. Interlanguage pragmatics. In Yan Huang (ed.), *The Oxford handbook of pragmatics*, 416–434. Oxford: Oxford University Press.
Félix-Brasdefer, J. César. 2019a. *Pragmática del español: contexto, uso y variación*. New York: Routledge Press.
Félix-Brasdefer, J. César. 2019b. Speech acts in interaction: Negotiating joint action in a second language. In Naoko Taguchi (ed.), *The Routledge handbook of second language pragmatics*, 17–30. New York: Routledge.
Huang, Yan. 2014. *Pragmatics*, 2nd edn. Oxford: Oxford University Press.
Kasper, Gabriele. 2006. Speech acts in interaction: Towards discursive pragmatics. In Kathleen Bardovi-Harlig, J. César Félix-Brasdefer, & Alwiya Omar (eds.). *Pragmatics and language learning* (vol. 11), 281–314. Manoa, HI: Second Language Teaching and Curriculum Center University of Hawaii.
Kasper, Gabriele & Kenneth R. Rose. 2002. *Pragmatic development in a second language*. Malden, MA: Blackwell.
Koike, Dale A. & J. César Félix-Brasdefer (eds.). 2021. *The Routledge handbook of Spanish pragmatics*. New York: Routledge.
Koike, Dale A. & Lynn Pearson. 2005. The effect of instruction and feedback in the development of pragmatic competence. *System* 33. 481–501.
Ishihara, Noriko & Andrew D. Cohen. 2010. *Teaching and learning pragmatics: Where language and culture meet*. Harlow, UK: Pearson.
Levinson, Stephen. 1983. *Pragmatics*. Cambridge: Cambridge University Press.
Pearson, Lynn & Maria Hasler-Barker. 2021. Second language acquisition of Spanish pragmatics. In Dale A. Koike & J. César Félix-Brasdefer (eds.), *The Routledge handbook of Spanish pragmatics*, 423–439. New York: Routledge.
Pérez Vidal, Carmen & Rachel L. Shively. 2019. L2 pragmatic development in study abroad settings. In Naoko Taguchi (ed.), *The Routledge handbook of second language pragmatics*, 355–371. New York: Routledge.
Rose, Kenneth R. & Gabriele Kasper. 2001. *Pragmatics in language teaching*. Cambridge: Cambridge University Press.

Sessarego, Cecilia. 2021. Advances in L2 Spanish pragmatics classroom instruction. In Dale A. Koike & J. César Félix-Brasdefer (eds.), *The Routledge handbook of Spanish pragmatics*, 441–454. New York: Routledge.

Shively, Rachel L. 2021. Pragmatics instruction and assessment in study abroad research. In Dale A. Koike & J. César Félix-Brasdefer (eds.), *The Routledge handbook of Spanish pragmatics*, 501–514. New York: Routledge.

Taguchi, Naoko. 2017. Interlanguage pragmatics: a historical sketch and future directions. In Anne Barron, Yueguo Gu, & Gerard Steen (eds.), *The Routledge handbook of pragmatics*, 153–167. New York: Routledge.

Part I: **Learning and teaching speech acts**

J. César Félix-Brasdefer
1 Pragmatic competence and speech-act research in second language pragmatics

Abstract: Speech act theory has been a predominant research topic in second language pragmatics. This chapter focuses on three key topics in the L2 pragmatics literature with regard to speech act production and comprehension: pragmatic competence, speech acts in interaction, and pragmatic instruction of speech acts. I examine the construct of pragmatic competence from the lens of L2 pragmatics, including ways to expand our understanding of this construct to interactional and intercultural competence. Using a pragmatic-discursive approach, I examine the learning and teaching of speech acts at the discourse level in various intercultural contexts. I conclude this chapter with directions for future research.

Keywords: awareness, pragmatic competence, pragmatic instruction, speech acts, study abroad

1 Introduction

Speech acts have been a predominant research topic in second language (L2) pragmatics since the late 1970s. Early studies include apologies (Cohen and Olshtain 1981; Olshtain and Cohen 1983), complaints (Olshtain and Weinbach 1987), compliments (Wolfson 1981), disagreements (Beebe and Takahashi 1989), requests (Koike 1989; Scarcella 1979; Walters 1979), and pragmatic routines (Coulmas 1981), to name but a few (for a review of L2 speech acts, see Bardovi-Harlig 2010; Félix-Brasdefer 2019a [Ch. 7], 2019b; Kasper and Rose 2002; Pearson and Hasler-Barker 2021). Most research in L2 pragmatics follows Andrew Cohen's contribution to speech act sets, which describes the strategies or semantic formulas that comprise the speech act itself (for a list of taxonomies of speech acts, see Félix-Brasdefer 2019a, Ch. 7 and Ishihara and Cohen 2010, Ch. 4). In addition, Andrew Cohen's work has been paramount in providing language instructors with resources for the teaching of speech acts in the classroom and in study-abroad environments (e.g., Cohen 2016, 2018a, 2018b; Félix-Brasdefer and Cohen 2012; Ishihara and Cohen 2010). However, with the exception of a few studies mentioned in Félix-Brasdefer (2019b) and Kasper (2006a) that take a pragmatic-discursive perspective, most research in L2 pragmatics still focuses on speech act strategies in non-interactive contexts.

In this chapter, I examine three topics in L2 pragmatics with regard to speech act research and language learning: pragmatic competence, speech acts in interaction, and the learning of speech acts as a result of pragmatic instruction. The ability to produce and comprehend speech acts in interaction represents one aspect of the learner's pragmatic competence.

2 Key issues

2.1 Pragmatic competence

What kind of pragmatic knowledge do learners need to develop to communicate effectively in a second language? Researchers in L2 pragmatics generally point to two types of pragmatic knowledge that allow learners to develop pragmatic competence over time (incidental learning) or to improve as a result of pedagogical intervention (for an overview, see Bardovi-Harlig 2001, 2013; Félix-Brasdefer 2017; Kasper and Rose 2002; Taguchi 2017). *Pragmalinguistic competence* refers to knowledge about and performance of the conventions of language use or the linguistic resources available in a given language that convey "particular illocutions" (Leech 1983: 11). It includes knowledge of strategies (e.g., directness, conventional indirectness) and the linguistic and non-linguistic resources (e.g., head nods and gesture, as well as prosodic features such as final intonation, loudness, and duration) used to convey pragmatic meaning. In contrast, *sociopragmatic competence* refers to knowledge about and performance consistent with the social norms in specific situations in a given society, as well as familiarity with assessments of (im)politeness and variables of social power and social distance. For example, to issue a request, learners not only need to know the various lexicogrammatical options available in the grammar (e.g., I need/want a letter of recommendation, Can/could/would you write a letter of recommendation?, I was wondering if you would have time to write a letter of recommendation), they must also have knowledge of the *where/who/when/how* these requests are used in particular situations. For example, they should understand appropriate degrees of directness and indirectness, appropriate degrees of politeness and impoliteness, as well as the sociocultural expectations of when to use a particular request.

In addition to pragmalinguistic and sociopragmatic knowledge, learners of an L2 or more languages must also develop other abilities in interaction: the ability to produce and comprehend speech acts at the discourse level, the ability to understand explicit and indirect meaning (e.g., implicature), the ability to learn the referential and social functions of address forms (deixis) and the sociocultural expectations of the appropriate degrees of (im)politeness, as well as a knowledge of the interactional mechanisms to communicate effectively with users of the target culture. According to Schneider (2017: 317), learners should also develop discourse-oriented macropragmatic competence, that is, "knowing how to behave in interaction" in a variety of formal and informal communicative events.

Following Timpe-Laughlin, Wain, and Schmidgall (2015), pragmatic competence encompasses other abilities, such as discourse (e.g., knowledge of cohesion and coherence) and sociocultural knowledge (e.g., knowledge of the communicative event such as a market transaction), that allow the learner to communicate effectively and appropriately in formal and informal situational contexts. Further, learners also need to develop intercultural competence so as "to interact with 'others', to accept other perspectives to be conscious of their evaluations of difference" (Byram, Nichols, and Stevens 2001: 5). Developing intercultural competence should include knowledge and discussion of cultural topics and global issues with speakers from other cultures. Finally, to expand on their ability to negotiate meaning in interaction, learners should develop interactional competence, which includes the ability to produce and comprehend social action in their sequential context, take turns, interrupt or yield the floor, and the ability to open and close an interaction in various discourse practices (Salaberry and Kunitz 2019; Young 2019). In fact, as noted in Barron (2020), interactional competence "recognises that competence in interactional practices, such as, for instance, repair, topic management and turn-taking, is an integral part of pragmatic competence" (p. 433).

Overall, pragmatic competence is understood as a composite of abilities that allow the intercultural speaker to understand and negotiate different aspects of communication such as speech acts in interaction, address forms in formal and informal situations, and direct and indirect meaning, based on knowledge of the sociocultural expectations of the target culture. It also includes awareness of the contextual factors and the status of participants that are part of the communicative event (social power and social distance, and degree of imposition). Pragmatic competence should also be examined within the field of intercultural communication which focuses on intercultural interaction (Taguchi 2017). Intercultural speakers are able to participate in different discourses such as oral interaction in L2 instructional settings (Félix-Brasdefer 2019a; Pearson and Hasler-Barker 2021; Sessarego 2021), service encounters (Félix-Brasdefer and Placencia 2020; Shively 2011), or computer-mediated discourse in a global world (e.g., Bou-Franch 2021; Félix-Brasdefer and Márquez Reiter forthcoming).

2.2 From utterances to extended sequences in discourse

2.2.1 Speech act theory: Main concepts

This section offers an abbreviated version of speech act theory as a precursor to the negotiation of speech acts in interaction in an L2. While speech act theory (Austin 1962; Searle 1969) was not conceptualized to examine stretches of talk, it provides the foundation for the analysis of speech acts in interaction, such as compliment-response sequences, offer-acceptance, or disagreement sequences. Austin proposed a three-way taxonomy of speech acts: 1. a locutionary act refers to the act of saying something meaningful in the literal sense (referring and predicating); 2. an illocutionary act is performed by saying something that has a conventional force such as informing, ordering, warning, complaining, requesting, and refusing (the speaker's intention); and 3. a perlocutionary act refers to what we achieve "*by* saying something, such as convincing, persuading, deterring, and even, say, surprising or misleading" (Austin 1962: 109 [emphasis in original]). Further, Searle (1969) proposed a set of felicity conditions that must be met before an utterance can be considered successful: the propositional content focuses only on the textual or content (literal meaning); the preparatory conditions emphasize the background circumstances or the prerequisites prior to the execution of the speech act; the sincerity condition reflects the speaker's psychological state; and, the essential condition centers on the illocutionary point of what is said (the speaker's intention). Further, inspired by Austin's original classification of illocutionary acts, Searle (1976) proposed a five-way taxonomy of speech acts: representatives (asserting, describing, reporting), directives (requesting, suggesting, asking questions), commissives (promising, refusing an invitation, taking an oath), expressives (apologizing, blaming, congratulating), and declarations (christening, naming, or declaring a marriage official).

However, researchers in pragmatics should be aware of some caveats when analyzing speech acts: some speech acts may belong to more than one category such as the act of complaining, which may include requests for clarification, assertions, and complaints. Searle's notion of context is cognitive and is restricted to the speaker's contribution without the expectation of the interlocutor's uptake (for additional limitations of speech act theory, see Huang 2017, Ch. 3; Félix-Brasdefer 2019a, Ch. 3; Levinson 2017). Unlike Searle's extension of speech act theory, which focused on the speaker's intention from a cognitive perspective, Austin's conceptualization of speech act theory underscored the importance of communicative action between the speaker and the hearer. He noted that the successful performance of an illocutionary act involves three conditions: securing an uptake, taking effects, and inviting response. First, in order to secure an uptake, the speaker must ensure that the interlocutor understands the pragmatic meaning and force of what is said. This concept opens the door to the analysis of speech acts in interaction because it considers both the speaker's utterances and the interlocutor's response to the utterances (e.g., A: I love your glasses; B: Thank you, I love this brand!). Second, illocutionary acts "take effect" by causing a change in the normal course of events. Third, the majority of illocutionary acts "invite by convention a response or a sequel" (Austin 1962: 117). A response can also be realized through non-verbal actions such as head nods, prosodic features (e.g., low or rising intonation), and gestures. The analysis of the illocutionary act suggests that speech acts are produced and interpreted under specific circumstances by two or more interlocutors, and within a sociocultural context.

Speech act theory makes fundamental contributions to our understanding of extended units of discourse, beyond the traditional analysis of isolated strategies that comprise a speech act. Notions such as uptake, illocutionary force, conventionality, felicity conditions, and indirectness have been adapted to examine a wide range of speech act sequences among native and non-native speakers and in different languages. The uptake of the illocutionary force is crucial to promote joint action among learners in formal and informal contexts, as well as in study abroad contexts during intercultural interaction. Finally, the notion of context should be extended to include both cognitive (shared knowledge) and sociocultural context (situational setting) where the speech event takes place, such as a sales transaction between an English-speaking US student and a Hebrew-speaking Israeli clerk at a supermarket in Jerusalem.

2.2.2 Negotiating joint action in a second language

Most recent research in L2 pragmatics still analyzes speech act strategies from the speaker's perspective and in isolated contexts (see Félix-Brasdefer 2017). Streeck (1980) and Edmonson (1981) were some of the first researchers to focus on the speaker's use of sequential resources to express intended illocutionary force during the co-construction of exchanged verbal messages or sequential actions. Following Kasper's (2006a) discursive perspective and Clark's (1996) approach to the analysis of joint actions, Félix-Brasdefer (2014, 2015, 2019b) proposed an approach for examining joint action at the discourse level in a variety of formal and informal contexts. The aforementioned pragmatic-discursive approach (Kasper 2006a; Félix-Brasdefer 2015, 2019b; see also Salaberry, Chapter 15, this volume) offers methodological resources for examining L2 speech acts in extended discourse.[1] First, it includes concepts and analytical tools from language use in social action (Clark 1996) and Conversation Analysis (CA) (Hutchby and Wooffitt 2008; Sacks, Schegloff, and Jefferson 1974; Schegloff 2007). The aim of CA is to examine talk in interaction: the analysis of sequential organization (e.g., openings, closings, speech act sequences, pre-/post-sequences), the organization of turn-taking in conversation, and preferred and dispreferred actions (e.g., acceptance and disagreement). CA is concerned with how participants co-construct an action sequentially, turn by turn, and how they design their turns to jointly perform communicative action. CA is ideal for examining speech acts in interaction across multiple sequences and multiple turns. For example, researchers in L2 pragmatics have examined social action using not only natural data, but also speech acts in elicited conversation (Taleghani-Nikazm and Huth 2010), as well as role plays to analyze classroom teaching (Félix-Brasdefer 2006, 2018) and L2 pragmatic development across multiple turns, including request sequences (Al-Gahtani and Roever 2012), direction-giving (Lee 2017), and acceptance and refusal sequences in invitation and offer interactions (Félix-Brasdefer 2004; Su and Ren 2017).

The second component of the pragmatic-discursive approach comprises Clark's (1996) joint actions. Clark examines communicative acts performed by at least two participants who engage in joint actions. He uses the concept of *joint activity* to refer to a speech event such as an advising session or a compliment-response. A joint activity is defined by the setting (e.g., a service encounter, student-professor advising session), the participants' roles (e.g., a clerk-customer, student-professor), and the allowable contributions for each activity (e.g., the rights and obligations of the interlocutors during the interaction).

The pragmatic-discursive model focuses on language use in social interaction. For example, it allows the researcher to examine social action in second and foreign language contexts such as invitation-refusal sequences (Félix-Brasdefer 2004; Gass and Houck 1999), directive sequences (Lee 2017), email request sequences (DiBartolomeo, this volume), compliment-response sequences (Hasler-Barker 2016), organizational structure request sequences (Al-Gahtani and Roever 2012, 2018), disagreements in native speaker-learner interactions (Bardovi-Harlig and Salsbury 2004), and advice-giving in written texts (Taguchi, Fernández, and Jiang, this volume). Félix-Brasdefer (2019b) offers an overview of speech acts in interaction including the interactional resources both the speakers and their interlocutors use to achieve common ground. Taguchi et al.

---

1 Kasper (2006a) reviewed previous approaches to the analysis of social action, including differences between rationalists and discursive approaches to speech acts in interaction, including research by conversation analysis (Bilmes 1986; see also Chapter 15, this volume).

(this volume) take a fresh look at written advice-giving sequences at the text level, and focus on individual clauses to examine the interpersonal meaning of the text as an exchange between a person who seeks advice and one who gives advice.

Finally, this approach to the analysis of speech acts in interaction uses data from interactive methods such as open role-plays, elicited conversation, and ethnographic methods such as ordinary conversation, and institutional discourse (Félix-Brasdefer and Hasler-Barker 2017; Koike 2021). The approach can also be used to analyze interactional data in online environments delivered through computer-mediated discourse in synchronous (chat), asynchronous (email), or a multimodal approach that blends oral and written modalities (Facebook, YouTube, Reddit) (Bou-Franch 2021; Herring and Antonopoulos 2015).

2.2.3 L2 speech act research and digital corpora

Speech-act research in L2 pragmatics has been informed by pragmalinguistic descriptions and sociopragmatic norms observed among NSs in cross-cultural and interlanguage discourse. The Cross-Cultural Speech Act Research Project (CCSARP, Blum-Kulka, House, and Kasper 1989) motivated empirical speech-act research in cross-cultural and ILP research. It is an analytical framework for the analysis of speech acts that is based on politeness theory (Brown and Levinson 1987) and a revised version of speech act theory (Bierwisch 1980), which situated the study of speech acts in linguistic communication. Using elicited data from Discourse Completion Tests (DCT) (see Chapters 4 and 8, this volume), Blum-Kulka *et al.* (1989) examined cross-cultural and intra-lingual variation in the realization of requests and apologies in seven countries (Australia, United States, England, Canada, Denmark, Germany, and Israel). As a result of this investigation, most research in ILP contrasted speech-act patterns between L2 learners and NSs of different languages (e.g., Bardovi-Harlig 1999; Félix-Brasdefer 2017; Félix-Brasdefer and Koike 2012; Gass and Houck 1999; Trosborg 1994; Wolfson 1989). Cross-cultural pragmatics, which contrasts speech-act patterns among NSs of different languages, has also influenced our understanding of speech acts in L2 contexts (e.g., Félix-Brasdefer 2008; Márquez Reiter 2000; Ogiermann 2009; Wierzbicka 2003). Finally, descriptions of NS interactions in different languages open the door to examining regional pragmatic variation in different varieties of a language (for an overview of speech acts across varieties of Spanish and English, see Félix-Brasdefer 2021 and Schneider and Placencia 2017, respectively).

There are three websites that offer speech-act descriptions with examples from NSs of different languages and varieties of Spanish. The Center for Advanced

Research on Language Acquisition (CARLA) website, led by Andrew Cohen, features descriptions of six speech acts (apologies, complaints, compliments and responses to compliments, requests, refusals, and expressions of gratitude), with examples from different languages (e.g., English, Spanish, German, Chinese, Japanese, and Hebrew) (https://carla.umn.edu/speechacts/index.html). The Indiana University Pragmatics and Discourse Website (https://pragmatics.indiana.edu/speechacts/index.html) includes descriptions of nine speech acts with examples from English and Spanish (e.g., requests, refusals, threats, promises, invitations, disinvitations, complaints, compliments, and advice) (Félix-Brasdefer 2020). Finally, the Multimodal Corpus of Spanish speech acts "Corpus Español Multimodal de Actos de Habla" (https://coremah-1a37f.firebaseapp.com/) includes descriptions of apologies, compliments, and refusals with elicited data from NSs from Spain and learners of Spanish at the intermediate and advanced levels. The NSs role-play situations (audio and video) offer excellent descriptions of pragmalinguistic expressions and sociopragmatic norms among NSs in Spain. Most researchers have collected speech-act data using corpora and elicited methods such as production questionnaires, Likert scales, and role plays (for a recent overview of data collection methods in pragmatics research see Koike [2021]; see also Félix-Brasdefer [2019a], Chapter 10). Overall, instructors should use speech-act descriptions to design lesson plans that raise learners' awareness of regional and situational variation that occurs in interactions with speakers in intercultural contexts. The following section offers an abbreviated review of the effects of pragmatic instruction in formal and informal contexts.

2.3 Teaching speech acts

Pragmatic competence is often late-acquired due to limited authentic pragmatic input in the classroom and limited awareness of differences between the L1 and the L2. There is considerable evidence to support the usefulness of instructional intervention to improve the production and comprehension of speech acts (e.g., Bardovi-Harlig, Mossman, and Vellenga 2015; Cohen 2016; Félix-Brasdefer and Cohen 2012; Hasler-Barker 2016; Kasper and Rose 2002; Sessarego 2021; Taguchi 2015; Taguchi and Roever 2017, Ch. 8). Taguchi (2015) reviewed 95 studies that looked at the effects of pedagogical intervention in L2 pragmatics over the last 30 years of research through explicit and implicit instruction, as well as a description of the methods used to assess pragmatic development as a result of instruction. The aim of explicit instruction is to direct the learner's attention to the pragmatic target (e.g., speech act strategies and internal/external modification) through a variety of awareness-raising activities and metapragmatic explanation. According to interlanguage pragmatics research (Kasper 2001), metapragmatic instruction includes explicit presentation of both pragmalinguistic forms and sociopragmatic norms in social interaction. Ishihara and Cohen (2010) provide a comprehensive overview of examples with lesson plans that can be used to raise awareness of the pragmatic target. Schmidt's (1993, 2001) noticing hypothesis has been used in instructional treatments that consider consciousness, pragmatic function, and contextual features. On the other hand, implicit instruction allows learners to induce the pragmalinguistic forms and sociopragmatic norms through a variety of input sources such as input enhancement (e.g., underlining, color, or bolding pragmatic features) and implicit feedback (e.g., recasts). Overall, while the instructor monitors the learner's development through metapragmatic explanation and practice, the learner is responsible for noticing the pragmatic forms available in the input through self-discovery of pragmalinguistic forms and sociopragmatic norms.

Research-based pedagogical models of speech acts provide instructors with lesson plans and effective ways to teach pragmatics in the classroom. For example, Tatsuki and Houck (2010) and Bardovi-Harlig and Mahan-Taylor (2003) offer lesson plans for teaching speech acts at various proficiency levels. Pedagogical models (e.g., Félix-Brasdefer and Cohen 2012; Félix-Brasdefer and Mugford 2017) provide instructors with approaches to the teaching of speech acts in the classroom that include raising awareness of pragmatic features (e.g., speech act strategies), focusing on the role of pragmatic input that students are exposed to in the classroom, teaching grammar as a communicative resource, and structuring communicative practice and feedback. In addition, Félix-Brasdefer (2020) offers online activities to teach speech acts, such as refusals and compliments, that can be used in the FL classroom and in study abroad settings (https://pragmatics.indiana.edu/teaching/index.html). In general, the goal of pedagogical intervention is to raise awareness of pragmalinguistic forms and sociopragmatic norms in interaction, as well as frequent practice and feedback.

A different line of research looks at the effects of pragmatic instruction in study abroad contexts with learners who receive instruction prior to and during exposure to the target culture (e.g., Cohen and Shively 2007; Hernández and Boero 2018; Mir, this volume; Paige et al. 2006; Shively 2010, 2011). Results show that learners who receive instruction improve their ability to produce different speech acts over time. For an in-depth review of L2 pragmatic development in study abroad settings, see Alcón-Soler (2015), Llanes (2021), Pérez Vidal and Shively (2019), and Shively (2021).

In sum, research in L2 pragmatics has consistently shown that pragmatic instruction is more beneficial than no instruction among learners in FL and study abroad contexts. Most studies to date also show that while groups of learners exposed to explicit and implicit instruction both outperformed the learners in the control group who did not receive pragmatic instruction, explicit instruction is generally more beneficial than implicit instruction, with the exception of Koike and Pearson (2005). These findings have been used to incorporate pragmatics in the language curriculum and to propose the development of textbooks for the teaching of pragmatics (for a recent description of ways to incorporate pragmatics in the curriculum, see Sessarego 2021).

3 Conclusion and future directions

This chapter examined three topics frequently discussed in L2 pragmatics: pragmatic competence, speech acts in interaction, and effective ways to deliver pragmatic instruction. The construct of pragmatic competence should be expanded to encompass the learner's ability to negotiate communicative action in written (see Chapter 2, this volume) and oral discourse, computer-mediated discourse (see Chapters 10–12, this volume), as well as the ability to negotiate joint actions in formal and informal contexts. Schneider (2017) argued that pragmatic variation should also be incorporated to the construct of pragmatic competence. Researchers in L2 pragmatics should focus on pragmatic variation, such as regional and social variation (e.g., age, gender). For a recent overview of regional pragmatic variation across varieties of Spanish and English, see Félix-Brasdefer (2021) and Schneider and Placencia (2017). The negotiation of meaning also includes interactional competence, such as competence to understand and produce social action in their sequential context (Kasper 2006b), open and close an interaction, the ability to repair misunderstandings in social interaction, and the ability to deploy interactional resources to co-construct social action across multiple turns (see Salaberry and Kunitz 2019; Young 2019; see also Chapter 15, this volume). According to Taguchi (2017), future research in L2 pragmatics should refine the notion of pragmatic competence to include the negotiation of meaning in intercultural contexts in formal and study abroad contexts.

Following Félix-Brasdefer and Lavin (2009), researchers in L2 pragmatics should further focus on the prosodic resources (e.g., final intonation, loudness, and duration) that learners use to produce and comprehend meaning in learner-NS speaker interactions. For a recent analysis of prosody and pragmatics, see

Escandell-Vidal and Prieto (2021). Finally, future studies should examine the effects of pedagogical intervention by comparing three groups of learners abroad, one receiving explicit instruction, a second receiving implicit instruction, and a third as a control group with no instruction on pragmatics. Specifically, the issue of the modality of instruction – explicit vs. implicit – in study abroad contexts, remains a *research desideratum*.

References

Alcón-Soler, Eva. 2015. Pragmatic learning and study abroad: Effects of instruction and length of stay. *System* 48. 62–74.

Al-Gahtani, Saad & Carsten Roever. 2012. Proficiency and sequential organization of L2 requests. *Applied Linguistics* 33(1). 42–65.

Al-Gahtani, Saad & Carsten Roever. 2018. Proficiency and preference organization in second language refusals. *Journal of Pragmatics* 129. 140–153.

Austin, John, L. 1962. *How to do things with words*. Cambridge, MA: Harvard University Press.

Bardovi-Harlig, Kathleen. 1999. Exploring the interlanguage of interlanguage pragmatics: A research agenda for acquisitional pragmatics. *Language Learning* 49(4). 677–713.

Bardovi-Harlig, Kathleen. 2001. Evaluating the empirical evidence: Grounds for instruction in pragmatics? In Gabriele Kasper & Kenneth Ross (eds.), *Pragmatics in language teaching*, 13–32. Cambridge, UK: Cambridge University Press.

Bardovi-Harlig, Kathleen. 2010. Exploring the pragmatics of interlanguage pragmatics: Definition by design. In Anna Trosborg (ed.), *Pragmatics across languages and cultures*, 219–259. (Handbook of Pragmatics 7). Berlin/Boston: de Gruyter Mouton.

Bardovi-Harlig, Kathleen. 2013. Developing L2 pragmatics. *Language Learning* 63(1). 68–86.

Bardovi-Harlig, Kathleen & Rebecca Mahan-Taylor, Rebecca (eds.). 2003. *Teaching pragmatics*. Washington DC: Office of English Language Programs, U.S. Department of State. https://americanenglish.state.gov/resources/teaching-pragmatics (accessed 5 August 2020).

Bardovi-Harlig, Kathleen, Sabrina Mossman & Heidi E. Vellenga. 2015. The effect of instruction on pragmatic routines in academic discussion. *Language Teaching Research* 19. 324–350.

Bardovi-Harlig, Kathleen & Tom Salsbury. 2004. The organization of turns in the disagreements of L2 learners: A longitudinal perspective. In Diana Boxer & Andrew D. Cohen (eds.), *Studying speaking to inform second language learning*, 199–227. Clevedon, UK: Multilingual Matters.

Barron, Anne. 2020. Developing pragmatic competence in a study abroad context. In Klaus P. Schneider & Elly Ifantidou (eds.), *Developmental and clinical pragmatics*, 429–474. (Handbook of Pragmatics 13). Berlin/Boston: De Gruyter Mouton.

Beebe, Leslie M. & Tomoko Takahashi. 1989. Sociolinguistic variation in face-threatening speech acts: Chastisement and disagreement. In Miriam R. Eisenstein (ed.), *The dynamic interlanguage: Empirical studies in second language variation*, 199–218. New York: Plenum Press.

Bierwisch, Manfred. 1980. Semantic structure and illocutionary force. In John R. Searle, Ferenc Kiefer, & Manfred Bierwisch (eds.), *Speech act theory and pragmatics*, 1–37. Dordrecht: D. Reidel.

Bilmes, Jack. 1986. *Language and behavior*. New York: Plenum.

Blum-Kulka, Shoshana, Juliane House, & Gabriele Kasper. 1989. *Cross-cultural pragmatics: Requests and apologies*. Norwood, NJ: Ablex.

Bou-Franch, Patricia. 2021. Pragmatics and digital discourse in Spanish research. In Dale A. Koike & J. César Félix-Brasdefer (eds.), *The Routledge handbook of Spanish pragmatics*, 533–547. New York: Routledge.

Brown, Penelope & Stephen C. Levinson. 1987. *Politeness: Some universals in language usage*. Cambridge: Cambridge University Press.

Byram, Michael, Adam Nichols, & David Stevens. 2001. *Developing intercultural competence in practice*. Clevedon, UK: Multilingual Matters.

Clark, Herbert H. 1996. *Using language*. Cambridge: Cambridge University Press.

Cohen, Andrew D. 2016. The teaching of pragmatics by native and nonnative language teachers: What they know and what they report doing. *Studies in Second Language Learning and Teaching* 6(4). 561–585.

Cohen, Andrew D. 2018a. *Learning pragmatics from native and nonnative language teachers*. Bristol: Multilingual Matters.

Cohen, Andrew D. 2018b. Reflections on a career in second language studies: Promising pathways for future research. *L2 Journal* 10(1).1–19.

Cohen, Andrew D. & Elite Olshtain. 1981. Developing a measure of sociolinguistic competence: The case of apology. *Language Learning* 31. 112–134.

Cohen, A. D. & Rachel L. Shively. 2007. Acquisition of requests and apologies in Spanish and French: Impact of study abroad and strategy building intervention. *Modern Language Journal* 91. 189–212.

Coulmas, Florian (ed.). 1981. *Conversational routine: Explorations in standardized communication situations and prepatterned speech*. The Hague: Mouton.

Edmonson, Willis. 1981. *Spoken discourse: A model for analysis*. London: Longman.

Escandell-Vidal, Victoria & Pilar Prieto. 2021. Pragmatics and prosody in research on Spanish. In Dale A. Koike & J. César Félix-Brasdefer (eds.), *The Routledge handbook of Spanish pragmatics*, 149–166. New York: Routledge.

Félix-Brasdefer, J. César. 2004. Interlanguage refusals: Linguistic politeness and length of residence in the target community. *Language Learning* 54. 587–653.

Félix-Brasdefer, J. César. 2006. Teaching the negotiation of multi-turn speech acts: Using conversation-analytic tools to teach pragmatics in the classroom. In Kathleen Bardovi-Harlig, J. César Félix–Brasdefer & Alwiya Omar (eds.), *Pragmatics and language learning* (vol. 11), 165–197. Honolulu: Second Language Teaching and Curriculum Center University of Hawaii.

Félix-Brasdefer, J. César. 2008. *Politeness in Mexico and the United States: A contrastive study of the realization and perception of refusals*. Amsterdam/Philadelphia: John Benjamins.

Félix-Brasdefer, J. César. 2014. Speech act sequences. In Klaus Schneider & Anne Barron (eds.), *Pragmatics of discourse*, 323–352. (Handbook of Pragmatics 3). Berlin/Boston: de Gruyter Mouton.

Félix-Brasdefer, J. César. 2015. *The language of service encounters: A pragmatic-discursive approach*. Cambridge: Cambridge University Press.

Félix-Brasdefer, J. César. 2017. Interlanguage pragmatics. In Yan Huang (ed.), *The Oxford handbook of pragmatics*, 416–434. Oxford: Oxford University Press.

Félix-Brasdefer, J. César. 2018. Role plays. In Andreas Jucker, Klaus Schneider, & Wolfram Bublitz (eds.), *Methods in pragmatics*, 305–332. (Handbook of Pragmatics 10). Berlin/Boston: de Gruyter Mouton.

Félix-Brasdefer, J. César. 2019a. *Pragmática del español: contexto, uso y variación*. New York: Routledge.

Félix-Brasdefer, J. César. 2019b. Speech acts in interaction: Negotiating joint action in a second language. In Naoko Taguchi (Ed.), *The Routledge handbook of second language pragmatics*, 17–30. New York: Routledge.

Félix-Brasdefer, J. César. 2020. Teaching speech acts. https://pragmatics.indiana.edu/teaching/index.html (accessed 5 August, 2020).

Félix-Brasdefer, J. César. 2021. Pragmatic variation across varieties of Spanish. In Dale A. Koike & J. César Félix-Brasdefer (eds.), *The Routledge handbook of Spanish pragmatics*, 269–287. New York: Routledge.

Félix-Brasdefer, J. César & Andrew D. Cohen. 2012. Teaching pragmatics in the foreign language classroom: Grammar as a Communicative Resource. *Hispania* 95(4). 650–669.

Félix-Brasdefer, J. C. & Maria Hasler-Barker. 2017. Elicited data. In Anne Barron, Yueguo Gu, & Gerard Steen (eds.), *The Routledge handbook of pragmatics*, 27–40. New York: Routledge.

Félix-Brasdefer, J. César & Dale A. Koike (eds.). 2012. *Pragmatic variation in first and second language contexts: Methodological issues*. Amsterdam: John Benjamins.

Félix-Brasdefer, J. César & Erin Lavin. 2009. Grammar and turn expansion in second language conversations. In Joseph Collentine, Maryellen García, Barbara Lafford, & Francisco Marcos Marín (eds.), *Selected Proceedings of the 11th Hispanic Linguistics Symposium*, 53–67. Somerville, MA: Cascadilla Proceedings Project. http://www.lingref.com/cpp/hls/11/paper2202.pdf (accessed 5 August 2020).

Félix-Brasdefer, J. César & Rosina Márquez Reiter. (forthcoming). Service encounter discourse. In Michael Haugh, Marina Terkourafi, & Daniel Kádár (eds.), *Handbook of sociopragmatics*. Cambridge: Cambridge University Press.

Félix-Brasdefer, J. César & Gerard Mugford. 2017. (Im)politeness: Learning and teaching. In Jonathan Culpeper, Michael Haugh, & Daniel Z. Kádár (eds.), *The Palgrave handbook of linguistic (im)politeness*, 489–516. Basingstoke, UK: Palgrave/McMillan.

Félix-Brasdefer, J. César & María Elena. Placencia (eds.). (2020). *Pragmatic variation in service encounter interactions across the Spanish-speaking world*. New York: Routledge.

Gass, Susan M. & Noel Houck. 1999. *Interlanguage refusals: A cross-cultural study of Japanese-English*. Berlin/Boston: de Gruyter Mouton.

Hasler-Barker, Maria. 2016. Effects of metapragmatic instruction on the production of compliments and compliment responses: learner-learner role play in the foreign language classroom. In Kathleen Bardovi-Harlig & J. César Félix-Brasdefer (eds.), *Pragmatics and language learning* (vol. 14), 125–152. Honolulu: Second Language Teaching and Curriculum Center University of Hawaii.

Hernández, Todd, A. & Paulo Boero. 2018. Explicit intervention for Spanish pragmatic Development during short-term study abroad: An examination of learner request production and cognition. *Foreign Language Annals* 51. 389–410.

Herring, Susan & Jannis Androutsopoulos. 2015. Computer-mediated discourse 2.0. In Deborah Tannen, Heidi E. Hamilton, & Deborah Schiffrin (eds.), *The Handbook of discourse analysis*, 127–151. Malden, MA: Wiley-Blackwell.

Huang, Yan. 2017. *Pragmatics*, 2nd edn. Oxford: Oxford University Press.
Hutchby, Ian & Robin Wooffitt, R. 2008. *Conversation analysis*, 2nd ed. Malden, MA: Polity.
Ishihara, Noriko & Andrew D. Cohen. 2010. *Teaching and learning pragmatics: Where language and culture meet*. Harlow, UK: Pearson.
Kasper, Gabriele. 2006a. Speech acts in interaction: Towards discursive pragmatics. In Kathleen Bardovi-Harlig, J. César Félix-Brasdefer, & Alwiya Omar (eds.). *Pragmatics and language learning* (vol. 11), 281–314. Honolulu: Second Language Teaching and Curriculum Center University of Hawaii.
Kasper, Gabriele. 2006b. Beyond repair: Conversation analysis as an approach to SLA. *Themes in SLA Research* 19. 83–99.
Kasper, Gabriele. 2001. Classroom research on interlanguage pragmatics. In Kenneth Rose & Gabriele Kasper (eds.), *Pragmatics in language teaching*, 33–60. Cambridge: Cambridge University Press.
Kasper, Gabriele & Kenneth R. Rose. 2002. *Pragmatic development in a second language*. Malden, MA: Blackwell.
Koike, Dale A. 1989. Pragmatic competence and adult L2 acquisition: Speech acts and interlanguage. *Modern Language Journal* 73(3). 279–289.
Koike, Dale A. 2021. Research methods for Spanish pragmatics study. In Dale A. Koike & J. César Félix-Brasdefer (eds.), *The Routledge handbook of Spanish pragmatics*, 567–582. New York: Routledge.
Koike, Dale A. & Lynn Pearson. 2005. The effect of instruction and feedback in the development of pragmatic competence. *System* 33. 481–501.
Lee, Ji Hye. 2017. Speech in direction-giving interactions in L2 English. *Korean Journal of Applied Linguistics* 33(2). 51–80.
Leech, Geoffrey. 1983. *Principles of pragmatics*. New York: Longman.
Levinson, Stephen. 2017. Speech acts. In Yan Huang (ed.), *The Oxford handbook of pragmatics*, 199–216. Oxford: Oxford University Press.
Llanes, Àngels. 2021. The impact of study abroad on L2 Spanish pragmatics development. In Dale A. Koike & J. César Félix-Brasdefer (eds.), *The Routledge handbook of Spanish pragmatics*, 485–499. New York: Routledge.
Márquez Reiter, Rosina. 2000. *Linguistic politeness in Britain and Uruguay: A contrastive study of requests and apologies*. Amsterdam/Philadelphia: John Benjamins.
Ogiermann, Eva. 2009. *On apologising in negative and positive politeness cultures*. Amsterdam: John Benjamins.
Olshtain, Elite & Andrew D. Cohen. 1983. Apology: A speech act set. In Nessa Wolfson & Elliot Judd (eds.), *Sociolinguistics and language acquisition*, 18–35. Rowley, MA: Newbury House.
Olshtain, Elite & Liora Weinbach. 1987. Complaints: A study of speech act behavior among native and non-native speakers of Hebrew. In Jeff Verschueren & Marcella Bertucelli-Papi (eds.), *The pragmatic perspective*, 195–208. Amsterdam: John Benjamins.
Paige, R. Michael, Andrew D. Cohen, Barbara Kappler, Julie Chi & James P. Lassegard, J. 2006. *Maximizing study abroad: A student's guide to strategies for language and culture learning and use* (2nd ed.). Minneapolis: Center for Advanced Research on Language Acquisition, University of Minnesota.
Pearson, Lynn & Maria Hasler-Barker. 2021. Second language acquisition of Spanish pragmatics. In Dale A. Koike & J. César Félix-Brasdefer (eds.), *The Routledge handbook of Spanish pragmatics*, 423–439. New York: Routledge.

Pérez Vidal, Carmen & Rachel L. Shively. 2019. L2 pragmatic development in study abroad settings. In Naoko Taguchi (ed.), *The Routledge handbook of second language pragmatics*, 355–371. New York: Routledge.

Sacks, Harvey, Emmanuel Schegloff & Gail Jefferson. 1974. A simplest systematics for the organization of turn-taking in conversation. *Language* 50. 96–735.

Salaberry, M. Rafael & Silvia Kunitz. 2019. *Teaching and testing L2 interactional competence bridging theory and practice*. New York: Routledge.

Scarcella, Robin. 1979. On speaking politely in a second language. In Carlos Yorio, Kyle Perkins, & Jacquelyn Schachter (eds.), *On TESOL '79: The learner in focus*, 275–287. Washington, DC: TESOL.

Schegloff, E. 2007. *Sequence organization in interaction: A primer in conversation analysis*. Cambridge: Cambridge University Press.

Schmidt, Richard. 1993. Consciousness, learning, and interlanguage pragmatics. In Gabriele Kasper & Shoshana Blum-Kulka (eds.), *Interlanguage pragmatics*, 21–42. Oxford: Oxford University Press.

Schmidt, Richard. 2001. Attention. In Peter Robinson (ed.), *Cognition and second language instruction*, 3–32. Cambridge: Cambridge University Press.

Schneider, Klaus P. 2017. Pragmatic competence and pragmatic variation. In Rachel Giora & Michael Haugh (eds.), *Doing pragmatics interculturally: Cognitive, philosophical, and sociopragmatic perspectives*, 315–333. Berlin/Boston: de Gruyter Mouton.

Schneider, Klaus & Maria Elena Placencia. 2017. (Im)politeness and regional variation. In Jonathan Culpeper, Michael Haugh, & Daniel Kádár (Eds.), *The Palgrave handbook of linguistic (im)politeness*, 539–570. London: Palgrave Macmillan.

Searle, John R. 1969. *Speech acts*. London, UK: Cambridge University Press.

Searle, John R. 1976. A classification of illocutionary acts. *Language in Society* 5. 1–23.

Sessarego, Cecilia. 2021. Advances in L2 Spanish pragmatics classroom instruction. In Dale A. Koike & J. César Félix-Brasdefer (eds.), *The Routledge handbook of Spanish pragmatics*, 441–454. New York: Routledge.

Shively, Rachel L. 2010. From the virtual world to the real world: A model of pragmatics instruction for study abroad. *Foreign Language Annals* 43. 105–137.

Shively, Rachel L. 2011. Pragmatic development in study abroad: a longitudinal study on Spanish service encounters. *Journal of Pragmatics* 43(6). 1818–1835.

Shively, Rachel L. 2021. Pragmatics instruction and assessment in study abroad research. In Dale A. Koike & J. César Félix-Brasdefer (eds.), *The Routledge handbook of Spanish pragmatics*, 501–514. New York: Routledge.

Streeck, Jurgen. 1980. Speech acts in interaction: A critique of Searle. *Discourse Processes* 3. 133–154.

Su, Yunwen & Wei Ren. 2017. Developing L2 pragmatic competence in Mandarin Chinese: Sequential realization of requests. *Foreign Language Annals* 50(2). 433–457.

Taguchi, Naoko. 2015. Instructed pragmatics at a glance: Where instructional studies were, are, and should be going. *Language Teaching* 48. 1–50.

Taguchi, Naoko. 2017. Interlanguage pragmatics: a historical sketch and future directions. In Anne Barron, Yueguo Gu, & Gerard Steen (eds.), *The Routledge handbook of pragmatics*, 153–167. London/New York: Routledge.

Taguchi, Naoko & Carsten Roever. 2017. *Second language pragmatics*. Oxford: Oxford University Press.

Taleghani-Nikazm, Carmen & Thorsten Huth. 2010. L2 requests: Preference structure in talk-in-interaction. *Multilingua* 29. 185–202.
Tatsuki Donna H. & Noel Houck. 2010. *Pragmatics: Teaching speech acts*. Alexandria, VA: TESOL.
Timpe Laughlin, Veronika, Jennifer Wain, & Jonathan Schmidgall. 2015. Defining and operationalizing the construct of pragmatic competence: Review and recommendations. *ETS Research Report Series*. 1–43.
Trosborg, Anna. 1994. *Interlanguage pragmatics: Requests, complaints, and apologies*. Berlin/Boston: de Gruyter Mouton.
Walters, Joel. 1979. Strategies for requesting in Spanish and English: Structural similarities and pragmatic differences. *Language Learning* 29. 277–293.
Wierzbicka, Ana. 2003. *Cross-cultural pragmatics: The semantics of human interaction*. Berlin: de Gruyter Mouton.
Wolfson, Nessa. 1981. Invitations, compliments and the competence of the native speakers. *International Journal of Psycholinguistics* 25. 7–22.
Wolfson, Nessa. 1989. *Perspectives: Sociolinguistics and TESOL*. Rowley, MA: Newbury House.
Young, Richard. 2019. Interactional competence and L2 pragmatics. In Naoko Taguchi (ed.), *The Routledge handbook of second language pragmatics*, 93–110. New York: Routledge.

Naoko Taguchi, Loretta Fernández and Yuechun Jiang

2 Systemic functional linguistics applied to analyze L2 speech acts: Analysis of advice-giving in a written text

Abstract: This study explores the application of systemic functional linguistics (SFL) to the analysis of second language (L2) speech acts. We illustrate how SFL helps us go beyond the traditional approach of coding isolated speech act forms by holistically analyzing the meaning making process. Twenty-two Chinese students studying English at a university in Beijing completed a writing task in which they read a personal problem described by a hypothetical peer and provided advice to the peer in writing. Participants' advice-giving texts were analyzed both at the utterance and discourse level. The utterance-level analysis involved a focus on form, coding and categorizing linguistic forms of advice-giving based on the existing coding framework (Martínez Flor 2003). The text-level, SFL-informed analysis involved a focus on meaning, analyzing individual clauses to examine the interpersonal meaning of the text as an exchange between the person who seeks advice and the person who gives advice. The text-level analysis involved two levels. At the lexical-grammatical level, we conducted a Mood analysis, while at the discourse-semantics level we completed an Appraisal analysis. These two approaches generated complementary information about L2 advice-giving ability in a written text.

Keywords: systemic functional linguistics, speech act, advice giving, assessment, pragmatics

1 Introduction

Data analysis methods in L2 pragmatics research have grown rapidly over the last decade. A recent trend has been the gradual shift from a speech-act centric approach to a discursive approach in analyzing L2 pragmatic competence (Cohen 2008; Taguchi and Roever 2017). Recognizing this shift, in this chapter we present an alternative, more discourse-focused approach to analyzing L2 speech acts. We refer to our approach as "alternative" because existing studies have predominantly focused on L2 learners' use of pragmalinguistic strategies and utterance-level forms in a speech act (e.g. using the modal "should" when giving advice). Studies analyzing a speech act in an extended written text are limited. This is a shortcoming in the field because a speech act is achieved not only by using utterance-level forms, but also by using text-level resources that help express intentions. Because utterance and text-level properties together determine the effectiveness of a speech act, both levels combined deserve more attention in L2 pragmatics analyses. Drawing on insights from systemic functional linguistics (SFL), this study illustrates how a text-level analysis can be performed on a speech act of advice-giving. An SFL-based analysis provides insights into the connection between the speech act forms and the discourse-semantic resources employed by the writers to convey their intentions.

Advice-giving essays collected from Chinese learners of English were analyzed both at the utterance- and the text-level. The utterance-level analysis exclusively focused on the forms, coding and categorizing of linguistic strategies used to provide advice. The text-level analysis involved identifying the interpersonal meaning of advice-giving texts as an exchange between the advice-giver and advice-receiver. To achieve this, we combined two levels of SFL analysis: the lexico-grammatical level (Mood analysis) and semantic-discourse level (Appraisal analysis). Unlike the coding approach that exclusively focused on forms, the SFL-based approach emphasized the connection between form and meaning. By comparing these two approaches, we examine how they are complementary to or distinct from one another in analyzing L2 English learners' ability to produce advice.

2 Background

2.1 Analyzing L2 speech acts in the traditional approach

Since the 1990s the field of L2 pragmatics has increasingly focused on how pragmatics can be taught in an L2 and how it can best be examined (Cohen 2004, 2008). Researchers have taken on a variety of units for instruction and analysis, including speech acts, implicatures, routines, interactional competence, speech styles, and address terms. Among these units, speech acts have been the primary focus of a number of studies. In his seminal paper, *Assessing Speech Acts in a Second Language*, Cohen (2004) presented a historical development of speech act tasks that have appeared since the 1980s. By far, discourse completion tests (DCT) and closed role plays have been the most popular (see also Nguyen 2019). Using these tasks, researchers have elicited L2 learners' speech acts and analyzed their linguistic forms. A common analytical method has been to identify linguistic strategies and categorize them using a coding framework (Blum-Kulka, House, and Kasper 1989). Frequencies of different strategy types are compared with those of native speakers to make a judgement about learners' speech act ability.

These tasks and analytical approaches have several limitations (e.g., Culpeper, Mackey, and Taguchi 2018). First, authenticity of language use is questionable in DCTs and closed role plays because they only elicit one-turn responses in an imaginary situation; thus, data do not reveal features of real-life interaction such as turn-taking, sequential organization, and co-construction of meaning. Coding and categorizing speech act strategies also undermine the interactive nature of a speech act, because in a real-life interaction, a speech act is not an individual act, but rather a collaborative act achieved among speakers. These limitations, along with the importance of a discursive approach to speech act analysis, were noted by Cohen (2008: 214):

> . . . . there is increasing interest in moving beyond a traditional approach to focusing on speech act theory and on speech acts in isolation from situated interaction. This new approach is referred to by Kasper (2006) as discursive pragmatics, which entails applying conversation analysis to speech act research.

As this quote shows, the discursive approach helps us move away from the traditional focus on select utterances isolated from discourse and instead examine a speech act in a situated interaction using conversation analysis as a method.

2.2 Analyzing speech acts in the discursive approach

The discursive approach to pragmatics underscores that meaning is fundamentally situated in a social context, arising among participants who are mutually oriented toward their communicative goals (Culpeper, Mackey, and Taguchi 2018). Recent literature has advocated *discursive pragmatics* as an approach to analyzing a speech act in a situated interaction (Kasper 2006). Parallel to this trend, a growing body of studies have adopted conversational analysis (CA) to study L2 speech acts (Félix-Brasdefer 2019; Mori and Nguyen 2019; see also Chapter 1, this volume). CA can reveal how a communicative act emerges in a conversation through sequences of talk, a sequence being a linguistic action co-constructed by participants over multiple turns (Schegloff 2007). From the CA perspective, a shortcoming of the utterance-level analyses of DCTs or role-play data is that they do not consider the meaning that emerges in sequential organization of talk-in-progress. Instead, the analyses focus on meaning in relation to a predetermined, intuition-based taxonomy of behavior, which makes inferences of real-world interactions difficult.

In the last decade, CA has started to show prominence in analyzing L2 speech acts (Taguchi and Roever 2017). For example, Youn (2015) developed CA-informed rating scales to assess L2 speech acts. Analyzing open role play data, Youn identified linguistic and interactional resources that learners used to co-construct a speech act with their interlocutors. Those resources were then used to develop several rating scales. For example, the scale of 'language use' focuses on the use of pragmalinguistic strategies, while the scales of 'contents delivery', 'turn organization', and 'engaging in interaction' address the discourse-level abilities of turn taking and turn construction. These rating criteria underscore the idea that a speech act is a product of extended discourse. Knowledge of isolated pragmalinguistic forms alone does not guarantee a successful speech act performance. Learners' ability to use the knowledge in unfolding interaction is essential for a successful speech act.

While the method of discursive pragmatics is apparent in spoken speech acts with the application of CA or other discourse analytic approaches, the discursive approach has not been used in the analysis of written texts. Speech acts in writing have largely been neglected in research (except for studies using a written DCT to elicit a speech act intended for speech). There are a few exceptions, however, such as Cohen and Tarone's (1994) early study that examined semantic strategies used by L2 English learners when writing an opinion essay. They identified a variety of strategies, including expressing change of opinion (e.g., "I would like to retract my previous position and state that . . . ."). More recent studies have explored technology-mediated contexts to examine speech acts in writing (e.g., emails, online forums). Alcón-Soler (2013) analyzed L2 English learners' email requests to their instructors. She found that, unlike native English speakers, L2 participants did not use many lexical and syntactic devices to soften the tone of their requests. Taguchi et al. (2016), on the other hand, examined the speech act of critiquing. Students in English composition classes in the U.S. and Hong Kong provided written comments for their classmates' essays online. Automated analysis of the comments revealed a range of linguistic devices used to add a personal or objective tone to the critiques (e.g., personal pronouns, imperatives, and abstract verbs).

While a small pool of studies has analyzed speech acts in written texts, these studies still focus on isolated, sentence-level forms and strategies without accounting for the meaning generated in written discourse. This is a shortcoming because, like in a spoken conversation, pragmatic meaning emerges in a written text at the discourse level from linguistic resources orchestrated throughout a text. Hence, the lower-level analysis of linguistic forms and strategies needs to be combined with the higher-level analysis of textual meaning in order to examine L2 learners' ability to achieve communicative purposes. To explore ways to analyze textual aspects of speech act production that take into account contextualized discourse, we will turn to systemic functional linguistics (SFL) as a method. The next section presents the basic tenets of SFL and illustrates the link between SFL and L2 pragmatics.

2.3 Systemic functional linguistics and its application to L2 pragmatics

2.3.1 Theoretical underpinnings

In SFL, language and other semiotic systems are considered as resources for making meaning (Halliday 1993). Meaning is created through texts that enact choices of the language users in the context of a particular situation and a specific culture. Meaning is thus enacted by the lexico-grammatical choices of the users of a language. Crucially in SFL, grammar construes our experience of the world (e.g., naming things, putting things in categories). Meaning is grammatically enacted and construed with three main functions in discourse (or more precisely, metafunctions): Ideational, Interpersonal and Textual (Halliday and Matthiessen 2014). The ideational metafunction refers to the representation of an action: who does what, to whom, when, and where. The Interpersonal metafunction enacts the relationship that the speaker or the writer has with the listener or the reader. Finally, the Textual metafunction enacts the discursive organization and flow of the sequences of discourse.

Under the SFL framework, language is not viewed as an abstract entity; rather, language can be analyzed according to the systematic enactment of three systems of meaning (Ideational, Interpersonal, and Textual). Hence, SFL investigates the way in which language is used to realize the three metafunctions. Based on this perspective, there is no distinction between meaning and structure or between grammar and pragmatics (Fernández 2018).

2.3.2 What does SFL offer to L2 pragmatics?

Rysina-Pankova (2019) claims that SFL can expand the scope of L2 pragmatics research with regard to methods and constructs of investigation. She contends that, although pragmatics and SFL have a common interest in language use as meaning-making in a social context, these two fields diverge in their views of what is entailed in the meaning-making ability and the methods examining that ability. Specifically, she argues that the SFL framework can enrich our understanding of pragmatics meaning-making in three ways. First, the traditional focus on interpersonal meanings in pragmatics research can extend to include ideational and textual meanings so that meaning-making can be understood more holistically, combining multiple perspectives. Second, SFL offers a method to analyze language use in the written mode, moving away from the focus on spoken interaction in L2 pragmatics research. By incorporating writing, we acquire ways to examine interaction in a variety of discourses and genres, including literature, academic prose, or fan fiction. Third, SFL provides a systematic tool to analyze connections between choices of linguistic systems and the context of use. This advantage is particularly appealing to L2 pragmatics because traditionally, researchers have identified certain linguistic forms as contributing to pragmatics meaning-making (e.g., the modal 'should' and imperative forms for advice-giving), but they have not specified the relationship among those forms, let alone how they contribute together toward a communicative goal. These benefits of SFL present new opportunities for researchers to detail the nature of pragmatic competence and methods for examining that competence at the discourse-level. This study is a preliminary effort to illustrate how the SFL framework can help us analyze a written text, focusing on the speech act of advice-giving.

Advice-giving closely reflects the pragmatics concerns of politeness and directness. Because the act of giving advice may threaten the hearer's negative face (i.e., the hearer's need for not being disturbed), the speaker uses a variety of linguistic and semantic strategies to mitigate the potential face-threat (Brown and Levinson 1987). Several coding frameworks have been developed to identify and categorize advice-giving strategies. For example, Hinkel (1997) classified L2 English learners' advice-giving strategies into three broad categories: the direct, hedged, and the indirect. Martinez-Flor (2003) presented a more comprehensive coding framework involving a number of strategies and linguistic forms for advice-giving (e.g., imperatives, modals, conditional sentences). DeCaptua and Dunham (2007), on the other hand, focused on semantic strategies of advice-giving in their coding framework (e.g., presenting several alternatives, expressing empathy). Despite its face-threatening nature, advice-giving is a common speech act, particularly in online communities and social networking sites (e.g., Yahoo Answers). Given the pervasiveness of advice-giving in online question and answer (Q&A) communities, this study examines how L2 learners of English express advice using their linguistic resources.

The present study addressed the following research questions:

RQ1: What pragmalinguistic resources do L2 English learners use to construct the speech act of advice-giving?

RQ2: What discourse-level resources do L2 English learners use to construct the speech act of advice-giving?

3 Method

3.1 Participants

Participants were 22 Chinese students enrolled in an English composition class at a university in Beijing. There were five males and 17 females, with an average age of 18.2 (range: 18–20). They were all freshmen majoring in law and had an average of 11 years of formal English study (range: 6–17 years). None of them had studied abroad. The participants' class focused on grammar, rhetorical structures, and conventions of academic writing; pragmatics (or speech acts) was not part of the instruction.

3.2 The advice-giving task

To collect samples of advice-giving writing, we developed a task that simulates a social Q&A community. We browsed several online Q&A sites (e.g., Yahoo Answers, Blurtit, Reddit) to identify a pool of postings describing a personal problem and seeking advice. We selected eight postings describing a variety of problems (e.g., game addiction, relationships) that were considered suitable for our participant population. In order to select the appropriate posting to use, a pilot study was conducted with students in the same Chinese university who were not involved in the main study (N=20). We administered a survey (in Chinese) that included the eight problem postings and asked the pilot participants to indicate the commonality of the problems and perceived difficulty in solving the problems on a scale of 1 to 5 ('5' indicating very familiar/difficult) (see Appendix A for sample survey questions).

Pilot results showed that the mean commonality rating of eight problems was 3.2 (range: 2.1–4.1), while the mean difficulty rating was 3.7 (range: 2.8–4.3). We selected the problem with the highest commonality rating (4.1) and the lowest difficulty rating (2.8) so we could elicit a sufficient amount of advice (see the abbreviated text describing a problem below). A Chinese speaker of L2 English developed the text for the problem posting used in the main task (about 300 words in length) because participants were all Chinese students learning English as a second language. Appendix B contains the complete advice-giving task.

> Problem posting (abbreviated version)
> I am a college student majoring in Chinese language and literature and have a double major in English. But I'm thinking of quitting English and only study Chinese. My mom is angry at me because she thinks I will get no job after I graduate, and all her time and money she spent on me will be wasted. But I really want her to respect my decision.

The task was administered via SurveyMonkey. Participants were asked to read the posting and type up their advice to the problem as if it had been posted by one of their classmates.

3.3 Data collection procedures

Data was collected during the eighth week of the participants' first semester at the university. We provided a link to the survey so they could complete the task online outside of their class. After completing the online consent form, the participants were directed to the background survey section and then to the task. The task instructions asked the participants to complete the task on their own without using any resources (e.g., dictionary). After completing the task, they submitted their writing online. There was no word or time limit imposed on the task.

3.4 Data analysis procedures

We analyzed 22 texts submitted by individual participants in response to the problem posted (see the previous section for the problem). The participants wrote 243 words on average, with responses ranging from 132 to 592 words ($SD=95$). The first research question addressed pragmalinguistic resources used in advice-giving (utterance-level analysis of advice-giving). To answer this question, we used a coding framework adapted from the existing literature (Martínez-Flor 2003; Salemi, Rabiee, and Ketabi 2012) (see Table 1). We analyzed each text for the strategies outlined below and tallied the frequency of each strategy. Two researchers checked the coding, achieving a 90% agreement rate. Discrepancies were resolved via discussion.

Table 1: Coding framework for advice-giving strategies.

Directness level	Strategy type	Example
Direct strategies	Performative verb	I suggest that you do X.
		I advise you to do X.
		I recommend that you do X.
	Noun of suggestion	My suggestion would be doing X.
	Imperative	Try to do X.
	Negative imperative	Don't try to do X.
	Formulaic expressions	Why don't you do X?
		How about X?
		What about X?
		Have you thought about X?
		Isn't it better for you to do X?
Conventionalized indirect strategies	Modals of possibility/ probability	You can X.
		You could X.
		You may X.
		You might X.
	Modal – should	You should/ought to do X.
	Modal – must	You must do X.
	Modal – need to	You need to do X.
	Conditional	If I were you, I would do X.
Indirect strategies	Impersonal	One thing (that you can do) would be X.
		Here's one possibility . . .
		There are a number of options that you can do.
		It would be helpful if you do X.
		X would help you.
		It might be better to do X.
		A good idea would be doing X.
		It would be nice if you do X.

The second research question addressed participants' advice-giving ability at the text level. We applied SFL to analyze how participants discursively construct their advice-giving text. After parsing an advice-giving text into clauses, we analysed the text on two aspects: Mood (lexico-grammatical analysis) and Appraisal (discourse-semantic analysis). Both aspects help us examine how participants create interpersonal meanings in their advice-giving text (Oteiza 2017).

The Mood system allows us to understand the clause as an exchange between the writer and reader (Halliday and Matthiessen 2014; see Table 2). The Mood conveys the validity of the claim the writer is making so the reader can accept it or reject it. The Mood analysis reveals the type of clause according to the subject and finite part of the verb (i.e., tense, number, person, modality), as well as the dependency of the clauses, namely independent clauses (declaratives, imperatives, interrogatives) or dependent clauses (e.g., embedded or bound clauses). Analyzing the clause type provides insights into how the writer positions herself in relation to the reader. We can examine whether writers are giving something to the reader or demanding something from the reader, and which grammatical resources they use to do so (e.g., modals). The use of bound clauses (i.e. dependent clauses that begin with a conjunction or a WH-element) can also create cohesiveness in discourse (Halliday and Matthiesen 2014).

Modality construes the writer's attitude and assessment around the claim he or she is making (Thompson 2014). There are two types of modality: modalization and modulation. Modalization regards the probability or the likelihood that the speaker/writer is telling the truth (e.g., "She might be wrong.") and the usuality (or frequency) of the claim to be true (e.g., "She seldom lies."). Modulation regards the degree of obligation the writer expresses in her proposal (e.g., "You should listen to her.") and the willingness or determination of the writer to fulfil her proposal (e.g., "I am willing to help you."). Modalization and modulation can be expressed explicitly or implicitly, as well as subjectively or objectively.

In addition to the Mood analysis, the Appraisal analysis (Iedema, Fez, and White 1994; Martin and White 2005) was conducted as a discourse-semantic analysis in this study. The Appraisal analysis addresses the negotiation of attitude between the sender and the receiver of information (Martin and Rose 2007). Three dimensions of Appraisal were analyzed: attitude, engagement, and graduation (Table 3). Attitude refers to the evaluative system (feelings, values, and aesthetic point of view) of the writer (or the speaker) about the reader (or the listener) or the content of the message. Engagement refers to the writer (or the speaker) acknowledging or ignoring diverse points of view. Graduation relates to the use of evaluative language to scale meaning. Within graduation, 'force' means a positive or negative grade given to a term (e.g., a big liar), while 'focus' signals a scale of closeness to the prototypical meaning of the term (e.g., a perfect gentlemen) (Martin and White, 2005). Thus, 'force' is a linguistic choice that intensifies the meaning of the text, while 'focus' is a linguistic choice that makes meaning more or less precise (Fernández, 2018.) Appraisal analysis can make it possible to understand the stance of the interactants because, through the analysis of the evaluative language (explicitly or implicitly used), we can analyse the writer's point of view in the text. Tables 2 and 3 present the dimensions of the Mood and Appraisal analysis conducted in this study.

Table 2: Mood analysis, dimensions.

Modality	Dimensions		Examples
	Type The writer's attitude around his/her claim	**Modalization:** Probability (likeliness to be true) and usuality (frequency to be true)	She might come. She often comes.
		Modulation: Obligation and willingness	She should come. She will help us.
	Responsibility The writer accepting or denying responsibility of his/her claim	**Explicit:** Modalization or modulation used in a separate clause	I am sure she will come. I don't think she will come.
		Implicit: Modalization or modulation used in the same clause	She might come. She must come.
		Subjective: personal	I am sure she will come.
		Objective: detached	It is said that she will come.

Table 3: Appraisal analysis, dimensions.

Appraisal	Dimensions		Examples
Resources used to position the writer inter-personally	**Engagement** Inclusion or exclusion of the reader	**Heterogloss:** Including the reader	I understand your point of view.
		Monogloss: Excluding the reader	It is hard for me to understand.
	Attitude Intersubjective value system	**Affect:** Expressing emotion	I love staring at stars. She was in tears.
		Judgement: Evaluating behaviors according to norms	She is a decent woman. The game was won fairly.
		Appreciation: Evaluating people/objects from an esthetic point of view	This is a gorgeous picture.
	Graduation Scaled meaning	**Focus:** Clarifying or blurring meaning	She is a true friend. She is sort of a friend.
		Force: Intensifying or weakening meaning	I like her very much. You are slightly wrong.

The first and second authors conducted the SFL-based coding of clauses, reaching an 80% agreement rate and revised it according to the reviewers' suggestions. Any discrepancies in the analysis were resolved via discussion. Then, the final analysis was checked by another researcher who has experience in SFL.

4 Results

4.1 Research question 1: Utterance-level resources in advice-giving

The first research question investigated the pragmalinguistic resources that learners used to construct their advice-giving texts. Table 4 displays the frequency distribution of the advice-giving strategies identified in the 22 writing samples.

Table 4: Frequency and percentage of advice-giving strategies.

Directness level	Strategy type	Frequency	%
Direct	Performative	4	2.8
	Suggestion (noun)	15	10.6
	Imperative	28	19.7
	Negative imperative	8	5.6
	Formulaic expressions	0	0
Conventionalized indirect	Modal- possibility/probability	18	12.7
	Modal – should	20	14.1
	Modal – must	5	3.6
	Modal – need to	4	2.8
	Conditional	28	19.7
Indirect	Impersonal	12	8.4
	TOTAL	142	100

The most frequent strategies were the imperative form (including the negative imperative) and the conditional (if + clause), which constituted about 20% of strategies. Among the modals used, modals of obligation (e.g., should, must, need to) appeared more frequently than those of possibility and probability (e.g., can, could, may) (about 20% vs. 13%). There was no use of formulaic expressions. Indirect strategies, particularly impersonal strategies (e.g., "One thing you could do is . . . ."), were not common (less than 9%).

Learners used multiple forms and strategies, as illustrated in Sample Text 1 below. When responding to the peer's problem (whether or not to change a major), this learner recommended that the peer stick to their current major of English. She used the imperative sentence in line 3 and the modal 'should' three times in line 6, 11, and 15. She also sparsely used impersonal expressions, such as, "the most important thing is that . . ." (line 2), "it is necessary for you to . . ." (line 6), and "it is possible for you to arrange your time well . . . " (line 13–14).

Sample Text 1

1 I'm very sorry to hear your bad situation. Everyone has a period which filled with
2 confusing and pressure both in study and life. <u>The most important thing is that</u> you
3 have to calm down at this time. <u>Then communicate more with your mother</u>. What
4 bother you is that you really don't English and it takes up too much of your time. You
5 even want to drop it and learn another skill. But as far as I am concerned, <u>it's</u>
6 <u>necessary for you to</u> learn English in collage and you <u>should</u> think highly of it. You
7 are thinking to develop another skill, but, you have to know English is the most
8 widely used language throughout the world. The more English skills you handle, the
9 more opportunities you can get in the future. Apart from that, everything worthwhile
10 is worth doing. When you get into the society, you will find the large demand of
11 professional English. Your future is unknown now and you <u>should</u> consider more for
12 yourself. Besides, because of your enthusiasm in Chinese, you are refusing to learn
13 English. As for the problem, I think <u>it's possible for you to</u> arrange your time well
14 and make a good study schedule. Only in this way can you be outstanding in your
15 filed. In short, I think you <u>should</u> keep learning English in case of you regret in the
16 future. What's more make a better use of time and your efforts will not in vain.

The coding framework used for the analysis is useful in that it revealed the scope of pragmalinguistic repertoire available to this learner, ranging from direct expressions (e.g., imperative forms), to conventional expressions (e.g., modals of obligation, impersonal expressions) and indirect expressions (e.g., hinting). Since the average use of impersonal expressions was low in this participant group, three different impersonal statements appearing in the text offering indirect advice indicate that this learner is capable of using a wide variety of linguistic forms in persuading someone to take a certain course of action.

However, we must note several limitations to this method of utterance-level coding. First, it does not consider the entire text for the force behind an act of advice-giving. The coded utterances occupy only about 60 words of a 240-word text, and the other 180 words (75% of the text) remain unanalyzed. In addition, the coding method treats the speech act as a collection of isolated linguistic forms and does not address the connection among those forms. For example, the modal 'should' appears three times throughout the text and is used in all cases to persuade the peer to continue studying English by emphasizing the importance of the language. On the other hand, the imperative form appears only once: at the beginning of the text when addressing the peer's immediate concern that his mother is angry with his decision of changing his major. Impersonal statements appear three times, but the degree of force differs each time. The first statement, "the most important thing is that you calm down", adds urgency by using "most" as emphasis, while in the other two cases the learner projects an objective stance by explaining what is necessary or possible for the peer to do. Between these two impersonal statements, the latter conveys a weaker intention with the adjective of 'possible' rather than 'necessary'.

In short, although several pragmalinguistic forms fall into the same category in the coding framework, the meaning and force conveyed through these forms are different, which is not captured by coding. In addition, the coding framework does not allow us to see how those forms are located in relation to each other to structure the overall argument. Most critically, using the coding framework limits our analyses to those forms pre-existing in the framework and does not allow for bottom-up analyses of how meaning emerges in discourse from a collection of linguistic resources. Those meaning-making resources include not just forms, but also other discourse-level features such as structures and resources for expressing attitude, affect, stance, or position. To address these limitations, the next section presents a text analysis using SFL. SFL can capture learners' meaning-making ability at discourse-level, going beyond the traditional analysis of isolated linguistic forms.

4.2 Research question 2: Text-level resources in advice-giving

This section demonstrates what the SFL approach reveals about L2 learners' advice-giving ability in a way that the traditional coding framework cannot. To illustrate the contrast between the two approaches, we selected two participants who produced the smallest number of advice-giving strategies. The text by Participant 9 below has only one strategy, the modal 'should' (underlined). The text by Participant 15 contains three, two conditional sentences and the performative verb "suggest" (underlined). Thus, using the coding framework, these participants would be judged as low-strategy users who have limited linguistic repertoire for advice-giving. However, the SFL-based analysis offers a different evaluation.

We first analyze Participant 9's text. Tables 2 and 3 (see Methods section) show the dimensions analyzed in the text (Mood and Appraisal), along with their definitions and examples (based on Thompson 2014). Table 5 presents the coding of the text based on these dimensions.

Participant 9, text

I am able to understand what you have gone through and sympathize with the condition you are in now. Everyone deserve to do their own choice and be out of control of others. So from my point of view, I'm convinced that you must have known all you want. However, your parents may got a different idea, which makes you feel unsatisfied. Generally speaking, your parents are trying to give you better suggestions in their opinions, so you <u>should</u> realize their concern with you. But on my personal level, it's very hard to make your own choices, and to stick to it is also very miserable. Believe it or not, your ambition will count one day. Only with your endeavors and hard-work could you succeed one day, and you will prove yourself to all the people who once look down to you at that time!

Table 5: Analysis of Participant 9's text.

Clause	Excerpt	Mood (subject + finite verb)	Clause type and modality type	Appraisal
1	I am able to understand what you have gone through	I am able to understand	Declarative Modalization Explicit Subjective	Heterogloss (understand you) Force (am able to)
2	and sympathize with the condition you are in now		Bound (and sympathize)	Heterogloss (sympathize, you) Affect (sympathize) Force (condition)
3	Everyone deserve to do their own choice and be out of control of others	Everyone deserves	Declarative Implicit Objective	Monogloss (everyone) Focus (their own)
4	So from my point of view, I'm convinced that you must have known all you want	I am (convinced)	Declarative Modulation Explicit Subjective	Monogloss (I'm convinced) Judgement (convinced) Force (must, all)
5	However, your parents may got a different idea		Declarative Modalization Implicit Objective	Heterogloss (your parents) Force (may got a different idea)

Table 5 (continued)

Clause	Excerpt	Mood (subject + finite verb)	Clause type and modality type	Appraisal
6	which makes you feel unsatisfied	(your parents' idea) which makes you feel	Bound (which makes)	Monogloss (which makes you) Affect (unsatisfied)
7	Generally speaking, your parents are trying to give you better suggestions in their opinions	Your parents are	Declarative	Heterogloss (their opinion) Judgement (suggestion, opinion) Focus (better suggestion)
8	so you should realize their concern with you		Bound (so) Modulation Implicit Subjective	Monogloss (you should realize) Judgement (concern with you)
9	But on my personal level, it's very hard to make your own choices	It is	Declarative	Heterogloss (my personal) Affect (personal, hard) Force (very) Focus (own choices)
10	and to stick to it is also very miserable		Bound (and)	Affect (miserable) Force (very)
11	Believe it or not, your ambition will count one day	Your ambition will (count)	Declarative Modulation Implicit Objective	Heterogloss (believe it or not) Judgement (ambition will count) Force (believe it or not) Focus (one day)
12	Only with your endeavors and hard-work could you succeed one day	You could	Declarative Modalization Explicit Subjective	Heterogloss (you will succeed) Judgement (endeavors and hard work) Force (only) Focus (one day)

Table 5 (continued)

Clause	Excerpt	Mood (subject + finite verb)	Clause type and modality type	Appraisal
13	and you will prove yourself to all the people who once look down to you at that time!	You will	Declarative Modulation Implicit Subjective	Heterogloss (you, all the people) Judgement (look down to you) Force (all)

As shown in the Mood analysis, Participant 9 uses declarative sentences most frequently. She also uses different modality types to give advice (obligation: "should" in Clause 8 and probability: "could" in Clause 12). She makes use of expressions such as "generally speaking" (Clause 7) and "believe it or not" (Clause 11) that strengthen the validity of her argument. Thus, this participant uses some lexical-grammatical devices that signal the interpersonal textual status of advice-giving.

In addition to the Mood analysis, we conducted the Appraisal analysis to retrieve a deeper level of information about the discourse-semantic resources used by this participant. From the graduation point of view (i.e., words that can raise or lower the intensity and preciseness of the text), this participant extensively uses "force" and "focus". For example, in Clause 1, she does not say simply, "I understand," but instead says, "I am able to understand." This linguistic choice gives more focus to the empathy that this participant is trying to convey. In Clause 2, she uses a bound clause to reinforce the emphasis of the first clause by saying, "and sympathize with you". This linguistic choice conveys more force because it is more emphatic than alternative expressions such as, "I understand you". It also implies an emotive involvement (e.g., "I sympathize with your sorrow."). Similarly, the linguistic choice of "must" and "all" in Clause 4 conveys force, emphasizing that the advice giver's understanding of the advice seeker's knowledge. From the "attitude" point of view, this participant initially sympathizes with the feelings of her friend (Clauses 2, 6, and 9), but ends her text with a judgement about what her friend's choice should be. In fact, the judgement appears in the last part of the text (Clauses 11, 12, and 13). From the "engagement" point of view, the feeling of empathy that she is trying to convey includes her friend dialogically and is thus mainly heteroglossic.

We now turn to the analysis of another text, Participant 15. Table 6 presents coding of the text for the dimensions of the Mood and Appraisal analysis.

Participant 15, text

I'm sorry to hear that you are having problems with issues about your future. In order to help you, I prepare two questions for you to ask yourself and answer from the bottom of your heart. The first question is: what's more important to you, your mother's wishes or your own dream? According to your description, your mother is unhappy about your choice of major, but you really like it and care a lot about your academic performance. It's quite simple to me, an outsider, that <u>if you want to satisfy your mother more, then keep up with your double major</u>; <u>if you are determined to learn Chinese courses better, then quit it</u>. The second question is: What's more unbearable to you, risks or regrets? It's true that Chinese major is not so useful to job-hunting in the market these days, but things are never definite – – I mean, if you are really outstanding in the field, it won't be a problem to find a job; if you fail to learn things well, English major is not that helpful. Risk certainly exists, but hope does, too. As you will surely regret your decision most if you sacrifice your Chinese major, <u>I suggest</u> you think hard about it. All in all, wish you could make the best decision for yourself!

Table 6: Analysis of Participant 15's text.

Clause	Excerpt	Mood (subject + finite verb)	Clause type and modality type	Appraisal
1	I'm sorry to hear that you are having problems with issues about your future.	I am	Declarative	Heterogloss (I am sorry to hear) Affect (sorry for your problems)
2	In order to help you, I prepare two questions for you	I prepared	Declarative	Heterogloss (including the reader in the reasoning) Focus (two questions)
3	to ask yourself and answer from the bottom of your heart	finite	Declarative	Heterogloss (ask yourself) Affect (answer from the heart) Force (bottom of your heart)
4	The first question is		Declarative	Focus (the first)

Table 6 (continued)

Clause	Excerpt	Mood (subject + finite verb)	Clause type and modality type	Appraisal
5	what's more important to you, your mother's wishes or your own dream?	What is . . . ?	Interrogative	Heterogloss (important to you) Judgement (important) Force (more) Focus (your own dream)
6	According to your description, your mother is unhappy about your choice of major	Your mother is	Declarative	Heterogloss (your description) Affect (unhappy)
7	but you really like it and care a lot about your academic performance		Bound (but)	Heterogloss (you care) Appreciation (like it) Affect (care about) Force (really, a lot)
8	It's quite simple to me, an outsider,	It is	Declarative	Judgement (it's simple) Force (quite) Focus (me, an outsider)
9	that if you want to satisfy your mother more	You want	Declarative	Heterogloss (you want) Affect (satisfy) Force (more)
10	then keep up with your double major		Bound (then) imperative	Monogloss (then do as I say)
11	if you are determined to learn Chinese courses better	You are	Declarative	Heterogloss (you are determined) Force (determined, better)
12	then quit it		Bound (then) imperative	Monogloss (then quit)
13	The second question is	The second question is	Declarative	Focus (second question)

Table 6 (continued)

Clause	Excerpt	Mood (subject + finite verb)	Clause type and modality type	Appraisal
14	What's more unbearable to you, risks or regrets?	What is . . . ?	Interrogative	Heterogloss (to you) Affect (unbearable) Force (more)
15	It's true that Chinese major is not so useful to job-hunting in the market these days	It is	Declarative	Heterogloss (it is true) Appreciation (not so useful) Force (not so) Focus (these days)
16	but things are never definite	Things are	Declarative	Monogloss (never) Judgement (definite) Force (never)
17	I mean, if you are really outstanding in the field	You are	Declarative	Heterogloss (I mean, if you) Judgement (outstanding) Force (really)
18	it won't be a problem to find a job	It will	Declarative Modulation Implicit Objective	Heterogloss (it won't be) Judgement (not a problem to find . . .)
19	if you fail to learn things well	You fail	Declarative	Monogloss (if you) Force (fail to, well) Judgement (fail to learn)
20	English major is not that helpful	Is not	Declarative	Monogloss (is not) Appreciation (helpful) Focus (not that helpful)
21	Risk certainly exists	Risk exists	Declarative	Heterogloss (certainly) Affect (conveying risk) Force (certainly)

Table 6 (continued)

Clause	Excerpt	Mood (subject + finite verb)	Clause type and modality type	Appraisal
22	but hope does, too	Hope does	Declarative	Heterogloss (disclaiming) Affect (hope)
23	As you will surely regret your decision most	You will	Declarative Modulation Explicit Subjective	Heterogloss (as you will) Judgement (regret) Affect (regret) Force (surely)
24	if you sacrifice your Chinese major	You sacrifice	Declarative Modulation	Heterogloss (if you) Affect (sacrifice)
25	I suggest you think hard about it	I suggest	Declarative	Heterogloss (I suggest) Force (hard)
26	All in all, wish you could make the best decision for yourself!	(I) wish	Declarative Modalization Implicit Subjective	Heterogloss (disclaim) Judgement (make the best decision) Force (all in all) Focus (best)

    The Mood analysis shows that Participant 15 uses the declarative sentence throughout the text. She also makes use of modal responsibility – accepting responsibility for what she is doing or directing the responsibility to an external entity – in a different way than Participant 9 did. Participant 15 utilizes less modalization and modulation and more bound clauses (Clauses 7, 10, 12) to make personal remarks about her point of view (Thompson 2014). In the case of implicit modal responsibility, she uses engagement strategies to include the reader by using expressions such as "in order to" (Clause 2), "according to" (Clause 6), and "it is true" (Clause 15) to soften the tone of her advice. Moreover, she uses interrogative clauses (Clauses 5, 14) which, according to Eggins and Slade (1997), are used to elicit missing information. The use of interrogative clauses highlights the interactive and persuasive nature of the advice-giving. In this case the interrogatives ask the advice seeker's judgement about what is "important" (Clause 5) and affect what is more "unbearable" (Clause 14). These are two main attitude strategies that Participant 15 uses in her text to give her advice.

Turning to the Appraisal analysis, from the "attitude" point of view, Participant 15 makes use of affect, appreciation, and judgement. She often gives a recommendation based on her friend's feelings rather than a logical assessment of the pros and cons of pursuing a certain path (Clauses 1, 3, 6, 7, 9, 14, 21, 22, 23). At the same time, she uses judgement about which course of action to take (Clauses 5, 7, 16–19, 23, 26). However, in those occasions of judgement, she employs an objective tone and appreciation to sustain her argument (e.g., "Chinese major is not so useful to job-hunting in the market these day" [Clause 15]). Nevertheless, she suggests that the reader must take into consideration her feelings to make her decision (e.g., "As you will surely regret your decision most if you sacrifice your Chinese major" [Clause 23]) and her judgement (Clauses 17 – 19). We can see the same pattern for "engagement". She moves from a predominantly heteroglossic discourse, using the pronoun "you" as referent, to a monoglossic discourse where she talks about her opinions (Clause 16, 18 – 20). Through these choices she makes a separation between the feelings of the reader, which are heteroglossically included in the discourse, and her general opinions that are external to the choice the reader should make.

Moreover, Participant 15 produces negative emotion words such as "unbearable" (Clause 14), "regret" (Clause 14, 23), "risk" (Clause 21), and "sacrifice" (Clause 24) to give force to her discourse. From the "graduation" point of view, she utilizes both force and focus in a number of clauses. Frequent use of force and focus, along with affect, serves to persuade the reader to make a certain choice. It seems that this participant's advice-giving approach involves reinforcing her point of view through linguistic choices that appeal to the reader's feelings.

5 Discussion

This study examined L2 English learners' written texts with a focus on examining their ability to construct the speech act of advice-giving. We first coded linguistic forms appearing in the texts based on the predetermined coding framework and tallied percentage distributions of the forms. Then, we adopted the SFL approach and conducted the Mood analysis (at the lexico-grammatical level) and the Appraisal analysis (at the discourse-semantic level) to reveal interpersonal meanings of the text as an exchange between the advice-giver and advice-seeker. These two types of analysis generated complementary information about L2 learners' advice-giving ability in a written text.

The form-focused coding approach revealed a scope of linguistic forms that the participants had as resources when giving advice. Except for the category of "formulaic expressions," all categories in the coding framework were found in the 22 texts (e.g., imperative forms, suggestion expressions, and a variety of modals), indicating that the participants were familiar with the forms serving the function of advice-giving. The analysis also revealed the learners' preference toward directness levels of the forms. Most forms fell in the level of "direct" and "conventionally indirect." The participants' sparse use of "indirect" strategies, particularly impersonal forms (e.g., "One possibility is . . . "), indicates that they had a means of giving suggestions in a more direct, transparent manner, rather than in an objective and distant manner.

Unlike the utterance-level, form-focused analysis using predetermined coding categories, the SFL-based analysis allowed us to examine an individual participant's text in its entirety, attending to all the clauses parsed in the text. Through the clause-by-clause analysis of the Mood and Appraisal, we were able to examine how the learner (advice-giver) tries to position herself in relation to the person who is reading her advice (advice-seeker). The position between the advice-giver and advice-seeker became evident in the type of clause used (i.e., declarative, imperative, and interrogative), as well as in the analysis of modalization and modularity (e.g., expressions of probability, obligation, and willingness). The two learners' texts were different in the extent of the modalization and modulation. While Participant 9 used modalization and modulation rather extensively, Participant 15 made minimal use of these resources.

The Appraisal analysis, on the other hand, revealed the advice-giver's attitude and stance toward her (imaginary) advice-seeker. We found that, although the two learners made minimal use of the forms based on the coding framework, they were actually capable of expressing various interpersonal meanings such as affect and judgement. These findings indicate that the learners appealed to both emotion (affect) and ethics (judgement) when trying to persuade someone to take a course of action. While they were sympathetic toward the reader's (advice seeker's) situation, they also remained objective (judgement), trying to present a fair and apt solution to the problem. In doing so, they employed linguistic resources to intensify and clarify their intention by adding "focus" and "force" throughout the text. The fact that the aspect of 'heterogloss' (nine clauses in Participant 9's text and 19 clauses in Participant 15's text) was more noticeable than 'monogloss' (4 clauses in Participant 9 and 5 clauses in participant 15) in both learners' texts shows that they were indeed focusing on the interpersonal needs of the advice-seeker. They closely attended to the reader's (advice-seeker's) situations and incorporated his/her perspective in the text. The inclusive text demonstrated in the heteroglossic language use is appropriate for the given genre – giving advice to a peer.

As summarized above, the SFL-based analysis helped us to apply a text-level, discursive pragmatics approach (Kasper 2006) to writing. The traditional approach of using a coding framework to identify speech act forms does not show how meaning is produced in relation to the other (dialogically) in discourse (Cohen 2008). As such, the SFL presents an alternative approach, prompting us to see how meaning emerges in a text holistically via a constellation of linguistic choices that signal the writer's interpersonal position vis-a-vis the reader. The writer does not just perform the communicative function of advice-giving without the presence of the reader; instead, the writer expresses a variety of meanings toward the reader throughout the text (e.g., emotion, judgement, stance, intensity, focus, and inclusiveness). These multiple levels of meanings all contribute to the communicative goal of advice-giving directed to the imagined reader. Hence, L2 learners' advice-giving ability needs to be evaluated beyond their knowledge of isolated linguistic forms. The focus should be placed instead on the types of meanings expressed using linguistic forms and their connection with the context of use. Degree of success in a speech act can be assessed in terms of the scope of meanings expressed – rather than the scope of linguistic forms – in relation to the context of discourse.

6 Conclusion

The present study illustrated how a speech act in written discourse can be analyzed using SFL as a method. The SFL approach was found to be useful, complementing the traditional, form-focused coding approach in the following ways:

1. SFL offers a means to analyse a speech act in a written text;
2. SFL helps us examine a speech act as a meaning-making process between the writer/speaker and the reader/listener, rather than as an illocutionary force produced by the writer/speaker via linguistic forms;
3. SFL helps us understand interpersonal meanings expressed in a text;
4. SFL offers a systematic tool to reveal connections among linguistic choices, meaning, and context of discourse.

We argue that the two approaches combined (utterance-level coding and SFL-based holistic analysis) could produce meaningful information about L2 speech acts.

While SFL presents a promising approach to analyzing how meaning is expressed, several challenges remain. One major challenge is how to conduct the group-level analysis using SFL. As presented in this paper, SFL requires parsing sentences into individual clauses and analysing each clause manually for various dimensions of the Mood and Appraisal, among others. This process is time-consuming and impractical. The process is particularly problematic in the area of assessment because it involves making a judgement of learners' ability at both individual and group-levels so that we can infer how a learner's performance compares to the group performing the same task. If we want to pursue a large-scale assessment using SFL in the future, we can explore the possibility of using technology to facilitate the process. Clauses, words, phrases, and sentence structures that typify specific features of the Mood and Appraisal can be tagged and programmed so that we can conduct an automated analysis of a large number of texts in one setting.

Related to this problem, another challenge is quantifying SFL analysis. The qualitative nature of the analysis presented in this paper does not yield a score easily. Hence, we need to explore ways to quantify the Mood and Appraisal analysis. For example, in the Appraisal analysis, we can count the frequency of key features appearing in a text (e.g., affect, force) and calculate their rate of appearance per text. In addition, we can have a group of expert raters assess texts for overall quality of advice-giving (e.g., effectiveness, clarity), and then cross-examine their ratings and the frequency of the Appraisal features. If certain features appear more often in higher-rated texts, those features can be considered as characteristics of high-quality advice giving. In turn, the meanings expressed through those features can serve as criteria for assessing advice-giving acts. The automated, computerized analysis mentioned in the previous section could facilitate the scoring process.

While major challenges exist when considering SFL for a quantitative, group-level analysis, SFL has great potential to expand the current scope of L2 pragmatics research. We hope that the interdisciplinary connection between pragmatics and SFL that Ryshina-Pankova (2019) advocated continues to grow as we find ways to overcome existing challenges, pushing the field forward to the next phase of developing useful tools to analyze L2 learners' pragmatic acts. Particularly promising in the future is to conduct a combined analysis of ideational, textual, and interpersonal meanings in pragmatics. Because the present study limited its analytical scope to interpersonal meaning, expanding the scope to three levels of meaning will help understand L2 learners' meaning-making ability in a more comprehensive manner.

References

Alcón-Soler, Eva. 2013. Mitigating E-Mail requests in teenagers' first and second language academic cyber-consultation. *Multilingua* 32(6). 779–799.

Blum-Kulka, Shohana, Julian House, & Gabriele Kasper. 1989. *Cross-cultural pragmatics: Requests and apologies*. Norwood, NJ: Ablex.

Brown, Penelope & Stephen Levinson. 1987. *Politeness: Some universals in language use*. Cambridge: Cambridge University Press.

Cohen, Andrew D. 2004. Assessing speech acts in a second language. In Diane Boxer & Andrew D. Cohen (eds.), *Studying speaking to inform second language learning*, 302–327. Clevedon: Multilingual Matters.

Cohen, Andrew D. 2008. Teaching and assessing L2 pragmatics: What can we expect from learners? *Language Teaching* 41. 215–237.

Cohen, Andrew D. & Elaine Tarone. 1994. The effects of training on written speech act behavior: Stating and changing an opinion. *MinneTESOL Journal* 12. 39–62.

Culpeper, Jonathan, Alison Mackey, & Naoko Taguchi. 2018. *Second language pragmatics: From theory to methods*. New York: Routledge.

DeCaptua, Andrea & Joan Findlay Dunham. 2007. The pragmatics of advice giving: Cross-cultural perspectives. *Intercultural Pragmatics* 4. 319–342.

Felix-Brasdefer, J. Cesar. 2019. Speech acts in interaction. In Naoko Taguchi (ed.), *The Routledge handbook of SLA and pragmatics*, 17–30. New York: Routledge.

Fernández, Loretta. 2018. Qualitative interview analysis: The use of systemic functional linguistics to reveal functional meanings. *Forum: Qualitative Social Research* 19(2) art. 6.

Eggins, Suzanne, & Diana Slade. 1997. *Analysing casual conversation*. London: Equinox.

Halliday, Michael A. K. & Christian M.I.M. Matthiessen. 2014 [1985]. *Halliday's introduction to functional grammar* (4th ed.). New York: Routledge.

Halliday, Michael A. K. 1993. Towards a language-based theory of learning. *Linguistics and Education* 5. 93–116.

Hinkel, Eli. 1997. Appropriateness of advice: DCT and multiple choice data. *Applied Linguistics* 18(1). 1–26.

Iedema, Rick, Susan Fez, Peter White. (1994). *Media literacy*. Sydney: Disadvantaged Schools Program, NSW Department of School Education.

Kasper, Gabrielle. 2006. Speech acts in interaction: Towards discursive pragmatics. In Kathleen Bardovi-Harlig, J. Cesar Felix-Brasdefer, & Alwiya S. Omar (eds.), *Pragmatics and language learning* (vol. 11), 281–314. Honolulu: Second Language Teaching and Curriculum Center University of Hawaii.

Martin, James Robert & David Rose. 2007. *Working with discourse meaning beyond the clause*. New York: Continuum.

Martin, James Robert & Peter White. 2005 *The language of evaluation: Appraisal in English*. New York: Palgrave-McMillan.

Martínez-Flor, Alicia. 2003. Non-native speakers' production of advice acts: The effects of proficiency. *Revista Española de Lingüística Aplicada* 16 139–153.

Mori, Junko Hanh thi Nguyen. 2019. Conversation analysis in L2 pragmatics research. In Naoko Taguchi (ed.), *The Routledge handbook of SLA and pragmatics*, 226–240. New York: Routledge.

Nguyen, Thi Thuy Minh. 2019. Data collection methods in L2 pragmatics research: An overview. In Naoko Taguchi (ed.), *The Routledge handbook of SLA and pragmatics*, 195–211. New York: Routledge.

Oteíza, Teresa. 2017. The appraisal framework and discourse analysis. In Tom Barlett & Gerard O'Grady (eds.) *The Routledge handbook of systemic functional linguistics*, 457–472. New York: Routledge.

Ryshina-Pankova, Marianna. 2019. Systemic functional linguistics and L2 pragmatics. In Naoko Taguchi (ed.), *The Routledge handbook of SLA and pragmatics*, 255–271. New York: Routledge.

Salemi, Azin, Mitra Rabiee & Saeed Ketabi. 2012. The effects of explicit/implicit instruction and feedback on the development of Persian EFL learners' pragmatic competence in suggestion structures. *Journal of Language Teaching and Research* 3 188–199.

Schegloff, Emanuel, A. 2007. *Sequence organization in interaction*. Cambridge: Cambridge University Press.

Taguchi, Naoko & Carsten Roever. 2017. *Second language pragmatics*. New York: Oxford University Press.

Taguchi, Naoko, David Kaufer, Pia M. Gomez-Laich, & Helen Zhao. 2016. A corpus linguistics analysis of on-line peer commentary. In Kathleen Bardovi-Harlig & J. Cesar Felix-Brasdefer (eds.), *Pragmatics and language learning* (vol. 14), 357–170. Honolulu: Second Language Teaching and Curriculum Center University of Hawaii.

Thompson, Geoff. 2014. *Introducing functional grammar*. New York: Routledge.

Youn, Soo Jung. 2015. Validity argument for assessing L2 pragmatics in interaction using mixed methods. *Language Testing* 32(2). 199–225.

Appendix A

Sample survey items

请您阅读以下有关提供建议的题目。根据您的判断，选出您认为为该问题提供建议的难易度，以及该问题的普遍性。判定难易度和普遍性的标准为：

非常容易 (1)：

您认为提供建议非常容易。您可以马上想出针对此问题的建议。

非常困难 (5)：

您认为提供建议非常困难。您完全不知道如何作答。

非常普遍 (1)：

您认为出现频率非常高。您或您的同学经常遇见此类问题。

非常罕见 (5)：

您认为出现频率非常低。您从来没有、甚至没听说过此类问题。

English translation: Please read each problem and rate the degree of difficulty in giving advice to each problem. Pease also rate the degree of commonality of each problem. Criteria to judge the difficulty and commonality are:

Very easy (1):
You have no problem with responding to this problem. There is no psychological pressure or uncomfortable feeling associated with the problem.
Very difficult (5):
There is great uncomfortable feeling associated with this problem I feel extremely ill at ease and nervous about talking about this problem.
Very common (1):
Similar problems often happen. I experienced this problem before, and/or I have seen people having the problem.
Very rare (5):
It is unimaginable to think that this problem could occur. It almost never happens.

Problem 1

My addiction to video and mobile games is getting out of control. I would skip classes and stop meeting my friends just to play the games. Now my grades do not look good, and my friends are leaving me. I really need to get my life back.

我的游戏瘾已经无法控制。我会翘课、不去见朋友，只是打游戏。现在我的成绩很差，朋友也不喜欢叫我玩了。我很想找回过去的生活。

您认为为该问题提出建议的难易度如何？	1	2	3	4	5
	非常容易				非常困难
您认为该问题出现的普遍性如何？	1	2	3	4	5
	非常普遍				非常少见

Problem 2

I've never had a relationship in my life. I am starting to think maybe there is something wrong with me. You know, maybe I don't look nice, or I'm not smart or anything. Looking at the happy couples on campus, I would feel so sad and anxious.

我从来没有谈过真正的恋爱。我想可能是我有什么问题。你知道，可能我长得不够好看，或者不够聪明什么的。看到学校里的情侣，我感到非常伤心和焦虑。

您认为为该问题提出建议的难易度如何？	1		2	3	4	5
		非常容易				非常困难
您认为该问题出现的普遍性如何？	1		2	3	4	5
		非常普遍				非常少见

Appendix B

Advice-giving writing task

Directions: Read the following paragraph which describes a problem that your classmate is having, and write your response to the problem. Your writing should show unity and use sufficient evidence to support your main ideas. Your response should be about 150 words (You can write more, if you'd like). Please also check your grammar, word choice, and use of punctuations (标点). You will receive feedback in terms of unity, support, and sentence skills.

NOTE: You may NOT use dictionary, class PPT slides, textbooks, or other resources for this task because we want to give feedback on what you can produce on your own.

Your classmate is asking you to give some advice. Here is his problem:
Prompt
Hi. I am a freshman at one of the top universities in China. When I started college, I majored in Chinese literature and had a double major in English. But I'm thinking of quitting English and only focus on studying Chinese. I found that I really don't like the English courses but developed a great interest for the Chinese courses. Studying English took so much of my time that I cannot find time to study Chinese as much as I want, or even take proper rest sometimes. But my mom is angry at my decision because she thinks I will get no job after I graduate. On the one hand, I want her be happy. But on the other, I also really want her to respect my decision. But to be honest, I have doubts about my decision, too. Since I don't know what I want to do with my life in the future, I am afraid that my decision will put me in a bad position in the future. I cannot re-enter the English program after I drop it. Moreover, I am thinking about using the extra time to equip myself with some new skills, but I am not sure what to do. So do I quit English and only pursue Chinese? I think if I make this decision, I

may have more time to study a major I like, and have more time for resting and learning some essential skills for the future. But I also risk limiting the job opportunities, which makes me feel anxious about my future. Do I change my major or not? How can I convince my mom? What if I have second thoughts? How do I use the extra time to equip myself with some useful skills?

Montserrat Mir
3 Learning about L2 Spanish requests abroad through classroom and ethnography-based pragmatics instruction

Abstract: The case for pragmatics instruction in second language (L2) learning has been confirmed by empirical research, although investigations within the context of study abroad are more limited. The objective of this paper is to discuss the impact of a pedagogical intervention on the learning of Spanish requests during a short-term (four-week) study abroad program. Despite the short time frame of their sojourn abroad, participants in this study demonstrated growth in requesting in Spanish. The results further suggest that maximizing exposure to the target language community as a complement to classroom-based pragmatics instruction during study abroad was beneficial.

Keywords: requests, pragmatics instruction, Spanish, study abroad

1 Introduction

In the field of interlanguage pragmatics, the teaching of pragmatics has been widely studied with positive results and an apparent advantage for explicit instruction (e.g., Cohen 2008; Taguchi 2015; Takahashi 2010). While an explicit approach appears to be more effective in raising learners' awareness of pragmatic forms and functions (Koike and Pearson 2005), an implicit approach can also be beneficial if learners' attention is drawn to the connections between target form, function, and context through in-class activities (Cohen 2016; Hasler-Barker 2016). We also know that in study abroad (SA) contexts, learners have the potential to find an abundance of opportunities to observe local norms of interaction, to practice and receive feedback from locals and peers, to experience real-life consequences of pragmatic failure, and to observe pragmatic variation (e.g., Taguchi 2018). However, because the development of pragmatic knowledge is slow in naturalistic settings, uninstructed learners often make only minor gains in target-like pragmatic competence after a stay abroad (Cohen and Shively 2007; Pérez-Vidal and Shively 2019). In the case of SA, pragmatic development not only varies by individual but also according to the complexity of pragmalinguistic forms,

https://doi.org/10.1515/9783110721775-004

degree of directness and conventionality, accuracy, and speed of pragmatic comprehension (Xiao 2015).

An SA experience that includes a pragmatics pedagogical intervention makes sense because classroom instruction can be extended to the community for learning practice, observation, and analysis of forms and functions. Specifically, the focus of the present investigation is to analyze how a pedagogical intervention that integrates the explicit teaching of speech acts with ethnographic field work impacts the learning of pragmatic features in the production of Spanish requests during a short-term SA program. This study differs from previous work in two ways. First, the pedagogical intervention includes learners in the role of ethnographers, and second, the immersion experience involves a short-term (four-week) program.

2 Review of existing research

2.1 Acquisition of Spanish requests in SA contexts

A review of the literature on the developmental patterns of acquisition of requests in SA contexts shows positive effects in approximating L2 norms over time. For example, we know that after at least one semester abroad, learners adopt target-like request strategies (Félix-Brasdefer 2007; Schauer 2007; Shively 2011), use more formulaic language (Bardovi-Harlig and Bastos 2011), and attempt to mitigate the illocutionary force of requests (Barron 2003).

In the case of the acquisition of Spanish requests, research findings indicate that learners move toward target-like request behavior in certain ways but retain non-target-like forms in other ways. For example, learners may abandon English strategies such as need statements (*Necesito* 'I need') and query permissions (*¿Puedo tener?* 'Can I have?') but fail to learn the most common Spanish request strategies such as the simple interrogative (*¿Me pones?* 'You give?') and/or the query ability (*¿Me puedes poner?* 'Can you give?') (Bataller 2010, 2016). This behavior may be due to learners' desire to "play it safe" (Barron 2003) by using a strategy that is correct even though another one would be more appropriate for the context. On the other hand, time and frequency of interactions with native speakers (NSs) may be responsible for approximating Peninsular Spanish norms by using formulaic imperatives (*ponme* 'give me') and assertive structures (*¿me pones?* 'you give me?') in service encounter scenarios (i.e., transactions with exchanges of goods and services in public settings) (Shively 2011).

Given the fact that short-term SA programs in the United States have been in the rise in the last few years (Institute of International Education 2018), a new line of research has emerged. While longer stays in the TL community are generally considered better than shorter stays, "[e]ven shorter lengths of stay might help learners become more target-like, particularly with respect to highly salient conversational functions" (Bardovi-Harlig 1999: 685), which supports research on highly formulaic speech acts such as apologies, compliments, and requests. Findings from the limited research on Spanish request development is contradictory, which may be due to differences in elicitation instruments, data analysis procedures, and request contexts. For example, while Spanish L2 learners' requests were rated higher after a four-week SA program, only advanced learners increased their use of internal mitigation and none of the participants switched to more target-like hearer-oriented requests (Hernández 2016). These results were very similar to Shively and Cohen's (2008) findings with a semester long SA program. However, in a six-week SA program in Spain, Czerwionka and Cuza's (2017a, 2017b) participants switched from speaker-oriented and declarative requests to hearer-oriented and imperative requests, although development was not the same in all contexts. Requests scenarios included three categories: food and drink in service encounters, general merchandise exchanges, and familial contexts. It was only in food and drink contexts that learners showed more improvement, perhaps due to the intensity of interaction in that communicative setting during the immersion experience (Czerwionka and Cuza 2017a).

2.2 Acquisition of Spanish requests in instructed SA contexts

Research in instructed SA contexts is also limited but evidence suggests that the incorporation of pragmatics instruction can positively affect learners' pragmatics knowledge and usage (e.g., Alcón-Soler 2017; Cohen and Shively 2007; Hernández and Boero 2018a, 2018b; Morris 2017; Mir 2020; Shively 2011).

Cohen and Shively's (2007) pedagogical intervention included a pre-departure orientation to speech acts, a self-training guidebook on developing language and culture strategies, and electronic journaling. The results indicated that the SA group who received pragmatic instruction during their one-semester experience abroad was rated more pragmatically appropriate in performing requests and used more mitigation than the uninstructed control SA group. However, the authors suggested that the self-directed nature of the pedagogical intervention may not have been enough to promote more pragmatic development.

Similar results were found in Shively's (2011) study where Spanish L2 learners participated in a brief orientation session on pragmatics, received 30 minutes of instruction on Spanish requests, and completed weekly journals during their semester in Spain. Some learners changed from indirect to direct requesting strategies, used elliptical forms, and shifted to hearer-oriented requesting strategies, approximating NS norms from the region. Shively (2011) highlights the different opportunities for socialization that learners had in Spain as key elements in pragmatic learning, although her participants reported not having many opportunities to practice in the community nor receiving corrective feedback on their pragmatic choices by Spanish NSs. Morris (2017) also found gains in the pragmatic knowledge of beginning Spanish L2 learners abroad during a 10-week program. Her results also demonstrated high retention of pragmatic competence one full year after the program ended. The pedagogical intervention included awareness-raising tasks in the classroom, practice with native conversation partners, completion of the task in the target-language (TL) community, and reflection and assessment on their own performance. Finally, Hernández and Boero (2018a, 2018b) explored the impact of pre-departure instruction accompanied by practice language tasks during short five-week programs in Argentina and Spain. Results indicated that their Spanish L2 participants shifted from speaker-oriented to hearer-oriented requests and increased their use of verbal downgrading.

2.3 Ethnography in language learning abroad

Ethnography seeks to provide a description of what people do in a setting, the outcome of their interactions, and the way they understand what they are doing (Watson-Gegeo 1988). The key element of an ethnographic paradigm is the extended, systematic, and detailed observation of a setting, where the observer also participates in the setting being studied (Jurasek, Lamson, and O'Maley 1996). Ethnography is also viewed as a natural way of learning. Since childhood, through observation and interaction, we build up an understanding of how things are done, what meanings they have, and how identities are expressed. We can train our students to follow this natural process of learning while abroad so they develop an ethnographic way of looking and working that will not only be useful for the period abroad, but will also have a lasting effect (Roberts 2003).

Research indicates that ethnography can promote learners' openness and curiosity toward the target culture and language and raise cross-cultural awareness (Bateman 2002; Roberts 2003). Lee (2012) used blogs and ethnographic interviews to explore the development of intercultural competence among a group of Spanish L2 learners abroad. One added benefit to the project was that her participants demonstrated their pragmatic competence by using a variety of speech acts (e.g., greetings, apologies, requests) in their interactions with NSs.

As the author described, "the ethnographic interviews exposed SA students to sociolinguistic dimensions of the Spanish language in a dynamic and authentic manner" (Lee 2012: 18).

The use of ethnography to examine pragmatic development abroad has not been widely studied. In one existing example, Shively (2011) used ethnographic data collection methods and analysis where learners recorded their use of requests in different service encounter scenarios in the TL community and completed reflective journals, interviews, and participant observations. Learners reported they learned about Spanish requests not only from explicit in-class instruction but also from observation in the TL community and their host families. Based on these results, Shively (2010) developed a model for pragmatics instruction in SA contexts that includes giving students practice in collecting and analyzing pragmatic features through ethnographic activities with NSs.

As seen, findings in previous research affirm the positive effect of pragmatic instruction in the development of pragmatic competence during a SA experience regardless of the length of the stay. However, given the rising popularity of short-term SA programs, more research is needed in these contexts. Additionally, very little is known about pragmatics instruction that goes beyond in-class lectures and activities and sends learners into the community to observe and analyze pragmatic features as participant observers, which is the goal of the present study. The following questions support this overall objective:
1. Does the requesting behavior of Spanish L2 learners change during a four-week SA experience with pragmatics instruction?
2. What factors contribute to the changes in the learners' requesting behavior and understanding of Spanish requests based on their perceptions?

3 Method

3.1 Participants

The participants for this study were 20 undergraduate students (3 male, 17 female) from a large midwestern university in the United States who participated in a four-week Spanish language program in Spain.[1] All participants were Spanish minors who had completed a minimum of four semesters of Spanish language

---

[1] Twenty-five students enrolled in the SA program, but some were Spanish heritage students and others did not complete all assessments, so their responses were excluded.

courses in addition to a Spanish writing course that was a prerequisite to participate in this SA program. Their level of proficiency was estimated at Intermediate-Low/Mid according to ACTFL guidelines and based on documented hours of instruction by empirical research (e.g., Rubio and Hacking 2019). They all consented to participate in the study by completing the corresponding IRB protocol. Their ages ranged between 18–21 years old and all had English as their native language.

3.2 Data collection instruments

An oral discourse completion test (DCT) was used at the start and at the end of the SA program.

The oral DCT consisted of 14 scenarios: four requests, four compliments, four compliment responses, and two distractors.[2] Participants read each scenario and recorded their responses orally. In order to maintain authenticity of the oral task, many scenarios depicted probable encounters between participants and host family members. Pre- and Post-DCTs included the same speech acts, but different scenarios. The request scenarios in this study are briefly described below.

Week 1 (Pre-DCT)
1. Ask to borrow an umbrella from your host parents
2. Order cookies at store
3. Ask your host brother to borrow his computer to show him a picture on the internet.
4. Ask for a second serving at the dinner table with your host family

Week 4 (Post-DCT)
1. Order a glass of wine at a bar
2. Ask to borrow a phone charger from your host parents.
3. Ask to borrow a fan for the room from your host parents.
4. Ask your host brother to pass the salt at the table while having a meal.

Learners were also asked to submit weekly journal entries in which they reflected on their overall experience in the SA program using a set of questions provided

---

[2] The data for this study come from a larger investigation on the learning of Spanish L2 compliments, compliment responses, and requests. The compliment data were examined in Mir (2020).

by the researcher. The following prompts were intentionally included in the third and fourth weekly journals to gather the participants' perceptions of Spanish requests and their own learning:
1. Reflect on your use of requests. Has your use of requests changed? How? What have you learned from watching how Spaniards use requests? How do you compare it to how Americans do it in the US? What difficulties do you have using requests in Spanish?
2. How confident do you feel now about using requests in Spanish? Did your host family correct you on how you used requests? Was that helpful? Please give details.

3.3 Immersion context and pedagogical intervention

The SA program took place in Ávila, Spain, a small town in the center of the country. Students completed a Spanish conversation class taught by Ávila faculty and an Introduction to Spanish Linguistics course offered by the researcher, totaling 20 hours of instruction per week. Each participant lived with a Spanish host family.

The instructional treatment used in this study was grounded in research-based models that focus on awareness-raising strategies and on training learners to observe, analyze, reflect, and practice pragmatics behaviors in the host community (Martínez-Flor and Usó-Juan 2006; Shively 2010). Participants received explicit teaching on the use of Spanish requests, compliments, and compliment responses as part of a pragmatics unit in the Spanish linguistics class. All explicit teaching in the classroom took place within the first two weeks of the program. In the first week, participants were introduced to the concept of Spanish pragmatics and speech acts. Using evidence from research in speech acts, they learned about pragmalinguistic forms and sociopragmatic factors first in general and then, with reference to the targeted speech acts in Spanish. Students participated in metapragmatic discussions using transcripts from movies and fictional dialogues (Mir 2001). They also engaged in controlled practice matching turns in dialogues and doing role plays in pairs. A first set of role plays included the type of answer expected. For example, one scenario required that the speaker ask an officemate for money to take a taxi, but the request had to be in the form of a question and had to offer compensation. A second round of role plays involved students in different requesting scenarios without any guidance on request strategy use.

As homework at the end of the first week, students were sent to conduct ethnographic research. Students were asked to record two members of their host family performing five given request scenarios, transcribe the dialogues, reflect on the responses, and bring them to class for discussion. Based on students' comments, this task engaged students in conversations about speech acts in Spanish with their host families. In addition, students recorded spontaneous conversations in the community, seeking examples of the targeted speech act, transcribed those conversations and made annotations about the social characteristics of the interaction. This material was also shared in the classroom to engage learners in metapragmatic discussions. Finally, during the second week students were encouraged to use compliments and requests with their host family and record a conversation with them. Prior to this family conversation, the researcher sent a letter to the host families explaining the research project, encouraging them to practice requests and compliments with their student, and requesting consent to use the recorded conversation for research purposes.[3] Overall, the explicit instructional treatment on Spanish requests in the classroom lasted approximately four to five hours.

3.4 Analysis of the data

The directness and orientation of the requests in the oral DCTs were coded following a scheme developed by Czerwionka and Cuza (2017a). Depending on the personal deictic orientation of the verb, requests were coded as hearer-oriented (i.e., second-person reference), speaker-oriented (i.e., first-person reference), or ambiguously-oriented (i.e., verbal ellipsis). With regard to directness, a division was made between direct requests (i.e., imperatives, declarative statements, and ellipsis) and conventionally indirect requests. The latter included various types of interrogatives such as simple interrogative clauses, ability, permission, or availability queries (Blum-Kulka, House, and Kasper 1989). Internal and external modification to mitigate the illocutionary force of the request was coded based on previous literature (Bataller 2016; Blum-Kulka, House, and Kasper 1989; Félix-Brasdefer 2007; Hernández 2016; Shively and Cohen 2008; Shively 2011). See Table 1 below for coding categories examples. Finally, the journal responses were analyzed by examining and recording themes within the data, which were used to answer our second research question.

---

[3] The recorded conversations with host parents are not analyzed here.

Table 1: Coding categories for requests with examples from SA students.

REQUESTS: HEAD ACTS		
ORIENTATION	DIRECTNESS	
	Direct	**Conventionally indirect**
Hearer-oriented	Imperatives *Oye, Rubén, pásame la sal* 'Listen, Ruben, pass me the salt'	Hearer-interrogatives *¿Me dan un paraguas, por favor?* (simple query) *'You give me an umbrella, please?'
Speaker-oriented	Declarative (want/need statements) *Quisiera una docena de galletas* 'I would like a dozen cookies'	Speaker-interrogatives *¿Puedo usar la computadora?* (ability query) 'Can I use the computer?'
Ambiguous	Ellipsis *Un poco más, por favor* 'A little bit more, please'	
REQUESTS: MITIGATION		
Internal Mitigation	Syntactic downgraders: Use of conditional or imperfect subjunctive tense. *¿Podría comprar una docena de galletas, por favor?* 'Could I buy a dozen cookies, please?'	
	Lexical/phrasal downgraders: Use of softeners (i.e., a little bit), consultative devices (i.e., is it okay if?), politeness devices (i.e., please, thank you), attention getters (i.e., hello, good morning, excuse me, Peter, Miss) *¿Puedo tener un poco más de arroz, por favor?* 'Can I have a little bit more rice, please?'	
External mitigation	Moves that check on availability, offer a disclaimer or a justification, or express exaggerated appreciation to sweeten the imposition on the hearer. *¿Tienes otro ventilador? Mi habitación hace mucho calor.* 'Do you have another fan? It is hot in my bedroom.' *Me gusta mucho el arroz. ¿Puedo repetir, por favor?* 'I like the rice very much. May I repeat, please?'	

4 Results

4.1 Research question 1: Spanish request development

Table 2 shows overall distribution of all request strategies found in the data.[4]

---

[4] Only one elliptical request form was found in the data and therefore, it was not included in the statistical analysis.

Table 2: Directness of request strategies before and after pedagogical treatment (N=20).

	Week 1 (pre-DCT)		Week 4 (post-DCT)	
	Total	%	Total	%
Imperative (hearer)	0	0	6	7.6
Interrogative (hearer)	11	14.5	39	49.4
Interrogative (speaker)	42	55.3	18	22.8
Declarative (speaker)	23	30.3	16	20.3
TOTAL	76	100	79	100

A chi-square test of independence showed that there was a significant association between strategy type and pedagogical treatment, X^2 (2, N = 155) = 30.0871, p = 0.00001. The presence of pragmatics instruction did influence the type of request strategies participants used during this SA program. In order to address the issue of directness alone, another chi-square analysis was conducted by collapsing the strategy types into two categories: direct and conventionally indirect. The statistical analysis was not significant (X^2 (2, N = 155) = 0.1097, p = 0.74). Overall, participants preferred conventionally indirect requests in both pre- and post-DCTs, which means the pedagogical intervention did not alter participants' pragmatic behavior with regards to directness.

A closer examination of strategy usage across each individual scenario was performed but no major deviations from the general results were observed. In all scenarios, except two, participants preferred conventionally indirect strategies. Hearer-oriented simple interrogatives (e.g., *¿Me dejas tu cargador?* 'You lend me your charger?') which are typical in Spanish, were used three times (3.9%) in the pre-DCT and six (7.5%) in the post-DCT, revealing a minor shift in approximation to Spanish norms. The most common conventionally indirect interrogatives used by participants in both DCTs were ability queries (e.g., *¿Puede prestarme un paraguas*? 'Can you lend me an umbrella?') (pre-DCT: N=43; 56.5%; post-DCT: N=34; 43%). The two scenarios where directness was favored was in the two service encounters included in the DCT. However, the directness displayed was with declarative statements. The first scenario in the pre-DCT involved ordering cookies at a store. Here 14 students (73.7%) used declarative statements such as (1) below. The use of *pedir* ('to order/ask for') in this scenario appeared in 6 of the 14 responses. Other declarative statements that students used included verbs such as *necesitar* ('to need') or *querer* ('to want').

(1) Week 1 (pre-DCT): Ordering cookies at a store
Pido una docena de galletas, por favor. Muchas gracias.
'I request a dozen cookies, please. Thank you very much'

The second service encounter appeared in the post-DCT and involved requesting red wine at a bar. Here also 14 students used declarative statements (70%), with eight of them using *pedir* in their requests, as in example (2).

(2) Week 4 (post-DCT): Ordering wine at a bar
Hola, pido un tinto de verano, ¿por favor?
'Hello, I order a summer red wine, please?'

The use of *pedir* or its English equivalent in service encounters is not common in American English or in Peninsular Spanish, which means these declarative statements may reflect an interlanguage phenomenon. In Peninsular Spanish, the verb *pedir* may appear in restaurant contexts when a waiter may ask for an order (e.g., *¿Qué van a pedir?* 'What are you going to order?') or among dinner guests as they discuss their order (e.g., *Oye, ¿qué vas a pedir tú?* 'Hey, what are you going to have?'), but it is not commonly used when placing an order. In shopping scenarios, as the one depicted in (1), the verb *pedir* is not pragmatically appropriate. The use of this verb in these service encounter scenarios may be due to the limited exposure and experience with these types of transactions during the short period abroad. Learners spent only four weeks in the TL setting which did not allow for many opportunities to go into stores or bars so that they could learn from observation how to order things and practice these forms in their own transactions.

There were only six imperatives and all of them appeared in the context of requesting salt at the dinner table in the post-DCT. In fact, in the pre-DCT, where students requested a second serving of rice, the directness of the request was obtained by want/need statements (N=4; 20%), in the "salt" context in the post-DCT, all direct requests were in the form of imperatives (N=6; 30%) as in example (3) below.

(3) Week 4 (post-DCT): Requesting salt at the table
Por favor, pasa la sal.
'Please, pass the salt.'

In contrast to directness, the orientation of the request was clearly impacted by the pedagogical intervention. In order to conduct statistical analysis, the four strategy types were collapsed into two categories: speaker- and hearer-oriented requests. A chi square test of independence resulted in significant results (χ^2 (2, N = 155) = 30.3032, $p < .05$). This change resulted in a drop from speaker-oriented requests (pre-DCT: 85.6%; post-DCT: 43%) to hearer-oriented requests (pre-DCT: 14.5%; post-DCT: 57%) after the pedagogical treatment. Excluding the two service encounter scenarios, prior to the pedagogical instruction, participants clearly favored speaker interrogatives in all contexts, as we see in example (4) below. After the treatment, in three of the four contexts, learners preferred hearer interrogatives in many of their responses as illustrated in the example in (5).

(4) Week 1 (pre-DCT): Request an umbrella from host family
¿Puedo usar una paraguas para afuera, por favor?
'Can I use an umbrella to go outside, please?'

(5) Week 4 (post-DCT): Request to use phone charger from host family
¿Puedes prestarme tu cargador?
'Can you lend me your charger?'

Table 3: Use of mitigation devices before and after pedagogical treatment (N=20).

	Week 1 (pre-DCT)		Week 4 (post-DCT)	
	Total	%	Total	%
Internal modification				
Imperfect subjunctive tense	2	2.0	1	0.7
Conditional tense	7	7.1	10	7.4
Politeness devices	41	41.4	48	35.6
Softeners	6	6.1	3	2.2
Attention getters	20	20.2	32	23.7
Consultative devices	5	5.1	3	2.2.
(Total)	81	81.8	97	71.9
External modification				
Justifications	10	10.1	31	23
Sweeteners	8	8.1	3	2.2
Disarmer	0	0	2	1.5
Preparator	0	0	2	1.5
(Total)	18	18.2	38	28.1
	99	100	135	100

The use of mitigation devices also revealed some changes in pragmatic behavior from the beginning to the end of the program. In order to get a clearer view, it was decided not to run statistical analyses across the two main types of mitigators (i.e., internal and external). The results in Table 3 show an increase in the number of mitigating devices from beginning (N=99) to end (N=135).

Before the pedagogical treatment, learners heavily relied on internal lexical modifications in the form of politeness devices (41.4%) and attention-getters (20.2%). By the end of the program, learners dropped the use of internal devices in favor of external mitigators as in the case of justifications (23%). The increase in the number of mitigating devices also resulted in longer request responses in week 4 (post-DCT).

At the syntactic level, we do not see many changes over time. The use of the imperfect subjunctive or the conditional to mitigate the imposition of the request was barely used. The category "politeness devices" included the expressions *por favor* ('please') and *gracias* ('thank you') and accounted for 41.4% of the data in the pre-DCT and 35.6% in the post-DCT. These two expressions have two different functions. The use of *por favor* in a request is expected as a way to minimize the imposition. The total number of times learners used *por favor* at program beginning and end was very similar, although their percentages changed due to the presence of an increase in mitigating devices in the post-DCT (pre-DCT: N=35; 35%, post-DCT: N=33; 24.4%).

On the other hand, the use of *gracias* in the learners' requests can be explained by the nature of the elicitation device. This politeness expression is expected after the addressee agrees to the request, but it does not make sense when added to the request head act. The oral DCT did not allow for a complete exchange between participants and therefore, learners may have felt motivated to include *gracias* because they only had one turn to complete the request as we see in (6) below.

(6) Week 1 (pre-DCT): Ask to borrow an umbrella from your host parents
Perdón, puede prestarme un paraguas? Muchas gracias.
'Excuse me, can you lend me an umbrella? Thank you very much.'

In order to illustrate the changes observed in the use of mitigation, we look at two parallel scenarios where a student requests to borrow an umbrella (pre-DCT) and a phone charger (post-DCT) from the host family. The number of mitigating devices in the 'umbrella' context was 25 compared to 35 in the "charger" scenario. The examples below exemplify typical responses:

(7) Week 1 (pre-DCT): Request to borrow an umbrella
¿Puedo usar un paraguas?
'Can I use an umbrella?'

(8) Week 4 (post-DCT): Request to borrow a phone charger
Perdón, mi cargador ha roto ahora. Necesito comprar una nueva mañana, ¿pero esta noche podría usar tuyo cargador?
'Excuse me, my charger is broken now. I need to buy a new one tomorrow, but tonight could I use your charger?'

Overall, these results reveal that the pedagogical intervention used during this short-term SA program altered learners' requesting behavior with regards to strategy type (i.e., learners used more hearer-oriented requests at program end) but not in terms of degree of directness. By the end of the program, learners increased the number of mitigating devices although they still preferred external support moves such as the lexical politeness form *por favor*, attention-getters, and justifications. These results have also revealed the role of the elicitation instrument and the importance of learner's familiarity with requesting scenarios in the DCT.

4.2 Research question 2: Perceptions of request behavior

All students completed weekly journals, but not all addressed all prompts. Based on the data, the following themes were present: a) change in use of requesting strategies, b) observation of Spanish norms, c) difficulties using Spanish requests, and d) host family help and/or correction.

Only two students (10%) reported no change in their requesting behavior, whereas the remaining 18 students (90%) highlighted their increased level of confidence, understanding, and actual use of Spanish requests as a result of what they had observed in the local community (N=11; 55%), learned through classroom instruction (N=5; 25%), or practiced in the community (N=4; 20%). Furthermore, in observing native Spanish speakers' requesting behavior, some students noticed that Spanish requests were direct or "straight to the point" (N=5; 25%) and involved simpler and more informal forms than requests in American English (N=4; 20%). It was the directness of Spanish requests that surprised some participants and, unfortunately, also complicated their requesting behavior, as Sonia explained in her entry:

> As far as requests, many Spaniards are very direct and do not waste much time asking for what they want. At first, this took me off guard and I took it as being rude, but now I have realized that it is simply the way that they do things. For example, when we were in Segovia yesterday, we stopped at an ice cream shop and the woman working there kept saying "Dime, dime." She wanted us to tell her what we wanted but we hadn't decided yet. It

> seemed a little rude and aggressive, but that is just how people ask for what they want . . . I am not good at being very direct with people. I prefer to ask in a polite way with lots of extra "fluff" and am not used to simply just asking what I want with a couple of words.

Participants were also asked whether their host family helped them with their Spanish requests. Half of them (N=10; 50%) noted that their family assisted with their learning as opposed to six (30%) who claimed no family assistance and/or correction. Those who claimed family help, also stressed its beneficial impact on their learning.

> I definitely asked my family for help and they would encourage me to say requests or compliments to get practice. This was definitely helpful . . . my mom would encourage me to compliment the food we were eating, or to ask her a request.   (Diana)

In order to examine the relationship between participants' opinions and their pragmatic behavior on the oral production task, we looked at responses from two participants: Dora and Kayla. In her journal entries, Dora positively commented on the amount of Spanish she was using every week as well as how much improvement she had observed in her language skills. However, she also indicated that she did not see much difference between Spanish and American English requests and stressed her family never helped her with her learning of requests. She also claimed that "my use of [requests] has changed a little in the sense that my form is better". However, her responses from the pre- and post-test are almost identical, revealing few changes in pragmatic development as seen in (9) and (10).

(9) Week 1 (pre-DCT):
 ¿Puedo usar un paraguas?
 'Can I use an umbrella?'
 ¿Puedo un poquito más arroz?
 '*Can I a little bit more rice?'

(10) Week 4 (post-DCT):
 Mi cuarto hace muy calor, ¿puedo usar una fan para mi cuarto?
 'My room is very hot, can I use a fan for my room?'
 Sí, quiero un vino tinto pero no ahora. Yo quiero un mojito
 'Yes, I want red wine but not now. I want a *mojito*'

On the other hand, Kayla observed differences in the Spanish requesting system. Kayla expressed an awareness that she needed to make an extra effort to engage in conversations with Spanish NSs and claimed that she spent 75% of the day speaking in Spanish. Kayla noticed Spanish requests were less formal and, in fact, said that "my requests are not as formal as they were when I started and are a lot shorter and to the point." In addition, she positively evaluated the assistance of her host family but also acknowledged her difficulty in adhering to Spanish speakers' norms: "My host family helped me with them. It is just hard for me because people in Spain literally say things that I would never say." A comparison of responses at both times shows the pragmatic development that Kayla claimed in her journal entries. She replaced the *¿puedo yo?* ('can I?') construction typical of many L2 learners with more natural hearer-oriented Spanish requests.

(11) Week 1 (pre-DCT):
¿Puedo usar sus paraguas?
'Can I use your umbrella?'
¿Puedo tener una docena de galletas?
'Can I have a dozen cookies?'

(12) Week 4 (post-DCT):
¿Puedes prestarme tu cargador?
'Can you lend me your charger?'
¿Puedes pasarme la sal?
'Can you pass me the salt?'

In sum, learners acknowledged that the classroom instruction they had received was a contributing factor in their learning of Spanish requests. They also stressed the ethnographic element of the instruction where they had to observe and analyze Spanish NSs' interactions in the community and at home with their host families, the latter of which led to assistance and/or correction at times.

5 Discussion

Our first research question examined changes in the requesting behavior of Spanish L2 learners over the course of a short-term SA program in Spain. The analysis of the data revealed only some pragmatic development, which is not surprising given the briefness of the sojourn abroad. As seen in previous research employing oral data (Czerwionka and Cuza 2017a, 2017b; Shively 2011), learners were able to switch to hearer-oriented requests by the end of the fourth week in Spain. While American English speakers rely on speaker-oriented requests (Fox and Heinneman 2016), Spanish speakers prefer hearer-oriented directives (Placencia 2005; Shively and Cohen 2008). In fact, speaker-oriented requests in the form of want/need statements and ability queries are quite typical in English (Fox and Heinemann 2016), contrary to Spanish where permission and ability queries are not as common (Pinto and Raschio 2007).

However, the directness of the learners' requests did not change much over time. Overall, learners preferred conventionally indirect requests, except in the two service encounter scenarios where direct declarative statements were common. In comparison with American English, Peninsular Spanish requests are more direct (Placencia 2005), although research has also indicated a preference for hearer-oriented interrogative requests (Bataller 2010). In service encounters in particular, Spaniards focus on the transaction at hand and, therefore, interactions tend to be quite brief and to the point, beginning with a greeting and followed by the service request (Shively 2011). Imperatives, hearer-oriented interrogatives, and elliptical forms are common, whereas declarative want-statements and conventionally indirect ability-queries are used much less frequently (Placencia 2005). Despite the preference for direct requests in Peninsular Spanish, learners' use of declarative statements at both the beginning and end of SA suggests that they were still uncertain after four weeks in Spain about local norms for these transactions, perhaps due to an overgeneralization of L2 pragmatic norms (Cohen 2012). Learners were aware that Spanish requests are more direct but were unaware of which forms are appropriate in public transactions. Switching from speaker to hearer-oriented requests requires a syntactic change in the formation of the request without impacting its politeness values. Choosing direct request forms strongly affects politeness values and given the short period of time abroad, learners were perhaps uncomfortable choosing a form that in their L1 would be considered less polite, indicating that learners were still transferring politeness norms from their L1.[5]

As seen in other research (Barron 2003; Cohen and Shively 2007; Félix-Brasdefer 2004), learners increased the use and variety of mitigating devices in their responses. Despite the fact that Spanish requests include verbal downgrading in the form of the conditional and past subjunctive (Bataller 2016; Cohen and Shively 2007; Shively and Cohen 2008), learners in this study did not incorporate these devices in their requests, perhaps due to the short duration of the program and/or their language proficiency level. Low/mid intermediate speakers still struggle with basic Spanish grammar rules, and the use of the conditional and/or subjunctive is more representative of language functions acquired at the

---

5 This point was made by one of the anonymous reviewers.

advanced and superior proficiency level (ACTFL 2012). In addition, while learners added more mitigation in the post-DCT requests, their use of the politeness marker *por favor* ('please') was maintained, perhaps due to its low propositional content and ease of use. However, this result contradicts the observation made in other studies that learners decreased the use of *por favor* over time (Bataller 2016; Félix-Brasdefer 2007). While L2 learners may lack the grammatical competence to add sophisticated internal and external modifications to their requests, they are equipped with the necessary sociopragmatic knowledge from their L1 to perform simple but effective and appropriate requests (Félix-Brasdefer 2007). In short, while learners used more mitigation at the end of week four, the nature of the mitigating devices seemed to be in accordance with their level of grammatical competence and the contexts in which mitigation was used. For example, the number of justifications seen in week 4 may be related to the types of scenarios in the instrument that led to the need to justify the request, as in the case of requesting a fan because it is hot in the room or asking for a phone charger because the learner's charger was broken.

The second research question addressed learners' perceptions of their own learning and understanding of Spanish requests. In the journal entries, many indicated that they learned primarily from observing Spanish speakers interact, such as in the case of the directness of Spanish requests. Some also mentioned the importance of their families' help in providing instruction and correction. In instructional pragmatics, and particularly in SA contexts, it is challenging to receive feedback on pragmatic issues from NSs (Shively 2011; Sykes 2009). Therefore, requesting assistance from host families in the current study was a potential resource for learners to acquire strategies to avoid negative transfer, overgeneralization of pragmatic rules, and the effect of instruction (Cohen 2012, 2017). Overall, the role of learners as ethnographers in this study assisted them in the development of their pragmatic competence as they engaged in interactions with Spanish NSs and in self-directed learning and reflection (Shively 2010). Additionally, allowing learners to engage in ethnographic tasks resulted in a sentiment of enjoyment and ownership (Cohen 2012, 2019), as well as intense involvement in their education (Jurasek, Lamson, and O'Maley 1996), as Jennifer explained in her journal entry:

> *I never spent so much time on this topic in a Spanish class before. It was nice to have some fresh material and to learn something about Spanish culture. A funny example of this is when we eat a meal I don't always ask for things. I let my shy personality take over and I would have rather wanted to go without than to ask. My host mom noticed and jokingly said, "If you don't ask, you can't eat!" I knew it was light-hearted, but I took it seriously. This made me ask questions and use what we learned in class. My host mom always corrected me with not only this but my grammar overall. I never felt offended by this. I knew*

> *that she was only helping me and what she told me always stuck and I was able to use the correct words/phrases the next time around.*

Based on the journal data, the participants reported spending a considerable amount of time interacting with their host families. The ethnographic component of the pedagogical intervention also contributed to the learners' noticing of Spanish requests in the community and in their own speech. In all, the language socialization that these learners experienced was a combination of an implicit (i.e., learning through interaction with native speakers) and explicit (i.e., instruction from an expert in the use of language forms and functions) processes of socialization (Ochs 1990). In the SA context, both kinds of socialization contribute to student learning (Shively 2011). This group of learners received explicit instruction and guided practice in the classroom. They also observed and practiced new forms as they interacted with local people in the community. They completed assignments with their host families, which led to conversations about speech acts and, in some cases, assistance through correction and feedback. Consequently, this pedagogical intervention helped to increase opportunities for explicit and implicit socialization as well as the amount and intensity of practice (Shively and Cohen 2008). However, approximation to Spanish NS norms was more apparent in the requesting scenarios that depicted typical situations with a host family. In the service encounters, learners did not show much improvement. Based on learners' feedback, their host families made them feel very comfortable and almost as part of the family. The time spent at home allowed for many more opportunities to socialize with family members and to observe and practice requests. However, the short duration of the SA context and, thus, the limited number of opportunities to engage in service encounters may have contributed to the learners' failure to pragmatically adhere to Spanish norms in these conditions. Given the length of the program, more focused ethnographic tasks around service encounters with assistance from family members might be beneficial.

This study has some limitations. Despite the abundance of research on Spanish requests, it is known that methodological differences in data collection and analysis may alter the comparison between studies (Bataller and Shively 2011). In fact, we do not know how NSs would respond in the given scenarios in the oral DCTs. Further, the lack of a control group of learners who studied abroad, but who did not receive the intervention, does not allow us to tease out the effects of instruction from incidental learning abroad. In addition, in order to increase the face validity of the elicitation instrument, many of the scenarios in the DCTs reflected typical situations between students and a host family. As observed, our conclusions are mainly limited to familiar contexts in the home.

6 Conclusion

This study has revealed that despite the short duration of a four-week SA experience, participants exhibited some changes in their use and understanding of Spanish requests. Previous studies revealed similar gains (Cohen and Shively 2007; Hernández and Boero 2018a, 2018b; Shively 2011), yet the pedagogical treatment in the current study differs from the prior research because of the presence of ethnographic tasks. Cohen has called for learners to be "proactive" in their own learning (Cohen 2017: 449) and strategic in the process of learning pragmatics. The benefits of teaching pragmatics abroad include not only access to authentic input but also the presence of NSs with whom they can learn. Learning can be enhanced through guided and purposeful ethnographic tasks that encourage learners to actively seek the type of explicit socialization that will provide them with instruction and feedback from the experts in the TL, especially their host families, with whom many students spend a considerasble amount of time and consequently develop quasi-familial ties. Given the intensity of practice and socialization in these familial contexts, pragmatics instruction with a strong ethnographic component could become the key to pragmatic development in short-term SA experiences.

References

Alcón-Soler, Eva. 2017. Pragmatic development during study abroad: An analysis of Spanish teenagers' request strategies in English emails. *Annual Review of Applied Linguistics* 37. 77–92.

ACTFL. 2012. ACTFL proficiency guidelines, Alexandria, VA: American Council on the Teaching of Foreign Languages. https://www.actfl.org/publications/guidelines-and-manuals/actfl-proficiency-guidelines-2 012 (accessed May 26, 2020).

Bardovi-Harlig, Kathleen. 1999. Exploring the interlanguage of interlanguage pragmatics: A research agenda for acquisitional pragmatics. *Language Learning* 49(4). 677–713.

Bardovi-Harlig, Kathleen & Maria-Thereza Bastos. 2011. Proficiency, length of stay, and intensity of interaction and acquisition of conventional expressions in L2 pragmatics. *Intercultural Pragmatics* 8(3). 347–384.

Barron, Anne. 2003. *Acquisition in interlanguage pragmatics: Learning how to do things with words in a study abroad context*. Philadelphia: John Benjamins.

Bataller, Rebeca. 2010. Making a request for a service in Spanish: Pragmatic development in the study abroad setting. *Foreign Language Annals* 43(1). 160–175.

Bataller, Rebeca. 2016. Por favor, ¿Puedo tener una Coca-cola, por favor? L2 development of internal mitigation in requests. *Issues in Applied Linguistics* 20. 1–34.

Bataller, Rebeca & Rachel L. Shively. 2011. Role plays and naturalistic data in pragmatics research: Service encounters during study abroad. *Journal of Linguistics and Language Teaching* 2(1). 15–50.

Bateman, Blair E. 2002. Promoting openness toward culture learning: Ethnographic interviews for students of Spanish. *The Modern Language Journal* 86(3). 318–331.

Blum-Kulka, Shoshana, Juliana House, & Gabriele Kasper (eds.). 1989. *Cross-cultural pragmatics: Requests and apologies*. Norwood, NJ: Ablex Publishing.

Cohen, Andrew. 2008. Teaching and assessing L2 pragmatics: What can we expect from learners? *Language Teaching* 41(2). 215–237.

Cohen, Andrew. 2012. Comprehensible pragmatics: Where input and output come together. In Miroslaw Pawlak (ed.), *New perspectives on individual differences in language learning and teaching*, 249–261. New York: Springer.

Cohen, Andrew. 2016. The teaching of pragmatics by native and nonnative language teachers: What they know and what they report doing. *Studies in Second Language Learning and Teaching* 6(4). 561–585.

Cohen, Andrew. 2017. Teaching and learning second language pragmatics. In Eli Hinkel (ed.), *Handbook of research in second language teaching and learning* (vol. 3), 428–452. New York: Routledge.

Cohen, Andrew. 2019. Strategy instruction for learning and performing target language pragmatics. In Anna Uhl Chamot & Vee Harris (eds.), *Learning strategy instruction in the language classroom: Issues and implementation*, 140–152. Bristol, England: Multilingual Matters.

Cohen, Andrew & Rachel L. Shively. 2007. Acquisitions of requests and apologies in Spanish and French: Impact of study abroad and strategy-building intervention. *Modern Language Journal* 91. 189–212.

Czerwionka, Lori & Alejandro Cuza. 2017a. A pragmatic analysis of L2 Spanish requests: Acquisition in three situational contexts during short-term study abroad. *Intercultural Pragmatics* 14(3). 391–419.

Czerwionka, Lori & Alejandro Cuza. 2017b. Second language acquisition of Spanish service industry requests in an immersion context. *Hispania* 100(2). 239–260.

Félix-Brasdefer, J. César. 2004. Interlanguage refusals: Linguistic politeness and length of residence in the target community. *Language Learning* 54. 587–653.

Félix-Brasdefer, J. César. 2007. Pragmatic development in the Spanish as a FL classroom: A cross-sectional study of learner requests. *Intercultural Pragmatics* 4. 253–286.

Fox, Barbara & Trine Heinneman. 2016. Rethinking format: An examination of requests. *Language in Society* 45(4). 499–531.

Hasler-Barker, Maria. 2016. Effects of metapragmatic instruction on the production of compliments and compliment responses: Learner-learner role-plays in the foreign language classroom. In Kathleen Bardovi-Harlig & J. César Félix-Brasdefer (eds.), *Pragmatics and Language Learning* (vol. 14), 125–152. Honolulu, HI: National Foreign Language Resource Center.

Hernández, Todd. 2016. Acquisition of L2 Spanish requests in short-term study abroad. *Study Abroad Research in Second Language Acquisition and International Education* 1. 186–216.

Hernández, Todd & Paulo Boero. 2018a. Explicit instruction for request strategy development during short-term study abroad. *Journal of Spanish Language Teaching* 5(1). 35–49.

Hernández, Todd & Paulo Boero. 2018b. Explicit intervention for Spanish pragmatic development during short-term study abroad: An examination of learner request production and cognition. *Foreign Language Annals* 51(2). 389–410.

Institute of International Education, 2018. Open Doors Report. https://www.iie.org/Research-and-Insights/Open-Doors/Data/US-Study-Abroad (accessed December 6, 2019).

Jurasek, Richard, Howard Lamson, & Patricia O'Maley. 1996. Ethnographic learning while studying abroad. *Frontiers: The Interdisciplinary Journal of Study Abroad* 2(1). 23–44.

Koike, Dale & Lynn Pearson. 2005.The effect of instruction and feedback in the development of pragmatic competence. *System* 33(3). 481–501.

Lee, Lina. 2012. Engaging study abroad students in intercultural learning through blogging and ethnographic interviews. *Foreign Language Annals* 41(1). 7–21.

Martínez-Flor, Alicia & Esther Usó-Juan. 2006. A comprehensive pedagogical framework to develop pragmatics in the foreign language classroom: The 6Rs approach. *Applied Language Learning* 16. 39–64.

Mir, Montserrat. 2001. Un modelo didáctico para la enseñanza de la pragmática. *Hispania* 84(3). 542–549.

Mir, Montserrat. 2020. Teaching and learning about Spanish L2 compliments in short-term study abroad. *Study Abroad Research in Second Language Acquisition and International Education* 5(2). 230–257.

Morris, Kimberly. 2017. *Learning by doing: The affordances of task-based pragmatics instruction for beginning L2 Spanish learners studying abroad*. CA: University of California, Davis dissertation.

Ochs, Elinor. 1990. Indexicality and socialization. In James Stigler, Richard Shweder & Gilbert Herdt (eds.), *Cultural psychology: Essays in comparative human psychology*, 287–308. Cambridge: Cambridge University Press.

Pérez Vidal, Carmen & Rachel L. Shively. 2019. L2 pragmatic development in study abroad settings. In Naoko Taguchi (ed.), *Handbook of SLA and pragmatics*, 355–371. New York: Routledge.

Pinto, Derrin & Ricaher Raschio. 2007. A comparative study of requests in heritage speaker Spanish, L1 Spanish, and L1 English. *International Journal of Bilingualism* 11(2). 135–155.

Placencia, María Elena. 2005. Pragmatic variation in corner store interactions in Quito and Madrid. *Hispania* 88(3). 583–598.

Roberts, Celia. 2003. Ethnography and cultural practice: Ways of learning during residence abroad. In Geof Alred, Michael Byram, & Mike Fleming (eds.), *Intercultural Experience and Education*, 114–130. Tonawanda, NY: Multilingual Matters.

Rubio, Fernando & Jane F. Hacking. 2019. Proficiency vs. Performance. What do the tests show? In Paula Winke & Susan Gass (eds.), *Foreign Language Proficiency in Higher Education*, 137–152. Switzerland: Springer Nature Switzerland.

Schauer, Gila. 2007. Finding the right words in the study abroad context: The development of German learners' use of external modifiers in English. *Intercultural Pragmatics* 4. 193–220.

Shively, Rachel L. 2010. From the virtual world to the real world: A model of pragmatics instruction for study abroad. *Foreign Language Annals* 43(1). 105–137.

Shively, Rachel L. 2011. L2 pragmatic development in study abroad: A longitudinal study of Spanish service encounters. *Journal of Pragmatics* 43. 1818–1835.

Shively, Rachel L. & Andrew Cohen. 2008. Development of Spanish requests and apologies during study abroad. *Íkala, revista de lenguaje y cultura* 13. 53–118.

Sykes, Julie. 2009. Learner requests in Spanish: Examining the potential of multiuser virtual environments for L2 pragmatics acquisition. In Lara Lomika & Gillian Lord (eds.), *The second generation: Online collaboration and social networking in CALL*, 199–234. San Marcos, Texas: CALICO, Texas State University.

Taguchi, Naoko. 2015. Instructed pragmatics at a glance: Where instructional studies were, are, and should be going. *Language Teaching* 48(1). 1–50.

Taguchi, Naoko. 2018. Data collection and analysis in developmental L2 pragmatics research: Discourse completion test, roleplay, and naturalistic recording. In Aarnes Gudmestad & Amanda Edmonds (eds.), *Critical reflections on data in second language acquisition*, 7–32. Amsterdam: John Benjamins.

Takahashi, Satomi. 2010. The effect of pragmatic instruction on speech act performance. In Alica Martínez Flor & Esther Usó-Juan (eds.), *Speech act performance: Theoretical, empirical and methodological issues*, 127–144. Amsterdam: John Benjamins.

Watson-Gegeo, Karen Ann. 1988. Ethnography in ESL: Defining the Essentials. *TESOL Quarterly* 22. 575–92.

Xiao, Feng. 2015. Adult second language learners' pragmatic development in the study-abroad context: A review. *Frontiers: The Interdisciplinary Journal of Study Abroad* 25. 132–149.

Tania Gómez and Luz Ede-Hernandez

4 Effectiveness of a post-study abroad pedagogical intervention in learning compliments and compliment responses in L2 Spanish

Abstract: Compliments and compliment responses have been widely studied in second language (L2) Spanish pragmatics pedagogical interventions. Results from previous research suggest that teaching the pragmatics of compliments is effective in increasing competence among learners of Spanish as an L2. This chapter examines the effects of Language Learning Strategy Instruction (LLSI) used to teach pragmatic strategies to students following a semester-long study abroad program. The instructional treatment included awareness-raising strategies, modeling, evaluation, and expansion of student self-directed learning. Student pragmatic competence was measured with a pre- and post-written discourse completion test. Additionally, qualitative student responses to a questionnaire were analyzed for the effectiveness of prescribed tasks to develop their pragmatic strategies. This study indicates that a combination of these tasks appears to be most advantageous in the learning of pragmatic strategies applied to compliments and compliment responses.

Keywords: pragmatic development, study abroad, Language Learning Strategy Instruction, compliments, compliment responses

1 Introduction

Paying someone a compliment (C) is a frequent way to begin a conversation. Cs are a means to increase the comfort between those speaking and to scaffold the conversation. This speech act, however, can be difficult for second language (L2) learners because they may transfer syntax from their native language to their target language, thereby distorting the meaning of the compliment. The evidence of this is abundant, therefore it is highly beneficial to teach pragmatics using explicit contexts for speech (Félix-Brasdefer 2008a, 2008b, 2012; Félix-Brasdefer and Hasler-Barker 2015; Hasler-Barker 2013; Grossi 2019). Knowing how to respond appropriately to compliments–that is, produce a compliment response (CR)–may also be challenging for L2 learners. Based on the findings of previous pedagogical interventions, researchers recommend that pragmatic instruction include: awareness activities, authentic language samples, input prior to interpretation (Bardovi-Harlig and Mahan-Taylor 2011; Félix-Brasdefer 2008a, 2008b), cross-cultural analysis (Cohen 2005; Félix-Brasdefer 2008b), form-focused instruction (Nguyen, Pham, and Pham 2012), controlled and guided practice (Hasler-Barker 2013), and communication strategies (Ishihara and Cohen 2010). The present study not only proposes how to implement the above activities in teaching the pragmatics of Cs and CRs, but also proposes how students can learn pragmatic strategies more effectively. To accomplish this, we followed Cohen's (2019) Language Learning Strategy Instruction (LLSI) recommendations, which provide tasks for instructors to use for teaching speech acts and pragmatic strategies. This approach has not previously been investigated empirically with L2 learners. Therefore the present study fills this gap by determining how effective LLSI tasks are for learners to gain pragmatic competence (see Chapter 1, this volume) and by providing instructors with reliable tools to teach pragmatics. This chapter begins with a review of existing research on Cs and CRs and then discusses studies concerning explicit interventions to foster speech act development. The subsequent sections include our research questions, methods, results, and discussion. The conclusion provides a discussion of the findings, as well as pedagogical implications, limitations, and areas for future research.

2 Literature review

2.1 Social benefits gained by compliments and compliment responses

Compliments in everyday conversations are defined as expressive speech acts that convey positive evaluations to the addressee (Searle 1976). Upon receiving a compliment, one usually responds with various forms of gratitude. Rejections of the praise also are common. Nonetheless, genuine compliments often facilitate kindness within conversations, express solidarity, generate appreciation of others, and enhance collaboration (Brown and Levinson 1987; Holmes 1986; Cohen 1996).

2.2 The L2 development of Spanish compliment culture in comparison to the English

In comparison to compliments in English,[1] compliments in Spanish are expressed in a variety of ways, as in the following examples:
1. Rhetorical questions: *¡Uy! ¿Compraste un computador?* ('Did you buy a computer?')
2. Impersonal sentences: *¡Qué chévere tener esa facilidad con los idiomas!* ('How cool to have such ability with languages!')
3. Ironic expressions: *¡Sabes mucho. No necesitas venir a la escuela!* ('You know so much. You don't even need to come to school!')

The most frequent syntactic patterns used in Spanish compliments are as follows:
1. Exclamatory sentences that include a form of *qué* ('how/what'): *¡Qué bebé tan lindo!* ('What a beautiful baby!')
2. Declarative sentences using the verb *quedar* or *ver* ('to look'): *¡Quedaste muy bien!* or *¡Te ves tan lindo!* ('You look nice!')
3. Copulative sentences often using the infinitive verb *estar* ('to be'): *¡Está muy vacano tu portátil!* ('Your laptop is cool!')

At least among Colombian and Mexican native speakers, exclamatory sentences using *qué* prevail (Félix-Brasdefer and Hasler-Barker 2015; Lopera Medina 2015; Nelson and Hall 1999). Regarding CRs in Spanish, the strategies appear to be more complex in form and function than those in English. Research by Herbert (1986) showed that more than half of CRs in American English were in the form of accepting the compliment with a "thank you." While in Spanish the common CR strategy is acceptance, research has revealed that Spanish CRs show a greater degree of creativity, verbosity, and unpredictability (Lorenzo-Dus 2001; Mack and Sykes 2009; Maíz-Arévalo 2010; Mir and Cots 2017). For instance, speakers from Spain living in the United States (Lorenzo-Dus 2001; Mack and Sykes 2009) and Mexican Spanish speakers (Valdés and Pino 1981) often employed ironic compliment responses or rejections that represented "fishing for further compliments" (Lorenzo-Dus 2001: 118). Spanish speakers rarely accept a compliment with just a token appreciation such as *gracias* ('thank you').

The use of Cs and CRs in Spanish varies greatly from region to region. Barros García (2018: 148) explains that "different cultures make different uses of

---

[1] The ethnographic work on compliments by Manes and Wolfson (1981) indicates that more than 85% of all compliments in American English are spoken using: 1) a copulative sentence (e.g., "Your blouse is beautiful") which accounts for more than 50% of the compliment data; 2) a declarative sentence (e.g., "I like your car"); or 3) an exclamatory sentence (e.g., "That's a nice wall hanging").

compliments, not only in the devices used to formulate them but also on their frequency of appearance, the contexts where they are considered appropriate, the responses of the complimentees, the recognition of an utterance as a compliment, and the functions performed by the speech act." Thus, when L2 speakers use pragmatic strategies that do not correspond to those that are expected in their L2, they can be unintentionally labeled as being "insensitive, rude, or inept" (Tello Rueda 2006: 169). Yousefvand, Yousofi, and Abasi (2014: 182) affirmed this, stating that "speakers need to know when and how it is appropriate to give one a compliment or respond to the received compliment."

2.3 Pedagogical interventions for pragmatic development

Researchers have confirmed that pedagogical intervention via explicit instruction of specific pragmatic elements is more effective than exposure alone in enhancing pragmatic competence (e.g., Hasler-Barker 2013, 2016; Félix-Brasdefer 2008a; Hasler-Barker 2016; Taguchi 2015). They propose that pragmatics instruction should incorporate many components: awareness activities (Kondo 2008), authentic language samples (Hasler-Barker 2013), input prior to student interpretation (Félix-Brasdefer 2008a, 2008b), cross-cultural analysis (Cohen 2005; Félix-Brasdefer 2008a), form-focused instruction and controlled and guided practice (Hasler-Baker 2013), and communication strategies (Ishihara and Cohen 2010). Cohen (2017: 449) stated that "while teachers can do lots of things to promote L2 pragmatics in the language classroom and beyond, the enormity of the learning task . . . means that learners would benefit highly from being proactive about their own learning in this domain."

Additional research shows that student involvement in their own learning produces positive results. For example, in Kondo's (2008) study, students reported that self-analyzing their responses improved their awareness strategies to express a refusal in their L2. Research by Sykes and Cohen (2008: 389) indicated that students learning grammar, turn-taking, syntax, and vocabulary while self-analyzing their ability to determine what speech to use in what context, reported better knowledge of "what to say, [and] also the skills needed for when and how to say it." The present study contributes to the body of research on explicit instruction for teaching pragmatics, including the LLSI approach which emphasizes the student's role in their own learning.

The LLSI targeting speech acts, first developed by Cohen (2019), gives students more responsibility in their learning of pragmatic strategies because instructors "can help raise and sharpen their awareness about the speech act before learners move on to practicing them for themselves" (144). Because

Cohen's LLSI has not yet been implemented – to our knowledge – in the present study we have assessed the effectiveness of the approach in teaching and learning pragmatic development of Cs and CRs in Spanish. Our study was guided by the following two research questions:
1. Does the production of Cs and CRs change after students experience an LLSI approach?
2. How do students perceive the effectiveness of the learning tasks included in the LLSI approach?

3 Method

3.1 Participants

The participants in this study were 10 undergraduate L2 Spanish learners from a small private university in the Midwest United States, who participated in a four-month study abroad program in Spain, Guatemala, or Chile during the semester prior to the present research. Language proficiency was not tested, but learners enrolled in the course were considered to be at the intermediate-high proficiency or advanced-low proficiency levels, having previously taken five semesters of college-level Spanish. Six of the participants were majors and four were minors in Spanish. All were enrolled in a topics course focused on the pragmatics of the Spanish language, as required of their major or minor program.

3.2 Instruments and data collection

The participants completed pre- and post-Written Discourse Completion Tests (WDCT) five weeks apart (see Appendix 1), responding to conversation scenarios (see Table 1) that included Cs, CRs, and distractors including apologies, requests, and refusals. Despite its documented limitations (e.g., Ogiermann 2018), the WDCT is a reliable tool to measure pragmatic knowledge (Félix-Brasdefer 2010). Kwon (2004: 342) indicates that the WDCT is an effective data collection instrument when the objective of the investigation is "to inform the speakers' pragmalinguistic knowledge of the strategies and linguistic forms by which communicative acts can be implemented." Students completed the pre-test in week five of the course, two weeks prior to the intervention and they took the post-test in week 12 of the course, two weeks after the intervention.

Table 1: Description of compliment and compliment response scenarios.

Speech act	Attribute praised	Relationship to interlocutor
Compliment	Appearance: New Hairdo Possession: New Jacket Skill: Host mother's cooking	Non distant-Friends Distant- Teacher Semi-distant
Compliment response	Responding to friend's compliment of learner's abilities playing soccer	Non distant-Friends
	Responding to a language tutor about learner's language skills	Semi-distant

The final instrument was a questionnaire administered one week after the intervention. It queried students about their perceptions concerning the effectiveness of each task and their degree of motivation to continue learning about the use of Cs and CRs in Spanish (see Appendix 2).

3.3 Treatment

The treatment was implemented at students' home university five months after students returned from studying abroad in a Spanish-speaking country. The setting to conduct this study was ideal as all the participants were part of a semester-long (15-week) topics course focused on the pragmatics of the Spanish language. The class was taught by a researcher who is a native speaker of Colombian Spanish with expertise in the pragmatics of the Spanish language. The class met for 10 weeks, three times a week for 55 minutes. During the first seven weeks of the course, the students learned basic concepts of pragmatics, including implicature and deixis, among others. During the last three weeks, for a total of eight hours and 15 minutes, students participated in the LLSI approach designed for the present study. Below, we provide a description of the course tasks organized in the order that they were implemented.

3.3.1 Awareness raising

In groups of two or three, students were asked to think about how they would respond, in English and Spanish, to five different scenarios that triggered the use of Cs and CRs. Students also discussed values and rules that apply to Cs and CRs.

3.3.2 Modeling presentation

To help participants develop awareness of strategies by native speakers using Cs and CRs, the instructor compiled four video clips showing the use of compliments. The clips were taken from two films, "María Full of Grace" (2004) and "Volver" (2006), and from the Center for Advanced Research on Language Acquisition (CARLA) website. For each clip, students identified and discussed with the teacher the pragmalinguistic strategies used. Though videos are not as authentic as spontaneous natural speech, they demonstrated simplified oral language that was accessible to our group of learners.

In addition, the instructor assigned readings of published research papers on Mexican Spanish compliments (Nelson and Hall 1999), Colombian Spanish compliments (Lopera Medina 2015), and compliment responses in American English and Peninsular Spanish (Mir and Cots 2017). The instructor requested students to pay attention to different types of compliments, preferred strategies, intensifying modifiers, and external factors affecting compliment strategies (e.g., degree of imposition, power, and social distance). The readings were done in groups to allow for collaboration and better understanding of the content. Each group read the articles at home and then prepared a presentation for the class. After each presentation, the instructor encouraged learners to identify connections between the findings of the readings, the video clips, and their previous study abroad experience.

3.3.3 Collaborative practice

Students participated in role playing to practice giving and responding to compliments. In doing so, they were encouraged to pay attention to sociolinguistic variables such as age, social status, and relationship between the interlocutors. Students practiced in groups several times. For this activity, there was a person assigned as a monitor who recorded the responses. Right after each role play was performed, the groups discussed and gave each other feedback as to how to make the Cs or CRs more native-like. Then they switched roles and practiced again.

3.3.4 Assessment

Although some informal assessment was conducted by the instructor while students worked on the collaborative practice activities, the students also assessed their own responses to the WDCTs. All the responses were grouped together to be analyzed. Using knowledge gained from previous tasks, students identified strategies that worked well and those which needed improvement. In groups, they discussed how Cs and CRs can be realized in ways that are closer to native Spanish speech.

3.3.5 Expansion

In small groups, students were asked to collect their own examples of Cs and CRs from films, soap operas, or online videos, and to work on different types of speech acts, such as reprimands and invitations. The goal was to encourage students to take more responsibility for their own learning and pique their curiosity about how to use appropriate speech acts in various situations they were interested in. Finally, students presented a brief summary of their research to the class.

3.4 Data analysis

To tabulate frequencies and percentages of strategy applications (Section 4.1), all instances of Cs and CRs that appeared in the pre- and post-WDCTs for each scenario were counted and categorized. Due to the sample size statistical analysis was not possible.

For compliment strategies, our classification used the syntactic patterns following Félix-Brasdefer's (2008a, 2008b) classification (see Section 4.1.1). For the compliment responses, the categorization (see Table 2) was based on the taxonomy created by Mir and Cots (2017). Those authors applied three macro strategies, including acceptance, mitigation, and rejection, along with several micro strategies, including appreciation, agreement, explanation, downgrading, self-praising, returning, credit shifting, seeking reassurance, and disagreement. Because *gracias*, a common token of appreciation, appeared in combination with other responses, it was coded by adding an "a" to the code number (as seen in Table 4). For example, qualifying/self-praising was coded differently when it was used without the appreciation strategy (see [1] below) than when it included the appreciation token (see [2] below).

(1) 1.6 *Practico mucho para jugar el fútbol.* ('I practiced soccer a lot to play like this.')
(2) 1.6a *Gracias. Estoy trabajando muy duro.* ('Thank you. I'm working really hard on this.')

Table 2: Compliment Response Strategies.

Macro strategies	Micro strategies	Examples
Acceptance	Appreciation	'Thanks', 'Thank you'
	Showing agreement	'I know' 'Yeah, I really like it'
	Giving an explanation or information	'I bought it in *Encantos*, Gloria's shop'
Mitigation	Downgrading	'It's nothing'; 'It's okay'
	Self-praising	'I worked hard on it'
	Returning	'Yours was good too'
	Reassuring	'Really?'
Rejection	Showing disagreement	'No way'

Finally, our research qualitatively analyzed student questionnaire responses to find out how effective the tasks were for learning the pragmatics of Cs and CRs, according to students.

4 Results

Results are presented here by each of the research questions that guided this study. Due to the small sample size, the findings are limited and need to be interpreted with caution.

4.1 Pragmatic variation of Cs and CRs after instruction

4.1.1 Compliments

Table 3 provides a summary of the frequency and percentages of the types of compliment strategies used by students in the pre-test and post-test as they apply to three scenarios: (1) complimenting one's appearance; (2) complimenting one's possession; and (3) complimenting one's skills. The results are presented by the percentage of total compliments. In the pre-test there were 47 compliments used in the three scenarios. In the post-test there were 51.

Three compliment strategies are highlighted: (1) the use of *me gusta/encanta* ('I like/love'); (2) declaratives using forms of the infinitive verb *ser/estar*

Table 3: Frequency of compliment strategies by WDCT scenario (N = 10).

Compliment strategy	Pretest				Posttest			
	#1 Appearance (n)%	#2 Possession (n)%	#3 Skills (n)%	Total (n)%	#1 Appearance (n)%	#2 Possession (n)%	#3 Skills (n)%	Total (n)%
Me gusta, encanta + (NP) (I like + NP)	(5) 35.7%	(9) 69.2%	(2) 10%	(16) 34.1%		(3) 17.6%	(1) 5.5%	(5) 9.8%
NP [*ser, estar, parecer*] +(*muy/tan*) +ADJ (NP [is, looks] (really) ADJ)	(1) 7.1%	(1) 7.7%	(6) 30%	(8) 17%	(1) 6.3%	(3) 17.6%	(5) 27.8%	(11) 21.6%
Qué + ADJ/ADV (NP) How/What ADJ/ADV NP	(4) 28.6%		(2) 10%	(6) 12.7%	(6) 37.5%	(5) 29.4%	(5) 27.8%	(16) 31.4%
(Intensifier) *Qué* + NP+ *tan*+ ADJ	(1) 7.1%			(1) 2.2	(1) 6.3%	(1) 6%		(2) 2.9%
(Intensifier) +ADJ	(2) 14.4%			(2) 4.3%				
Other (includes sarcasm, questions)	(1) 7.1%	(3) 23.1%	(2) 10%	(6) 12.7%	(5) 31.2%	(5) 29.4%	(6) 33.4%	(16) 31.4%
Appreciation token (thank you)			(8) 40%	(8) 17%			(1) 5.5%	(1) 1.9%
Total	(14) 100%	(13) 100%	(20) 100%	(47) 100%	(16) 100%	(17) 100	(18) 100%	(51) 100%

('to be'); and (3) declaratives using *qué* ('what'). The appreciation token *gracias* ('thanks') also was used by participants, but mostly as a way to introduce the compliment, which is why *gracias* is included in Table 3 as a compliment strategy, rather than only a CR strategy.

The pre-test results indicate that the most common strategy employed by students was *me gusta/encanta* ('I like/love'), chosen 34.1% of the time. This strategy was preferred when presenting compliments to praise appearance or possession. However, it was not a preferred strategy when complimenting skills. In the pre-test totals, participants used the token *gracias* attached to the skills compliment 40% of the time (8 of 47 total strategies used). While a stand-alone *gracias* 'thank you' is literally a compliment response rather than a compliment per se, students would attach *gracias* to the actual compliment to enhance the message of appreciation. For example, in the context of appreciating a mother in a study-abroad host family: *Gracias Mamá, me gusta su cocinando* ('Thank you mother, I love your cooking'). The strategy using *ser/estar* ('to be') was chosen 17% of the time (8 of 47 strategies). The strategy using *qué* ('how/what') was chosen 12.7% of the time (6 of 47).

In the post-test following the intervention, learners drastically reduced the use of *me gusta/encanta*, using that strategy only 9.8% (5 of 51 total), compared to the pre-test results of 34.1% (16 of 47). This suggests the LLSI increased student awareness of native speakers' frequent forms of compliments and reduced their reliance on English forms. Learners also slightly increased their use of *ser/estar* from 17% (8 of 47) in the pre-test, to 21.6% (11 of 51) in the post-test. Compliments for appearance increased from 7.1% (1 of 47) to 18.7% (3 of 51). Compliments for possessions increased from 7.7% (1 of 47) to 17.6% (3 of 51). These findings suggest that the intervention affected the use of copulative sentences in compliments for appearance and possessions.

In the pre-test, the strategy using *qué* with adjectives or adverbs and noun phrases, was only chosen in compliments for appearance or skills (possessions). Pre-test results involving *qué* showed appearance compliments were used 28.6% (4 of 47) and skills compliments were used 10% (2 of 47). But compliments including *qué* tended to be used in any scenario in the post-test, on average 31.4% of the time. Further, in the post-test, we noted an increase in the use of other strategies, such as questions or sarcasm, in all three scenarios. While the use was sporadic in the pre-test at 12.7% (6 of 47), the use of these other strategies increased in the post-test to 31.4% (16 of 51).

4.1.2 Compliment responses

Now we turn to analysis of the frequency of CRs about two skill examples: one's ability to speak Spanish well and one's ability to excel at playing soccer. Table 4 presents the frequency results for the pre-test and post-test following the three-strategy taxonomy: acceptance, mitigation, and rejection. The results are presented by the percentage of the total CRs and number of strategies, followed by the percentage for each of the two scenarios above. Note that there were a total of 48 CRs used by 10 learners: 20 in the pre-test and 28 in the post-test.

Table 4: Frequency of compliment responses by WDCT scenario (N = 10).

Micro strategies	Pretest			Posttest		
	Skill # 1 (n) %	Skill # 2 (n) %	Total	Skill # 1 (n) %	Skill # 2 (n) %	Total
Acceptance						
1.1 Appreciation		(1) 10%	(1) 5%	(1) 7.1%		(1) 3.6%
1.2 Showing agreement				(1) 7.1%		(1) 3.6%
1.3 Giving an explanation				(1) 7.1%		(1) 3.6%
1.3a Giving an explanation		(3) 30%	(3) 15%			
Total Acceptance		(4) 40%	(4) 20%	(3) 6.2%		(3) 10.8%
Mitigation						
1.4 Downgrading					(1) 7.1%	(1) 4%
1.5 Self-praising	(1) 10%	(1) 10%	(2) 10%		(3) 21.4%	(3) 12%
1.5a Self-praising	(8) 80%	(4) 40%	(12) 60%	(1) 7.1%	(2) 14.2%	(3) 12%
1.6 Returning				(1) 7.1%		(1) 4%

Table 4 (continued)

Micro strategies	Pretest			Posttest		
	Skill # 1 (n) %	Skill # 2 (n) %	Total	Skill # 1 (n) %	Skill # 2 (n) %	Total
1.7 Credit-shifting	(1) 10%		(1) 5%		(3) 21.4%	(3) 12%
1.7a Credit-shifting		(1) 10%	(1) 5%	(2) 14.2%	(1) 7.14%	(3) 12%
1.8 Reassuring				(3) 21.4%		(3) 12%
Total Mitigation	(10) 20%	(6) 60%	(16) **80%**	(7) 14.5%	(10) 20.8%	(17) **68%**
Rejection						
1.9 Showing disagreement				(4) 28.5%	(4) 28.5%	(8) 29%
Total Rejection				(4) 8.3%	(4) 8.3%	(8) **29%**
Total	(10) 100%	(10) 100 %	**(20)** 100%	(14) 100%	(14) 100%	**(28)** 100%

* The "a" is coded to reflect the use of the appreciation token + another strategy.

As Table 4 indicates, learners preferred the mitigation CR strategy in both pre-tests and post-tests: 80% of the time (N=16) in the pre-test, and 68% (N=17) in the post-test. In the pre-test, learners favored the use of the self-praising micro strategy, with or without an appreciation token, 70% (N=14). But the self-praising tendency diminished in the post-test to 24% (N=5). The micro strategies of seeking reassurance and downgrading appeared only in the post-test 12% (N=3) and 4% (N=1), and the rejection strategy appeared solely in the post-test at 29% (N=8). These findings suggest that the intervention provided these strategy options for the learners in the post-test. However, because of the low frequency of these strategies, our study indicates that the LLSI approach had just a moderately positive effect, slightly increasing the overall use of variable and more native-like CRs.

4.2 Student perceptions of the LLSI approach tasks

All students reported the task aimed at developing awareness of compliments in English compared to Spanish was valuable based on their discussions during class. One student stated that comparing and self-evaluating the forms they used to give and respond to compliments was "an eye-opening experience because [we] had no idea it was different. [We] just focused so much on grammar that [we] forget that there is more than that when learning Spanish." Another student stated, "It was interesting to discuss that even in English you compliment someone differently according to age."

Students were also tasked with watching video clips and identifying strategies to use in Cs and CRs as demonstrated by native Spanish speakers. In this modeling task, 70% of the students reported the task was effective because the clips provided a rich context for them to learn about natural pragmatics, speech in a real context, and gestures and facial expressions. For instance, one student commented, "It was interesting to see the lady touching the piece of jewelry while giving the compliment. I wouldn't touch it, but it seems appropriate to native speakers [of Spanish]."

On the other hand, 30% of students reported that this task was not effective because of their difficulty with the vocabulary and phonetic variations of the language by Spanish native speakers in the videos. One student stated, "I was not able to understand what they were saying [in the videos]." This particular statement was not connected with the tasks for learning pragmatics, but with the language proficiency of the student. Although this is a variable we did not analyze, language proficiency even in advanced courses of Spanish fluctuates from student to student.

Another task involving modeling was reading research studies on the use of Spanish and English Cs and CRs. Eighty percent of the students commented that the readings had developed their awareness about the cross-cultural and linguistic differences of compliments. One student stated, "Compliments really stuck out to me because they are so complex and different from English, and I wasn't aware of the differences at all before this." This comment reveals that time spent abroad had not been enough for students to become aware of such pragmatic differences. Another student commented, "I wish I knew this before going to Spain. Now, it makes more sense." The other 20% of the students noted that they found the readings too complex due to the scientific jargon and the statistical analysis content.

Collaborative practice was in the form of the role playing. All students agreed that role playing was productive because it allowed them to practice and perform some of the strategies studied in class. However, students expressed the need for more practice, but in a different context. For example, one student commented, "Practicing in class was OK, but I wish we could practice with native speakers to see how they react."

In the self-assessment strategy, students assessed their own performance of Cs and CRs, including comparing their pre- and post-test responses. Ninety percent of the students agreed that it was important to monitor their speech to avoid transferring inappropriate pragmalinguistic forms used in English to Spanish. The following response illustrates this: "Doing the test before and then analyzing all the students' responses helped me a lot because I realized that I tend to say the same thing in English and Spanish, for example, I say, *Amo tu pelo* ['I love your hair']."

Expansion learning involved individual student research in which they each collected and analyzed additional examples of Cs and CRs. Only 40% of the participants perceived the task positively because it allowed them to further their language proficiency as they were planning on travelling abroad again. The other 60% of students' comments regarding the expansion task assessed the type of work done. These students found more value from working in groups instead of alone. As noted by a student,

(1) "[Working in groups] produced more ideas, and it was helpful to hear multiple explanations of the topic."

Students in this group also reported that gathering specific examples of speech uses was too challenging and frustrating. One student said,

(2) "I like that we study something that you don't normally focus on when learning a language. . . . However, [it] was difficult to find examples in videos. It is very time consuming."

Another student stated that they still lacked language abilities to accurately pinpoint the correct examples needed for the analysis:

(3) "The most difficult part of the work was getting examples in videos because I watched a movie in Spanish from Spain and was not able to understand what they were saying."

These statements are a reminder that language proficiency is a factor that prevents learners from achieving certain goals (Félix-Brasdefer 2008a, 2008b; Félix-Brasdefer and Hasler-Barker 2015).

Regarding their level of motivation to continue studying speech acts, 70% of the students reported that the pedagogical intervention increased their motivation to conduct more research to expand their understanding of a topic. For example, one student reported that because he plans to travel again to Chile, he would like to read more about speech acts. Other students were motivated to strengthen their use of learning strategies by using those that better serve their learning styles. For example, one student found it difficult to collect samples in video clips and instead decided to replicate the WDCT scenarios with students from another class. "For my research, I collected data from my Latino class, and I found that the Latino students also use *gustar* ['to like'] as the structure to give compliments and *gracias* to respond to compliments. Now I've learned that there are other forms. Getting the examples from movies was difficult, and that is why I decided to reach out to Latino students because it was much easier to collect the data." This reveals that giving students tools and encouraging them to do research is effective in cultivating learner autonomy (Kubota 2017). Students can take responsibility for their own learning by going beyond what has been asked of them.

The other 30% of the participants reported no motivation to continue learning about speech acts. They appeared to be stuck on the idea that language learning must be focused on grammar. One student found that "there were [simply] too many details to study [the pragmatics of the language]." The formulas to use Cs and CRs were too complex and they preferred to memorize formulaic structures. Indeed, as they learn, sociopragmatic variables also need to be considered even when learning formulaic structures.

5 Discussion

The present study combined a quantitative and a qualitative methodology to explore the effects of the LLSI approach in teaching the use of compliments and compliment responses to English speakers learning Spanish after they completed a study abroad experience. We based our teaching and research design on Cohen's (2019) proposal.

5.1 Evidence of pragmatic change

Our study's first research question was: Does the production of Cs and CRs change after returned study abroad students experience an LLSI approach? Our answer is that this study's quantitative findings support previous studies on the immediate effects of pragmatic instruction to increase L2 variability of compliment uses as spoken among native speakers (Félix-Brasdefer and Hasler-Barker 2015; Hasler-Barker 2013, 2016). One clear finding was the increased use of the Spanish compliments that include the *qué* ('what/how') form, which predominates in native Spanish compliments.

Unlike previous studies that revealed a pervasive use of the form *me gusta/encanta* ('I like/love') (e.g., Félix-Brasdefer and Hasler-Barker 2015), our study observed a decrease in the frequency of this form. While *me gusta/encanta* was the preferable form in the pre-test, we argue that the decrease of its use is likely a result of the instruction helping learners develop awareness of the forms and providing them with strategies to understand how and why certain forms are not used by native Spanish speakers. In addition, their study abroad experience along with the time frame dedicated to the instruction were valuable tools that served learners with optimal understanding of the sociopragmatic rules needed in using compliments.

Similarly, evidence of change was noted in the variability of CR forms and a decrease of the frequency of the token *gracias* ('thanks') as acceptance to a compliment. We argue that the work learners did with input, research, and expansion tasks allowed them to move away from the English self-praising CR form (e.g., "I worked really hard on my project"), and instead showed more intimacy and sociability by using downgrading, questioning, and rejecting strategies.

5.2 Effectiveness of the LLSI tasks

Our second research question was: How do students perceive the effectiveness of the learning tasks included in the approach? Our answer is that analysis of student responses reveals one clear pattern; working on different tasks provided learners with a more holistic experience that helped them learn pragmatic strategies and allowed them to take more control of their own learning. This is something instructors and previous researchers in L2 learning support (e.g., Cohen 2017, 2019; Sykes and Cohen 2008).

The content of student discussions in class after analyzing their own speech performance, samples from other speakers, and research data taken from different cultural groups, revealed that the LLSI raised awareness concerning various pragmatic aspects related to using Cs and CRs. The findings show that learners can do metapragmatic analyses and become linguists and make discoveries themselves by being actively involved in analyzing and reflecting on their own speech performance. In addition, tasks aimed at providing modeling or authentic input lends support to existing literature that suggests that audiovisual and multimedia input enhances both sociopragmatic and pragmalinguistic awareness (e.g., Cohen and Ishihara 2005; Sykes and Cohen 2008; Russel and Vásquez 2018).

The modeling presentations along with the expansion tasks proved to be challenging but also rewarding for some learners. Learners demonstrated understanding of research material and designed their own research on speech acts. As expected, however, collecting the data was troublesome for participants. Cohen (2019: 144) foresaw this by asserting, "While it is undoubtedly challenging for students to collect such data on their own, it may give them more ownership of the task, and hence more motivation to do it and contribute to the learning process." In fact, in our study, students who had difficulties collecting data from videos found a different way to collect different data. By doing this, students recognized the value of using a broad range of strategies in language learning.

Another important finding of the implementation of the LLSI approach, consistent with previous research (e.g., Kondo 2008; Sykes and Cohen 2008), is the importance of the instructor's role. One student said, "I like the videos that show the speech act demonstrating in real scenarios; however, [the teacher explanations] were always really helpful, because sometimes as learners we don't notice stuff." Providing feedback, as studies suggest (e.g., Sykes and Cohen 2008), makes a difference because it focuses the students on what is relevant and appropriate and what is not.

In summary, unlike previous studies (Félix-Brasdefer 2008a; Hasler-Barker 2013, 2016), we were able to demonstrate that even learners who had already studied abroad still lacked pragmatic competence and benefitted from an LLSI approach. A remarkable feature of our study is the intensity of the learning process. Previous studies actively engaged students in a narrow time frame (Félix-Brasdefer 2008a; Hasler-Barker 2016; Kondo 2008), but because our students were participating in a course dedicated to the study of pragmatics of the Spanish language, we were able to work on Cs and CRs for two hours and 45 minutes per week for three weeks. We argue that this time frame for teaching pragmatics needs to be considered in future interventions.

6 Conclusion

The present study adds to the body of research on teaching pragmatics explicitly by indicating that the LLSI approach for teaching speech acts proposed by Cohen (2019) is effective because it provides a variety of tasks that allow learners to truly understand the reasons, context, and examples for specific speech choices native speakers make. The approach gives learners an advantage by allowing them to become more involved in their own learning.

L2 learners in our study showed an increase in the variability of their use of Cs and CRs that resembled native Spanish forms. Results from the questionnaire underlined the effectiveness of some of the LLSI tasks. Those that required students to collect data and read research studies appeared to increase students' motivation to work with Cs and CRs. The findings suggest that even students who have already participated in a study abroad experience can benefit from the LLSI approach. It is beyond the scope of the present study to assert that one particular task, among the role playing, reading of research studies, presentations, and self-evaluations, had the greatest impact on learning variability in the use of Cs and CRs. However, implementing a variety of LLSI tasks gives us a better sense of adjustments needed to make learning effective.

The present study has its limitations based on the number of participants and the design of the instruments. A small number of participants and a lack of a control group limited our ability to compare speech frequencies that could provide more robust statistical results. Also, we did not apply a post-test instrument after the completion of each task, which prevented us from identifying which of them had more impact on learners. Additionally, the questions in the final instrument needed refinement so that students could provide more in-depth answers as to how the tasks influenced their pragmatic strategies. Regardless of its limitations, we hope that the findings have shed light on the kinds of LLSI tasks that are helpful to students and show the value of students becoming more active participants in their own learning.

References

Bardovi-Harlig, Kathleen & Rebecca Mahan-Taylor. 2011. Proficiency, length of stay, and intensity of interaction and the acquisition of conventional expressions in L2 pragmatics. *Intercultural Pragmatics* 8(3). 347–384.

Barros García, María Jesús. 2018. Face-enhancing compliments in informal conversations in Valencian Spanish. *Borealis: An International Journal of Hispanic Linguistics* 7(1). 147–168.

Brown, Penelope & Stephen Levinson. 1987. *Politeness: Some universals in language use.* Cambridge: Cambridge University Press.

Center for Advanced Research on Language Acquisition. 2006. *Dancing with Words: Strategies for Learning Pragmatics in Spanish.* https://carla.umn.edu/speechacts/sp_pragmatics/home.html (accessed 10 October 2019).

Cohen, Andrew D. 1996. Speech acts. In Sandra L. McKay & Nancy H. Hornberger (eds.), *Sociolinguistics and language teaching*, 383–420. Cambridge: Cambridge University Press.

Cohen, Andrew D. 2008. Teaching and assessing L2 pragmatics: What can we expect from learners? *Language Teaching* 41(2). 213–235.
Cohen, Andrew D. 2017. Teaching and learning second language pragmatics. In Eli Hinkel (ed.), *Handbook of research in second language teaching and learning*, 428–452. New York: Routledge.
Cohen, Andrew D. 2019. Strategy instruction for learning and performing target language pragmatics. In Ana Uhl Chamot & Vee Harris (eds.), *Learning strategy instruction in the language classroom: Issues and implementation*, 140–152. Bristol, England: Multilingual Matters.
Cohen, Andrew D. & Noriko Ishihara. 2005. *A web-based approach to strategic learning of speech acts*. http://www.carla.umn.edu/speechacts (accessed 10 October 2019).
Félix-Brasdefer, J. César. 2008a. Teaching Spanish pragmatics in the classroom: Explicit instruction mitigation. *Hispania* 91(2). 477–492.
Félix-Brasdefer, J. César. 2008b. Pedagogical intervention and the development of pragmatic competence in learning Spanish as a foreign language. *Issues in Applied Linguistics* 16(1). 47–82.
Félix-Brasdefer, J. César. 2010. Data collection methods in speech act performance: DCTs, role plays, and verbal reports. In Esther Usó-Juan & Alicia Martínez-Flor (eds.), *Speech act performance: Theoretical, empirical, and methodological issues*, 41–56. Amsterdam: John Benjamins Publishing.
Félix-Brasdefer, J. César. 2012. Complimenting and responding to a compliment in the Spanish FL classroom: From empirical evidence to pedagogical intervention. In Leyre Ruiz de Zarobe & Yolanda Ruiz de Zarobe (eds.), *Speech acts and politeness across languages and cultures*, 241–271. Bern, Switzerland: International Academic Publishers.
Félix-Brasdefer, J. César & Maria Hasler-Barker. 2015. Complimenting in Spanish in a short-term study abroad context. *System* 48. 75–85.
Grossi, Vittoria. 2019. Teaching pragmatic competence: Compliments and compliment responses in the ESL classroom. *Prospect: An Australian Journal of Teaching/Teachers of English to Speakers of Other Languages* 24(2). 54–62.
Hasler-Barker, Maria. 2013. *Effects of pedagogical intervention on the production of the compliment-compliment response sequence by second language learners of Spanish*. Indianapolis, IN: Indiana University dissertation.
Hasler-Barker, Maria. 2016. Effects of metapragmatic instruction on the production of compliments and compliment responses: Learner-learner role-plays in the foreign classroom. *Pragmatics and Language Learning* 14. 125–152.
Herbert, Robert K. 1986. Say "thank you" or something. *American Speech* 61(1). 76–88.
Holmes, Janet. 1986. Compliments and compliment responses in New Zealand English. *Anthropological Linguistics* 28(4). 90–121.
Ishihara, Noriko & Andrew D. Cohen. 2010. *Teaching and learning pragmatics: Where language and culture meet*. New York, NY: Longman.
Kondo, Sachiko. 2008. Effects of pragmatic development through awareness-raising instruction: Refusals by Japanese EFL learners. In Eva Alcón Soler & Alicia Martínez-Flor (eds.), *Investigating pragmatics in foreign language learning, teaching and testing*, 153–177. Bristol, UK: Channel View Publications.
Kubota, Maki. 2017. Post study abroad investigation of Kanji knowledge in Japanese as a second language learners. *System* 69. 143–152.

Kwon, Jinyun. 2004. Expressing refusals in Korean and in American English. *Multilingua* 23. 339–364.

Lopera Medina, Sergio Alonso. 2015. La caracterización de los cumplidos en una población universitaria. *Ikala, Revista de Lenguaje y Cultura* 20(1). 61–77.

Lorenzo-Dus, Nuria. 2001. Compliment responses among British and Spanish university students: A contrastive study. *Journal of Pragmatics* 33(1). 107–127.

Mack, Sara & Julie Sykes. 2009. *¡Qué feito estás tú también, cariño!*: A comparison of the response to the use of 'positive' irony for complimenting in Peninsular and Mexican Spanish. *Studies in Hispanic and Lusophone Linguistics* 2. 305–345.

Maíz-Arévalo, Carmen. 2010. Intercultural pragmatics: A contrastive analysis of compliments in English and Spanish. In María Luisa Blanco Gómez & Juana Marín-Arrese (eds.), *Discourse and communication: Cognitive and functional perspectives*, 175–208. Madrid: Dykinson.

Manes, Joan & Nessa Wolfson. 1981. The compliment formula. In Florian Coulmas (ed.), *Conversational routine*, 115–132. The Hague: Mouton.

Mir, Montserrat & Joseph M. Cots. 2017. Beyond saying thanks: Compliment responses in American English and Peninsular Spanish. *Languages in Contrast* 17. 128–150.

Nelson, Gayle & Christopher Hall. 1999. Complimenting in Mexican Spanish: Developing grammatical and pragmatic competence. *Spanish Applied Linguistics* 3(1). 91–121.

Nguyen, Thi Thuy Minh, Thi Hanh Pham, & Minh Tam Pham. 2012. The relative effects of explicit and implicit form-focused instruction on the development of L2 pragmatic competence. *Journal of Pragmatics* 44(4). 416–434.

Ogiermann, Eva. 2018. Discourse completion tasks. In Andreas Jucker, Klaus Schneider, & Wolfram Bublitz (eds.), *Methods in pragmatics*, 229–255. Berlin: De Gruyter.

Russell, Victoria & Camilla Vásquez. 2018. Assessing the effectiveness of a web-based tutorial for interlanguage pragmatic development prior to studying abroad. *Journal of Language Learning Technologies* 48. 69–95.

Searle, John. 1976. A classification of illocutionary acts. *Language and Society* 5. 1–23.

Sykes, Julie & Andrew D. Cohen. 2008. Observed learner behavior, reported use, and evaluation of a website for learning Spanish pragmatics. In Melissa Bowles, Rebecca Foote, Silvia Perpiñán, & Rakesh Bhatt (eds.), *Selected Proceedings of the 2007 Second Language Research Forum*, 144–157. Somerville, MA: Cascadilla Proceedings Project.

Taguchi, Naoko. 2015. Instructed pragmatics at a glance: Where instructional studies were, are, and should be going. *Language Teaching* 48. 1–50.

Tello Rueda, Yined. 2006. Developing pragmatic competence in a foreign language. *Colombian Applied Linguistics Journal* 8. 169–182.

Valdés, Guadalupe & Cecilia Pino. 1981. Muy a tus órdenes: Compliment responses among Mexican-American bilinguals. *Language and Society* 10. 53–72.

Yousefvand, Elaheh, Nouroddin Yousofi, & Mohsen Abasi. 2014. The study of compliment speech act responses: A study based on status and gender in Persian. *Journal of Applied Environmental and Biological Sciences* 4(3). 182–196.

Appendix 1

Scenarios in discourse completion test
1. As soon as you meet your best friend, you notice s/he has a new haircut.
   You say: _____
2. You scored the winning goal at last night's soccer game and your classmates tell you they are impressed with your skills.
   You say: _____
3. Your teacher is wearing a jacket you really like.
   You say: _____
4. Your Spanish tutor tells you that they are impressed with your progress.
   You say: _____
5. Your host mom prepared the best meal for you today. You are at the table.
   You say: _____

Appendix 2

Questionnaire

For each task on compliments and compliment responses, please state your opinion, perception, and/or comment as to how the task helped you learn more about the speech act. If you believe the task was not effective tell us why you think so.

I. Tasks
1. Completion of scenarios in English and Spanish and discussion of rules
2. Examination of CARLA video clips and clips from the movies "María Full of Grace" and "Volver"
3. Discourse Completion Test comparison to research collected at the beginning of the course
4. Reading and discussion of research studies on compliments in different varieties of Spanish
5. Gathering your own data
6. Practicing speech acts by role playing

II. Tasks overall
7. Among all the tasks, which one, in your opinion, gave you the best experience to learn about the speech act? Why do you think so?
8. How motivated were you after completing the course to continue learning about speech acts and why?

Enrique Rodríguez

5 ¡Madre mía de mi alma!: Pragmalinguistic variation and gender differences in perception of *piropos* in Badajoz, Spain

Abstract: *Piropos* are a discourse practice in Spanish-speaking communities which consists of unsolicited flirtatious remarks, traditionally said by men to women in a public setting in the past. However, progressive global and regional movements in recent years critical of traditional gender roles and gender discrimination seem to be influencing the way *piropos* are produced and perceived by speakers across different Spanish-speaking speech communities. The present study analyzes pragmalinguistic and gender differences in perception of *piropos* in the speech community of Badajoz, Spain. Results indicate that wh-phrasal exclamatives and vocatives are preferred in contexts of higher social distance between interlocutors, while more intimate settings yield linguistic patterns that resemble other types of compliments in Spanish. In terms of gender differences in perception, men rated *piropos* more favorably than women, but all participants perceived those *piropos* that are structurally similar to other compliment types in Spanish as the most appropriate.

Keywords: piropos, speech acts, pragmalinguistic variation, perception, gender differences

1 Introduction

The purpose of this chapter is to analyze pragmalinguistic variation and gender differences in the perception of *piropos* in the speech community of Badajoz, Spain. In lay terms, a *piropo* is an unsolicited flirtatious remark traditionally said by a man to a woman in a public setting, though this heteronormative situation might be facing some societal changes. A subtype of expressive speech acts (Searle 1976), *piropos* are considered to be a discourse practice that is present in much, if not all, of the Spanish-speaking world (Achugar 2001; Félix-Brasdefer 2018). The interaction they bring about between language and cultural issues can generate conflicts not only among members of these speech

https://doi.org/10.1515/9783110721775-006

communities, but also in terms of intercultural communication among native and non-native speakers (Cohen 2012; Ishihara and Cohen 2010).

In the past, *piropos* were seen as a flattering comment by heterosexual men towards women (Calvo Carrilla 2000), but this practice slowly became outdated and began to be perceived as a violation of someone's privacy (Malaver and González 2008), an insult, or harassment (Achugar 2002). Issuing *piropos* now, especially those based on metaphors, is seen as an old-fashioned practice that reinforces sexist and patriarchal attitudes in society (Níkleva 2016). While *piropos* are still part of Spanish cultures and traditions, the perception of this speech act in Spanish speech communities has changed, leading to innovations in the ways Spanish speakers produce it in context and interaction with others (Bailey 2017). Therefore, periodic investigations that examine innovative ways of issuing *piropos* are needed in order to describe the current production and perception patterns of this speech act in different Spanish speech communities.

The present study aims to explore pragmalinguistic variation and differences in perception between men and women in the region of Badajoz, Spain. Badajoz is a region in the autonomous community of Extremadura in Southwestern Spain. Located on the border with Portugal on the east and the region of Seville, Spain, to the south, Badajoz is traditionally considered part of the Western Andalusia dialectal division (Lipski 2012). Badajoz is a largely overlooked region in terms of pragmatic variation research, and to date there are no studies in the field that have focused on speakers from Badajoz, despite its strategic location and the possible influence that migration from Portugal and Seville might engender. This study, therefore, aims to contribute to filling the gap in pragmalinguistic variation studies in the region of Badajoz by investigating current production and perception patterns among men and women in the discourse practice of *piropos*.

2 Literature review

2.1 From compliments to *piropos*

Following Searle's (1969, 1976) classification of speech acts, a compliment is an expressive act that a speaker uses to indicate approval and express a positive evaluation about their hearer, normally in relation to their possessions, skills, achievements, or physical appearance (Holmes 1988; Manes and Wolfson 1981). They are used in conversation for different reasons, including praising and criticizing (Goddard and Wierzbicka 2014), but also apologizing, thanking, or greeting (Wolfson 1983). Compliments are traditionally related to sociocultural values associated with a speech community, which helps to define what attributes are worth being complimented by others (Manes 1983). While their main function in conversation is to keep social harmony, create solidarity ties between speakers, and lessen a potential face-threatening act on the hearer, not all compliments are equally accepted by speakers of a speech community, and the context and interpersonal relations between interlocutors can affect the way they are perceived (Mills 2003). In terms of syntactic and semantic patterns, studies on complimenting strategies in different languages have highlighted their conventionality and restricted nature in adjective and noun selection, making them easily identifiable by speakers and, therefore, increasing the likelihood that this expressive act is effective in building and maintaining solidarity in social interactions (Golato 2005; Wolfson and Manes 1980). American English speakers, for example, have been found to show a preference for adjectives such as 'nice', 'good', 'beautiful', 'pretty' and 'great', verbs like 'love' and 'like', and noun phrases with 'to be' and 'to look' (Manes and Wolfson 1981).

Studies on Spanish compliments have also reported that this expressive speech act follows a conventional and formulaic nature (Lorenzo-Dus 2001). More specifically, Spanish compliments show a preference for adjectives such as *lindo/a* ('lovely'), *bonito/a* ('pretty'), *guapo/a* ('good-looking'), and verbs like *gustar* ('to like') and *encantar* ('to love') (Hernández Herrero 1999; Placencia and Yépez 1999). Maíz-Arévalo (2010) collected naturally recurring data from English and Spanish, and proposed the following lexical-grammatical categorization for compliments in Spanish:

a) Wh- exclamative clause with an adjective as a modifying complimented item (e.g., *¡Qué vestido más bonito!* 'What a beautiful dress!').
b) Declarative clause with a copulative verb and a positive adjective modifying the subject, who is usually the person being complimented (e.g., *Eres preciosa* 'You're pretty').
c) Declarative clause with a mental process verb such as *gustar* 'to like' or *encantar* 'to love' and the complimented item as the direct object (e.g., *Me gusta/encanta tu reloj* 'I like/love your watch').

These formulas have also been found in explicit compliments in Spanish in other studies such as Maíz-Arévalo (2012), who used naturally occurring conversational data from Peninsular Spanish to analyze the degree of explicitness speakers from that speech community have in their complimenting routines. This study reported that Spanish speakers tend to compliment more on appearance and physical attributes, both explicitly and implicitly. Barros García (2018) analyzed compliments in informal conversations by Valencian Spanish speakers and found that this speech act is highly formulaic in nature, containing a short repertory of positive adjectives such as *bonito/a* ('pretty') and *guapa* ('beautiful'). Also, declarative, copulative, and exclamative sentences modified by intensifiers were reported to be the preferred syntactic patterns when issuing face-enhancing compliments. Compliments by Peninsular Spanish speakers have also been analyzed in computer-mediated environments such as Facebook, where Maíz-Arévalo and García-Gómez (2013) found that exclamative sentences were used more often for appraising beauty and intelligence (e.g., *¡Pero qué guapísima eres!* 'But how very pretty you are!'), whereas declarative sentences (e.g., *Sobrino, eres un artista* 'nephew, you're an artist') were reserved for complimenting someone's personalities and skills. In Peru, De los Heros (2001) compared speakers from two communities, Cuzco and Lima, through a discourse completion task, and found that speakers from Cuzco, especially men, paid more compliments than those from Lima. Regarding the target of these compliments, speakers from Cuzco showed a preference for complimenting the interlocutor's appearance, while Lima residents tended to compliment possessions more frequently. Women, however, preferred the use of explicit compliments, while men favored indirect, implicit ones.

Spanish-speaking countries show a very specific type of compliment, the *piropo*, even though it has sociocultural and historical factors that make it its own category within the larger schema of speech acts (Bailey 2017). A *piropo* is traditionally defined as an unsolicited compliment that a speaker, usually a male, gives their interlocutor, typically a woman, with the intention of appraising their appearance and/or clothing (Achugar 2001, 2002; Bailey 2017). *Piropos* tend to be flirtatious and have sexual connotations, but they can also be lighthearted and complimenting, which makes the recipient perceive them more positively (Mitchell 2015). The content and the syntactic structures of *piropos* vary according to the situation and the social distance between interlocutors. The most prototypical *piropos* seem to be metaphors related to food (e.g., *Mira, mira, qué perita enconfitada* 'Look, look, what a little sugared pear', in Andalucia, Spain) and movement (e.g., *¡Qué curvas, y yo sin frenos!* 'What curves, and I without brakes!' in El Salvador), even though cars and religion are two other common topics among *piropos* in some Spanish-speaking communities such as the River Plate area, Chile, El Salvador, and Andalucía, Spain (Achugar 2001, 2002). However, *piropos* are not reduced to these conventionalized expressions only, as they can also take the form of single words (e.g., *¡Guapa!* 'Beautiful!') or explicit formulaic compliments such as *¡Qué ojazos!* ('What beautiful eyes!') in the region of Granada, in southern Spain, among other Spanish-speaking regions (Bailey 2017; Níkleva 2016).

Though *piropos* were widely considered a deep-seated part of Spanish-speaking cultures as a mechanism to create solidarity among speakers through a personal evaluation of the interlocutor's possessions, skills, or appearance, this perception is now shifting, especially among women (Achugar 2016). Traditionally, women are reported to have generally found *piropos* that highlighted their beauty through metaphors and flattering remarks culturally and socially acceptable, but those with sexual connotations were deemed as impolite and a form of harassment (Bailey 2017). In this regard, *piropos* can be face-threatening to the addressee's face as they represent an unsolicited comment on someone's physical appearance and an invasion of their own privacy, especially if uttered in a public setting (Schreier 2005).

2.2 Pragmatic variation of *piropos*

Despite being a common discourse practice in Spanish-speaking communities (Achugar 2001), research on *piropos* is largely underdeveloped in terms of pragmalinguistic variation and less explored with regard to different gender pairings (i.e., women to men, or among non-heterosexual interlocutors). *Piropos* have been the object of study in various Spanish-speaking regions, and such investigations show that the linguistic strategies speakers use to issue them, as well as the ways they are perceived by members of those regions, reveal some pragmatic variation. Achugar (2002) analyzed *piropos* among Uruguayan women through a written perception questionnaire and found that older women accepted this practice more favorably than younger women, who perceived them as harassing remarks. This finding suggests that generational differences and changes in politeness practices in society play a role in the ways women experience *piropos*. In Achugar's study, those *piropos* that included food and movement metaphors were perceived more negatively, while *piropos* with religious undertones were seen as more polite. Sykes (2006), on the other hand, collected data through a social acceptability scale and six semi-structured interviews in the region of Yucatan, Mexico, and found similar results in terms of semantic content as well as age and gender differences to those reported in Achugar (2002). In this study, women also showed a less positive perception of *piropos*, while men stated that they are part of Spanish-speaking cultures.

Gónzalez's (2009) study yielded similar results to Achugar (2002). She analyzed the perception of *piropos* among young women in Caracas, Venezuela, by means of a rating scale in which participants had to evaluate 14 *piropos* that were addressed to women on the street by men. *Piropos* that referenced body parts or bodily functions were systematically rated as ruder and more impolite, whereas those that included a divine metaphor were seen as polite and more preferable among Venezuelan women. Mitchell (2015) focused on Buenos Aires Spanish and analyzed women's production and perception of *piropos* through ethnographic methods and sociolinguistic interviews. The findings suggest that the current perception of *piropos* among women in that region is mixed, ranging from regarding them as harassment and gender-based violence to harmless and innocuous. Chilean *piropos* were analyzed by Abarca Millán (2016), who collected 67 *piropos* from a Chilean repository source online and grouped them according to the conceptual metaphor they belonged to, including religion, crime, food, nature, and transfiguration. A syntactic and pragmatic analysis revealed that women are always the passive object of the idealization and that they were usually addressed in the formal second person singular pronoun *usted* (formal 'you'). Finally, in Bogotá, Colombia, Ramírez-Cruz, Correa and Mancera (2017) carried out an ethnographic study on *piropos* produced by construction workers and directed to female passers-by on the street and found that the men displayed an array of discourse features such as vowel lengthening and rhyming sounds when uttering a *piropo*. The structures the speakers used, on the other hand, were both creative and conventionalized to a certain degree, suggesting that *piropos* issued on the street are more formulaic than in other settings, with a tendency to use metaphorical content. In follow-up interviews with these men, they stated that *piropos* are flirtatious remarks said with no intention to harm women, but since female participants were not included in these surveys, it is not clear whether men and women show variation in terms of how *piropos* addressed to them were perceived.

In Spain, Níkleva (2016) investigated the current situation of *piropos* among university students in the city of Granada through a written production questionnaire. Her results indicate that men prefer the use of words such as *bombón* ('stunner'), *guapa* ('beautiful') and *sol* (lit. 'sun'), and favor word classes such as nouns, pronouns and verbs when addressing *piropos* to women. One of the methodological innovations of this study was the elicitation of *piropos* said by women, which had not been previously explored in the literature. In this study, women showed a preference for the use of adjectives such as *bueno* ('hot') and *guapo* ('handsome') and reported that they would only issue *piropos* in situations of familiarity with their interlocutor, usually a man. Moreover, Fridzilius (2009) carried out an ethnographic study on the streets of Madrid and found that *piropos* are most frequently said between strangers, from men to women, and with a tendency to use words such as *guapa* ('beautiful') or *hermosa* ('pretty'). These studies, therefore, suggest that the traditional view of *piropos* as metaphorical and creative flirtatious remarks is rapidly changing in Spanish-speaking communities, where this expressive speech act is adopting linguistic features that resemble explicit compliments.

Table 1 below presents a summary of the empirical studies from 2000 to 2017 discussed here. While it seems that the study of *piropos* from a pragmalinguistic point of view has become more frequent in the last few years, the lack of research done on the pragmatic variation of *piropos* makes it difficult to come to conclusions about the current situation of this speech act in Spanish-speaking countries.

Table 1: Empirical studies on pragmatic variation of *piropos* (2000–2017).

Author(s)	Year	Region	Instrument	Findings	Gender variation
Ramírez-Cruz, Correa and Mancera	2017	Bogotá (Colombia)	Ethnographic observation Semi-structured interviews	Vowel lengthening, rhymes, and metaphors were frequent strategies when saying *piropos* on the street	Men deemed *piropos* as harmless flirtatious remarks
Bailey	2016	Lima (Perú), Barranquilla (Colombia), New York (United States), Rome (Italy), and Cairo (Egypt)	Video recorded naturally-occurring street remarks	Addressing, greetings, expressing admiration, summoning, and asking rhetorical questions were the most frequent speech acts included in the street remarks by men and women	Women categorically rejected street remarks by ignoring them
Níkleva	2016	Granada (Spain)	Written production questionnaire	*Piropos* are turning into compliments in terms of syntactic and lexical patterns	Men prefer words such as *bombón* 'stunner', *guapa* 'beautiful', and *sol* (lit. 'sun'), while women use adjectives such as *bueno* 'good' and *guapo* 'handsome'

Table 1 (continued)

Author(s)	Year	Region	Instrument	Findings	Gender variation
Abarca Millán	2016	Chile	Corpus study	Religion, crime, food, nature, and transfiguration as most common metaphors. Use of social distance second person pronouns ('usted')	NA
Mitchell	2015	Buenos Aires (Argentina)	Ethnographic observation Sociolinguistic interviews	*Piropos* frequently took the form of staring, car honking, and whistling rather than linguistic utterances	Mixed perception by women
Fridzilius	2009	Madrid (Spain)	Ethnographic observation	Formulaic, traditional *piropos* were not heard frequently. *Piropos* seem to be adopting compliment structures	Adjectives such as *guapa* 'beautiful' or *hermosa* 'pretty' were common among men.
González	2009	Caracas (Venezuela)	Rating scale	*Piropos* with references to body parts and body functions were seen as rude and impolite. Religious *piropos* were accepted more often.	Half of the female participants found *piropos* acceptable; the other half thought they are rude

Table 1 (continued)

Author(s)	Year	Region	Instrument	Findings	Gender variation
Sykes	2006	Yucatan (Mexico)	Rating scale Semi-structured interviews	Food and movement metaphors were seen as rude. *Piropos* with divine and world references were understood as compliments.	Men accepted *piropos* more often than women
Achugar	2002	Montevideo (Uruguay)	Rating scale Interviews	*Piropos* with religious metaphors were seen as more polite. Food and movement metaphors were deemed as rude.	Older women found *piropos* more acceptable

As illustrated in Table 1, most studies on pragmalinguistic variation of *piropos* have been carried out in Latin America, and ethnographic observations and semi-structured interviews are the most common means of data collection. Out of these eight studies, onlyNíkleva (2016) asked her participants for their pragmalinguistic knowledge of *piropos* through a written questionnaire, albeit her goal was to create an inventory of *piropos* in the target region, Granada, Spain rather than analyzing their production in specific situations according to pragmatic variables. However, to date there are no empirical studies that have investigated how social factors such as gender or social distance among speakers affect the production and perception of *piropos* in controlled situations. Such data would offer researchers insights into potential pragmalinguistic variation in the performance of this speech act among men and women, and whether context and speaker intent play a role in the perception of *piropos*.

The present study, therefore, aims to contribute to the body of research on the pragmalinguistic variation of *piropos* by analyzing production and perception patterns of this speech act in the region of Badajoz, Spain. Drawing from a variational pragmatics framework (Barron 2017), this study looks at variation in the actional level (i.e., speech acts) by investigating how men and

women produce and perceive *piropos* according to the micro-social variable of social distance. The research questions that motivate this study are the following:
1. What are the strategies used by men and women when producing *piropos* in Badajoz, Spain?
2. Which *piropos* are perceived more favorably by men and women in the community of Badajoz, Spain?

3 Method

3.1 Participants

A total of 60 participants, 30 women and 30 men, completed a computer-delivered online questionnaire. All participants were current members of the speech community of Badajoz, and their ages ranged from 18 to 50 years old, with an average age of 24 years. The vast majority of them were university students in their fourth year of undergraduate studies or their first year of a master's degree program. However, a few participants reported different educational levels, which ranged from a high school diploma to a Ph.D. Participants filled out the questionnaire online, and none reported having issues during the completion of the task.

3.2 Instrument and procedures for data collection

The instrument[1] consisted of a computer-delivered written production questionnaire and a perception task in the form of a Likert scale. Written-production questionnaires are a common means to collect data in variational pragmatics studies, as they give comparable data across participants and are useful for

---

[1] Prior to the data collection stage, an online preliminary questionnaire was distributed among members of the speech community of Badajoz in order to gain insights about the current situation of *piropos* in that region. This pilot questionnaire consisted of an open-ended question in which participants were asked to provide examples of *piropos* they hear frequently in Badajoz, both from man to women, and from women to man. Seventeen participants completed the questionnaire and produced a total of 87 *piropos*. All *piropos* were collected and quantified, and the seven most frequent ones in each pairing (man to woman, woman to male) were used to inform the design of the final instrument for this study. Using the most common *piropos* among the initial participants gives us a better basis for comparison among items, as they are representative of what speakers hear and/or use in their interactions with others.

assessing pragmalinguistic knowledge (Ogiermann, 2018). They have been extensively employed in the literature to analyze speech act variation, such as in compliments (Golato 2003), refusals (Félix-Brasdefer 2008a), and requests (Lorenzo and Bou 2003). The written-production questionnaire for the present study included four situations that were manipulated according to one macro-social factor, the genders of the speakers, and one micro-social factor, the social distance between interlocutors (+/− social distance). The micro-social factor of social distance is operationalized in the present study as situations that involve speakers who do not know each other and are catcalled by the other in public setting (+ social distance), and situations that describe two speakers who are somewhat familiar with each other and might or might not continue talking after that social interaction (− social distance). This distinction was explained in lay terms in the instructions of the written-production questionnaire in order to avoid confusion among the participants. These two variables, gender and social distance, were chosen as they are hypothesized to play a role not only in the linguistic structure of the *piropo* produced but also in its semantic content (Níkleva 2016; Ramírez Cruz, Correa, and Mancera 2017). While there are also situations in which non-heterosexual speakers issue *piropos* to each other, the focus here is heterosexual relationships. The analysis of pragmalinguistic variation of *piropos* in LGBTQ communities falls outside the scope of the present study, and represents a possible direction for future research.

The second part of the data collection instrument consisted of a perception task in which participants were asked to evaluate seven *piropos* uttered by men to women, and seven *piropos* issued by women to men in two contexts that differed in the social distance between speakers. Therefore, each situation in the perception task controlled for the micro-social factor of social distance in order to assess whether *piropos* are perceived differently depending on the relationship the receiver has with the speaker.[2] A total of 28 situations were evaluated using a numerical Likert scale as in the following example:

Mujer a hombre: "¡Guapo!"   Woman to male: Handsome!
Muy apropiado (1)   Very appropriate (1)
Apropiado (2)   Appropriate (2)
No lo sé (3)   I don't know (3)
Poco apropiado (4)   Not appropriate (4)
Nada apropiado (5)   Not appropriate at all (5)

---

[2] These fourteen different *piropos* were taken from the most common ones listed in the original pilot questionnaire.

The last section of the instrument included demographic questions about the participants regarding their age, hometown, level of education, and their current city of residence.

Data were collected by means of a computer-delivered questionnaire on Google Forms that was distributed to members of the speech community of Badajoz. The instrument was shared with a convenience sample of participants first, and it was then sent to others by using a snowballing effect. Only those participants who reported being members of the speech community of Badajoz were included in the data reported in this chapter.

3.3 Data analysis

For the written production questionnaire, *piropos* were analyzed following specific syntactic structure and adjective and verb selections (Félix-Brasdefer 2018; Lorenzo-Dus 2001; Maíz Arévalo 2010). Exclamative particles such as *vaya*, *qué* and *menudo,* all of which belong to the wh- phrasal exclamatives 'what a X', were grouped together due to their similarities in syntactic and pragmatic functions. Traditional formulaic *piropos* such as *Los bombones al sol se derriten* ('Chocolates melt in the sun') that cannot be broken down into smaller semantic components were categorized as *piropos*. Non-verbal features such as whistling, gaze, or clicks were included in the "Other" category.

Data collected using the perception instrument were coded on a scale from 1 (most appropriate) to 5 (least appropriate). *T*-tests were carried out to determine whether there was a significant difference in how each gender group rated these *piropos* according to the pragmatic variable of +/− social distance with their interlocutor.

4 Results

4.1 Strategies used by men and women when producing *piropos*

The first research question addressed pragmalinguistic variation in the production of *piropos* between men and women according to the parameter of +/− social distance. Four situations were chosen for this part of the instrument: a man issuing a *piropo* to a passing woman on the street (+ social distance), a woman directing a *piropo* to a passing man on the street (+ social distance), a man uttering a *piropo* to a woman in a bar (– social distance), and a woman giving a *piropo* to a man in a bar (– social distance). A total of 60 answers were collected and grouped in their corresponding category following their syntactic structure and the semantic content of the *piropo*. Several answers were a *no piropo* option, that is, situations in which the participant did not think a *piropo* would be said. Those answers were also included in the analysis. A summary of the results for both men and women in the first situation (+ social distance) is shown in Table 2 below.

Table 2: Piropos by men and women in + social distance situations.

Situation 1: Piropos from a man to a passing woman (+ social distance)	Results
¡Vaya/Qué/Menudo + body part! ('What a + female body part')	16 (53.4%)
Vocative	10 (33.3%)
Other	3 (10%)
Nothing	1 (3.3%)
Total	30 (100%)
Situation 2: *Piropos* from a woman to a passing man (+ social distance)	**Count**
Vocative	11 (36.7%)
Other	7 (23.3%)
Nothing	5 (16.7%)
¡Vaya/Qué/Menudo + body part! ('What a + body part')	5 (16.7%)
¡Qué + ADJ + VP! ('What + ADJ + VP')	2 (6.6%)
Total	30 (100%)

The results suggest that men show a clear preference for wh- phrasal exclamatives followed by an explicit reference to a woman's body part (53.4%) and vocatives such as *guapa* ('beautiful') or *preciosa* ('pretty') (33.3%) when using *piropos* in a situation of little to no familiarity with their interlocutor. The "Other" category includes more formulaic *piropos* (*¡Que ese cuerpo no pase hambre!* 'I better not find out that body is starving!') and rhymes (*Rojo que te cojo* 'I'll take the one in red').

Among women, vocatives such as *guapo* ('handsome') or *tío bueno* ('hottie') are the most preferred answers (36.7%). 23.3% of the responses were classified into the "Other" category, which included non-verbal *piropos* such as interjections

(¡*Guau!* 'Wow!'), whistling, and gazing, as well as flirtatious remarks that are not traditionally considered part of formulaic *piropos* (e.g., ¡*Así me lo recetó el doctor!* 'Just what the doctor ordered!'). Finally, wh- phrasal exclamatives, which are the most common *piropo* structure among men, are also produced by women (16.7%), suggesting that this particular construction might be undergoing a process of conventionalization for this speech act in the region of Badajoz.

Table 3 shows the distribution for *piropos* by men and women in – social distance settings.

Table 3: Distribution for piropos by men and women in – social distance situations.

Situation 3: Piropos from a man to a woman (- social distance)	Results
¡*Qué bien bailas/te mueves!* ('You dance/move your body very well!)	12 (40%)
Other	9 (30%)
Vocative	5 (16.7%)
¡*Eres/estás (muy) guapa!* ('You're (very) pretty!')	3 (10%)
Nothing	1 (3.3%)
Total	30 (100%)
Situation 4: Piropos from a woman to a man (- social distance)	**Results**
¡*Qué + ADJ + eres!* ('You're + ADJ!')	9 (30%)
¡*Qué sonrisa/ojos más/tan bonita/os!* ('What (a) beautiful smile/eyes!')	7 (23.3%)
Other	5 (16.7%)
Me gusta/encanta + body part ('I like/love your + body part)	4 (13.3%)
Eres/Estás muy + ADJ ('You're + ADJ!')	3 (10%)
Nothing	2 (6.7%)
Total	30 (100%)

Results show that a situation in which the interlocutors are more familiar with each other yields a greater range of variety of *piropos* than those contexts where the speakers are mutually strangers. Among men, the "Other" category, and ¡*Qué bien bailas/te mueves!* ('You dance/move your body very well!') emerge as the most frequent piropos for this situation (40%). The "Other" category includes approaching strategies such as greetings (*Hola, guapa, ¿qué tal?* 'Hi, gorgeous, what's up?'), requests to dancing (*¿Bailamos?*, 'Shall we dance?'), and invitations

(*Ven, que te invito a una copa* 'Come here, let me buy you a drink'), as well as more traditional compliments like *¡Qué bien te sienta el vestido!* ('That dress looks great on you!') or *'¡Qué ojos más bonitos!* ('Such pretty eyes!').

Women, on the other hand, show greater variation in their inventory of *piropos* for this situation. *¡Qué + ADJ + eres!* ('You're + ADJ!') (30%) and *¡Qué sonrisa/ojos más/tan bonita/os!* ('What (a) beautiful smile/eyes!') (23.3%) are the preferred means of performing this speech act in contexts where they are familiar with their male interlocutor. The "Other" category (16.7%) for this situation includes approaching strategies such as greetings (¿*Qué tal?*, 'What's up?') and flirting remarks (e.g., *Creía que ya no existían hombres como tú* 'I didn't think men like you existed anymore'). Finally, *Me gusta/encanta + body part* ('I like/love your + body part') (13.3%) and *Eres/Estás muy + ADJ* ('You're + ADJ!') (10%) were also produced in these data.

4.2 *Piropos* that are perceived more favorably by men and women

The second research question set out to analyze variation in perception of *piropos* by men and women according to the pragmatic variable +/– social distance. The second section of the computer-delivered instrument asked participants to rate seven frequently heard *piropos* in the speech community of Badajoz, Spain, in terms of their appropriateness depending on the setting and the grade of familiarity between interlocutors. Table 4 below shows a summary of results of men's variation in perception of *piropos* directed to women according to the variable +/– social distance and again employing the scale very appropriate (1) to not appropriate at all (5).

The results show that *piropos* said between strangers are perceived more inappropriately (3.28) than those said to a friend or acquaintance (2.82). *¡Quién fuera suelo para verte el mochuelo!* (Lit.: 'I wish I were the floor so that I could see your owlet') (7), a traditionally conventionalized *piropo* in this speech community, was perceived as the most impolite in both situations. The other formulaic *piropo*, *Los bombones al suelo se derriten* ('Chocolate melts when left in the sun') in (5), was also deemed as inappropriate in both settings. Finally, men found *¡Qué guapa!* ('You're so pretty!') in (2) and *¡Qué bien te queda ese vestido!* ('You look good in that dress!') in (3) as the most appropriate *piropos* to say to women in both contexts, suggesting that complimenting strategies are perceived most favorably and are less face-threatening in this region. An independent-sample t-test was calculated in order to analyze differences between gender groups and the micro-social variable of + social distance. No significant differences between gender and social distance means were found in the data.

Table 4: Rating scale average results of *piropos* said from men to women.

	+ social distance	– social distance
(1) ¡Pibón! ('Headturner!')	3.51	2.53
(2) ¡Qué guapa! ('You're so pretty!')	2.37	1.76
(3) ¡Qué bien te queda ese vestido! ('You look good in that dress!')	1.92	1.5
(4) ¡Madre mía! ('Wow!')	3.22	2.88
(5) Los bombones al suelo se derriten ('Chocolate melts when left in the sun')	3.62	3.57
(6) ¡Tía buena! ('*Hot chick!*')	3.77	3.3
(7) Quién fuera suelo para verte el mochuelo (Lit.: 'I wish I was the floor so that I could see your owlet')	4.55	4.26
Average	3.28	2.82

Shown in Table 5 is a summary of women's perception ratings of *piropos* said by women to men following the variable of +/– social distance: very appropriate (1) to not appropriate at all (5).

Table 5: Rating scale average results of *piropos* said by women to men.

	+ social distance	– social distance
(8) ¡Guapo! ('Handsome!')	2.66	2.13
(9) ¡Qué bien te queda esa camisa! ('You look good on that shirt!')	2.40	1.86
(10) ¡Morenazo! ('Hunk!')	3.63	2.80
(11) ¡Tío bueno! ('Hottie!')	4.26	3.36
(12) ¡Estás para chuparte los dedos! ('You're finger-licking good!')	4.46	4.26
(13) ¡Qué ojazos! ('What (beautiful) eyes!')	2.43	1.90
(14) ¡Qué culito! ('What a nice rear end!')	4.53	4.33
Average	3.48	2.94

Item (9), where a woman would address the *piropo ¡Qué bien te queda esa camisa!* ('That shirt looks good on you') to a passing male, and item (13), which included *¡Qué ojazos!* ('What (great) eyes!'), were rated more favorably among the participants. *¡Qué culito!* ('What a nice rear end!') in (14), which follows the syntactic structure *Qué + body part* and was found to be one of the most frequent options in the written production questionnaire, is rated highly inappropriate in this situation (4.53). The phrase *¡Estás para chuparte los dedos!* ('You're finger-licking good!') in (12), a commonly heard flirting remark in Spain, was similarly deemed unfavorable for women to say to unknown men (4.46). In situations of − social distance among speakers, women found complimenting routines such as *¡Qué bien te queda esa camisa!* ('That shirt looks good on you!') in (9) and *¡Qué ojazos!* ('What great eyes!') in (13) as the most suitable strategies to give a *piropo* to men, while the phrase *¡Qué culito!* in (14) was still considered inappropriate for such a context. An independent sample *t*-test was administered, but no significant differences between gender groups were found.

5 Discussion

5.1 Pragmalinguistic variation of *piropos* in men and women

Regarding the first research question, among men, wh- phrasal exclamatives combined with a reference to a woman's body part (e.g., *¡qué cuerpo!* 'what a body!') emerged as the most preferred strategy to give *piropos* (53.4%) in situations of less familiarity among speakers (+ social distance). This finding is surprising, as such a pattern has not been reported in previous studies, suggesting that the linguistic structures used to issue *piropos* in Spanish-speaking communities might be in constant evolution. Vocatives (e.g., *guapa* 'beautiful') were also produced frequently by men for this situation (33.3%), following similar results reported in the literature (Fridzilius 2009; Níkleva 2016), which found that vocatives and more direct structures are preferred over metaphors or more traditionally formulaic *piropos*. A possible hypothesis that would explain these results has to do with the context in which they are produced: a public setting with passing interlocutors as receivers of the *piropos* favoring the use of quick comments due to the immediacy of the situation. Another difference with regard to gender variation in the production of this speech act is found in the semantic content of the *piropo*, that is, in what is being appraised in the utterance. Men produced a greater variety of references to a woman's body parts (i.e., *culo* 'butt', *piernas* 'legs', *cuerpo* 'body') in wh- phrasal exclamatives, while women only targeted one, *culo*.

In contexts of more familiarity among speakers, men prefer the use of *¡Qué bien bailas/te mueves!* ('You dance/move your body very well!') (37%) as well as other complimenting strategies like '*¡Me gusta tu sonrisa!* ('I like your smile') or *¡Qué ojos más bonitos!* ('Such pretty eyes!'). Surprisingly, only one *piropo* produced by men in this situation targeted a woman's clothing and/or accessories, *¡Qué bien te sienta el vestido!* ('That dress looks great on you!'), while the majority of them referenced physical attributes such as *sonrisa* ('smile'), *ojos* ('eyes'), or *pelo* ('hair'). Some of the *piropos* reported also included pragmatic routines such as greetings (*¿Qué tal, guapa?* 'What's up, gorgeous?'), requests (*¿Bailamos?* 'Shall we dance?'), and invitations (*Ven, que te invito a una copa* 'Come here and I'll get you a drink') (30%). These results suggest that the context in which a *piropo* is said has important implications regarding how it is ultimately realized. Whereas *piropos* said by men to a passing woman on the street were found to be vocatives and wh- phrasal exclamatives including explicit references to their bodies, situations of more intimacy among interlocutors yielded structures that resemble those of Spanish compliments (Maíz-Arévalo 2010).

Women, on the other hand, showed a wider variety of *piropo* strategies for situations of higher social distance. Vocatives were the most common form for women in this situation (40%), followed by non-verbal gestures such as gazing or whistling. This finding adds support to the results of Mitchell's (2015) research in terms of the use of non-linguistic structures when using *piropos* on the street, albeit that study only reported on men's non-verbal *piropos*. Though this expressive speech act has traditionally been considered a male practice (Achugar 2001, 2002), only 16.7% of the women surveyed in the present study revealed that they would not issue a *piropo* in such a situation, suggesting that this discourse practice might be undergoing some changes in society. However, as this study only analyzes elicited data, it is difficult to make any strong claims about what these women would say and do in real life. Since previous ethnographic studies (Fridzilius 2009; Mitchell 2015) only reported on men giving *piropos* to women, the findings of the present study need to be interpreted considering the limitations of the data collection instrument.

Finally, wh- phrasal exclamatives like *¡Vaya/Qué/Menudo + body part!* ('What a + body part') were also found in the women's data, albeit much less frequently than in the male corpus, indicating that this linguistic structure seems to be recognized by members of this speech community as a conventionalized way of saying *piropos* in contexts of less familiarity among speakers. However, the women's production data, much like the men's data, also show an overwhelming preference for *piropos* that target body parts such as *ojos* ('eyes'), *boca* ('mouth'), and *sonrisa* ('smile'). The fact that women did not produce any *piropos* that targeted the addressee's clothing or accessories was somewhat surprising, considering that the perception data showed that utterances with a less sexually-explicit semantic content were systematically perceived as more appropriate by both men and women.

In situations of lower social distance between interlocutors, women show a preference for linguistic patterns that resemble those structures for other types of Spanish compliments proposed by Maíz-Arévalo (2010), such as *¡Qué + ADJ + eres!* ('You're + ADJ!'), *¡Qué sonrisa/ojos más/tan bonita/os!* ('What (a) beautiful smile/eyes!'), and *Me gusta/encanta + NP* ('I like/love + NP'). These results seem to align with what other studies in Spain have found in that *piropos* are slowly adopting complimenting structures (Fridzilius 2009; Níkleva 2016). However, one of the contributions of the present study is that this is the first to report the differences in these complimenting structures, showing which ones are used predominantly by each gender. While both men and women tend to use less face-threatening structures in this situation, the syntactic patterns reported by each group are different, with women showing a wider array of *piropo* strategies that mirror other types of Spanish compliments.

5.2 Gender differences in perception of *piropos*

The second research question examined gender differences in perception of *piropos* in two different settings (+/− social distance). Men evaluated the same seven *piropos* for women in both contexts and reported that those said in situations of less familiarity between speakers are perceived more negatively on average (3.28) than those in more intimate settings (2.82). The expression *¡Quién fuera suelo para verte el mochuelo!* (Lit.: 'I wish I was the floor so that I could see your owlet') and *Los bombones al suelo se derriten* ('Chocolate melts when left in the sun') were perceived less favorably by men in both settings, suggesting that metaphors, formulaic *piropos*, and those whose semantic content targets a traditionally sexually-objectified body part are highly dispreferred in the speech community of Badajoz, Spain, in these two settings. This finding is corroborated by the results reported in the written-production questionnaire, where male participants did not provide any of these *piropos* for any of the two situations. Fridzilius (2009) found similar results in her ethnographic study of *piropos* in Madrid, where metaphors and formulaic phrases were rarely heard. These results also add support to those found by Sykes (2006) in Mexico, who reported that food and movement metaphors were perceived more negatively.

Piropos that resemble complimenting structures were rated more favorably in both contexts, though they were seen more positively in situations of less social distance between speakers.

These results give us insights regarding how men perceive *piropos* directed to women in the speech community of Badajoz, Spain. First, men find *piropos* to be less appropriate with women who are strangers, even though they are not perceived as highly undesirable overall (3.28). Second, men perceive complimenting strategies as a favorable and suitable way of giving *piropos* to a woman. These results, however, are not supported by the written-production questionnaire, where men revealed a high preference for vocatives, which are rated more negatively in the perception instrument.

With respect to female participants, *piropos* were perceived less favorably in situations of more social distance, that is, when said to a passing man on the street (3.48). Similar to previous studies (Fridzilius 2009; Níkleva 2016; Sykes 2006), *piropos* that are structurally closer to compliments were perceived more positively, whereas vocatives and food metaphors were rated less favorably. An interesting contrast is found between *¡Qué ojazos!* ('What beautiful eyes!') and *¡Qué culito!* ('What a nice rear end!'), which despite presenting similar syntactic structures that resemble those of compliments, the latter is perceived more negatively in both situations. A possible hypothesis for this is that since the semantic content of *¡Qué ojazos!* is traditionally associated with compliments (i.e., eyes are body parts that are normally accepted to be commented on), speakers perceive this *piropo* more favorably than *¡Qué culito!*, which references a body part that has sexual connotations and is normally not the target of Spanish compliments (González 2009). Finally, *piropos* uttered in situations of lower social distance with their interlocutor were rated by women similarly to men, suggesting that this setting leads participants to perceive *piropos* as more complimenting than flirtatious.

Another finding that is illustrated by these data is the relationship between semantic content and how a *piropo* is perceived by its interlocutor. Those *piropos* that target a body part of the addressee are categorically rated more negatively than utterances that mention clothing or accessories. *¡Qué bien te queda ese vestido!* ('You look good on that dress!') and *¡Qué bien te queda esa camisa!* ('You look good on that shirt!') were perceived more favorably, while *Quién fuera suelo para verte el mochuelo* (Lit. 'I wish I was the floor so that I could see your owlet') and *¡Qué culito!* ('What a nice rear end!'), which target one of the addressee's body parts were clearly viewed as the least appropriate utterances in the data.

6 Limitations and future directions

This study is not without limitations. First, the modest sample size of participants made it difficult to explore gender differences in both production and perception of *piropos* more in depth. However, this study takes a first step toward analyzing current trends in *piropos* according to the micro-social factor of social distance and the macro-social variable of gender. Second, the computer-delivered questionnaire, while easy to distribute online, was written and untimed, which may have prompted participants to produce *piropos* that they would not say in real life. Future studies should investigate other data elicitation instruments such as timed, oral production tasks, as well as retrospective verbal protocols that explore the participants' perceptions of the *piropos* they issued. Finally, the present study only analyzed the production and perception of *piropos* in two specific settings and with regard to gender and situational variation, but there is also the possibility that *piropos* are produced in other contexts such as among close friends and family members, or between same-gender and/or non-binary interlocutors. Thus, more studies that investigate interlocutors' characteristics are needed in order to have additional evidence regarding *piropos* in today's society.

7 Pedagogical implications

The findings of the present study have several pedagogical implications for the teaching and learning of *piropos* and compliments in the second language (L2) Spanish classroom, especially for students in study abroad contexts. Since *piropos* are a discourse practice that is specific to Spanish-speaking cultures, L2 learners of Spanish need to be aware of what strategies are used by native speakers to produce this speech act in context, and how and why they are different from traditional compliments. The present study shows that native speakers of Spanish in Badajoz, Spain, use different strategies to produce *piropos* and compliments according to the situation and the gender of their interlocutor, suggesting that L2 speakers would benefit greatly from classroom activities that tackle these speech acts in context. Metapragmatic instruction in particular has been found to have a positive impact on speech act production by L2 learners (Félix-Brasdefer and Hasler-Barker 2013; Hasler-Barker 2016), as it allows them to explore their pragmatic competence and develop their interactional strategies in the L2 (Kasper and Rose 2012).

Previous studies have highlighted the need for explicit, cross-cultural comparison in the instruction of pragmatics in the L2 classroom (Cohen 2017;

Félix-Brasdefer 2008b). Given that compliments and *piropos* are produced in different settings and with different interlocutors, pragmalinguistic awareness-raising activities that explore these two types of speech acts with authentic examples from the target variety (i.e., Peninsular Spanish, Mexican Spanish) might be an initial step for the comparison of L1 and L2 norms (Ishihara and Cohen 2010; Taguchi and Roever 2017). Transcripts of authentic interactions, as well as audiovisual materials such as audio or video recordings, would be particularly helpful for the teaching and learning of compliments and *piropos*, especially in classroom activities that encourage students to discuss the differences between the two speech acts, the settings in which they are produced, the reason why they are issued, the semantic content of each, their degree of appropriateness, and how they are perceived by their interlocutor (e.g., whether they are accepted or ignored). Metapragmatic instruction and awareness-raising activities could prove especially beneficial for learners in study abroad contexts, as exposure to the sociocultural target norms during a pedagogical intervention might improve their pragmatic competence prior to their abroad stay and, consequently, sensitize learners to gender and situational variation in the production of compliments and *piropos* in the L2 setting.

8 Conclusion

This chapter contributes to the work on the pragmatic variation of *piropos* by examining gender differences in production and perception of this speech act in the region of Badajoz, Spain. This study offers a novel approach to pragmatic variation research on *piropos*, as it is the first one that (a) examines pragmalinguistic variation at the levels of production and perception, (b) explores how the micro-social variable of +/− social distance affects pragmatic variation of *piropos*, and (c) focuses on an under-researched region. Results from the written-production questionnaire suggest that wh-phrasal exclamatives and vocatives are the preferred linguistic structures in situations of higher social distance between interlocutors, while more intimate settings yield linguistic patterns resembling traditional Spanish compliments. Regarding gender differences in perception, men rated *piropos* as more favorably than women in both settings, but all participants perceived *piropos* that are structurally similar to Spanish compliments as more appropriate than any other type. Finally, metaphors and formulaic *piropos* were deemed as highly dispreferred in all settings, indicating that this expressive speech act is slowly adopting new linguistic structures in this speech community.

References

Abarca Millán, Erika. 2016. ¡Quién fuera noche para caerle encima! Piropos in Chile: Sexual harassment or flirtation? *Sociolinguistic Studies* 10(4). 509–527.

Achugar, Mariana. 2001. Piropos as metaphors for gender roles in Spanish speaking cultures. *Pragmatics* 11(2). 127–137.

Achugar, Mariana. 2002. Piropos: Cambios en la valoración del grado de cortesía de una práctica discursiva. In María Elena Placencia & Diana Bravo (eds.), *Actos de habla y cortesía en español*, 175–192. Munich: LINCOM EUROPA.

Achugar, Mariana. 2016. Piropos and other forms of flirtatious street talk as contested discursive practices. *Sociolinguistic Studies* 10(4). 499–507.

Bailey, Benjamin. 2016. Street remarks to women in five countries and four languages: Impositions of engagement and intimacy. *Sociolinguistic Studies* 10(4). 589–609.

Bailey, Benjamin. 2017. Piropo [Amorous Flattery] as a cultural term for talk in the Spanish-speaking world. In Donal Carbaugh (ed.), *The handbook of communication in cross-cultural perspective*, 195–207. New York: Routledge.

Barron, Anne. 2017. Variational Pragmatics. In Anne Barron, Yueguo Gu, & Gerard Steen (eds.), *The Routledge handbook of pragmatics*, 91–104. Abingdon/New York: Routledge.

Barros García, María Jesús. 2018. Face-enhancing compliments in informal conversations in Valencian Spanish. *Borealis: An International Journal of Hispanic Linguistics* 7(1). 147–168.

Calvo Carrilla, José Luis. 2000. *La palabra inflamada. Historia y metafísica del piropo literario en el siglo XX*. Barcelona: Península.

Cohen, Andrew. 2012. Research methods for describing variation in intercultural pragmatics for cultures in contact and conflict. In César Félix-Brasdefer & Dale Koike (eds.), *Pragmatic variation in first and second language contexts: Methodological issues*, 271–294. Amsterdam: John Benjamins.

Cohen, Andrew. 2017. Teaching and learning second language pragmatics. In Eli Hinkel (ed.), *Handbook of research in second language teaching and learning*, 428–452. New York: Routledge.

De los Heros, Susana. 2001. *Discurso, identidad y género en el castellano peruano*. Lima: Pontifica Universidad Católica del Perú.

Félix-Brasdefer, J. César. 2008a. *Politeness in Mexico and the United States: A contrastive study of the realization and perception of refusals*. Amsterdam/Philadelphia: John Benjamins.

Félix-Brasdefer, J. César. 2008b. Teaching Spanish pragmatics in the classroom: Explicit instruction of mitigation. *Hispania* 91(2). 477–492.

Félix-Brasdefer, J. César & Maria Hasler-Barker. 2012. Compliments and compliment responses: From empirical evidence to pedagogical application. In Leyre Ruiz de Zarobe & Yolanda Ruiz de Zarobe (eds.), *Speech acts and politeness across languages and cultures*, 650–669. Bern: Peter Lang.

Félix-Brasdefer, J. César. 2018. *Pragmática del español: Contexto, uso y variación*. New York: Routledge.

Fridzilius, Noemí. 2009. *Me gustaría ser baldosa . . . Un estudio cualitativo sobre el uso actual de los piropos callejeros en España*. Gothenburg: Gothenburg University bachelor's thesis.

Goddard, Cliff & Anna Wierzbicka. 2014. *Words and meanings: Lexical semantics across domains, languages, and cultures*. Oxford: Oxford University Press.

Golato, Andrea. 2003. Studying compliment responses: A comparison of DCTs and recordings of naturally occurring talk. *Applied Linguistics* 24. 90–121.

Golato, Andrea. 2005. *Compliments and Compliment Responses: Grammatical structure and sequential organization*. John Benjamins Publishing.

González, Carla Margarita. 2009. *Si así eres en rayas cómo serás en pelotas: Piropos y antipiropos caraqueños*. Caracas: Fundación para la Cultura Urbana.

Hasler-Barker, María. 2016. Effects of metapragmatic instruction on the production of compliments and compliment responses: Learner-learner role plays in the foreign language classroom. In Kathleen Bardovi-Harlig & Julio César. Félix-Brasdefer (eds.), *Pragmatics and language learning* (vol. 14), 125–152. Honolulu: Second Language Teaching and Curriculum Center University of Hawai'i.

Hernández Herrero, Annabelle. 1999. Analysis and comparison of complimenting behavior in Costa Rican Spanish and American English. *Kañina, Revista de Artes y Letras* 23(3). 121-31.

Holmes, Janet. 1988. Paying compliments: A sex-preferential politeness strategy. *Journal of Pragmatics* 12. 445–465.

Ishihara, Noriko & Andrew D. Cohen. 2010. *Teaching and learning pragmatics: Where language and culture meet*. Harlow, UK: Longman/Pearson Education.

Kasper, Gabriele & Kenneth Rose. 2002. *Pragmatic development in a second language*. Malden, MA: Wiley-Blackwell.

Lipski, John. 2012. Geographical and social varieties of Spanish: An overview. In Juan Ignacio Hualde, Antxon Olarrea, & Erin O'Rourke (eds.), *Handbook of Spanish linguistics*, 1–26. Wiley-Blackwell.

Lorenzo-Dus, Nuria. 2001. Compliment responses among British and Spanish university students: A contrastive study. *Journal of Pragmatics* 33(1). 107–27.

Lorenzo, Nuria & Patricia Bou. 2003. Gender and politeness: Spanish and British undergraduates. In José Santaemilia (ed.), *Género, lenguaje y traducción*, 187–199. Valencia: Universidad de Valencia/Dirección General de la Mujer.

Maíz Arévalo, Carmen. 2010. Intercultural pragmatics: A contrastive analysis of compliments in English and Spanish. In María Luisa Blanco Gómez & Juana Marín Arrese (eds.), *Discourse and communication: Cognitive and functional perspectives*, 107–127. Madrid: Servicio de Publicaciones, Universidad Rey Juan Carlos.

Maíz Arévalo, Carmen. 2012. "Was that a compliment?" Implicit compliments in English and Spanish. *Journal of Pragmatics* 44. 980–996.

Maíz Arévalo, Carmen & Antonio García-Gómez. 2013. "You look terrific!" Social evaluation and relationships in online compliments. *Discourse Studies* 16(6). 735–760.

Malaver, Irania & Carla González. 2008. El antipiropo: El lado oculto de la cortesía verbal. In Antonio Briz, Antonio Hidalgo, Marta Albelda, Josefa Contreras, & Nieves Hernández Flores (eds.), *Cortesía y conversación: De lo escrito a lo oral. III Coloquio Internacional del Programa EDICE*, 267–282. Valencia: Universitat de València.

Manes, Joan. 1983. Compliments: A mirror of cultural values. In Nessa Wolfson & Elliot Judd (eds.), *Sociolinguistics and language acquisition*, 96–102. Rowley, MA: Newbury House.

Manes, Joan & Nessa Wolfson. 1981. The compliment formula. In Joan Manes & Nessa Wolfson (eds.), *Conversational routine: Explorations in standardized communication situations and prepatterned speech*, 115–132. The Hague: Mouton Publishers.

Mills, Sara. 2003. *Gender and politeness*. Cambridge: Cambridge University Press.

Mitchell, Mia Lael. 2015. *Who controls the streets? Piropos in Buenos Aires: Women's experiences and interpretations*. Tempe, Arizona: Arizona State University MA thesis.

Níkleva, Dimitrinka. 2016. Tendencias actuales en los piropos españoles. *Onomázein* 34. 322–350.

Ogiermann, Eva. 2018. Discourse completion tasks. In Andreas Jucker, Klaus Schneider, & Wolfram Bublitz (eds.), *Methods in pragmatics*, 301–325. Berlin: de Gruyter.

Placencia, Maria Elena & Yépez, María. 1999. Compliment responses: Compliments in Ecuadorian Spanish. *Lengua* 9. 83–121.

Ramírez-Cruz, Héctor, Nataly Correa, & Jennifer Mancera. 2017. '¡*Uy!, ¿quién pidió pollo?*' A qualitative analysis of the piropo practice among construction workers in Bogotá, Colombia. *Sociolinguistic Studies* 10(4). 563–588.

Schreier, Judith. 2005. Quién fuera mecánico . . . Un estudio sociopragmático sobre la aceptación social del piropo. *Revista Internacional de Lingüística Iberoamericana* 3(1). 65–78.

Searle, John. 1969. *Speech acts*. Cambridge: Cambridge University Press.

Searle, John. 1976. A classification of illocutionary acts. *Language in Society* 5(1). 1–23.

Sykes, Julie. 2006. *Pragmatic evolution: An examination of the changing politeness perceptions of piropos in Yucatán, México*. Paper presented at the Hispanic Linguistic Symposium (HLS), University of Minnesota, 15–17 October.

Taguchi, Naoko & Carsten Roever. 2017. *Second language pragmatics*. Oxford University Press.

Wolfson, Nessa. 1983. An empirically based analysis of complimenting in American English. In Nessa Wolfson & Elliot Judd (eds.), *Sociolinguistics and Language Acquisition*, 82–95. Rowley, MA: Newbury House.

Wolfson, Nessa & Joan Manes. 1980. The compliment as a social strategy. *Papers in Linguistics* 13(3). 391–410.

Part II: **Assessing pragmatic competence**

Rachel L. Shively
6 Assessing L2 pragmatic competence

Abstract: This chapter offers an overview of key issues and current debates related to the assessment of second language (L2) pragmatics. It begins by examining definitions of pragmatic competence and how the underlying construct of these definitions affects how and what is assessed. This discussion is followed by a consideration of the dimensions of pragmatics that have been assessed and a review of assessment methods, highlighting recent innovations and the role of learner agency. The concluding section of this chapter suggests future directions in L2 pragmatics assessment.

Keywords: second language pragmatics, pragmatics assessment, pragmatics testing

1 Introduction

It is through assessment that teachers and researchers are able to collect information about what second language (L2) speakers know about a language, are able to do with the language, or have accomplished in a period of time (e.g., Kasper and Ross 2013). Assessment includes both traditional standardized testing, but also classroom-based assessment administered by teachers to determine learning outcomes in a particular setting and to support students' continued development (e.g., Ishihara and Cohen 2010). Although work on assessing L2 pragmatics goes back more than two decades, neither standardized testing nor classroom-based assessment of pragmatics has been widely implemented in practice (e.g., Taguchi and Roever 2017; Youn 2018). Large-scale tests commonly employed to measure global L2 competence such as the American Council on the Teaching of Foreign Languages Oral Proficiency Interview (ACTFL OPI) or the Test of English as a Foreign Language (TOEFL) do not include assessment of pragmatics (Taguchi and Roever 2017). In the case of classroom-based assessment, a challenge that teachers face is that pragmatic skills are often not included in the foreign language (FL) curriculum or in textbook materials, so teachers are typically left to their own devices if they want to assess pragmatic competence in the FL classroom (e.g., Bardovi-Harlig 2017; Dumitrescu and Andueza 2018; Gironzetti and Koike 2016). The lack of attention to pragmatics is problematic given that this domain is one component of communicative competence (e.g., Bachman and Palmer 2010; Timpe-Laughlin, Wain, and Schmidgall 2015) and, consequently, if we do not assess pragmatics, we cannot obtain a full picture of L2 speakers' abilities. Further, there is a lack of research demonstrating that pragmatic competence is not subsumed under more general listening or speaking abilities. In this context, it is crucial to continue to develop and refine approaches to the assessment of various dimensions of pragmatics and the chapters in Section II do just that.

In order to contextualize and introduce Section II, the goal of this chapter is to provide an overview of key issues in the assessment of L2 pragmatics and to discuss the evolution of assessment methods from the early days of the field when Andrew Cohen and his colleagues pioneered the discourse completion task (e.g., Cohen and Olshtain 1981) to the present. The chapter will begin by examining how the underlying construct of pragmatic competence impacts what and how we assess in pragmatics. In terms of what aspects of pragmatic competence can be assessed, the chapter outlines various dimensions such as receptive and productive skills, oral and written modes, implicit and explicit knowledge, and pragmalinguistic and sociopragmatic skills. We also highlight a shift in the field from an early focus on assessing single-utterance, isolated speech acts to the more recent surge in pragmatics-in-interaction studies, which analyze longer stretches of contextualized and co-constructed talk (e.g., Félix-Brasdefer 2019; Kasper 2006). The chapter then turns to how to assess pragmatic competence, describing various assessment methods and spotlighting recent innovations in these methods. We conclude by suggesting future directions for assessment in L2 pragmatics.

2 Key issues

An essential issue in the assessment of L2 pragmatics is defining both pragmatics and pragmatic competence (see Chapter 1, this volume), since various definitions of both terms have been put forth that reflect specific traditions (e.g., Schneider 2017). A broad view of pragmatic competence is that of Fraser (2010: 15), who defined pragmatic competence as "the ability to communicate your intended message with all its nuances in any socio-cultural context and to interpret the message of your interlocutor as it was intended." Some of the specific knowledge and skills that have been outlined as components in pragmatic competence include sociocultural knowledge about social norms and language use in different contexts, mapping of forms with the social meanings that they index, understanding implicit meaning, and being able to participate in extended discourse, among other aspects (e.g., Kasper and Rose 2002; Taguchi and Roever 2017; Timpe-Laughlin, Wain, and Schmidgall, 2015). The distinction between pragmalinguistic competence (i.e., being able to link specific language forms with their functions and meanings) and sociopragmatic competence (i.e., knowing in what circumstances and with whom specific language forms are culturally appropriate) has also been made to differentiate aspects of pragmatic competence. Although previous research has predominantly focused on productive skills in oral language, receptive skills (e.g., comprehension of implicit meaning) and writing skills are also aspects of pragmatic competence.

2.1 Theoretical frameworks and assessment

The way that L2 pragmatics and pragmatic competence are defined is crucial to assessment because theoretical orientation influences the target constructs. The earliest work on the assessment of L2 pragmatics was grounded in speech act theory (e.g., Searle 1976), which resulted in a narrow focus on communicative actions at the utterance level in spoken language. This approach further involves an etic perspective (i.e., the analyst interprets the intentions of the participants), does not look beyond individual utterances in isolation, and reflects a "rational actor model" or "rationalist approach," which conceives of an ideal speaker who acts rationally to achieve communication goals and who possesses a static base of knowledge and skills that are not affected by the interlocutor or by the sequential unfolding of an interaction (e.g., Kasper 2006; Kasper and Ross 2013). In this theoretical framework, the target construct are speech acts, which was operationalized in assessments that tested L2 speakers' ability to recognize or produce socially appropriate speech acts at the utterance level.

An example of early pragmatics tests that adopted what has been termed the rationalist approach are those developed by Hudson, Detmer, and Brown (1995). Hudson et al., for instance, in their ground-breaking test battery, assessed the speech acts of apologies, refusals, and requests using a variety of item types. Apart from multiple-choice questions, the test included both written and oral discourse completion tasks (DCTs), that is, an item in which test-takers are given the description of a situation and then asked to write or speak what they would say in response. Hudson and his colleagues also included role plays (i.e., spontaneous simulated oral interactions) in their battery, but they only examined the specific speech act in question, not the entire interaction. For the DCTs and role plays, pragmatic competence was measured using various criteria including production of the appropriate speech act, amount of language provided, formality, politeness, and directness.

Some have argued that the speech act framework under-specifies pragmatic competence, reducing the target construct in assessment to isolated communicative acts at the utterance level (e.g., Roever 2011; Scheider 2017). Consequently, various authors have worked to broaden the construct of pragmatic competence to assess features beyond speech acts. Roever and colleagues (e.g., Roever 2005, 2006; Roever, Fraser, and Elder 2014), for example, developed a series of web-based tests to assess both pragmalinguistic and sociopragmatic skills related to L2 speakers' ability to recognize formulas, understand implicature, judge pragmatic appropriateness, and provide a turn in a multiple-rejoiner DCT. These efforts expanded the focus from a small number of isolated speech acts to other aspects of pragmatics, as well as began to examine speech acts in more extended discourse.

More recent work in L2 pragmatics assessment has gone even further in its focus on pragmatics in interaction. This discursive approach to L2 pragmatics theorizes that pragmatics is an interactional phenomenon and that pragmatic competence includes being able to participate in extended interaction and to accomplish social actions in the unfolding discourse context (e.g., Kasper 2006; Kasper and Ross 2013; Roever and Kasper 2018). This view is grounded theoretically in traditions such as interactional sociolinguistics and conversation analysis (CA), approaches which take an emic perspective – that is, they focus on how the participants themselves orient to the talk, not the analyst's interpretation – and conceive of pragmatic meaning and social actions as jointly accomplished by the participants, rather than solely the performance of an individual rational actor (e.g. Kasper 2006; Kasper and Ross 2013; Mori and Nguyen 2019). Within a discursive approach, the construct of pragmatic competence is expanded to L2 speakers' ability to produce speech acts in their sequential context, to co-construct meaning with others, and to use interactional skills such as turn-taking, alignment, and repair (e.g. Roever and Kasper 2018). The assessment method employed in this tradition has typically been role plays (e.g., Félix-Brasdefer 2018). Grabowski (2009) and Youn (2015) are two researchers who have designed role plays to assess pragmatics skills in extended discourse.

2.2 Assessment methods

As theoretical orientations have shifted over time, so too have assessment methods. Written DCTs with a single turn that were intended to elicit speech acts in spoken language dominated early work on L2 pragmatics. While DCTs are still a widely-employed method, role plays have become more common as the focus has changed to examining interactional skills and pragmatic actions in extended discourse. Written DCTs have been critiqued for producing data that do not serve as strong validity evidence for making inferences about pragmatic competence (e.g., Youn and Bogorevich 2019). Research has indicated that written DCTs do not always capture the same range and types of strategies that are found in real-life interactions, nor does the written mode reflect characteristics of oral speech such as hesitation, repetition, and prosodic and nonverbal information (e.g., Economidou-Kogetsidis 2013; Golato 2003; Kasper 2008; Yuan 2001). Furthermore, written DCTs elicit what test-takers think they would say and draw on their explicit knowledge (i.e., knowledge of which a person is conscious and aware), rather than their implicit knowledge (i.e., rapidly accessible knowledge of which a person is unaware), that is, what they would actually do in a spontaneous oral interaction (e.g., Kasper and Dahl 1991; Bardovi-Harlig 2013).

The primary reason why written DCTs continue to be popular, however, is that they allow systematic control of situational and social factors, they are easy to administer, and can be used to collect large amounts of data in a relatively short amount of time. Recent research has also offered innovations to the original format of the DCT, such as that provided in Cohen and Olshtain (1981). Oral DCTs (also termed closed role plays) ask participants to speak their turn rather than write it, which makes the task a direct measure of spoken language rather than indirect in the case of written DCTs that intend to project oral responses. Some authors have developed technology-enhanced DCTs that provide images, audio, video, and/or animation (e.g., Halenko 2013; Winke and Teng 2010), which may make the task more appealing and authentic for test-takers (e.g., Culpeper, Mackey, and Taguchi 2018; Rockey, Tiegs, and Fernández 2020). Another innovation in the DCT format are collaborative DCTs in which two participants construct a dialogue together (Taguchi and Kim 2016). In any type of DCT, the responses collected must be scored by trained raters using well-developed and clear rating criteria in order for the data to have a reasonable level of reliability (i.e., consistency in scoring) (e.g., Youn and Bogorevich 2019).

Role plays (also called open role plays) involve a simulated verbal interaction between two or more people. Although the participants' roles and the setting are controlled by the researcher, the interactional outcomes of the role play are not predetermined (e.g., Félix-Brasdefer 2018). The data that result can be analyzed for interactional features and co-construction of meaning over multiple turns. While role plays have been employed for decades in L2 pragmatics (e.g., Rintell 1979), only more recently have interactional resources – rather than speech acts – been the focus in assessing L2 speakers' performance in role plays. Because role play performances are more complex than DCT responses, developing clear and valid rating criteria for interactional data is crucial – for example, by using CA to analyze interactional features as a first step in developing data-driven rating criteria (e.g., Youn, 2015). A further consideration when assessing interaction within a theoretical framework such as interactional competence (e.g., Young 2011, 2019), is how or whether to give an individual a rating when theoretically speaking, interactional competence is co-constructed and not only related to the skills of one individual. Young (2019) argues that examining the participation framework and how individuals establish intersubjectivity within that framework is key.

Although role plays have the advantage of eliciting interactional data in a controlled context (i.e., setting and roles are crafted by the researcher to target particular contextual variables), they have the disadvantage of being less practical than DCTs to administer and analyze. Further, role plays tend to reflect naturalistic interaction better than DCTs, but still constitute dialogue between people who are acting and using their imaginations to construct the scenario, who typically do not have real-life relationships, and whose behavior will not have any real social consequences.[1] A further challenge in developing role play scenarios and rating criteria is ensuring that the task and the assessment of the performance reflect the characteristics of the real-life setting being represented (e.g., Taguchi and Roever 2017). Some innovative techniques have attempted to improve on some of the limitations of role plays. For instance, Vilar-Beltran and Melchor-Couto (2013) asked participants to complete role plays as avatars in the virtual world Second Life, which provided a richer visual context through graphic images and animation, reducing the need for participants to rely on their imaginations. Another strategy is to include a speech act not described in the role play scenario, so that participants are unaware and do not expect that speech act and, therefore, may respond to it more naturalistically. An example is Cheng (2011), who included compliments in role plays in which participants were expecting other speech acts.

While role plays and DCTs are the most common methods to assess pragmatic production, multiple-choice questions (MCQs) is a method that has been employed to examine receptive skills in pragmatics. Researchers have assessed comprehension and recognition of various pragmatic features such as conversational implicatures, routine formulas, and speech acts (e.g., Hudson et al. 1995; Taguchi 2009; Timpe-Laughlin and Choi 2017). Although MCQs have high practicality due to ease of administration and scoring, they sometimes suffer from low reliability, if distractor options are not clearly incorrect for all test-takers or

---

[1] In naturally-occurring interactions, there are also instances in which participants do not have relationships beyond a brief transaction, for example, service encounters between strangers.

partial credit is not given. Taguchi and Roever (2017) point out that one challenge in creating MCQs, as well as other assessment methods in L2 pragmatics, is making items difficult enough for higher proficiency learners to avoid ceiling effects. Steps to address this challenge highlighted by these authors include creating more difficult test items, recruiting test-takers with a range of proficiency levels (previous research is dominated by intermediate and advanced L2 speakers), and identifying the degree of difficulty of various pragmatic features.

A final assessment method that has been employed occasionally in classroom-based assessment is collecting samples of L2 use in real-life settings beyond the classroom. Morris (2017), for instance, assessed the learning of L2 speech acts in oral communication by asking her students to audio-record themselves using the L2 out in the community to complete tasks such as ordering food in restaurants and asking people on the street for directions. In another case, Alcón-Soler (2015) assessed the use of requests in writing by collecting and analyzing authentic emails that students had written to their professors. A considerable benefit of this method is that we can assess what L2 speakers actually do with language in a real-life encounter with potential material and social consequences, but drawbacks include lack of practicality in many situations (e.g., difficulty getting ethics board approval or consent from community members, few opportunities for L2 interactions outside the FL classroom) and the challenge of comparability, since in real life, the researcher cannot always control social and contextual variables. Finally, when assessing productive skills in the classroom context, Ishihara (2019) and Ishihara and Cohen (2010) have advocated for innovative assessment techniques to respect L2 speakers' agency and identity. For instance, teachers can measure performance not in comparison to L2 native speakers – whom L2 speakers may not wish to emulate – but rather, L2 speakers can be assessed in relation to how successful they were in a given task in achieving their own communicative goals in the L2.

In sum, this section has provided an overview of historical trends in L2 pragmatics assessment, has touched upon current debates in the field, and has reviewed common assessment methods. We conclude in the following section by offering some future directions.

3 Conclusion and future directions

This chapter has traced developments in assessing L2 pragmatics over the past four decades, from the early 1980s when Andrew Cohen and his colleagues began implementing DCTs to assess speech acts to more recent interest in discursive pragmatics and pragmatic abilities beyond speech acts. Looking toward the future, the remainder of this section highlights some areas for research going forward.

The potential for digital technologies to enhance assessment is a key consideration. In pragmatics, it is imperative to contextualize interaction physically, discursively, and socially, yet as we discussed earlier, providing this real-life context for assessment tasks can be challenging in terms of practicality. Creating pragmatics assessments that are administered within digital spaces such as virtual environments, in which individuals role play via avatars or test-takers interact with a bot (i.e., an artificial intelligent agent), are potential ways to not sacrifice practicality while improving contextualization and standardization of assessment tasks (see Chapter 10, this volume). More research on the creation and implementation of assessment tasks in digital spaces is needed.

Another direction for future research is to expand on what has previously been assessed in order to measure dimensions of pragmatic competence that have heretofore received little attention, such as humor (see Chapter 8, this volume), strategic competence (see Chapter 9, this volume), and gesture and prosody. While assessing areas such as humor and gesture may create challenges for scoring and inter-rater reliability, broadening our focus to encompass such areas has the potential to provide a fuller picture of L2 learners' pragmatic abilities. Chapters 8 and 9 in this volume provide examples of how to approach assessing the underexplored areas of humor and strategic competence.

Various authors (e.g., Cohen 2019; Taguchi and Roever 2017; Youn and Bogorevich 2019) have pointed out the need for empirical research that establishes the features and range of pragmatic norms expected in different domains (e.g., retail service encounter, advising session) and in different target languages. For instance, in the case of retail service encounters in Spanish, previous research has documented the expected social actions and their sequential organization, norms for requesting, and a range of ways that speakers express politeness in this domain in various Spanish-speaking communities (e.g., Félix-Brasdefer 2015). Such information is crucial for assessment because, in order to determine the degree of appropriateness of pragmatic performance in a particular domain, we need to have an empirically-based understanding of how competent speakers behave in that domain in the real world.

Finally, we have seen efforts in recent years to make pragmatics-focused instructional materials easily accessible to FL teachers – Andrew Cohen, for instance, was involved in developing websites for learning Japanese (http://carla.umn.edu/speechacts/japanese/introtospeechacts/index.htm) and Spanish (http://carla.umn.edu/speechacts/sp_pragmatics/home.html) pragmatics and a wiki for sharing pragmatics materials (http://wlpragmatics.pbworks.com). As we continue this push for pragmatics instruction in the FL classroom, we need a greater focus on the design and implementation of classroom-based assessments in order to support teachers as they incorporate pragmatics instruction into their curricula (e.g., Ishihara and Cohen 2010).

References

Bachman, Lyle F., & Adrian S. Palmer. 2010. *Language testing in practice*. Oxford: Oxford University Press.
Bardovi-Harlig, Kathleen. 2013. Developing L2 pragmatics. *Language Learning* 63. 68–86.
Bardovi-Harlig, Kathleen. 2017. Acquisition of L2 pragmatics. In Shawn Loewen & Masatoshi Sato (eds.), *The Routledge handbook of instructed second language acquisition*, 224–245. New York: Routledge.
Cheng, Dongmei. 2011. New insights on compliment responses: A comparison between native English speakers and Chinese L2 speakers. *Journal of Pragmatics* 43. 2204–2214.
Cohen, Andrew D. 2019. Considerations in assessing pragmatic appropriateness in spoken language. *Language Teaching* 53(2). 183–202.
Cohen, Andrew D. & Elite Olshtain. 1981. Developing a measure of socio-cultural competence: The case of the apology. *Language Learning* 31. 113–134.
Culpeper, Jonathan, Alison Mackey, & Naoko Taguchi. 2018. *Second language pragmatics: From theory to research*. New York: Routledge.
Dumitrescu, Domnita & Patricia L. Andueza (eds.). 2018. *L2 Spanish pragmatics: From research to practice*. New York: Routledge.
Economidou-Kogetsidis, Maria. 2013. Strategies, modification and perspective in native speakers' requests: A comparison of WDCT and naturally occurring requests. *Journal of Pragmatics* 53. 21–38.
Félix-Brasdefer, J. César. 2015. *The language of service encounters: A pragmatic-discursive approach*. Cambridge: Cambridge University Press.
Félix-Brasdefer, J. César. 2018. Role plays. In Andreas Jucker, Klaus Schneider, & Wolfram Bublitz (eds.), *Methods in Pragmatics*, 305–332. (Handbook of Pragmatics 10). Berlin: De Gruyter Mouton.
Félix-Brasdefer, J. César. 2019. Speech acts in interaction: Negotiating joint action in a second language. In Naoko Taguchi (ed.), *The Routledge handbook of second language acquisition and pragmatics*, 17–30. New York: Routledge.
Fraser, Bruce. 2010. Pragmatic competence: The case of hedging. In Gunther Kaltenböck, Wiltrud Mihatsch, & Stefan Schneider (eds.), *New approaches to hedging*, 15–34. Bingley, UK: Emerald.
Gironzetti, Elisa & Dale Koike. 2016. Bridging the gap in Spanish instructional pragmatics: from theory to practice. *Journal of Spanish Language Teaching* 3. 89–98.
Golato, Andrea. 2003. Studying compliment responses: A comparison of DCTs and recordings of naturally occurring talk. *Applied Linguistics* 24. 90–121.
Grabowski, Kirby. 2009. *Investigating the construct validity of a test designed to measure grammatical and pragmatic knowledge in the context of speaking*. New York: Columbia University dissertation.

Halenko, Nicola. 2013. Using computer animation to assess and improve spoken language skills. In Pixel (ed.), *ICT for language learning conference proceedings*, 286–290. Florence: Libreriauniversitaria.

Hudson, Thom D., Emily Detmer, & J. D. Brown. 1995. *Developing prototype measures of cross-cultural pragmatics* (Technical Report #7). Honolulu: Second Language Teaching and Curriculum Center University of Hawaii.

Ishihara, Noriko. 2019. Identity and agency in L2 pragmatics. In Naoko Taguchi (ed.), *The Routledge handbook of second language acquisition and pragmatics*, 161–175. New York: Routledge.

Ishihara, Noriko & Andrew D. Cohen. 2010. *Teaching and learning pragmatics: Where language and culture meet*. Harlow: Longman.

Kasper, Gabriele. 2006. Speech acts in interaction: towards discursive pragmatics. In Kathleen Bardovi-Harlig, J. César Félix-Brasdefer, & Alwiya Omar (eds.), *Pragmatics and language learning* (vol. 11), 281–314. Honolulu: Second Language Teaching and Curriculum Center University of Hawaii.

Kasper, Gabriele. 2008. Data collection in pragmatics research. In Helen Spencer-Oatey (ed.), *Culturally speaking: Culture, communication and politeness theory*, 279–303. London: Continuum.

Kasper, Gabriele & Merete Dahl. 1991. Research methods in interlanguage pragmatics. *Studies in Second Language Acquisition* 13. 215–247.

Kasper, Gabriele & Kenneth Rose. 2002. *Pragmatic development in a second language*. Malden, MA: Blackwell.

Kasper, Gabriele & Steven J. Ross. 2013. Assessing second language pragmatics: An overview and introductions. In Steven J. Ross & Gabriele Kasper (eds.), *Assessing second language pragmatics*, 1–40. New York: Palgrave Macmillan.

Mori, Junko & Hanh thi Nguyen. 2019. Conversation analysis in L2 pragmatics research. In Naoko Taguchi (ed.), *The Routledge handbook of second language acquisition and pragmatics*, 226–240. New York: Routledge.

Morris, Kimberly. 2017. *Learning by doing: The affordances of task-based pragmatics instruction for beginning L2 Spanish learners studying abroad*. Davis, CA: University of California, Davis, dissertation.

Rintell, Ellen. 1979. Getting your speech act together: The pragmatic ability of second language learners. *Working Papers on Bilingualism* 17. 97–106.

Rockey, Catherine, Jessica Tiegs, & Julieta Fernández. 2020. Mobile application use in technology-enhanced DCTs. *CALICO Journal* 73(1). 85–108.

Roever, Carsten. 2005. *Testing in ESL pragmatics*. Frankfurt: Peter Lang.

Roever, Carsten. 2006. Validation of a web-based test of ESL pragmalinguistics. *Language Testing* 23. 229–256.

Roever, Carsten. 2011. Testing of second language pragmatics: Past and future. *Language Testing* 28. 463–481.

Roever, Carsten, Catriona Fraser, & Catherine Elder. 2014. *Testing ESL sociopragmatics: Development and validation of a web-based battery*. Frankfurt am Main: Peter Lang.

Roever, Carsten & Gabriele Kasper. 2018. Speaking in turns and sequences: Interactional competence as a target construct in testing speaking. *Language Testing* 35. 331–355.

Schneider, Klaus. 2017. Pragmatic competence and pragmatic variation. In Rachel Giora & Michale Haugh (eds.), *Doing pragmatics interculturally: Cognitive, philosophical, and sociopragmatic perspectives*, 315–333. Berlin: De Gruyter Mouton.

Searle, John. (1976). A classification of illocutionary acts. *Language in Society* 5. 1–23.
Taguchi, Naoko. 2009. Corpus-informed assessment of comprehension of conversational implicatures in L2 English. *TESOL Quarterly* 43. 739–750.
Taguchi, Naoko & YouJin Kim. 2016. Collaborative dialogue in learning pragmatics: Pragmatics-related episodes as an opportunity for learning request-making. *Applied Linguistics* 37. 416–437.
Taguchi, Naoko & Carsten Roever. 2017. *Second language pragmatics*. Oxford: Oxford University Press.
Timpe-Laughlin, Veronika & Ikkyu Choi. 2017. Exploring the validity of a second language intercultural pragmatics assessment tool. *Language Assessment Quarterly* 14. 19–35.
Timpe-Laughlin, Veronika, Jennifer Wain, & Jonathan Schmidgall. 2015. Defining and operationalizing the construct of pragmatic competence: Review and recommendations. *ETS Research Report Series 2015(l)*, 1–43. Princeton, NJ: ETS.
Vilar-Beltrán, Elina & Sabela Melchor-Couto. 2013. Refusing in second life. *Utrecht Studies in Language and Communication* 25. 23–40.
Winke, Paula & Chunhong Teng. 2010. Using task-based pragmatics tutorials while studying abroad in China. *Intercultural Pragmatics* 7(2). 363–399.
Youn, Soo Jung. 2015. Validity argument for assessing L2 pragmatics in interaction using mixed methods. *Language Testing* 32. 199–225.
Youn, Soo Jung. 2018. Second language pragmatics. In Aek Phakiti, Peter De Costa, Luke Plonsky, & Sue Starfield (eds.), *The Palgrave handbook of applied linguistics research methodology*, 829–844. London: Palgrave Macmillan.
Youn, Soo Jung, & Valeriia Bogorevich, V. 2019. Assessment in L2 pragmatics. In Naoko Taguchi (ed.), *The Routledge handbook of second language acquisition and pragmatics*, 308–321. New York: Routledge.
Young, Richard F. 2011. Interactional competence in language learning, teaching, and testing. In Eli Hinkel (ed.), *Handbook of research in second language teaching and learning* (vol. 2), 233–268. New York: Routledge.
Young, Richard F. 2019. Interactional competence and L2 pragmatics. In Naoko Taguchi (ed.), *The Routledge handbook of second language acquisition and pragmatics*, 93–110. New York: Routledge.
Yuan, Yi. 2001. An inquiry into empirical pragmatics data-gathering methods: Written DCTs, oral DCTs, field notes, and natural conversations. *Journal of Pragmatics* 33. 271–292.

Carsten Roever and Rod Ellis

7 Testing of L2 pragmatics: The challenge of implicit knowledge

Abstract: The testing of L2 pragmatics has been a core part of Andrew Cohen's work. This area has seen steadily increasing research interest with several testing instruments being developed based on both a speech act perspective and an interactional competence perspective. One issue that has received very little attention is the distinction between implicit and explicit pragmatic knowledge. This is in contrast to more general SLA work where these types of L2 knowledge and their implications for language learning and teaching have been thoroughly discussed. This paper intends to raise the profile of the distinction between explicit and implicit pragmatic knowledge and show how different assessment instruments in L2 pragmatics testing differentially engage these knowledge types. An argument is presented for a greater emphasis on measures of implicit pragmatic knowledge in pragmatics assessment.

Keywords: explicit and implicit knowledge, discourse completion tests, role plays, testing, validity, interactional competence

1 Introduction

Andrew Cohen has contributed to the testing of second language (L2) pragmatics from the very beginning of this burgeoning research area (Cohen and Olshtain 1981), throughout its development (Cohen 2004; Ishihara and Cohen 2010), and to the present day (Cohen 2019). His formative influence was all the more important given the recency of work on testing of L2 pragmatics. Apart from some early attempts (Farhady 1980; Shimazu 1989), systematic development of test batteries did not start until 1995 when Hudson, Detmer, and Brown (1995) introduced their test development project. Since then, research on testing L2 pragmatics has been lively with multiple tests having been developed and trialed for research purposes (see below for a brief summary, and Roever and Ikeda, 2020 for more detail).

However, a risk is emerging for the real-world relevance of pragmatics tests; with the exception of a small number of recent instruments which test interactional abilities, most pragmatics tests tap explicit knowledge (see Chapter 13, this volume, for an in-depth review on explicit knowledge in L2

https://doi.org/10.1515/9783110721775-008

pragmatics). These tests may fail on the Extrapolation inference in an argument-based validity framework (Kane 2013) since their tasks do not reflect the fast, non-monitored, intuitive processing which is overwhelmingly required in real-world language use settings. In the real world, language users need to interpret implicature, recognize and produce routine formulae, and formulate appropriate speech acts quickly and automatically based on implicit pragmatic knowledge. Moreover, they do not have the extensive time to plan, analyze, and recall explicit knowledge afforded by all but the most interactional of tests.

In the following, we will first briefly review the concept of implicit and explicit knowledge as well as existing pragmatics tests, followed by a more detailed discussion of testing tools used and their potential for eliciting implicit knowledge.

2 Key issues

2.1 Implicit and explicit knowledge

There is a long-standing debate in L2 acquisition about how second language knowledge is represented, which has significant consequences for pedagogy and assessment but has had little uptake in second language pragmatics. The main debate is around implicit and explicit knowledge, with implicit knowledge being equivalent to intuition, which is rapidly accessible, unreportable, and outside the language user's awareness (R. Ellis and Roever 2018). By contrast, explicit knowledge encompasses conscious knowledge, which is within awareness, can be verbalized and consciously manipulated, and requires slower, more effortful access. Native speakers rely nearly exclusively on implicit knowledge in their language production and comprehension, while learners tend to rely much more heavily on explicit knowledge, especially in the early stages of L2 development.

The two knowledge types appear to be distinct and represented in two different areas of the brain (N. Ellis 2017), but it can be difficult to discern whether a particular second language performance truly relies on implicit knowledge, since explicit knowledge can become highly automatized through repeated practice (Suzuki and DeKeyser 2015) and can then be accessed quickly and effortlessly without conscious awareness. While this is problematic for studies that try to clearly differentiate the knowledge types, it is less of a concern for language assessment since it can be argued that adequate performance on a task is all that matters, regardless of whether it is reliant on truly implicit or highly automatized explicit knowledge. Therefore, we will only distinguish implicit and explicit knowledge in our discussion, and not separately consider highly automatized explicit knowledge, which is functionally equivalent to implicit knowledge.

Due to (unautomatized) explicit knowledge requiring slow, effortful retrieval and cognitive operations in working memory (e.g., recall of grammatical or pragmatic rules), reliance on explicit knowledge is at odds with the need to produce language quickly in natural interaction; Levinson and Torreira (2015) show that the typical gap between turns in a conversation is 0.2 seconds with speech planning starting even before the gap. In other words, interactants must construct their next utterance before the interlocutor has completed his/her turn, which necessitates production and comprehension to place little burden on working memory, which would otherwise quickly get overloaded. Recourse to implicit knowledge requires little involvement of working memory, and thereby preserves precious processing space.

Little research has been done on explicit and implicit knowledge in L2 pragmatics and interaction. Ellis (2004) raised the issue that most pragmatics research instruments seem to tap explicit knowledge, and Bardovi-Harlig (2013) encouraged L2 pragmatics researchers to consider the explicit-implicit distinction to understand what pragmatics research instruments actually measure (see also Chapter 13, this volume). This issue is just as relevant for pragmatics assessments, which tend to use similar instruments as research studies and whose results are intended to predict real-world performance. It is therefore important to consider what kinds of claims about test takers and their abilities can be made based on data elicited from different instruments used in pragmatics assessment.

2.2 Testing L2 pragmatics: A brief overview

In the testing of L2 pragmatics, two major research streams exist, which have developed assessment instruments for somewhat different constructs of L2 pragmatics. The older stream focuses on pragmatic competence, as conceptualized by Leech (1983, 2014) and Thomas (1983), and incorporates research on speech acts and politeness (Brown and Levinson 1987), routine formulae (Coulmas 1981), and implicature (Grice 1975). Testing instruments generally follow an analytic psychometric tradition (Klein-Braley 1997), consisting of multi-item batteries, and include Discourse Completion Tests (DCTs), multiple-choice comprehension / recognition tasks, and rating scales.

Within this first research stream, two generations of tests can be distinguished. The first generation of pragmatics assessment focuses on speech acts and politeness, and takes off from Hudson et al.'s (1995) pioneering test battery. Hudson et al. developed three different types of DCTs (written, oral, and multiple choice), role play tasks, and two self-assessment scales. They investigated learners' knowledge of appropriateness for requests, apologies and refusals. Their instrument was contrastively designed for L1 Japanese-speaking learners of English, and it led to several spin-offs. Yamashita (1996) adapted the test battery for L1 English speaking learners of Japanese, Yoshitake (1997) used it with EFL learners in Japan, and Brown and Ahn (2011) adapted it for L2 Korean. Liu (2006) addressed the challenge of developing reliable multiple-choice DCTs with Chinese learners of English, while Tada (2005) used video-based scenarios to contextualize his productive and multiple-choice DCTs for Japanese learners of English.

The second generation of tests is also situated in traditional pragmatics but broadens the construct from speech acts to other aspects of pragmatics, notably implicature and routine formulae. It emphasized practicality of measurement through web-based delivery to facilitate wider uptake of pragmatics assessment. Roever (2005, 2006) developed a test of English L2 pragmatics with a pragmalinguistic focus as opposed to Hudson et al.'s (1995) sociopragmatic focus, assessing knowledge of implicature, routine formulae, and speech acts. In the same tradition, Itomitsu (2009) developed a test of Japanese as an L2, assessing knowledge of speech acts, speech styles, routine formulae and grammar. Roever, Fraser, and Elder (2014) expanded this line of work by focusing on sociopragmatics in a test including dialogue completion, appropriateness judgments and corrections, and comprehension of extended discourse. Finally, Timpe (2013) and Timpe-Laughlin and Choi (2017) tested speech act comprehension, routine formulae, and idiomatic language use, supplemented by role plays.

The second, more recent stream of pragmatics assessments emphasizes extended interaction, most commonly following the conceptualization of interactional competence by Hall and Pekarek Doehler (2011), which is infused with the research approach of Conversation Analysis (Sacks 1992; Schegloff 2007). It assesses learners' ability to manage extended conversations, create interpersonal meanings, and design contributions that fit the addressee's epistemic and social status. Testing instruments are role plays, elicited conversations and extended monologues, and scoring is done by raters.

Two tests have been developed in this tradition which are squarely situated in the interactional competence paradigm. Youn (2015, 2019) developed a role-play based test and created scoring criteria bottom-up from the test takers' interactions. Ikeda (2017) expanded on Youn, also employing role plays and creating scoring criteria based on the data, but with an additional focus on the possible use of monologue tasks and the role of proficiency and exposure. Working outside interactional competence as a framework, Grabowski (2009, 2013) also employed role plays and scored them following Purpura's (2004) model of language ability.

Finally, Walters (2007, 2009) attempted to measure aspects of interactional ability receptively and productively but his test suffered from extremely low reliability.

The two streams of pragmatics testing have addressed related constructs but used quite different instruments and scoring procedures. The instruments used determine the type of pragmatic knowledge elicited. In the following section, we will discuss instruments in more detail, which will demonstrate that the first stream has mostly assessed explicit pragmatic knowledge, and the second stream implicit pragmatic knowledge.

2.3 Test instruments and knowledge types

2.3.1 Discourse completion tasks (DCTs)

The Discourse Completion Test (DCT) has been the primary assessment tool in the older stream of pragmatics tests, used by Hudson, Detmer and Brown (1995) and its spin-offs, Roever (2005, 2006), Liu (2006), and Tada (2005). In their most typical form, DCTs consist of 12–24 paragraph-length scenarios that encapsulate different settings of social context factors (Power / Distance / Imposition). In testing of L2 pragmatics, they commonly elicit a request, apology, or refusal, but can also elicit other speech acts. Test takers are asked to imagine themselves in the scenario and produce an utterance directed at the imaginary interlocutor.

This basic DCT can be administered as a written task, where input and test taker production are in writing, or a spoken task, where input is aural and output is oral. Test takers can also be given multiple-choice response options for the gap and choose the most appropriate one. All these varieties were used by Hudson, Detmer, and Brown (1995), Yamashita (1996), and Yoshitake (1997) with the overall finding that written and oral DCTs are reliable, but multiple-choice DCTs suffer from very low reliability (Brown 2001). However, Liu (2006) developed a multiple-choice DCT that functioned reasonably reliably. Variations on the basic DCT include the use of a rejoinder (response from the imaginary interlocutor) after the gap (Roever 2005, 2006), or dialogues with gaps, where the imaginary interlocutor's turns are provided and test takers fill in the missing turns (Roever, Fraser, and Elder 2014).

Traditional written DCTs and untimed spoken DCTs allow learners to engage explicit knowledge as there is time to reflect, and, with written DCTs, even to go back and revise. Implicit knowledge may be involved, but explicit knowledge cannot be limited or excluded and is likely to dominate, especially with lower-level learners.

Of the instruments used so far, the only DCT which could tap implicit knowledge is the production part of Tada's (2005) video-based instrument. Tada played 24 short video clips to test takers with the last utterance replaced by a multiple-choice task ("perception test"), or an instruction to produce the missing utterance orally ("production test"). He attained satisfactory reliability of his perception test (α = .75), which was the focus of his study, and a reasonable interrater agreement after Fisher-Z transformation of .74 among his three raters. Tada did not enforce a time limit on test taker responses for his production part, only instructing test takers to "start to speak immediately after the video clip finishes" (Tada 2005: 246). Enforcing a time limit would potentially lead to this task type eliciting implicit or highly automatized explicit knowledge. However, even if implicit knowledge could be tapped, this would not overcome the inherent limitations of DCTs as research or testing instruments. The most serious limitation is that most DCTs only allow a one-shot response (with the exception of some experimental tasks by Cohen and Shively 2002/2003 and Roever, Fraser and Elder 2014) and therefore do not capture how social actions unfold over several turns in real-world interaction. In addition, concerns abound about possible dissimilarities between performance on DCTs and real-world language use (Golato 2003; Taguchi and Roever 2017).

Overall, DCTs have primarily been used for the assessment of explicit pragmatic knowledge, and it is difficult to modify them for the assessment of implicit pragmatic knowledge though options exist with oral DCTs administered under time pressure.

2.3.2 Metapragmatic judgment tasks

Metapragmatic judgments, also known as "appropriateness judgments," have had limited use in pragmatics assessment (e.g., in Roever, Fraser and Elder 2014), but occur quite frequently in pragmatics research (e.g., Bardovi-Harlig and Dörnyei 1998; Li and Taguchi 2014; Takimoto 2009, 2012). Metapragmatic judgments usually present a scenario similar to a DCT scenario together with a target utterance, which is typically a request, apology or refusal. Respondents then judge the appropriateness of the utterance on a Likert scale (Roever, Fraser, and Elder 2014; Takimoto 2009).

Variations to this standard methodology include binary judgments, which were also used by Roever, Fraser, and Elder (2014) followed by a productive correction task. Similarly, in Bardovi-Harlig and Dörnyei's (1998) research, respondents first indicated whether a target utterance was grammatically and pragmatically accurate or problematic, and if they decided it was problematic, they rated the severity of the problem on a Likert scale. While Bardovi-Harlig and Dörnyei did not require participants to indicate whether the problem was grammatical or pragmatic, Li and Taguchi (2014) required their participants to choose whether a target utterance was pragmatically inaccurate, grammatically inaccurate, or accurate on both counts.

Metapragmatic judgment tasks are the pragmatics task type most similar to grammaticality judgment tasks, a mainstay in explicit / implicit studies of grammatical knowledge. In their typical format, where test takers are shown a written scenario with a target utterance which they are asked to judge, metapragmatic judgment tasks enable use of explicit knowledge. However, they could be redirected towards implicit knowledge by being set up as listening tasks in a speeded environment with a binary choice (appropriate / not appropriate) displayed immediately after completion and response times captured, as shown in example (1):

(1) Metapragmatic judgment item for implicit knowledge
Decide whether the woman's utterance is appropriate (A) or inappropriate (I).
1. Susan is visiting her friend Mark's house. She accidentally knocked over an empty cup, which fell to the floor and broke.
(Female voice) "Oh no, I'm so sorry. I'll clean it up."
2. Susan is at a store. She just bought an item, and the cashier hands it to her.
(Female voice) "I want a bag."

Such tasks force reliance on implicit knowledge, and would likely lead to fast response times. However, they would be primarily suitable for learners with well-developed listening comprehension as lack of linguistic comprehension might otherwise impact pragmatic judgments and lead to construct-irrelevant variance.

2.3.3 Multiple-choice tasks

Multiple choice tasks have been widely used in second language pragmatics assessment and research to gauge learners' comprehension of implicature and recognition of routine formulae, and to a somewhat lesser extent for the judgment of speech act appropriateness.

In implicature comprehension tasks, learners are presented with a contextualized short (two-turn) conversation, and select the correct interpretation of the final utterance from four response options (Roever 2005, 2006; Taguchi 2008). For routine formula tasks, a scenario is usually given and learners are asked to identify the one formula most likely to occur from four response options (Roever 2005, 2012). In both cases, explicit knowledge can be involved because learners have time to compare possible answers.

However, for implicature, a variation on this methodology by Taguchi (2008) opens up the possibility of eliciting performance based on implicit knowledge. She showed dialogues with the final (target) utterance being a refusal or indirect opinion, followed by a yes-no question, e.g., *A: "Can you go answer the phone?" – B: "I'm in the bath." Can B answer the phone?* Such an item type can be administered aurally in a speeded computer-based environment, which reduces the likelihood that learners can access explicit knowledge. However, all the items in the set would need to follow the same response patterns so that no question occurs between the target utterance and the response (which would introduce time for reflection), as shown in example (2):

(2) Implicature comprehension item for implicit knowledge
Indicate whether the man agrees (press A) or disagrees (press D) with the woman.
1. Susan and her friend Mark just had dinner at a new restaurant.
(Female voice) "That meal was absolutely delicious."
(Male voice) "It couldn't have been better."
2. Susan and her friend Mark just attended a public lecture about ancient pottery.
(Female voice) "Man, that lecture was boring."
(Male voice) "I got a lot out of it."

For routine formulae, learners can be asked to give a binary judgment of whether the formula is appropriate in the situation, similar to the metapragmatic judgment tasks described in example (1). This would also be the only option for testing implicit knowledge of speech act appropriateness, replacing multiple-choice DCTs as they have been used in pragmatic assessment (Hudson et al. 1995; Liu 2006; Tada 2005) and research (Matsumura 2001, 2003; Takimoto 2009). Only by deploying time-limited tasks will it be possible to assess to what extent learners are able to make judgments expeditiously and accurately, which is what is required in real-world language use.

2.3.4 Role plays and monologues

Role plays (see Félix-Brasdefer 2018 for a recent overview) are the main instrument used in the more recent stream of pragmatics assessments, whose target construct is the ability to engage in extended discourse, rather than ability to perform or comprehend isolated speech acts, implicature, and routine formulae. Ability to engage in extended discourse is most commonly viewed from the perspective of interactional competence (Pekarek Doehler & Pochon-Berger 2011) or discursive pragmatics (Félix-Brasdefer 2019; Kasper 2006). Assessment of interactional competence crucially involves interaction, so the two major studies (Ikeda 2017; Youn 2013, 2015) in this area have been primarily based on data generated by role plays but have also included monologic tasks. Other studies have been role-play based (Grabowski 2009; Timpe 2013), with Walters's (2007, 2009) study featuring multiple-choice tasks in addition to role plays. A less common instrument is elicited conversation (Galaczi 2014), where test takers discuss a predetermined topic.

Role-play performances rely heavily on implicit knowledge, as talking in real time requires both online processing with little or no planning time as well as responsiveness to aural input. While there is little opportunity to plan an individual utterance, role-play interactants may pre-plan the overall structure of a conversation in terms of how to bring up a particular topic. However, the sequential organization of requests and refusals, as well as turn design and fine-tuned recipient design, are likely beyond conscious control and rely entirely on implicit knowledge (Kasper 2006; Taleghani-Nikazm and Huth 2010).

As scoring of role play performances frequently happens through a rating rubric, the degree to which scores represent implicit knowledge depends on the rubrics as well. For example, Youn (2013, 2015) scored on five criteria:
1. content delivery: smoothness of topic transitions and clarity of social actions;
2. language use: use of modals and other pragmalinguistic features as well as overall linguistic accuracy;
3. sensitivity to the situation: display of pre-expansions and supportive social actions;
4. engagement with the interaction: demonstrating understanding and active listening;
5. turn organization: appropriateness of responses and conventional turn transitions.

Youn's criteria are likely to represent implicit knowledge well. Language users generally have no awareness of how they do topic transitions (content delivery), how to organize disaffiliative social actions (like requests) sequentially (sensitivity to the situation), how to show engagement with interlocutor talk (engagement with the interaction), and how to predict and embark upon turn transitions (turn organization). The only criterion potentially affected by explicit knowledge is language use, where test takers might consciously recall particular expressions they have learned to express a request.

Monologues might allow more conscious planning and reliance on explicit knowledge as they do not involve unpredictable interactions with an interlocutor. However, Ikeda (2017) found a very large degree of overlap (correlation of $r = .94$) between test taker scores on role played dialogues and monologues based on four non-interactive rating criteria, which indicates that the kinds of knowledge involved in both are likely similar.

Overall, role plays primarily require learners to rely on implicit knowledge, as interactants are not usually conscious of turn-taking and sequential organization of talk. Monologues are also likely to rely mostly on implicit knowledge, though an explicit component is possible. These instruments are therefore highly suited for making implicit knowledge visible in assessment.

3 Conclusion and future directions

Past approaches to testing speech acts, routines, and implicature allowed learners to rely on explicit knowledge, whereas the testing of interactional abilities elicits performances based largely on implicit knowledge. The latter type is likely to stand up better in a validation exercise, as it more closely simulates language use in real-world settings, but it suffers from limited practicality due to role plays being time- and resource-intensive to administer and score. By contrast, multiple choice, metapragmatic judgment tasks, and DCT-type short response tasks are more practical to administer and score as they can be computerized, simultaneously administered to large numbers of test takers, and automatically scored (though this would be more difficult for spoken responses). For large-scale tests, this is an attractive proposition, and might enable the integration of pragmatics components in large-scale computerized test batteries. A greater emphasis on the elicitation of implicit knowledge in pragmatics testing would be highly desirable to ensure strong real-world extrapolation and, if widely integrated in general language proficiency assessments, can generate positive washback onto classroom instruction and self-study courses (see Cohen 2019 for a recent discussion of washback of pragmatics assessments on instruction).

A precondition for this to happen is greater research on measurement of implicit pragmatic knowledge and the extent to which such measurement provides support for the extrapolation inference in an argument-based framework. Instrument development is a crucial first step, and some of the time-pressure instruments suggested above may constitute a starting point for measurements of implicit pragmatic knowledge. Investigating the degree to which such instruments replicate real-world use of pragmatic abilities is the second step, and such investigations provide evidence for an extrapolation inference. By comparing measures addressing explicit and implicit pragmatic knowledge (see Ellis and Roever 2018 for a first study), studies can also investigate the differential importance of both knowledge types for different real-world usage contexts. For example, explicit pragmatic knowledge may be useful in real-world tasks like email writing, whereas implicit pragmatic knowledge is likely to play a central role in spontaneous production. However, the exact balance is unclear and could motivate research in both second language pragmatics as well as language testing.

In summary, we argue for researchers developing increased awareness of the difference between explicit and implicit pragmatic knowledge, which should influence development and validation of pragmatic measures. The development of measures specific to these two aspects of L2 learners' pragmatic competence is likely to improve the value of pragmatics measures for all stakeholders, i.e., researchers, learners, and score users.

References

Bardovi-Harlig, Kathleen. 2013. Developing L2 Pragmatics. *Language Learning* 63. 68–86.

Bardovi Harlig, Kathleen & Zoltán Dörnyei. 1998. Do language learners recognize pragmatic violations? Pragmatic versus grammatical awareness in instructed L2 learning. *TESOL Quarterly* 32(2). 233–259.

Brown, James Dean & Russell Changseob Ahn. 2011. Variables that affect the dependability of L2 pragmatics tests. *Journal of Pragmatics* 43(1). 198–217.

Brown, James Dean. 2001. Six types of pragmatics tests in two different contexts. In Kenneth Rose, & Gabriele Kasper (eds.) *Pragmatics in language teaching*. 301–325. New York: Cambridge University Press.

Brown, Penelope & Stephen C. Levinson. 1987. *Politeness: some universals in language usage*. Cambridge: Cambridge University Press.

Cohen, Andrew D. 2004. Assessing Speech Acts in a Second Language. In Andrew D. Cohen & Diana Boxer (eds.). *Studying speaking to inform second language learning*. 302–327. Clevedon: Multilingual Matters.

Cohen, Andrew D. 2019. Considerations in assessing pragmatic appropriateness in spoken language. *Language Teaching* 53(2). 183–202.

Cohen, Andrew D. & Elite Olshtain. 1981. Developing a measure of sociocultural competence: The case of apology. *Language Learning* 31(1). 113–134.

Cohen, Andrew D. & Rachel L. Shively. 2002/2003. Measuring speech acts with multiple rejoinder DCTs. *Language Testing Update* 32. 39–42.

Coulmas, Florian. 1981. *Conversational Routine*. The Hague: Mouton.

Ellis, Nick C. 2017. Implicit and Explicit Knowledge About Language. In Jasone Cenoz, Durk Gorter, & Stephen May (eds.), *Language Awareness and Multilingualism*, 113–124. Cham: Springer International Publishing.

Ellis, Rod. 2004. The definition and measurement of L2 explicit knowledge. *Language Learning* 54(2). 227–275.
Ellis, Rod & Carsten Roever. 2018. The measurement of implicit and explicit knowledge. *The Language Learning Journal*. DOI: 10.1080/09571736.2018.1504229.
Farhady, Hossein. 1980. *Justification, development, and validation of functional language testing*. Los Angeles, CA: University of California dissertation.
Félix-Brasdefer, J.César. 2018. Role plays. In Andreas H. Jucker, Klaus P. Schneider, & Wolfram Bublitz (eds.), *Methods in pragmatics*, 305–331. (Handbook of Pragmatics 10). Berlin: De Gruyter Mouton.
Félix-Brasdefer, J.César. 2019. Speech acts in interaction: negotiating joint action in a second language. In Naoko Taguchi (ed.), *The Routledge handbook of second language acquisition and pragmatics*, 17–30. New York: Routledge.
Galaczi, Evelina D. 2014. Interactional Competence across Proficiency Levels: How do Learners Manage Interaction in Paired Speaking Tests? *Applied Linguistics* 35(5). 553–574.
Golato, Andrea. 2003. Studying compliment responses: A comparison of DCTs and recordings of naturally occurring talk. *Applied Linguistics* 24(1). 90–121.
Grabowski, Kirby C. 2009. *Investigating the construct validity of a test designed to measure grammatical and pragmatic knowledge in the context of speaking*. New York: Teachers College, Columbia University dissertation.
Grabowski, Kirby C. 2013. Investigating the construct validity of a role-play test designed to measure grammatical and pragmatic knowledge at multiple proficiency levels. In Gabriele Kasper & Steven Ross (eds.), *Assessing second language pragmatics*, 149–171. New York: Palgrave.
Grice, H. Paul. 1975. Logic and conversation. In Peter Cole & Jerry L. Morgan (eds.), *Syntax and semantics 3: speech acts*, 41–58. New York: Academic Press.
Hall, Joan Kelly & Simona Pekarek Doehler. 2011. L2 Interactional competence and development. In Joan Kelly Hall, John Hellermann, & Simona Pekarek Doehler (eds.), *L2 interactional competence and development*, 1–15. Bristol: Multilingual Matters.
Hudson, Thom, Emily Detmer, & James Dean Brown. 1995. *Developing prototypic measures of cross-cultural pragmatics* (vol. 7). Honolulu: National Foreign Language Resource Center.
Ikeda, Naoki. 2017. *Measuring L2 oral pragmatic abilities for use in social contexts: Development and validation of an assessment instrument for L2 pragmatics performance in university settings*. Melbourne: The University of Melbourne dissertation.
Ishihara, Noriko & Andrew D. Cohen. 2010. *Teaching and learning pragmatics*. London: Longman.
Itomitsu, Masayuki. 2009. *Developing a test of pragmatics of Japanese as a Foreign Language*. Columbus, OH: Ohio State University dissertation.
Kane, Michael T. 2013. Validating the Interpretations and Uses of Test Scores: Validating the Interpretations and Uses of Test Scores. *Journal of Educational Measurement* 50(1). 1–73.
Kasper, Gabriele. 2006. Speech acts in interaction: Towards discursive pragmatics. In Kathleen Bardovi-Harlig, J. César Félix-Brasdefer, & Alwiya S. Omar (eds.), *Pragmatics and language learning* (vol. 11), 281–314. Honolulu: Second Language Teaching and Curriculum Center University of Hawaii.
Klein-Braley, Christine. 1997. C-tests in the context of reduced redundancy testing: an appraisal. *Language Testing* 14(1). 47–84.
Leech, Geoffrey. 1983. *Principles of politeness*. New York: Longman.
Leech, Geoffrey. 2014. *The pragmatics of politeness*. Oxford: Oxford University Press.

Levinson, Stephen C. & Francisco Torreira. 2015. Timing in turn-taking and its implications for processing models of language. *Frontiers* 6. 10–26.

Li, Shuai & Naoko Taguchi. 2014. The effects of practice modality on pragmatic development in L2 Chinese. *The Modern Language Journal* 98(3). 794–812.

Liu, Jianda. 2006. *Measuring interlanguage pragmatic knowledge of EFL learners*. Frankfurt: Peter Lang.

Matsumura, Shoichi. 2001. Learning the rules for offering advice: A quantitative approach to second language socialization. *Language Learning* 51(4). 635–679.

Matsumura, Shoichi. 2003. Modelling the relationships among interlanguage pragmatic development, L2 proficiency, and exposure to L2. *Applied Linguistics* 24(4). 465–491.

Pekarek Doehler, Simona & Eva Pochon-Berger. 2011. Developing 'methods' for interaction. In Joan K. Hall, John Hellermann, & Simone Pekarek Doehler (eds.), *L2 interactional competence and development*, 206–243. Bristol: Multilingual Matters.

Purpura, James E. 2004. *Assessing grammar*. Cambridge: Cambridge University Press.

Roever, Carsten. 2005. *Testing ESL pragmatics*. Frankfurt: Peter Lang.

Roever, Carsten. 2006. Validation of a web-based test of ESL pragmalinguistics. *Language Testing* 23(2). 229–256.

Roever, Carsten. 2012. What learners get for free (and when): Learning of routine formulae in ESL and EFL environments. *ELT Journal* 66(1). 10–21.

Roever, Carsten, Catriona Fraser, & Catherine Elder. 2014. *Testing ESL pragmatics: Development and validation of a web-based assessment battery*. Frankfurt: Peter Lang.

Roever, Carsten & Naoki Ikeda. 2020. Testing L2 pragmatic competence. In Klaus P. Schneider & Elly Ifantidou (eds.), *Handbook of developmental and clinical pragmatics*, 475–496. (Handbook of Pragmatics 13). Berlin: de Gruyter Mouton.

Sacks, Harvey. 1992. *Lectures on conversation*. Malden, MA: Blackwell.

Schegloff, Emanuel A. 2007. *Sequence organization in interaction: A primer in conversation analysis*. Cambridge: Cambridge University Press.

Shimazu, Yoshi-Mitsu. 1989. *Construction and concurrent validation of a written pragmatic competence test of English as a second language*. San Francisco, CA: University of San Francisco dissertation.

Suzuki, Yuichi & Robert DeKeyser. 2015. Comparing elicited imitation and word monitoring as measures of implicit knowledge. *Language Learning* 65(4). 860–895.

Tada, Masao. 2005. *Assessment of EFL pragmatic production and perception using video prompts*. Tokyo: Temple University dissertation.

Taguchi, Naoko. 2008. Cognition, language contact, and the development of pragmatic comprehension in a study-abroad context. *Language Learning* 58(1). 33–71.

Taguchi, Naoko & Carsten Roever. 2017. *Second language pragmatics*. Oxford: Oxford University Press.

Takimoto, Masahiro. 2009. The effects of input-based tasks on the development of learners' pragmatic proficiency. *Applied Linguistics* 30(1). 1–25.

Takimoto, Masahiro. 2012. Metapragmatic discussion in interlanguage pragmatics. *Journal of Pragmatics* 44(10). 1240–1253.

Taleghani-Nikazm, Carmen & Thorsten Huth. 2010. L2 requests: Preference structure in talk-in-interaction. *Multilingua* 29. 185–202.

Thomas, Jenny. 1983. Cross-cultural pragmatic failure. *Applied Linguistics* 4(2). 91–112.

Timpe, Veronika. 2013. *Assessing intercultural language learning*. Frankfurt: Peter Lang.

Timpe-Laughlin, Veronika & Ikkyu Choi. 2017. Exploring the Validity of a Second Language Intercultural Pragmatics Assessment Tool. *Language Assessment Quarterly* 14(1). 19–35.

Walters, F. Scott. 2007. A conversation-analytic hermeneutic rating protocol to assess L2 oral pragmatic competence. *Language Testing* 24(2). 155–183.

Walters, F. Scott. 2009. A Conversation Analysis-Informed Test of L2 Aural Pragmatic Comprehension. *TESOL Quarterly* 43(1). 29–54.

Yamashita, Sayoko. 1996. *Six measures of JSL pragmatics*. Honolulu, HI: University of Hawai'i at Mānoa, National Foreign Languages Resource Center.

Yoshitake, Sonia. 1997. *Interlanguage competence of Japanese students of English: A multi-test framework evaluation*. San Rafael, CA: Columbia Pacific University dissertation.

Youn, Soo Jung. 2013. Validating task-based assessment of L2 pragmatics in interaction using mixed methods. Honolulu, HI: University of Hawai'i at Manoa dissertation.

Youn, Soo Jung. 2015. Validity argument for assessing L2 pragmatics in interaction using mixed methods. *Language Testing* 32(2). 199–225.

Youn, Soo Jung. 2019. Managing proposal sequences in role-play assessment: Validity evidence of interactional competence across levels. *Language Testing*. doi:10.1177/0265532219860077.

Nancy Bell, Maria Shardakova and Rachel L. Shively
8 The DCT as a data collection method for L2 humor production

Abstract: Humor is a pervasive feature of everyday interaction among friends, in the workplace, and in the classroom. Although previous research indicates that L2 users do, indeed, understand and employ humor in various settings, no previous studies have elicited L2 humor data with a large number of participants, which, in turn, would facilitate making broader generalizations regarding L2 humor use. A method that may lend itself to large-scale collection of L2 humor data is the discourse completion task (DCT). This study sought to develop a DCT to elicit humor, explore when L2 users employ humor in the DCT, and evaluate the DCT as a method for collecting L2 humor data. The results indicate that the instrument was effective in eliciting humor from L2 speakers, that perception of humor encouraged creation of humor, and that target language, mother tongue, and humor directionality (i.e., self- vs. other-directed) affected humor perception and production.

Keywords: second language humor, discourse completion task, second language pragmatics, language play

1 Introduction

In contrast to other areas of second language (L2) pragmatics, such as speech act research (see Chapter 1, this volume), the database of previous studies concerning L2 humor production is somewhat of an outlier in terms of methodology: much of what we know about producing L2 humor is based on qualitative studies that employed authentic discourse samples rather than quantitative research involving elicited data. For instance, despite the fact that the discourse completion task (DCT) has been a mainstay of L2 speech act research for decades, to our knowledge, this instrument has never previously been employed to collect L2 humor data. On the one hand, the prevalence of qualitative studies that have collected naturally-occurring instances of L2 humor is clearly a strength of this database, since through rich and multilayered analyses we are able to see how L2 speakers co-construct humor with others for enjoyment, to build and navigate relationships, and to negotiate identities in social interaction. On the other hand, there are also some limitations to qualitative analyses of naturally occurring L2 humor, including the issue of comparability over time and across speakers, proficiency levels, and settings, and the fact that most previous research in this vein involves small numbers of participants. Furthermore, while there is no question that L2 speakers from beginning to advanced levels of proficiency can and do produce humor in social interaction both inside and outside of the classroom (e.g., Bell 2017; Bell and Pomerantz 2015, 2019; Shardakova 2017; Shively 2018), one difficulty that L2 speakers have reported in using humor in their L2 is not having enough time in spontaneous oral interactions to formulate and deliver a humorous quip (e.g., Bell and Attardo 2010). L2 users may have the ability to create humor in ways not captured heretofore in spontaneous verbal interactions.

With these considerations in mind, we wanted to explore whether a DCT might be a useful instrument to elicit L2 humor data that would complement what is already known, allow researchers to tackle new problems, and facilitate broader generalizations about L2 humor use. The potential benefits of the questionnaire format of the DCT for our purposes included collecting large amounts of data in a short period of time; conducting a systematic and quantitative analysis of patterns in L2 humor; making comparisons of humor use across time, proficiency, and language; and allowing L2 speakers sufficient time to craft their humorous utterances by doing so in the written mode. Hence, the goal of this paper is, first, to describe the development of a new DCT designed to elicit humor and, second, to assess its effectiveness for collecting humor based on the results of a pilot study in which 60 L2 speakers of English, Russian, and Spanish completed this questionnaire. We begin with a review of existing studies, which is followed by an overview of the creation of the instrument and the design of the pilot study. In light of the findings of the pilot study, we then evaluate the potential of the DCT to elicit humor and conclude by discussing how the instrument might be improved and different ways it might be used to contribute new insights to the field of L2 humor studies. Note that the purpose of this chapter is to examine the DCT as an instrument for humor data collection, not to analyze the humor produced by L2 users on the DCT.

2 Review of existing research

2.1 Previous research on L2 humor

Humor can be defined as a mode of communication by which a speaker attempts to amuse a hearer. The humorous effect is generally understood to be created by the perception of incongruity, that is, something unexpected, exaggerated, illogical, or inappropriate (e.g., Attardo 2001). Although amusement is its primary function, humor also serves other social goals such as displaying affiliation, creating rapport, and negotiating power relations. The production of humor in an L2 has been researched in a variety of settings including the foreign language classroom, everyday conversation, interviews, coaching sessions, business negotiations, and computer-mediated chat rooms (e.g., Adelswärd and Öberg 1998; Ahn 2016; Bell, Skalicky, and Salsbury 2014; Cheng 2003; Vandergriff and Fuchs 2012). In most cases, L2 speakers' use of humor has been assessed by examining instances of humor as they emerged in authentic discourse contexts, whether that be in interactions between teachers and students in the foreign language classroom (e.g., Pomerantz and Bell 2011; Reddington and Waring 2015; Shardakova 2017; Sterling and Loewen 2015) or among age peers in informal conversations (e.g., Bell 2007; Davies 2003; Shively 2018). Only occasionally have other methods been employed in previous studies to research L2 humor production apart from collecting samples of discourse. Petkova (2013), for instance, employed role plays to assess use of humor as part of a pedagogical intervention to teach humor in an English as a foreign language course. Further, DCTs designed to elicit speech acts such as apologies and compliments have, in certain cases, generated humorous responses from some speakers (e.g., Mir and Cots 2017; Shardakova 2010, 2012).

This body of research has revealed how L2 speakers from beginning to advanced proficiency levels creatively deploy the verbal and non-verbal resources in their L2 repertoire for humorous purposes and for a variety of social functions. Previous studies have also examined issues such as how L2 speakers' humor is perceived by expert speakers, whether emergent bilinguals are positioned as legitimate humorists, and the ways in which L2 users develop humor over time (e.g., Bell 2006; Bell, Skalicky, and Salsbury 2014; Shardakova 2013; Shively 2018). But just as other areas of L2 pragmatics have been studied using a variety of methods (e.g., DCTs, role plays, authentic discourse samples), so too can humor be researched using a variety of methods that can reveal different aspects of the phenomenon. To date, most research in this area has been qualitative in nature and no large-scale studies have been conducted specifically to elicit L2 humor. Such studies could add to our understanding of L2 humor by uncovering developmental patterns with regard to, for instance, the link between L2 proficiency and the linguistic, paralinguistic, and non-verbal resources that speakers employ to create humorous utterances. Shardakova's (2010) data pointed to advanced proficiency as necessary to be able to manipulate grammar for humorous purposes. Large-scale studies could confirm this observation as well as investigate other developmental patterns. Another area that could benefit from quantitative research is the comparison of humor use and development across a variety of target languages and with L2 speakers with different first language backgrounds.

2.2 DCTs

One method that may be useful for large-scale L2 humor research is the DCT. A written production questionnaire consisting of a series of scenarios (e.g., Kasper and Dahl 1991; Ogiermann 2018) in which test-takers typically provide a single-turn response, DCTs have their origins in early work on L2 speech acts by Andrew Cohen and Elite Olshtain (Cohen and Olshtain 1981; Olshtain and Cohen 1983). The main advantages of DCTs as a method are: (1) they produce a large corpus of data that are comparable among participants and over time; (2) data can be collected from a large participant pool in a short period of time; and (3) DCT scenarios can be translated into any language, which allows cross-cultural and cross-linguistic analyses to be conducted. An additional advantage of this method is that DCTs allow researchers to include scenarios and gather humor data from situations to which real-life access for researchers is difficult. Even though DCT responses do not reflect naturally occurring interaction in all respects, Ogiermann (2018: 246) argues that "there does seem to be a general agreement . . . that DCT responses do contain a similar range of linguistic expressions to those found in other types of data." Although rare in the literature, DCT-like instruments have been employed successfully to elicit humor from L1 speakers (e.g. Gibson 2019; Holmes 2000) and one potential benefit of using a written measure with L2 speakers is, as we highlighted above, the provision of sufficient time to craft a humorous utterance.

We are, of course, well aware of the many critiques and limitations of DCTs underscored by recent scholarship (see e.g., Culpeper, Mackey, and Taguchi [2018] for an overview). Theoretically speaking, DCTs were developed hand in hand with speech act theory, in which communicative actions are examined in isolation and the hearer's role in the interaction is not considered (e.g., Walters 2013). This theoretical orientation is based on the "rational actor model," in which an ideal speaker acts rationally and is presumed to have static knowledge of linguistic forms that is not shaped by interlocutor or context (e.g., Kasper and Ross 2013). This rationalistic approach compares to a discursive approach, which focuses on how participants orient to utterances, how an interaction unfolds sequentially, and how participants co-construct meaning across multiple turns.

Another limitation of DCTs that has been revealed through empirical research is that they do not necessarily capture what happens in real life interactions.

Pragmatic features that have been shown to differ in DCTs compared to naturalistic interactions include the strategies employed, the range of strategies represented in the data, the length of responses, and the number of repetitions (e.g., Beebe and Cummings 1996; Economidou-Kogetsidis 2013; Golato 2003; Hartford and Bardovi-Harlig 1992; Yuan 2001). Similarly, written responses that are intended to reflect oral speech lack characteristics of spoken interactions such as turn-taking, hesitation, and prosodic and non-verbal information (e.g., Kasper 2008). Bardovi-Harlig (2010) further points out that unlike in real life interactions, how a participant responds in an elicited task like a DCT does not pose any social consequences which, in turn, may influence an individual's response. DCTs capture participants' intuitions or what they think they would say in a given scenario and, therefore, primarily measure metapragmatic competence (Walters 2013).

While the DCT has considerable limitations, we wondered whether it might have useful applications for the study of L2 humor, principally, in giving researchers a tool to explore aspects of L2 humor that are difficult to study through qualitative research. For instance, one can investigate interlanguage developmental patterns in humor use by learners of various target languages or who have different proficiency levels and make systematic comparisons and derive generalizations about L2 humor that qualitative research cannot effectively address. Hence, while it is certainly true that DCTs have important drawbacks, we wanted to explore their potential benefits for assessing L2 humor production. As the field of L2 humor studies continues to grow, it is advantageous to make use of all available methods in order to address a variety of problems.

2.3 Aims of the study and research questions

The main purpose of this study was to evaluate the effectiveness of the DCT as an instrument for eliciting L2 humor and, subsequently, to explore whether collected humor samples could be used for broader generalizations and cross-sectional comparisons across different target and native languages, L2 proficiency levels, humor types and characteristics, and other dimensions that could be identified in further research. Capitalizing on the DCT's capability to generate large amounts of data, we particularly wanted to carry out quantitative analysis and focused on the following research questions:
1. Can a DCT be an effective instrument for collecting L2 humor from emerging bilinguals of different backgrounds?
2. Does L2 speakers' graded perception of the humorousness of a situation affect their production of L2 humor?

3. Does the target of the humor (self or other) affect L2 speakers' perception and production of L2 humor?
4. Does the target language affect L2 speakers' perception and production of L2 humor?
5. Do L2 speakers with a shared mother tongue but who study different target languages differ in their perception and production of L2 humor from those with different mother tongues?

3 Method

3.1 Creating humorous DCTs

Mindful of the considerations elucidated above, we set about constructing DCT scenarios that we hoped would encourage humorous responses. Because we wanted to collect data from learners of Russian and Spanish at two U.S. universities, as well as from a variety of international students learning English in the U.S., potentially amusing situations first needed to not be culturally specific. Thus, we tried to avoid situations that relied upon current topics in the news or popular culture with which not everyone might be familiar. Rather, we sought to exploit events and interactions that seemed likely to arouse one or more feelings of excitement, discomfiture, diversion, pleasure, and, of course, amusement across a broad swath of people. In doing so, we began by brainstorming amusing real life interactions that we had experienced or witnessed, as well as drawing on existing corpora (e.g., Eisenstein and Bodman 1993).

As we expanded our search for appropriate scenarios, we also considered Cook's (2000: 123) description of language play (a related, but broader category than humor) as often involving "vital" topics. He provides, as examples of such subjects, "birth, death, sexual relations, health, etc." Cook notes that it is precisely these areas that are largely excluded from the formal curriculum of the language classroom, which favors utilitarian discourse, with the effect that students are not exposed to the type of language that is most engaging to many people: "Indeed, publishers' lists of what should *not* go into a language teaching textbook could be read as recommendations for what *should* go into a best-selling novel, lead news story, or blockbuster TV series" (Cook 2000: 159; emphasis in original). Despite our recognition that exciting topics would be more likely to elicit humor, we also needed to balance the "vitality" of the scenarios with the need to obtain Institutional Review Board approval for our pilot study and to avoid offending any of our participants. Given that the language classroom tends to avoid controversial or salacious topics, even alluding to these areas, we hoped, would trigger participants to respond humorously. Thus, we developed scenarios around, for example, lack of bodily control (burping), alcohol, and taboo language (accidentally breaking a bottle of beer and swearing), and mild sexual content (sending a flirtatious text to the wrong person). Other scenes involved mild public embarrassment, for instance through accidentally entangling desks, mispronouncing a name, and arriving at class soaking wet from a rainstorm. The full instrument is available for free download from the IRIS database: http://www.iris-database.org.

Once we had developed 10 scenarios that we hoped would encourage participants to respond with humor, we constructed the DCT. First, in order to capture the extent to which self- versus other-directed humor influenced participants' willingness and ability to come up with funny remarks, we rewrote each situation to alter the target. Thus, the sample question below, in which your friend is searching for her glasses, which are on her face, was also rewritten to make the participant the target of the joke (self-directed humor), as follows:

> You have been looking for your glasses for a few minutes. You ask your friend if she has seen them and when she looks up, she tells you that you are wearing your glasses.

We then created two versions of the DCT, in which all the questions had the same content, but half were self-directed and half were other-directed. Thus, in one DCT version, the glasses scenario would target the friend, while in the other version the participant would be the target. We included this design of varying the target because we hypothesized that the target (i.e., self vs. an interlocutor) had the potential to influence humor use. For instance, some participants might not want to make fun of someone else, but would be willing to joke about themselves.

In addition to asking participants to write what they thought they would say in each situation, we asked them to make two assessments: first, they named the extent to which they found the scenario amusing and second, whether their own response should be understood as funny. In the first instance, we sought feedback on the effectiveness of our scenarios, with the assumption that a funny situation would encourage a funny response. We provided participants with a scale of responses, asking them to choose among "very funny," "somewhat funny," or "not funny" immediately following their reading of the situation. Below that, they were provided with several blank lines where they were asked to write their response. Finally, rather than rely on our own interpretations, we asked participants to explicitly state whether their intention in that answer was to amuse. This was done not only to assess the value of the DCT and each question within it as an instrument for eliciting humor from L2 users, but also to circumvent any need for the researchers to interpret the participants' intentions. Below we provide an example of an item as it appeared on the questionnaire.

Sample DCT question

1. Your friend has been looking for her glasses for a few minutes. She asks you if you have seen them and when you look up, you see that she is wearing her glasses.
    1. I would think this was very funny.
    2. I would think this was somewhat funny.
    3. I would not think this was funny.

You say:

_____
_____
_____
_____

Is your response funny? (circle one)   yes   no

For our DCT items, we used Comic Sans font, which was one of several strategies we drew on to try to induce a playful mood in participants and thus encourage amusing responses. In a series of classroom-based experiments designed to examine the relationship between humor and creativity, Ziv (1976) found that showing students a funny movie, cartoon, or audio recording prior to taking a test of creativity significantly increased their scores on that test. Furthermore, Ziv (1983) found that these scores were also raised simply by instructing the participants to provide as many funny responses, as they were able to on this test. Given the strong relationship between humor and creativity, we hoped that priming students similarly to Ziv would facilitate a greater number of humorous responses, as well as more creative attempts at humor. Thus, for our study, in addition to opting for a less serious and institutional font for our questionnaires, we primed students in two additional ways. First, our brief instructions explicitly asked them to attempt to be funny: "Here are some situations that many people find funny. Read them and answer the questions. Please try to respond with humor as often as possible." We also incorporated simple clip art on each page as a visual reminder of the goal of the task. See below for examples.

Visual cues to prime participants to use humor

3.2 Participants

The participants in the pilot study were undergraduate students who were enrolled in foreign language coursework in English, Russian, or Spanish at three different large or mid-sized public universities in the U.S. Demographics of the participants are presented in Table 1. The 16 L2 speakers of Russian and 21 L2 speakers of Spanish were all American nationals living in the U.S. at the time of data collection, whereas the 23 learners of English were from a variety of countries (e.g., Brazil, China, Saudi Arabia) and were studying at an Intensive English Program in the U.S. when the survey was administered. In the case of the Russian and Spanish students, three were heritage speakers of their respective target language. As Table 1 indicates, gender was balanced in the sample as a whole, but not for individual languages (i.e., many more men were studying English and many more women were studying Spanish). The amount of time participants had studied their target language is indicated in Table 1 for Russian and Spanish learners and spanned three years or less to 10 years or more. For English learners, the number of months they had been in the U.S. at the time of data collection is provided in Table 1. Finally, the researchers were not able to obtain proficiency scores for all learners, but OPI and TOEFL results are provided in Table 1 for some participants and reveal that the sample was diverse proficiency-wise.

3.3 Data collection and analysis

The written humor DCT was administered to participants in a paper-and-pencil format. The instructions, descriptions of the scenarios, and questions on the instrument were provided to all participants in English, but participants were asked to respond with humor in their target language. We kept the instrument in English for the American participants to ensure comprehension. In that

Table 1: Participant demographics.

		Target language			
		English	Russian	Spanish	Total
Participants		23	16	21	60
Gender	Female	5	6	17	28
	Male	18	10	4	32
Age	18–20	11	1	6	18
	21–22	4	5	11	20
	23–24	4	4	3	11
	25+	4	6	1	11
Number of years of formal study of target language	0–3		5		5
	4–5		5	3	8
	6–7		4	8	12
	8–9		2	7	9
	10+			3	3
Studied abroad?	Yes		13	12	44
	No		3	9	16
Time living in the US (ESL students)	0–5 months	14			
	6–12 months	5			
	1+ year	3			
Native language	English		16	19	35
	Spanish			1	1
	Russian		2		2
	Other	23		1	24
Country of origin	Brazil	9			9
	China	2			2
	Japan	1			1
	Libya	1			1
	Oman	3			3

Table 1 (continued)

		Target language			
		English	Russian	Spanish	Total
	Saudi Arabia	7			7
	US		16	21	37
OPI	No score			16	
	Intermediate Mid		1	1	
	Intermediate High		2	1	
	Advanced Low		5	2	
	Advanced Mid		6	1	
	Advanced High		1		
	Superior		1		
TOEFL	No score	12			
	430–450	3			
	473–480	4			
	Over 500	4			

regard, the English L2 speakers had a more difficult task, since they also completed the English version, yet English was their L2.

Respondents all volunteered to complete the questionnaire, consented to participate in the study, and were given as much time as they wanted to provide their responses to both background questions provided at the beginning of the instrument and to the 10 scenarios designed to elicit humor and assess perception of the scenarios. After collecting all the questionnaires, the researchers entered participants' responses into a database. Self-directed humor and other-directed humor were categories that were coded and quantified. Finally, perception data regarding how funny the situation appeared and whether they thought their responses were funny were tallied and analyzed quantitatively. A series of statistical procedures were then selected to address each research question.

4 Results

4.1 RQ1: Can a DCT be an effective instrument for collecting L2 humor from emerging bilinguals of different backgrounds?

Responses on the DCT that participants marked as funny were combined and a one-sample t-test was performed to determine whether the number of collected responses was higher than we would expect to see by chance. With no prior research available on the frequency of humorous responses to DCT questionnaires featuring playful scenarios, we assumed a 50% chance of such responses and compared our sample against a hypothetical sample in which participants would offer funny responses in 50% of situations. The test confirmed that the DCT designed for this study yielded significantly more humorous responses than we would have otherwise collected (t(59)=19.92, p=.000). When we further compared the two versions of the DCT (see Figure 1), Version B seemed to be more effective at prompting students' playful responses (M=20.4, SD=5.6) than Version A (M=16.6, SD=3.68). While not statistically significant, this difference suggests that some scenarios were perceived as more humorous when participants were encouraged to joke about themselves (e.g., looking for glasses that are perched on one's own head), while other scenarios were seen as funnier when someone else was featured as the butt of a joke (e.g., someone comes to class soaking wet from the rain). The data also supported our decision to have students mark their responses as "funny" or "not funny." Without their intentions clearly stated, it would often have been impossible to detect humor in many of the collected responses. For instance, in the scenario in which a friend is wearing her glasses while looking for them, the following English as a second language (ESL), Russian, and Spanish student responses would likely not have been coded as amusing, but participants indicated that their responses were intended to amuse:

> ESL: Your glasses is on your face.
>
> Russian: *Nu chto*? ('So what?')
>
> Spanish: ¿*Es possible que sea en tu cara*? ('Is it possible it's on your face?')

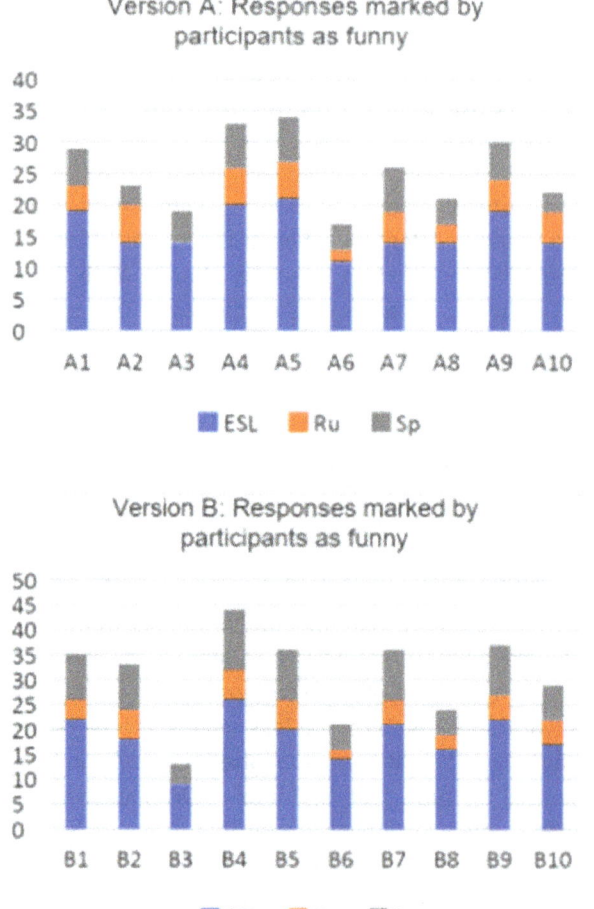

Figure 1: Number of humorous responses in each scenario and version of the DCT.

4.2 RQ2: Does L2 speakers' graded perception of the humorousness of a situation affect their production of L2 humor?

Our second research question considered the possibility of a causal relation between participants' graded perception of the humorousness of DCT scenarios and humor production (Figure 2). A generalized linear model was used to test whether the graded perception of the scenario as "very funny," "somewhat funny," or "not funny" predicted participants' production of humor. The results suggest that seeing a scenario as "very funny" had the strongest effect on students' humor production (p=.02). A second strong effect, although not statistically significant, came from perceiving a scenario as "somewhat funny" (p=.19). Not surprisingly, seeing a scenario as "not funny" did not affect participants' production of humor and, therefore, was excluded from other statistical tests. To increase the effect size of subsequent statistical tests, the "very funny" and "somewhat funny" responses were combined into one category "funny."

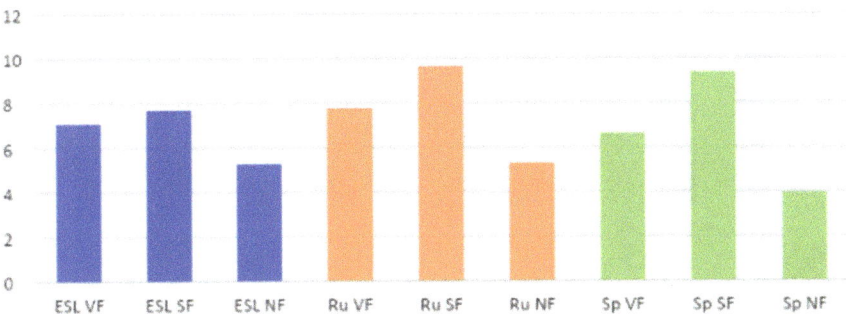

Figure 2: Perception of DCT scenarios as "very funny" (VF), "somewhat funny" (SF), and "not funny" (NF).

4.3 RQ3: Does the target of the humor (self or other) affect L2 speakers' perception and production of L2 humor?

In our third research question, we tackle the issue of whether humor directionality – that is, whether the speaker (self) or their interlocutor (other) was featured as a target of the playful scenario – affected L2 users' perception and production of humor. We broke down this question into two sub-questions: (a) the effect of humor directionality on perception of humor and (b) the effect of humor directionality on production of humor. Given a noticeable difference in humor perception across the groups (see Figures 3a and 3b), with ESL and L2 Spanish participants finding other-directed scenarios more amusing than self-directed scenarios and L2 Russian participants favoring self-directed humor, we constructed a generalized linear model to test the combined effect of humor directionality and participants' target language. Both variables were significant, with the target language having the strongest main effect (p=.000) on participants' perception of DCT scenarios as "funny."

Just as both humor directionality and the target language were implicated in participants' perception of the scenario as funny, these same variables affected production of humor (see Figure 3). A generalized linear model confirmed that both variables were significant, with the target language exerting a stronger main effect (p=.000).

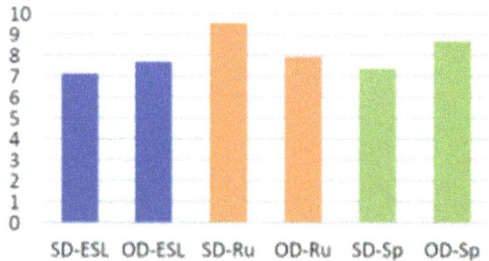

(3a) Perception of DCT scenarios as 'funny' across study groups

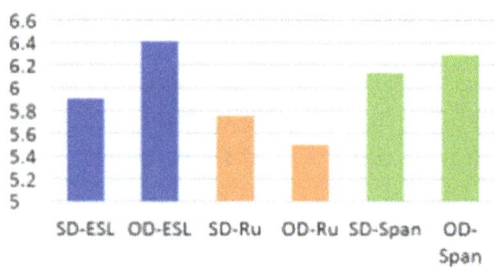

(3b) Production of humor across study groups

Figure 3: Humor target (self- [SD] vs. other-directed [OD]) and perception and production of humor.

4.4 RQ4: Does the target language affect L2 speakers' perception and production of L2 humor?

The fourth research question focused on the causal role of a target language on learners' perception and production of humor. In the previous paragraphs, we have already positively answered this question when the two general linear models unequivocally pointed to the target language as a variable exerting a strong main effect on humor perception and production. That accomplished, we wanted to take a closer look at the study groups and see whether participants in these groups do indeed differ in their perception and production of humor and that these differences are not accidental.

First, we carried out a one-way between subjects ANOVA to determine whether study groups differ in their perception of humor. The results were significant (F=4.32, p=.018), with the post hoc Turkey HSD test highlighting the difference between the L2 Russian (M=5.9, SD=1.8) and L2 Spanish (M=8.45, SD=3.83) groups (Figure 4). These results indicate that further qualitative analysis is needed to explore possible variables affecting differentiated perception of humor among learners who study different languages.

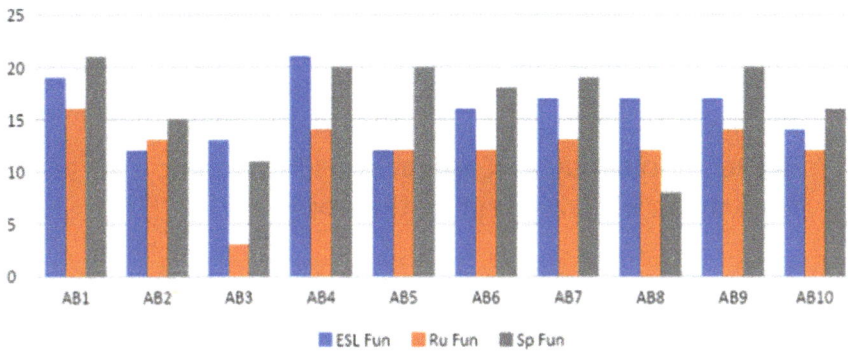

Figure 4: Perception of scenarios as "funny" in DCT scenarios (Versions A and B combined).

A second one-way between subjects ANOVA confirmed that the study groups also significantly differ in their propensity to produce humor [F(2, 57) =14.2, (p=.000)]. Post hoc comparisons using the Turkey HSD test were carried out. There was a significant difference between ESL (M=7.25, SD=1.997) and L2 Russian (M=4.6, SD=1.76) groups (p=.000) and between L2 Russian and L2 Spanish (M=6.65; SD=2.62) groups (p=.000). Taken together, these results suggest that L2 Russian participants produced fewer humorous responses than their L2 Spanish and ESL counterparts (Figure 5).[1]

---

[1] Although we did not assess all participants' L2 proficiency for this study, it does not appear that this result can be attributed to lower L2 proficiency on the part of the Russian participants compared to the other L2 groups.

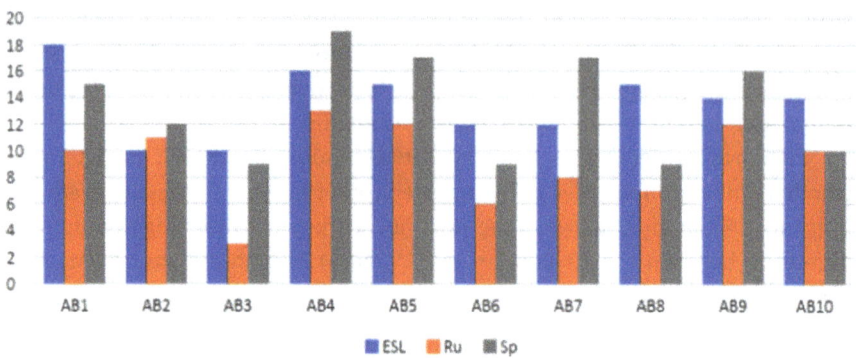

Figure 5: Number of humorous responses across study groups in the DCT scenarios (Versions A and B combined).

4.5 RQ5: Do L2 speakers with a shared mother tongue but who study different target languages differ in their perception and production of L2 humor from those with different mother tongues?

To answer our final question, we combined the Russian and Spanish groups, both of which were comprised of U.S.-born English speakers, with a negligible exception of four bilingual students who came to the U.S. at a young age and compared this new L1 American-English group with the ESL group.

Two independent-samples t-test were administered. The first t-test showed that the difference in humor perception between the American group (M=7.8, SD=3.09) and the ESL group (M=6, SD=1.89) was statistically significant ((t(58)=4.53, p=.000). The second independent-samples t-test contrasted the amount of humor produced by the American group (M=6.05; SD=2.6) and ESL participants (M=5.95, SD=1.73). The difference in humor production did not reach statistical significance (p=.106).

5 Discussion

As our analysis has demonstrated, the DCT proved to be a useful instrument for collecting a large set of humor from L2 users relatively quickly and easily. Not only did the scenarios elicit more humor than would be expected under non-humor-stimulating situations, but those that were rated the funniest by participants elicited the greatest number of responses labeled as humorous. We were also able to identify important differences among the groups in their assessments of the scenarios, and in the number of humorous responses that they constructed to each scenario or type of scenario (self versus other as target).

With regard to perception of the scenarios, the results indicated that L1 speakers of American English found the DCT scenarios to be significantly funnier than did the participants with other mother tongues (i.e., ESL participants), which may reflect cultural differences in the salience of humor in these situations (e.g., Vaid et al. 2008). Additionally, the target language groups differed in their perception of how funny self-directed humor was compared to other-directed humor, which may also point to variation in cultural preferences. In terms of humor production, L2 speakers of Russian provided significantly less humor than their peers who were emerging bilinguals of English or Spanish. Additional analysis is needed to unravel the relationship between target languages and linguistic playfulness. There are a few variables related to the target language and the learning context that may prompt learners' propensity for humor: the relative simplicity of the target language, the cultural appropriateness of humor, as well as the copiousness of conventional humor routines, instructional materials, and/or instructors encouraging humor.

Although the DCT that we developed was, indeed, effective in collecting humorous responses from our participants, in the following sections we discuss ways in which the instrument could potentially be improved, as well as suggestions for how DCTs might be used to help us better understand whether, how, and under what conditions L2 users choose to be funny in their additional language.

5.1 Ways to modify the humor DCT

Given that our pilot study pointed to cultural differences regarding how funny the DCT scenarios were perceived, when crafting a DCT to collect humor data, it seems advisable to conduct extensive pilot-testing to pinpoint situations in which humor is not consistently salient cross-culturally and which may need to be modified to avoid cultural specificity. Another change that could be made to the DCT format that we employed is to provide pictures and word balloons in the scenarios rather than use the exclusively text-based items based on the classic DCT, similar to what has been done to contextualize tasks in more recent computerized DCTs (see e.g., Culpeper, Mackey, and Taguchi 2018). Adjusting the DCT format in this way would provide additional visual cues that could be perceived as funny which, in turn, could further encourage participants to create amusing responses. Pictorial depictions of the scenes might also have the effect of enhancing the comprehensibility of the scenarios for lower-proficiency L2 speakers if the DCT is to be delivered in the target language as was the case with the ESL group in our study.

A more substantive modification to our instrument would be to employ an oral DCT. While giving L2 speakers sufficient time to formulate a humorous response was viewed as a benefit of the written DCT, a limitation is that written DCTs do not capture non-verbal and paralinguistic cues, which are resources that contribute to creating humor in verbal interactions. Indeed, as we read participants' responses to our DCT scenarios, some that were intended to be funny did not seem humorous, but could have potentially been made humorous if produced with, for instance, exaggerated intonation or a wry facial expression. Hence, a possible change to the procedure that we employed would be to ask participants to first read the scenarios and write down a humorous response and then, after being given sufficient time to jot down what they would say, ask them to verbally produce their humorous utterances, as in an oral DCT (e.g., Bardovi-Harlig 2013). This method would combine the benefit of giving participants time to draw on their explicit knowledge with the opportunity to deliver their humor with their full paralinguistic and non-verbal repertoire. Of course, the practicality of data collection would be somewhat diminished by the need to video-record and subsequently transcribe the non-verbal characteristics of participants' responses.

5.2 Ways to use the DCT to advance our understanding of L2 humor

Since our research indicates that the DCT is a viable instrument for collecting samples of L2 efforts at humor, it seems reasonable to begin to use it in the ways that traditional, speech-act-based DCTs have been used. For instance, the scenarios could easily be altered to investigate how such sociolinguistic variables as age or gender of interlocutor, role relationships, and context influence the amount and types of humor created. The DCT might also be designed in such a way as to analyze L2 responses to target language humor, rather than initiations of humor. It might also be worth constructing DCTs in a similar style as ours, but that target specific types of humor, such as teasing, wordplay, or self-deprecating humor.

Also, following on well-established uses of DCTs, a cross-sectional study using this instrument might help us understand the strategies used by L2 users at different levels of proficiency for creating humor. Although there is likely to be a wide range of idiosyncratic attempts at humor, given individual differences in humor tastes and styles, the DCT would allow for the creation of a data set that would be large enough to identify patterns. Such data could be used to examine trends in the types of humor, formulaic expressions, and linguistic mechanisms that L2 speakers employ in each scenario. In addition to coding specific types of humor strategies, responses to the DCT scenarios could be rated as to how funny they are, data which could point to degree of communicative success in attempts to amuse. Further, engaging both monolingual and bilingual raters might reveal that some humor is only enjoyed when both speaker and hearer have two languages in common or when they share the experience of learning the same L2 (e.g., Vaid 2006). Finally, a longitudinal design could examine changes in individuals' humor practices over time, for instance, before and after studying abroad or receiving instruction about L2 humor. These types of analyses would represent an important complement to the qualitative studies that, as we have noted, currently dominate this area of inquiry.

The language-humor-culture interface could also be an area of study using this type of DCT. A large data set like that described above could be employed to detect common, or "default" types of humor in specific situations that could be identified as culturally-specific and traceable to either the L1 or L2. This type of information would be particularly helpful in designing additional DCTs, as well as for constructing classroom materials. The DCT might also be used to test L2 users' cultural competence. Reactions to scenarios that are very likely to be culturally inappropriate would gauge their ability to detect and assess culturally appropriate humor. Similarly, some playful reactions are conventional and this instrument could help us assess the extent to which learners are able to detect and/or produce such responses. Again, both of these types of DCTs would also yield useful information for instructional materials development, as well as function as methods for assessing learning outcomes of instruction targeting humor in an L2.

6 Conclusion

As our data showed, not only was the DCT for humor effective, it was sensitive enough to sieve the most unambiguously humorous situations and enticing enough to spur English, Russian, and Spanish L2 speakers' linguistic playfulness. Moreover, during this pilot study it became evident that DCTs can be used to (rather quickly) identify topics, themes, and situations that are perceived as universally versus locally humorous. Further investigation is needed to reveal whether such responses are traceable to the first language and culture or learned in the process of L2 acquisition, or further yet, whether they are an example of interlanguage. A quantitative perspective on humor would complement existing qualitative work that has documented in rich detail the multilayered and co-constructed nature of L2 humor. While written DCTs certainly have limitations, as we have outlined above, our analysis suggests that this instrument does, indeed, have the potential to provide new insights regarding cultural patterns in humor practices, sociolinguistic variation concerning when and with whom we joke, and can further elucidate the relationship between humor and L2 proficiency.

References

Adelswärd, Viveka & Britt-Marie Öberg. 1998. The function of laughter and joking in negotiation activities. *Humor: International Journal of Humor Research* 11. 411–429.

Ahn, So-Yeon. 2016. Exploring language awareness through students' engagement in language play. *Language Awareness* 25. 40–54.

Attardo, Salvatore. 2001. *Humorous texts: A semantic and pragmatic analysis.* Berlin: De Gruyter Mouton.

Bardovi-Harlig, Kathleen. 2010. Exploring the pragmatics of interlanguage pragmatics: Definition by design. In Anna Trosborg (ed.), *Pragmatics across languages and cultures*, 219–260. (Handbook of Pragmatics 7). Berlin: De Gruyter Mouton.

Bardovi-Harlig, Kathleen. 2013. Developing L2 pragmatics. *Language Learning* 63. 68–86.

Beebe, Leslie & Martha Cummings. 1996. Natural speech act data versus written questionnaire data: How data collection method affects speech act performance. In Sue Gass & Joyce Neu (eds.), *Speech acts across cultures: Challenges to communication in a second language*, 65–86. Berlin: De Gruyter Mouton.

Bell, Nancy D. 2006. Interactional adjustments in humorous intercultural communication. *Intercultural Pragmatics* 3. 1–28.

Bell, Nancy D. 2007. How native and non-native English speakers adapt to humor in intercultural interaction. *Humor* 20. 27–48.

Bell, Nancy D. 2017. Humor and second language development. In Salvatore Attardo (ed.), *The Routledge handbook of language and humor*, 444–455. New York: Routledge.

Bell, Nancy D. & Salvatore Attardo. 2010. Failed humor: Issue in non-native speakers' appreciation and understanding of humor. *Intercultural Pragmatics* 7. 423–447.

Bell, Nancy D. & Anne Pomerantz. 2015. *Humor in the classroom: A guide for language teachers and educational researchers.* New York: Routledge.

Bell, Nancy D. & Anne Pomerantz. 2019. Humor in L2 pragmatics research. In Naoko Taguchi (ed.), *The Routledge handbook of second language acquisition and pragmatics*, 63–77. New York: Routledge.

Bell, Nancy D., Stephen Skalicky, & Tom Salsbury. 2014. Multicompetence in L2 language play: A longitudinal case study. *Language Learning* 64(1). 72–102.

Cheng, Winnie. 2003. Humor in intercultural conversations. *Semiotica* 146. 287–306.

Cohen, Andrew D. & Elite Olshtain. 1981. Developing a measure of socio-cultural competence: The case of the apology. *Language Learning* 31. 113–134.
Cook, Guy. 2000. *Language play, language learning*. Oxford: Oxford University Press.
Culpeper, Jonathan, Alison Mackey, & Naoko Taguchi. 2018. *Second language pragmatics: From theory to research*. New York: Routledge.
Davies, Catherine E. 2003. How English-learners joke with native speakers: An interactional sociolinguistic perspective on humor as collaborative discourse across cultures. *Journal of Pragmatics* 35. 1361–1385.
Economidou-Kogetsidis, Maria. 2013. Strategies, modification and perspective in native speakers' requests: A comparison of WDCT and naturally occurring requests. *Journal of Pragmatics* 53. 21–38.
Eisenstein, Miriam & Jean Bodman. 1993. Expressing gratitude in American English. In Gabriele Kasper & Shoshana Blum-Kulka (eds.), *Interlanguage pragmatics*, 64–81. New York: Oxford University Press.
Gibson, Janet. 2019. Cognition, creativity, and humor. Paper presented at the Conference of the International Society for Humor Studies, University of Texas, Austin, TX, 24–28 June.
Golato, Andrea. 2003. Studying compliment responses: A comparison of DCTs and recordings of naturally occurring talk. *Applied Linguistics* 24. 90–121.
Hartford, Beverly S. & Kathleen Bardovi-Harlig. 1992. Closing the conversation: Evidence from the academic advising session. *Discourse Processes* 15. 93–116.
Holmes, Janet. 2000. Politeness, power, and provocation: How humor functions in the workplace. *Discourse Studies* 2. 159–185.
Kasper, Gabriele. 2008. Data collection in pragmatics research. In Helen Spencer-Oatey (ed.), *Culturally speaking: Culture, communication and politeness theory*, 279–303. London: Continuum.
Kasper, Gabriele & Merete Dahl. 1991. Research methods in interlanguage pragmatics. *Studies in Second Language Acquisition* 13. 215–247.
Kasper, Gabriele & Steven J. Ross. 2013. Assessing second language pragmatics: An overview and introductions. In Steven J. Ross & Gabriele Kasper (eds.), *Assessing second language pragmatics*, 1–40. New York: Palgrave Macmillan.
Mir, Montserrat & Josep M. Cots. 2017. Beyond saying thanks: Compliment responses in American English and Peninsular Spanish. *Languages in Contrast* 17. 128–150.
Ogiermann, Eva. 2018. Discourse completion tasks. In Andreas H. Jucker, Klaus P. Schneider, & Wolfram Bublitz (eds.), *Methods in pragmatics*, 229–255. Berlin: De Gruyter.
Olshtain, Elite, & Andrew Cohen. 1983. Apology: A speech act set. In Nessa Wolfson & Elliot Judd (eds.), *Sociolinguistics and language acquisition*, 18–36. Rowley, MA: Newbury House.
Petkova, Maria. 2013. *Effects and perceptions of a humor competence curriculum in an intensive English program in Southern California*. San Diego, CA: Alliant International University dissertation.
Pomerantz, Anne & Nancy D. Bell. 2011. Humor as safe house in the foreign language classroom. *Modern Language Journal* 95. 148–161.
Reddington, Elizabeth & Hansun Waring. 2015. Understanding the sequential resources for doing humor in the language classroom. *Humor* 28. 1–23.
Shardakova, Maria. 2010. How to be funny in a second language: Pragmatics of L2 humor. In Richard D. Brecht, Ludmila A. Verbitskaja, Maria D. Lekic, & William P. Rivers (eds.), *Mnemosynon. Studies on language and culture in the Russophone world: A collection of*

papers presented to Dan E. Davidson *by his students and colleagues*, 288–310. Moscow: Azbukovinik, Institut russkogo jazyka.

Shardakova, Maria. 2012. Cross-cultural analysis of the use of humor by Russian and American English speakers. In Leyre Ruiz de Zarobe & Yolanda Ruiz de Zarobe (eds.), *Speech acts and politeness across languages and cultures*, 197–235. New York: Peter Lang.

Shardakova, Maria. 2013. "I joke you don't": Second language humor and intercultural identity construction. In Celeste Kinginger (ed.), *Social and cultural aspects of language learning in study abroad*, 207–238. Amsterdam: John Benjamins.

Shardakova, Maria. 2017. Politeness, teasing, and humor. In Salvatore Attardo (ed.), *The Routledge handbook of language and humor*, 219–233. New York: Routledge.

Shively, Rachel L. 2018. *Learning and using conversational humor in a second language during study abroad*. Berlin: de Gruyter Mouton.

Sterling, Scott & Shawn Loewen. 2015. The occurrence of teacher-initiated playful LREs in a Spanish L2 classroom. *System* 53. 73–83.

Vaid, Jyotsna. 2006. Joking across languages: Perspectives on humor, emotion, and bilingualism. In Anita Pavlenko (ed.), *Bilingual minds: Emotional experience, expression, and representation*, 152–182. Clevedon, UK: Multilingual Matters.

Vaid, Jyotsna, Hyun Choi, Hsin-Chin Chen, & Michael Friedman. 2008. Perceiving and responding to embarrassing predicaments across languages: Culture influences on the emotion lexicon. *The Mental Lexicon* 3. 121–147.

Vandergriff, Ilona & Carolin Fuchs. 2012. Humor support in synchronous computer-mediated classroom discussions. *Humor* 25. 437–458.

Walters, F. Scott. 2013. Interfaces between a discourse completion test and a conversation analysis-informed test of L2 pragmatic competence. In Steven J. Ross & Gabriele Kasper (eds.), *Assessing second language pragmatics*, 172–195. New York: Palgrave Macmillan.

Yuan, Yi. 2001. An inquiry into empirical pragmatics data-gathering methods: Written DCTs, oral DCTs, field notes, and natural conversations. *Journal of Pragmatics* 33. 271–292.

Ziv, Avner. 1976. Facilitating effects of humor on creativity. *Journal of Educational Psychology.* 68(3). 318–22.

Ziv, Avner. 1983. The influence of humorous atmosphere on divergent thinking. *Contemporary Educational Psychology* 8(1). 68–75.

Steven J. Ross and Qi Zheng
9 Strategic competence and pragmatic proficiency in L2 role plays

Abstract: Building on the varied work of Andrew Cohen in the domain of second language (L2) pragmatics and assessment, this chapter examines the assessment of strategic competence in role plays devised for the oral proficiency interview. Strategic competence develops in both instructed and naturalistic L2 acquisition contexts. Evidence for stages of development for this aspect of pragmatic competence has been inconsistently available, and to a large degree has been observable in more direct assessment techniques, such as interactive role plays, rather than in indirect methods such as discourse completion tasks. This chapter explores overlooked aspects of strategic and pragmatic competence made observable in interactive open role plays. In such role plays the candidate is provided a transactional scenario and is asked to pursue a specific goal in light of constraints implied in the scenario itself, or imposed by the interlocutor as a complication introduced to assess the candidate's strategic competence. The analyses focus on examples of interaction from role plays that provide evidence of pragmatic abilities beyond the usual focus on speech act realization. We focus on four facets of pragmatic proficiency that have not been formally assessed in the oral proficiency interview.

Keywords: oral proficiency interview, role plays, strategic competence, second language pragmatics, pragmatic competence

1 Introduction

Oral proficiency interviews often feature simulations of second language (L2) pragmatic and strategic competency display in the form of role plays. The role plays are crafted to simulate "authentic" contextualized situations which a second or foreign language learner would be expected to encounter in transactional service settings and, in more advanced level interviews, simulations of interpersonal situations requiring deference, indirectness, and recipient design. While role playing as simulation of specific forms of institutional talk often differs from actual workplace interaction (Stokoe 2013), in proficiency interviews they are primarily used to elicit specific speech acts such as requests, complaints, or suggestions. As Cohen (2014) has noted, the assessment of L2 pragmatics, in terms of theory and practice, is a relatively new area in language assessment. Besides the focus on situated speech acts, role plays within oral proficiency interviews can provide evidence of strategic and interactional competence, and possibly, as we will argue, other important aspects of a L2 speaker's pragmatic abilities. Strategic competence encompasses the candidate's schematic knowledge of the world, which, as will be outlined in this chapter, involves reference to pertinent and realistic facts marshalled to support options the candidate chooses to achieve transactional or interactional goals (Felix-Brasdefer 2018; Ross and O'Connell 2013). Strategic competence to some degree overlaps with interactional competence, which entails more minute phenomena such as sequence organization (Al-Gahtani and Roever 2012, 2018; Roever 2011), turn-taking (Ducasse and Brown 2009), repair, posture, gaze (Jenkins and Parra 2003), and listener responses (Galaczi 2014; Ross 2018). Strategic competence, we argue, influences what role play candidates do to achieve their goals, while interactional competence accounts for how candidates perform them.

We differentiate role plays for formal assessment, as they have been used in some versions of the oral proficiency interview (OPI), from role plays devised for research purposes, with no stakes for the candidates. Our focus is on role play as a formal assessment task, in light of the fact that role plays in OPIs have been conventionally scored in a criterion-referenced, pass or fail, manner (Ross 2017). Role playing on conventional oral proficiency interviews has mainly focused on speech act realization, leaving other aspects of a L2 speaker's strategic and interactional competence largely unassessed. It will be argued in this chapter that there are a number of other aspects of a L2 speaker's strategic competence that can be revealed through assessment of role plays, and that these can provide additional criteria increasing the validity of role plays as assessments.

The starting point for the expansion of assessment criteria is a quantitative analysis of the relative difficulties of tasks appearing on more than 850 English as a foreign language OPIs rated on the Interagency Language Roundtable (ILR) scale by certified raters. Candidates' proficiencies ranged from high intermediate (ILR 1) to general working proficiency (ILR 3). Role play tasks, commonly assessed as pass or fail, are observed to have calibrated difficulties that are not consonant with the proficiency level the role plays are designed to indicate. In short, role play tasks devised to indicate candidates' transactional, strategic, and pragmatic competence do not serve to discriminate between levels of proficiency, and are weakly correlated with other OPI tasks. To this end, the analyses to follow start with a quantitative analysis devised to estimate the relative difficulty of OPI tasks on the ILR scale, with a particular focus on the relative difficulties of role play tasks. The difficulty estimation analysis is then the starting point for micro-analyses of interactions within the role play excerpts, with the goal of identifying overlooked aspects of pragmatic abilities currently not formally assessed in the OPI.

2 Role plays as strategic competence

Strategic competence is generally understood to be both intentional and volitional and, depending on the test type and task format, entails test-taking strategies. Cohen (2006, 2013) observed that such test-taking strategies tend to be less effective in speaking tests. In speaking tests such as the oral proficiency interview, where topical focus and task selection is adaptive and contingent on previous turns, there are relatively few opportunities for candidates to deploy test-taking strategies. Indeed, when interviewers detect a prepared topic, or suspect that a candidate is attempting to subvert the current interview task as an avoidance strategy, there is a greater likelihood that the interviewer will maneuver away from the candidate's preferred topic. We add the observation that non-interactive speaking tests designed for automated scoring are more likely to provoke test-taking strategies such as rehearsing chunks for insertion into narratives. Scoring algorithms must detect evidence of overall incoherence by comparing the content of the narratives to the expected range of synonymous lexical content most likely to appear. For interactive assessments with live interlocutors, rehearsal is not likely to be effective, as the topics of talk and segues to new tasks are less predictable.

While it is a fact that not all versions of OPIs, such as the Foreign Service Institute oral assessment, the ACTFL oral interview, and other OPI variants used by U.S. Government agencies include role plays, there is a subset that does include the role play as an indicator of a candidate's ability to formulate a recognizable speech act. At higher levels of proficiency, role plays are crafted to reveal strategic competence in routine and non-routine situations, and at the most advanced levels of proficiency, the adaptive role plays focus on a candidate's capacity to accommodate to the interlocutor in terms of role relations, politeness requirements, and stance towards an issue set down in the role play scenario.

When interview tasks are rated individually as having fulfilled the requirements of fluency, accuracy, and coherence, they are awarded a pass, consonant with a criterion-referenced scoring procedure. Interviews produce in many rating systems a pattern of passed and failed tasks, with the selection and articulation of each task adaptively and uniquely varying by interviewer and candidate.

Interview tasks, including the various forms of role plays, are amenable to quantitative analysis. Figure 1 provides a plot of oral proficiency interview tasks from more than 850 English as a foreign language interviews from the Test of English for International Communication that were subjected to a many-facet Rasch analysis. The vertical axis shows the probability of candidates succeeding on the tasks appearing in any given interview. The horizontal axis shows the tasks by level and implied difficulty. Of particular interest here are three role-play tasks. The two tasks that were easiest to pass are the L1RP and L2RP, which are the transactional role play and the role play with a complication, respectively. The L2RP is designed to assess if a candidate can deploy strategic competence after the interlocutor makes unavailable the information, object, or service the candidate seeks in the simulated transaction. The assessment focus is on how the candidate can independently come up with a resolution of the transactional problem.

Also noteworthy is the relative difficulty of the L3RP, which is the non-routine role play devised to assess a speaker's ability to resolve a novel problem using tact and a more elaborate display of strategic competence. The level 3 role play in a non-routine situation appears in Figure 1 to have an out-of-order difficulty, and is in fact as easy as ILR level 2 tasks such as the present and future narratives. The relative difficulty of the three role plays suggests that the rating criteria for role plays do not sufficiently differentiate the pragmatic and strategic competence of the candidates. The focus of this paper is to explore other aspects of pragmatic competence that might be overlooked in current role play rating practices.

In this paper we will focus on examples of role plays in which, in addition to the main speech act, suggest that four other indicators of the L2 speaker's pragmatic competence could be included as assessment criteria. In addition to the main speech act, we explore overlooked facets of strategic and pragmatic competence. Of particular interest is evidence of the degree of assistance the interlocutor provides to keep the role play on track and re-frame the intended speech act in conjunction with candidate's strategy for co-constructing the thematic context for the main speech act, as well as how the candidate reveals a strategy for achieving the desired transactional end. We examine how the candidate deploys knowledge of the world (Thomas 1983) in formulating the speech act. This forms the basis of realism, because the constraints normally expected in typical transactional exchanges serve to make the contrived interaction in the role play more, or less, authentic. Further, whether the candidate's framing of the intended speech act provokes the interlocutor to modify the interaction through scaffolding will be considered an assessable aspect of the role play interaction. The candidate's anticipation of what the interlocutor would be expected to know or not know given the scenario as well as the candidate's meta-pragmatic knowledge–as revealed in affective alignment to the

9 Strategic competence and pragmatic proficiency in L2 role plays — 183

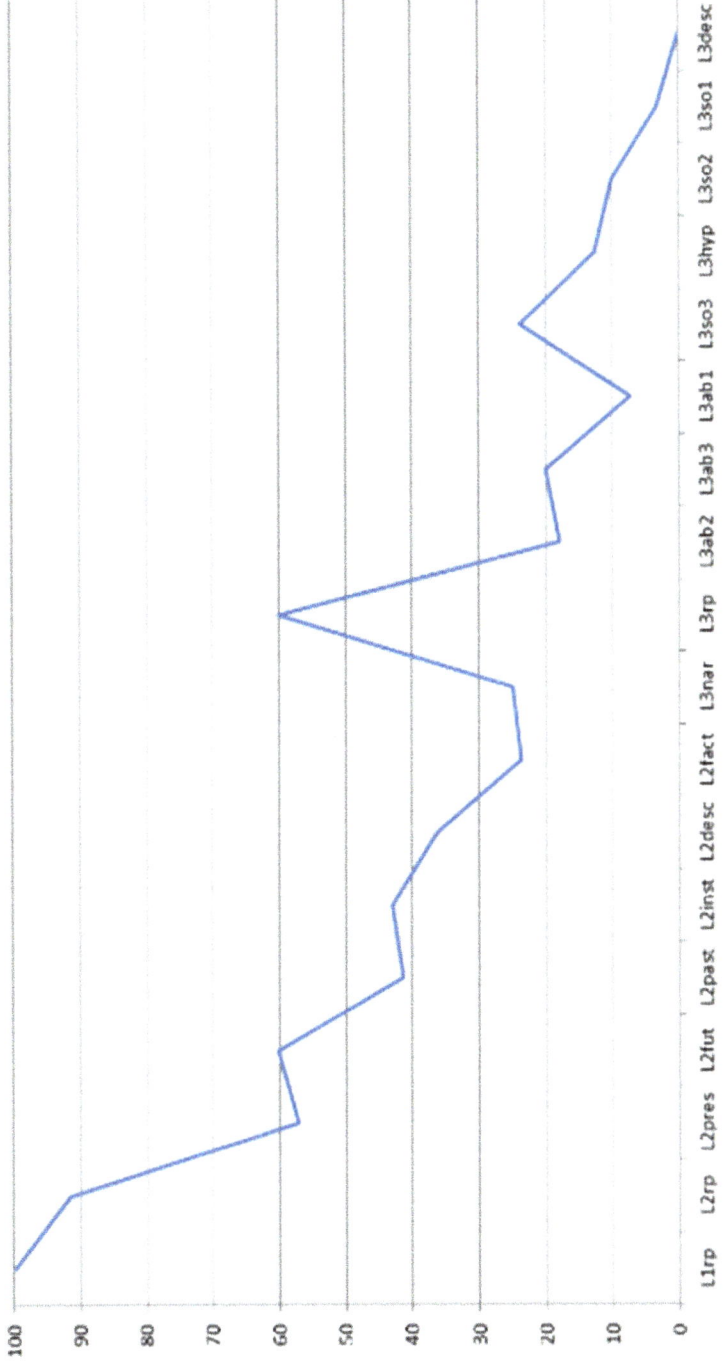

Figure 1: Probability of success on interview tasks.

interlocutor and to the facts of the role play scenario–are considered. The fourth assessable aspect of the candidate's contribution to the role play is the candidate's alignment to the situational conditions set down in the role play scenario and to the mood of the interlocutor. The four putative ratable aspects of strategic and pragmatic competence are exemplified and discussed in turn.

2.1 Interlocutor support

Excerpt 1 of a world-knowledge factor in a transactional role play features the candidate's ("C") apparent difficulties in formulating the request to a hotel concierge for an early morning taxi to the airport. The focus of this assessment task is on how the candidate can understand the facts stated in written and spoken form from the scenario description before formulating a speech act such as a request. The candidate is first given a verbal description of the scenario in English, and is then allowed to read a summary of the scenario in her native language.

Excerpt 1: Taxi to the airport

```
4   I:  Can I help you m'am
5   C:  (.)yes ahh I like to::(.) get on:: taxi ah!-get on taxi (.) please(.) call me a
        taxi
6   I:  Okay-where would you like to go.
7   C:  (.) ah to Buffalo
8   I:  (.).hhh (.) you want to [take a taxi to    ←Repetition of C's request
9   C:  [hahehaah
10  I:  [=Buffalo
11  C:  [hehhe ah nohhoo sorry ahh (.) t-to the airport
12  I:  =to the airport-I see(.) do you want to go now.  ←Conflict with RP
        Scenario Details
13  C:  (.)yes(.)°hum°
14  I:  you want to go now.   ←Repetition of Previous Corrective Move
15  C:  now? (.) yeah (2) noh-heh.hh tomorrow morning
16  I:  =tomorrow morning(.)°okay° what time would you like to go.
17  C:  (.) six-six o'clock
18  I:  =six o'clock(.) okay(.) ah so let me (.) your name is::: ahm(.) is Nishida
        Room 1211
19  C:  yes uhm
21  I:  okay(.) so(.) would you:: ah like a wake up call in the morning.
22  C:  °ahh° yes please
```

While the speech act is partially formulated (line 5) and is recognizable as a formulaic rendering of the request "please call me a taxi," the supporting details of the request are not specifically stated. The candidate's strategic competence–or ability to organize her linguistic resources to achieve the transactional goal–are taxed in this interaction, and require some degree of interlocutor support and scaffolding to help the candidate revise the errant details of the request (lines 7 to 10), and the trouble in specifying the time for the departure from the hotel (lines 12 to 14).

Under a binary scoring rubric based on whether the speech act was recognizable, the candidate would have most likely received a pass for the role play. It is evident that there is a shortcoming in the strategy for achieving the goal, however, as it requires considerable repair effort by the interlocutor (I) to sort out the facts of the scenario details. The need for interlocutor intervention apparently stems from the candidate's trouble in arranging the factual details of the request in terms of the details set down in the role play scenario. The extra effort the interlocutor takes to guide the candidate back to the schematic details suggests that scoring more than articulation of the request speech act itself presents a potentially meaningful additional criterion for assessment.

2.2 Realism

When candidates are presented with a role play scenario, they must initiate the interaction by introducing the problem or transactional goal as specified in the scenario description. Realism refers to the candidate's recognition of the factual, practical, and plausible constraints associated with the transactional schema provided to set up the role play task. The particular details of the speech act, typically a request for service in transactional role plays, are left up to the candidate. In Excerpt 2, wherein the candidate requests repair of a broken camera, the candidate is required to provide factual details about the camera and why it is in need of repair.

Excerpt 2: Instant camera

```
4   C:  (.)ah °ehhtoh° my cam-my camera (.) is ah(.) is breaken
6   I:  Oh I see-I see how did that happen.
7   C:  Oh(.) when I walk around here
8   I:  uhum
9   C:  I (.)(dropped (.)my camera
10  I:  uhum
11  C:  ah(.) ou(.)yes droheheppehed my camera
12  I:  I see-I see(.) what kind of camera is it?
```

13 C: (.)ah(.) my(.) ah camera is (.)ah instanto (.) cahahme(.) my camera is in-
     stant camera
14 I: uhum
15 C: I bought it in(.) I bought it in the airport(1) in Japan
16 I: uhum uhum (1) wha-what would you like me to do.
17 C: ah (.) I want to::I want to::re(.)repair (.)my camera ←Conflict with
     Realistic Request
18 I: (.) I see(.) its an instant (.)camera
19 C: =hehehahe ahh::
20 I: (.)probably we can't repair [an instant camera
21 C: [hehehaheha(.) of course
22 I: =[HHEHAHHEHE hhehehheh
23 C: [°hhehehehe°] (.) .hhah
24 I: (1) wha-wha-what would you like me-I am sorry I I I [can't repair an
25   hehhheinstant camera
26 C: [hhehhehehheh

While such transactional role plays are easily passed as long as the candidate articulates a recognizable request, the other pertinent details revealing the realism of the request itself are not currently assessable aspects of the interaction. In Excerpt 2, lines 13 through 19 suggest that while the request for repair is clearly made (line 17), the lack of the realism of the repair request clashes with normal expectations about what constitutes a reasonable request. The interlocutor (interviewer posing as camera repairer) points out that instant cameras are not, in most circumstances, considered repairable objects.

That the request is not a realistic one is made evident by the candidate and interlocutor laughing after realizing the oddness of the request, and a repetition that such a request could not realistically be fulfilled. Again, if articulation of the request speech act were the only assessable point of the role play interaction, the candidate would have passed the task, as indeed, he does in fact formulate an identifiable request. The implausibility of the request given real-world constraints on what would be deemed feasible could, we argue, also be considered a fault in the candidate's strategic competence.

The two excepts examined thus far suggest that if, after their articulation of the main speech act, candidates exhibit trouble in formulating the specific details of their requests, the interlocutors may feel compelled to restructure the interaction into question and answer sequencing so that the factual details of the request are rearranged into a more plausible version. Likewise, if the details of the request are unlikely to represent real-world constraints, the interaction in the role play will deviate from a realistic facsimile of a transaction to one that is overtly accommodative, or even comical. As noted above, given the conventional binary rating rubric for transactional role plays, in both instances a passing mark would have been awarded. If assessed with a more stringent scoring rubric, one that brings in a consideration of the realism about the situational conditions and actors in it, as well as the extent and formulation of interlocutor interventions provided to the candidates, neither of the candidates in the two excerpts examined thus far would have unambiguously demonstrated strategic competence.

2.3 Theory of mind

Implicit in typical transactions is the participants' anticipation of their interlocutor's schematic and situated state of knowledge. The role relations set out in a role play scenario, for instance, imply that the role-playing interlocutor possesses a delimited scope of conceptual knowledge as well as procedural abilities associated with the roles defined in a scenario. When engaging the interlocutor in a transactional role play devised to assess strategic competence, the candidate needs to anticipate what the interlocutor would and would not be expected to know about whatever is to be requested. Excerpt 3 provides an example of how a transactional role play, one requiring the candidate to get assistance from a librarian, reveals another assessable aspect of the candidate's strategic and pragmatic competence–that is, formulating the target request speech act in light of what the interlocutor would be expected to know about the contents of the library.

Excerpt 3: Omniscient Librarian

```
2   I:  hi-how can I help you.
3   C:  I'd like to read the ah::hah:::car magazine
4   I:  okay
5   C:  =published recently
6   I:  ahuh
7   C:  from the ah:: International Car Association
8   I:  ahright-do you know the name of the magazine er
9   C:  tha:ahh()Modern Cars
10  I:  =[Modern Cars]
11  C:  [>Modern Cars ]
12  I:  okay yes we have that magazine ahm do you know what issue
13  I:  you're looking for.
14  C:  ah the issue was ah ah:: eh() about ah ah hm about
```

15 C: recommendation-about the ah: criticism about the-To-Toyota ←Theory of Mind
16 C: ar-ah recent car
17 I: Okay
18 C: hn
19 I: that magazine is published mont-published monthly-what
29 C: [ah yes
21 I: [what month edition are ya lookin for.
22 C: ahh unnn I'd like to read the newest one
23 I: alright-so that would be May
24 C: =May

In the library role play, there is evidence of a cognitive misalignment (Potter and te Molder 2005) between the candidate and the interlocutor. Here, the candidate makes an assumption about the extent of the specific knowledge that the "librarian" would have about periodical contents. Speakers in the real world anticipate what their interlocutors would and would not already know, and accordingly formulate the introduction of pertinent information to frame the details of the intended request. In example (3), the term "issue" in lines 12–13 is possibly misinterpreted, as the topical content of the sought after article, rather than the more likely interpretation (given the cognitive constraints on a typical librarian) of the "issue" referring to the serialization of the year and month of publication. A librarian could be expected to know the location of magazines and where earlier issues are stored, but probably would not know the specific table of contents of any given issue of a particular magazine. Theory of mind, or what the candidate anticipates the interlocutor in the role play would and would not know, we claim, can be an additional assessable aspect of L2 pragmatic ability.

2.4 Situational and affective concordance

Role plays presume that the participants are attuned to the goals of the simulated interaction and can switch from the context of the assessment interview to a facsimile of an interaction removed in imaginary time and space. Some speaking assessment candidates appear less able to engage in imaginary interaction, and are variably misaligned to the interlocutor in adhering to the roles set down in the scenario. Stokoe (2011) observed, as a case in point, that in role playing police interviews, officers in training regularly deviated from the core tasks of simulating interviews with actors posing as suspects by adding off-task commentary and behaviors unlike those appearing in authentic police interviews. Stokoe noted that unless participants are aligned fully to the details set down in the role play scenarios, off-task talk and behaviors will undermine the authenticity of role play as a facsimile of in-the-workplace interaction. Stokoe's observation brings up a possibly overlooked aspect of role plays as a language assessment device – one that presumes participants recognize the role play as a simulation of the real world of interaction, and that their comportment within it needs to align to it accordingly.

In the stomach-ache role play, Excerpt 4, the interviewer devised a role play in which the candidate comes to a pharmacy complaining of a serious stomach ache:

Excerpt 4: Stomach ache

1   I: tseh yess: well I don't think I should give you medicine
2   I: I think you should go to a doctor
3   C: aohh
4   I: because it was an oyster
5   C: uhuh
6   I: and you-you may have food poisoning
7   C: aohh hah
8   I: so I don't want to give you something which would ahm
9   I: damage your stomach more and make you feel worse
10 C: =AOHH HAH HA ←Lack of Concordance with Implied Affect
11 I: so I think that ahm its not () a good idea for me to give
12 I: somethings [to you
13 C: [AOH ha
14 I: so there is a ahm a hospital near by() and there is also a
15 I: very very good internist
16 C: uhum
17 I: just down the road

The interviewer takes the role of the pharmacist and throughout retains a serious professional demeanor with the "customer." The interviewer declines the request for over-the-counter medication for the ailment, but does not inject a complication for which the candidate must seek resolution. This fact, along with the recommendation that a doctor be seen (line 2) suggests that the role play was devised to be straightforwardly transactional. Evidence that the candidate is not aligned to the tone adopted by the pharmacist, or possibly to the pragmatic constraints that this particular interaction could be expected to impose is made evident by his frequent laughter. The candidate's loud laughter (line 10) in particular clashes with the advice the pharmacist is giving him about the danger of taking medicine without first seeing a physician. The interviewer pursues the task goal by extending the advice-giving turn through a paraphrase of the pre-laughed interviewer turn, and thus attempts to reorient the candidate to the role play task in such a way that repairs his pragmatic miscue: people with food poisoning would not be so jolly.

The evidence of misalignment of affect is revealed in the candidate's differential footing to that of the serious "pharmacist." The interaction in Excerpt 4 may be indicative of the candidate's lack of meta-pragmatic ability to assume a different, albeit fictitious, identity (Zimmerman 1998) to match the requirements of the role play situation. Misalignment of affect in the role play interaction provides another assessable criterion for scoring role play performances.

Of interest central to assessment practice is how role plays should be scored. In current practice, both transactional and complicated role plays are scored in a holistic and binary manner; the candidate either passes or fails the role play. The binary scoring system, as seen in Figure 1, does not sufficiently differentiate the quality of role-play performance if the only criterion for passing is whether or not the intended speech act has been articulated. Concordance with the affective stance of the interlocutor and to the situation presents another criterion for assessment. While it could be argued that affective concordance requires some degree of an aptitude for acting, it is also plausible to consider recognition of the requirements imposed by a situation, even one fabricated for assessment purposes, entails pragmatic competence.

3 Implications for assessment

Like no other part of an oral proficiency assessment, the role play provides a window to candidates' strategic and pragmatic proficiency. Our thesis in this chapter is that role plays have not been exploited sufficiently to serve as assessment devices that differentiate strategic and pragmatic levels of competence. For this reason we propose a revision to the way role plays should be scored, as shown in Table 1.

Table 1: Proposed role play scoring criteria.

Scoring Criteria		Survival	Complication	Non-Routine	Tailored
Speech Act	0	1	2	3	4
Scaffolding	0	-1	-1	-1	-1
Realism	0	-1	-1	-1	-1
Theory of Mind	0	-1	-1	-1	-1
Affect Alignment	0	-1	-1	-1	-1

Specifically, in addition to the main speech act as a focus for scoring, we propose that *scaffolding* (interlocutor support), the degree of *realism* in the manner candidates formulate their requests, *theory of mind* (the evidence that candidates accurately anticipate what their interlocutors could be expected to know), and how candidates align to the *affective tone* of their interlocutors, are important facets for the assessment of pragmatic competence. These added criteria for role play scoring, we argue, can serve to make role plays a more valid assessment technique.

As role plays are usually formulated along the continuum of candidate proficiency in the ILR framework, they can be weighted differentially. Most proficiency interviews are pitched at the ILR 1 (high-intermediate) through ILR 3 (working proficiency) range such that a successful speech act realization at each level would be awarded a score weight reflecting the level of task difficulty. The four criteria outlined in this paper would be used to adjust the baseline speech act rating. For instance, a survival or transactional role play would be awarded the baseline rating of rating of "1" if the candidate successfully articulated a speech act such as a request appropriate for the role play scenario. If the candidate required substantive interlocutor intervention in the form of restructuring such as that seen in Excerpt 1, a demerit of –1 would apply resulting in a role play score of zero. To take another example, if a candidate is assessed at the ILR level 2, with a role play involving a complication, but the interaction reveals that the candidate presumes the interlocutor has conceptual or procedural knowledge recognizable to raters as extraordinary and unlike the state of knowledge normally associated with the interlocutors role (e.g., as in Excerpt 3), the successful display of strategic ability, negotiating a resolution, would be downgraded from a rating of 2 to 1. Our working hypothesis is that finer differentiation of the quality of role play performances will make them more discriminating and ultimately more highly correlated with other interview tasks.

4 Conclusion

Andrew Cohen's career and research agenda in the assessment of strategic and pragmatic competence in an L2 has laid a firm foundation for successive generations of language assessment researchers. Strategic competence research (Cohen 1994) has from its early days striven to merge more from the real world into assessment practice. The inclusion of interactional phenomena in assessment role plays, we argue, may provide additional assessment criteria for finer gradations of L2 strategic and pragmatic competence. This goal remains a formidable challenge. It could be argued that knowledge of the world is a construct independent of L2 proficiency. Role playing as an assessment technique, while overlapping in some aspects of conversational interaction (Okada and Greer 2013), is at best a contrived form of interaction delicately vulnerable to misalignments with real world constraints. Further, as role playing is removed in time and space from the immediate context of the interaction, its representativeness is contingent on the participants' ability to insert themselves into the scenarios and speak as if they were there in real time. It could also be claimed that role plays require some degree of aptitude for acting, and that variation in outcomes may be attributable to an array of skills not directly related to L2 speaking ability.

At this point, there is little evidence to refute potential claims about non-linguistic influences on role play outcomes. We build our thesis rather on the observation that role plays insufficiently discriminate among levels of proficiency and are at best weakly correlated with other generative speaking assessment tasks appearing on oral proficiency assessments. We observe that realization of the target speech act alone will not constitute a sufficiently useful basis for L2 pragmatics assessment. The sub-components of strategic competence we have outlined here may to varying degrees correlate with existing components of L2 pragmatics. Indeed, some higher level role plays designed for tailoring language to interlocutors are devised to assess socio-pragmatic competence. Candidates also differ in the range of their grammatical, lexical, and formulaic resources, leaving open the influence of pragmalinguistic limitations affecting the performances of strategic competence we outline here.

The practical issue considered here is what constitutes sufficient and valid criteria for determining success on a role play. We see that the transactional goal is the obvious first requirement: whether the main speech act is recognizably articulated. Variation in how candidates introduce the intended speech acts, how they understand what other information is relevant given the details set down in the scenario, their knowledge of specific procedural scripts, and the relevant schemata associated with them, what interlocutors could be expected to know or not know, and what mood fits the scenario, are all factors that account for variation in role play quality (see also, Félix-Brasdefer and Koike 2012). Based on the excerpts selected for this paper, we infer that if the more subtle and discriminating strategic and pragmatic criteria had been used in the rating process, a more fine-grained and ultimately valid assessment outcome would be observed. What we have outlined here is a launching point for further research into more detailed scoring of role plays devised to assess L2 pragmatics and proficiency. If the additional criteria indeed serve to differentiate finer gradations of strategic and pragmatic competence, we would expect the near-perfect success rates for role plays to decline and result in a more coherent implicational ordering of oral proficiency interview tasks.

References

Al-Gahtani, Saad & Carsten Roever. 2012. Proficiency and sequential organization of L2 requests. *Applied Linguistics* 33. 42–65.

Al-Gahtani, Saad & Carsten Roever. 2018. Proficiency and preference organization in second language refusals. *Journal of Pragmatics* 129. 140–153.

Cohen, Andrew D. 1994. *Assessing language ability in the classroom*. Boston: Heinle and Heinle.

Cohen, Andrew D. 2006. The coming of age of research on test-taking strategies. *Language Assessment Quarterly* 3(4). 307–331.

Cohen, Andrew D. 2013. Using test-wiseness strategy research in task development. *The Companion to Language Assessment* 2. 893–905.

Cohen, Andrew D. 2014. *Strategies in learning and using a second language*. New York: Routledge.

Ducasse, Ana Maria & Annie Brown. 2009. Assessing paired orals: Raters' orientation to interaction. *Language Testing* 26(3). 423–443.

Félix-Brasdefer, J. César & Dale A. Koike. 2012. *Pragmatic variation in first and second language contexts: Methodological issues*. Philadelphia: John Benjamins.

Félix-Brasdefer, J. César. 2018. Role Plays. In Andreas H. Jucker, Klaus P. Schneider, & Wolfram Bublitz (eds.), *Methods in pragmatics*, 305–331. (Handbook of Pragmatics 10). Berlin: De Gruyter Mouton.

Galaczi, Evelina D. 2014. Interactional competence across proficiency levels: How do learners manage interaction in paired speaking tests. *Applied Linguistics* 35(5). 553–574.

Jenkins, Susan & Isabel Parra. 2003. Multiple layers of meaning in an oral proficiency test: The complementary roles of nonverbal, paralinguistic, and verbal behaviors in assessment decisions. *Modern Language Journal* 87(1). 90–107.

Okada, Yusuke & Tim Greer. 2013. Pursuing a relevant response in oral proficiency interview role plays. In Steven Ross & Gabriele Kasper (eds.), *Assessing second language pragmatics*, 288–310. Basingstoke: Palgrave MacMillan.

Potter, Jonathan & Hedwig te Molder. 2005. Talking cognition: Mapping and making the terrain. In Jonathan Potter & Hedwig te Molder (eds.), *Conversation and cognition*, 1–54. Cambridge: Cambridge University Press.

Roever, Carsten. 2011. Testing of second language pragmatics: Past and future. *Language Testing* 28(4). 463–481.

Ross, Steven J. 2017. *Interviewing for proficiency: Interaction and interpretation*. Basingstoke: Palgrave MacMillan/Springer.

Ross, Steven J. 2018. Listener response as a facet of interactional competence. *Language Testing* 35(3). 357–375.

Ross, Steven J. & Stephen P. O'Connell. 2013. The situation with complication as a site for strategic competence. In Steven J. Ross & Gabriele Kasper (eds.), *Assessing second language pragmatics*, 311–326. Basingstoke: Palgrave MacMillan.

Stokoe, Elizabeth. 2011. Simulated interaction and communication skills training: The 'conversation-analytic role-play method'. In Charles Antaki (ed.), *Applied conversation analysis*, 119–139. Basingstoke: Palgrave MacMillan.

Stokoe, Elizabeth. 2013. The (in)authenticity of simulated talk: Comparing role-played and actual interaction and the implications for communication training. *Research on Language & Social Interaction* 46(2). 165–185.

Thomas, Jenny. 1983. Cross-cultural pragmatic failure. *Applied Linguistics* 4(2). 91–112.

Zimmerman, Don H. 1998. Identity, context, and interaction. In Charles Antaki & Steve Widdicombe (eds.), *Identities in Talk*, 87–106. London: Sage.

Part III: Analyzing discourses in L2 digital contexts

Julie M. Sykes
10 Researching digital discourse in second language pragmatics

Abstract: Current advances in emergent technologies for communication, combined with the ever-present notion of globalization, continually complexify the teaching and learning of second language (L2) pragmatics. As a result, a synthesized approach critical to researching and teaching various dimensions of L2 pragmatics. This chapter explores the role of digital technologies in L2 pragmatics in two areas: (1) extended content and contexts and (2) research capabilities. It first explores the necessity of research on digital discourse(s) to equip learners to develop a comprehensive L2 repertoire. The chapter then highlights ways in which digital technologies can facilitate this exploration, while also enhancing, shaping, and changing L2 pragmatics research more broadly. Ranging from digital analytics, eye-tracking, and simulations research, insightful research approaches are both possible and necessary. Future directions for research and classroom implementation conclude the chapter.

Keywords: computer-mediated contexts, digital discourses, second language pragmatics

1 Introduction

Technological innovation has fundamentally shaped the world in which we live and, with increasing frequency and intensity, permeates all aspects of daily life and person-to-person communication. From a trip to the grocery store to pick up an online "click" order to a 'thank you' text to a food delivery person in a time of physical distancing, digital tools fundamentally change the way humans behave in the world. Concurrently, those behaviors shape the next generation of tools (see Thorne 2003; Thorne, Sauro, and Smith 2015 for further discussion). With this ever-evolving interplay of tools and human behavior comes a critical need to examine language and expand our understanding of the language skills needed for multilingual communication (e.g., Aiken 2016; Thorne, Black, and Sykes 2009), as well as research tools available for studying such phenomena (Taguchi and Sykes 2013; Sykes 2018). For example, discourse has been mediated by the use of hashtags to catalyze social movements, kids are teaching their grandparents how to Facetime across time zones, while the power of complex algorithms and databases driving analytical systems for data analysis has facilitated researching these practices. Identifying pragmatic patterns (i.e., the way speakers and learners communicate and interpret meaning) is all the time more complex and necessary (Sykes 2016, 2019; Thorne, Sauro, and Smith 2015). Furthermore, teaching language learners how to maneuver these contexts in a second or third language becomes critical to their full participation in the communities where those languages are spoken.

In addition to their powerful role in human interaction, digital tools also change how and what can be researched, thereby increasing our analytical capabilities (e.g., the use of computing power for "big data" analysis and modeling, eye-tracking to study gaze, real-time metapragmatic analysis). At the same time, these capabilities extend the types of research questions being asked while concurrently expanding our view of pragmatic competence (e.g., movement away from elicited pragmalinguistic features towards a sequential view of L2 pragmatic ability) (see Chapter 1, this volume).

This chapter briefly explores each of these areas–the pragmatics of digital discourse(s) and L2 pragmatics research possibilities–by summarizing key challenges and current insights. It then concludes with implications for future teaching and research in L2 pragmatics.

2 Key issues

2.1 Digital discourse(s)

Technological advances offer an ever-increasing number of interactional contexts for speakers and listeners to maneuver. Digital discourse(s) are "language patterns occurring in digitally-mediated interactions, or, as a result of, digitally-mediated interaction, even if those occur by analog means" (Sykes 2019: 129). As such, for the purposes of this discussion, digital discourse(s) merge the notion of online and offline, moving away from separate realms and, instead, focus on the hybridity of human communication. A reporter live tweeting a political rally from her seat, a family sitting around the table using online travel guides and reviews to plan a vacation, or two people in their respective living rooms planning their next strategic move in an online game using paper and pencil all offer examples of the hybrid nature of today's discursive practices. From this perspective, technology is more than a facilitative tool to learn something "more important." Instead, wielding digitally-mediated communication has become a critical language skill (i.e., pragmatic skill) used for high stakes interactions in social, educational, and professional domains.

Key challenges when researching and teaching pragmatic patterns within digital discourse(s) are two-fold: (1) the number of contexts to explore is immense with new tools for interaction emerging every day and (2) within those contexts, interactional dynamics evolve rapidly. Each day, it seems, a new social media platform (e.g., Marco Polo) or feature (e.g., live streaming) is developed for online interaction. In 2019, there were 3.4 billion social media users and that number is projected to grow to over 4 billion by 2021 (Lambert 2020). This number does not include other digitally-mediated contexts, such as platforms for collaborative social management (e.g., Asana, Trello), email (e.g. Gmail, Hotmail), or video chatting (e.g., Zoom, Microsoft Teams). The immensity of growth, the diversity of user groups, and the infinite number of options can make navigation of digital discourse(s), at best, challenging to maneuver and, at worst, overwhelmingly impossible. To add to this complexity, the pragmatic norms of interaction within each of these spaces is also dynamic and rapidly changing. While especially salient since the confinement orders put in place in late 2019/early 2020, in light of the novel coronavirus pandemic, one does not actually have to look at such unprecedented times to find evidence of these rapidly shifting interactional expectations. For two examples among many, consider the evolution of the use of Facebook away from a personal sharing site towards a site where the majority of users now share news on current events or political perspectives (Hoadley et al. 2010; Stal and Fiebert 2013) or the increased interest in Twitter and hashtags (see, for example, Scott 2015; Steiglitz and Dang-Xuan 2012; Sykes 2019, for recent work specifically focusing on the pragmatics of hashtags). In addition to the sheer immensity of possibilities, the rapid dynamicity of interaction and pragmatic expectations within these spaces can be especially challenging for language learners. To address these challenges, the sections that follow highlight current work being done along with implications for the researching and teaching of L2 pragmatics as related to digital discourse(s).

2.2 Research tools

In addition to shaping our notion of L2 pragmatic patterns and the need to explore digital discourse(s), digital technologies also extend research capabilities. This expanded potential enables both the analysis of digital discourse patterns and face-to-face interaction (Taguchi and Sykes 2013; Sykes and González-Lloret 2020). Capturing key pragmatic data such as fluency, intonation, and gesture, while also collecting and analyzing sufficiently robust data sets to extrapolate generalizable patterns is an ongoing challenge in pragmatics research. These new technologies enable researchers to expand the types of research questions they can address. The comparison across types of L2 pragmatic data reveal significant differences among the types of information available to researchers based on varying elicitation methods (e.g., Félix-Brasdefer 2010, 2018; Golato 2003; Taguchi 2018). The goal here is not to provide a comprehensive review of L2 pragmatic research methodologies. Instead, this chapter aims to further explore the potential of digital tools to increase the ability to analyze large data sets, consider different types of data, study sequential discourse, and facilitate real-time data collection. As such, digital tools increase the feasibility of examining more contexts and extending our understanding of pragmatic behavior across time. A key challenge remains the timely collection and analysis of comprehensive and comparable data sets that can be analyzed for generalizable patterns and that reflect the complexity of pragmatic patterns as they occur in the world, across a wide variety of contexts. The section that follows explores current advances in this area.

3 Current trends

3.1 L2 pragmatic content

In response to the critical L2 pragmatic skills needed for interaction in digital spaces, this section highlights current work on digital discourse(s) and language learning. Drawing on Yus' (2010) call for the study of "cyberpragmatics," this section illustrates ways in which digitally-mediated discourse is dynamic, co-constructed, relevant, high stakes, and impactful and, therefore, essential for any learner's multilingual repertoire (Bou-Franch and Garcés-Conejos Blitvich 2018; Thorne, Black, and Sykes 2009; Thorne, Sauro, and Smith 2015). While still relatively limited from an explicitly L2 pragmatics learning perspective,[1] an interdisciplinary look at communication research offers significant pragmatic insight. Work directly relevant to the learning of L2 pragmatics is synthesized here with a focus on two digital discourse practices as examples: hashtags and Reddit.

Hashtags (i.e., a traditionally digital practice in which words or phrases follow a # symbol to indicate a topic, emotion, or context) are a ubiquitous discursive behavior, starting online, but also more recently integrated into face-to-face conversation. Prolific in other disciplines, the research on hashtags and language learning is sparse. To address the need for explicit attention to digital discourse behavior in

---

[1] For notable exceptions see Law, Barney, and Poulin 2020; Scott 2015, Shakarami, Hajhashemi, and Caltabiano 2016; and Yeh and Swinehart 2020.

world language classrooms, Sykes (2019) offers an analysis of three pragmatic functions of hashtags: (1) marketing and public relations, (2) interpersonal interaction, and (3) organizing text around a topic, movement, or phenomena. Each is a high stakes function with specific uses and purposes, arguably both financially and socially significant. For example, in the marketing and public relations sphere, much of the work focuses on building sentiment and public appeal, requiring sophisticated hashtags that serve a critical function across domains (e.g., the success or failure of political campaigns, as well as musicians and sports teams connecting with fans and boosting ticket sales). In the interpersonal sphere, hashtags are used to identify interpersonal jokes and connect with smaller communities. However, the ways in which this is done varies greatly across languages, requiring explicit attention on the part of the language learner in multilingual interactions. The third pragmatic function is that of topics, movements, or phenomena, where a specific hashtag is used to tie posts about an event together. This function has been used to catalyze social movements around the world (e.g., #metoo, #blacklivesmatter, #amoresamor) and target areas in need of humanitarian aid via geotagging. For each function, Sykes (2019) offers tools for analysis and suggests ways to guide learners' exploration in their dominant language as well as in the language(s) they are learning. Identifying similarities and differences in each language can help to build critical pragmatic skills.

Reddit (https://www.reddit.com/), an online social site where users share news and curated content, is a thriving multilingual space well suited to learners with specific hobbies and interests. In an effort to explore the pragmatic behaviors of Reddit, as well as consider it as a pedagogical tool, Yeh and Swinehart (2020) suggest that Reddit and, more specifically subreddits, are noteworthy contexts for L2 pragmatic development. Though specific in its nature, the study offers specific insight into L2 pragmatic learning and digital discourse, warranting discussion here. In the study, the authors first explore digital discourse(s) in Reddit, suggesting it is best understood as a compilation of affinity spaces (Gee 2004). To examine the role of Reddit in L2 pragmatic learning, fifteen Chinese-speaking learners of English participated in a Reddit subgroup over a period of six weeks. Engaging in a Reddit subgroup of their choice, the learners completed an analysis of the genre and the space while also posting weekly. Through analysis of the posts themselves, the upvotes and downvotes, and a post-questionnaire, the authors analyzed learners' L2 pragmatic development. The results demonstrate that, over the course of the six weeks, students became aware of pragmatic patterns in the Reddit subgroup. Evidence suggests the learners could identify relevant content as well as identify appropriate pragmatic practices. Yeh and Swinehart then offer ways in which L2 learners can continue to build their L2 pragmatic repertoire, both through the exploration of a specific social media platform, as well through autonomous engagement with digital communities of their choice.

Researching and teaching the specifics of every digital practice and online community is impractical and not in learners' best interests. Instead, the study of digital discourse(s) as a skills-based approach to learning, through inquiry, analysis, and exploration, can facilitate the development of L2 pragmatic analysis critical to a learners' L2 repertoire. This could include, for example, the use of a hashtag aggregator to compare similar hashtags in two languages and the development of the language skills to extract critical information from that analysis. Moreover, it builds learner independence so they can tackle digital discourse(s) independently. Critical to furthering this discussion is an empirical look at the effectiveness of a variety of means for giving explicit attention to digital discourse practices in classrooms and beyond.

3.2 Research capabilities

In addition to the expansion of L2 pragmatic inquiry to include digital discourse(s), digital technologies also facilitate new approaches to research (Taguchi and Sykes 2013; Sykes and González-Lloret 2020). Current work demonstrates a wide variety of research possibilities in L2 pragmatics, all enabled by technological advancements. These entail models for improving existing research paradigms, examining new pragmatic features, and analyzing large, complex data sets.

First, digital tools have been used to enhance classic experimental measures. Discourse Completion Tasks (DCTs) are being delivered digitally, overcoming some of the challenges involved in the creation of the contextual context (e.g., Roever 2013; see also Chapter 6, this volume). Along this vein, multimodal DCTs enable the capacity for oral responses as well as the analysis of gesture and prosodic features across languages (Rockey, Tiegs, and Fernández 2020). These DCTs are video-recorded, instead of the more traditional written format, allowing researchers to analyze a larger set of data markers, such as gesture and pause.

In addition, a number of researchers have expanded methods to analyze key pragmatic features that are not possible to study without advances in digital technology. These advances include the analysis of performance fluency as a result of using digital simulations (Li 2013; Taguchi 2013), metapragmatic analysis and learner behavior patterns via digital simulations (Sykes 2009, 2013), systematic investigation of sociopragmatic awareness and impact via place-based mobile games (Douglass 2009; Holden and Sykes 2013), and hashtag analysis (Scott 2015). Furthermore, researchers are beginning to redefine coding schema and methods of analysis for digital spaces. For example, Haythornthwaite et al. (2018) describe a coding schema for the analysis of informal learning in Reddit.

Researchers also point to the role of technology in the complex research via large data sets through the genre analysis of written texts and automated scoring mechanisms for pragmatic evaluation of textual artifacts (Taguchi et al. 2017; Zhao and Kaufer 2013) and L2 corpora with concordancing, structural tagging, and pragmatic notations (Fung and Carter 2007; Geyer 2007; Vyatkina and Belz 2005). Especially relevant to the discussion in the previous section is the work of Choi et al. (2015), who demonstrated the value of a large data set (i.e., 700K threaded conversations from 1.5 million users) to analyze volume, responsiveness, and virality of user behavior in relation to Reddit posts. While not specifically related to pragmatics, similar types of analysis around questions of digital discourse(s) and L2 pragmatics are critical moving forward.

Finally, as we look further into the future, researchers will have the opportunity to continue to utilize human-machine interaction to study interactional pragmatics (e.g., Sydorenko et al. 2020). As noted by González-Lloret (2019), Google has tapped pragmatics research for the development of their Google Duplex (i.e., an artificial intelligent system used in service encounters) to make the system seem more human-like with elements of interaction (e.g., pauses, latches, and corrections). One could easily imagine this system also being used as a data collection tool for L2 pragmatics. Using a bot (i.e., artificial interactional agent), researchers would be able to create meaningful data collection instruments that would be balanced across all participants and reflective of the interactional scenario created.

4 Conclusion and future directions

As the digital world continues to grow and the field moves toward an extended understanding of L2 pragmatics, both in terms of pragmatic content and research capabilities, a nimble approach is fundamental. No one would have predicted the especially prominent role digital discourse(s) would play in 2020, with the rapid implementation of remote learning and shelter-in-place living due to the coronavirus pandemic. This global event, occurring as this chapter is written, further emphasizes the critical role of digital tools to facilitate human interaction in unexpected and unique ways. The impact on digital discourse(s) and pragmatic behaviors is still unknown, but undoubtedly evolving every day. As we look toward the future, a responsive approach to L2 pragmatics will enable learners to respond to a rapidly changing world, adding to their multilingual

abilities across a wide variety of contexts. It is still unknown if, as was the case in March 2020, terms like *zoombombing* and *waiting room* will remain common dinner conversation, or if unprecedented collaborations in art and media will continue to proliferate online engagement. Regardless, digital discourse(s) will continue to evolve and remain core to human interaction. As technological advances continue, understanding these practices and continuing to refine our ability to research them will, undoubtedly, remain fundamental. As a response, Sykes and González-Lloret (2020) advocate L2 pragmatics research that:
- addresses the ways users engage with digital discourse(s) over time;
- examines how those practices shift based on contextual factors (internal and external);
- analyzes how patterns vary and/or remain similar across, for example, languages, socioeconomic factors, race, and gender; and
- identifies systems and approaches for using big data and algorithms to gain insight not feasible through other means of analysis.

Each of these areas offers significant insight into the ways in which human communication occurs and evolves over time, while also enabling a comprehensive understanding of L2 pragmatics as part of a learner's language repertoire. Added to this list is the need for a comprehensive research agenda that examines the role of various instructional interventions for the teaching and learning of L2 pragmatics, and more specifically, digital discourse(s), as part of the language learning process.

In addition, it is essential that we continue to refine and examine research methodologies based on the technological tools available. This could include:
- *the continuance of multimodal discourse completion tasks to capture more comprehensive pragmatic behavior*. This next generation of DCTs could include the use of video-conferencing, multimedia prompts and responses, and a variety of digital contexts that would be "real world;"
- *refined role-play protocols and an increased inclusion of simulations for the measurement of L2 pragmatic abilities*. Role plays via digital simulations can re-emphasize the context and characters of the role play through digital communication, thereby increasing the validity of the measure (see, e.g., Sykes, Malone, Forrest, and Sağdıç 2020);
- *complex analysis of large data sets through corpora and machine learning technologies*. This includes the analysis of sets of learner data corpora as well as data sets which capture the multitude of digitally-mediated utterances;
- *a refined understanding of human-machine interaction and how that impacts pragmatics research*. This includes the incorporation of pragmatic elements in natural language processing and artificial intelligence systems;

- *automatic scoring and genre analysis to increase analytical capabilities.* This approach enables the analysis of a large amount of data that can identify patterns in complex discourse relatively quickly;
- *real-time data collection via wearables and mobile technologies.* For example, participants could wear voice activated devices the size of *Fitbits* or *Apple Watches* to record and track L2 interaction that could then be analyzed from an L2 pragmatic development perspective.

Digital tools are a ubiquitous part of everyday life, and, as such, warrant intentioned understanding as tools to facilitate human communication and expand research possibilities. Moving forward, addressing these critical needs will not only expand learners' language repertoires, but also the field's general notions of what can, and should, be better understood.

References

Aiken, Mary. 2016. *The cyber effect: A pioneering cyber-psychologist explains how human behavior changes online.* New York: Spiegel & Grau.

Bou-Franch, Patricia & Pilar Garcés-Conejos Blitvich (eds.). 2018. *Analyzing digital discourse: New insights and future directions.* London: Palgrave-Macmillan.

Choi, Daejin, Jinyoung Han, Taejoong Chung, Yong-Yeol Ahn, Byung-Gon Chun, & Ted "Taekyoung" Kwon. 2015. Characterizing conversation patterns in Reddit: From the perspective of content properties and user participation behaviors. COSN 15 Conference proceedings, 233–243. Palo Alto, CA.

Douglass, Kate. 2009. Second-person pronoun use in French-language blogs: Developing L2 sociopragmatic competence. In Lee Abraham & Lawrence Williams (eds.), *Electronic discourse in language learning and language teaching*, 213–240. Amsterdam: John Benjamins.

Félix-Brasdefer, J. César. 2010. Data collection methods in speech act performance. In Alicia Martinez-Flor & Esther Usó-Juan (eds.), *Speech act performance: Theoretical, empirical and methodological issues*, 41–56. Amsterdam: John Benjamins.

Félix-Brasdefer, J. César. 2018. Role plays. In Andreas H. Jucker, Klaus P Schneider, & Wolfram Bublitz (eds.), *Methods in Pragmatics*, 305–331. (Handbook of Pragmatics 10). Berlin/Boston: De Gruyter Mouton.

Fung, Loretta & Ronald Carter. 2007. Discourse Markers and Spoken English: Native and Learner Use in Pedagogic Settings, *Applied Linguistics* 28(3). 410–439.

Gee, James. P. 2004. *Situated language and learning: A critique of traditional schooling.* New York: Routledge.

Geyer, Naomi. 2007. The grammar–pragmatics interface in L2 Japanese: The case of contrastive expressions. *Japanese Language and Literature* 41(1). 93–117.

Golato, Andrea. 2003. Studying compliment responses: A comparison of DCTs and recordings of naturally occurring talk. *Applied Linguistics* 24(1). 90–121.

González-Lloret, Marta. 2019. Technology and L2 Pragmatics Learning. *Annual Review of Applied Linguistics* 39. 113–127.

Haythornthwaite, Caroline, Priya Kumar, Anatoliy Gruzd, Sarah Gilbert, Marc Esteve del Valle, & Drew Paulin. 2018. Learning in the wild: coding for learning and practice on Reddit. *Learning, Media and Technology* 43(3). 219–235.

Hoadley, Christopher, Heng Xu, Joey Lee, & Mary Beth Rosson. 2010. Privacy as information access and illusory control: The case of the Facebook News Feed privacy outcry, *Electronic Commerce Research and Applications* 9(1). 50–60.

Holden, Christopher & Julie. M. Sykes. 2013. Complex L2 pragmatic feedback via place-based mobile games. In Naoko Taguchi & Julie M. Sykes (eds.), *Technology in interlanguage pragmatics research and teaching*, 155–183. Amsterdam: John Benjamins.

Lambert, Sebastian. 2020. Number of social media users in 2020: Demographics and predictions. *Finances Online: Reviews for Business*. https://financesonline.com/number-of-social-media-users/ (accessed 31 March 2020).

Law, James, David Barny, & Rachel Poulin. 2020. Patterns of peer interaction in multimodal L2 digital social reading. *Language Learning & Technology* 24(2). 70–85.

Li, Shuai. 2013. Amount of practice and pragmatic development of request-making in L2 chinese. In Naoko Taguchi & Julie M. Sykes (eds.), *Technology and interlanguage pragmatics research and teaching*, 43–70. Amsterdam: John Benjamins.

Rockey, Catherine, Jessica Tiegs, & Julieta Fernández. 2020. Mobile application use in technology-enhanced DCTs. *CALICO Journal* 73(1). 85–108.

Roever, Carsten. 2013. Testing implicature under operational conditions. In Steven J. Ross & Gabriele Kasper (eds.), *Assessing second language pragmatics*, 43–64. Palgrave Advances in Language and Linguistics. London: Palgrave Macmillan.

Scott, Katie. 2015. The pragmatics of hashtags: Inference and conversational style on twitter. *Journal of Pragmatics* 81. 8–20.

Shakarami, Alireza, Karim Hajhashemi, & Nerina Jane Caltabiano. 2016. Digital discourse markers in an ESL learning setting: The case of socialization forums. *International Journal of Instruction* 9(2). 167–182.

Stal, Mikhail & Martin Fiebert. 2013. Changes in Facebook behavior over time. *Global Journal of Computer Science and Technology* 9, np. https://computerresearch.org/index.php/computer/article/view/158 (accessed 4 August, 2020).

Stieglitz, Stefan & Linh Dang-Xuan. 2012. Social media and political communication: A social media analytics framework. *Social Network Analysis and Mining*. DOI: 10.1007/s13278-012-0079-3.

Sydorenko, Tetyana, Zachary Jones, Phoebe Daurio, & Steven Thorne. 2020. Beyond the curriculum: Extended discourse practice through self-access pragmatics simulations. *Language Learning & Technology* 24(2). 48–69.

Sykes, Julie M. 2009. Learner requests in Spanish: examining the potential of multiuser virtual environments for l2 pragmatics acquisition. In Lara Lomicka & Gillian Lord (eds.), *The next generation: social networking and online collaboration*, 119–234. San Marcos, TX: CALICO.

Sykes, Julie M. 2013. Complex L2 pragmatic feedback via place-based mobile games. In Naoko Taguchi & Julie Sykes (eds.), *Technology and interlanguage pragmatics research and teaching*. 155–184. Amsterdam: Benjamins.

Sykes, Julie M. 2016. Technologies for Teaching and Learning Intercultural Competence and Interlanguage Pragmatics. In Carol A. Chapelle & Shannon Sauro (eds.), *Handbook of technology and second Language teaching and learning*, 119–133. New York: Wiley.

Sykes, Julie M. 2018. Review article: Interlanguage Pragmatics, Curricular Innovation, and Digital Technologies. *CALICO Journal* 35(2). 120–141.

Sykes, Julie M. 2019. Emergent digital discourses: What can we Learn from hashtags and digital games to expand learners' second language repertoire? *Annual Review of Applied Linguistics* 39. 128–145.

Sykes Julie M. & Marta González-Lloret. 2020. Exploring the interface of interlanguage (L2) pragmatics and digital spaces. *CALICO Journal* 37(1). i–xv.

Sykes, Julie, Margaret Malone, Linda Forrest, & Ayşenur Sağdıç. 2020. Affordances of digital simulations to measure communicative success. In Okim Kang & Alyssa Kermad (eds.), *Transdisciplinary innovations for communicative success*, n. p. Singapore: Springer. Available at: https://link.springer.com/referenceworkentry/10.1007/978-981-13-2262-4_90-2 (accessed 4 August, 2020).

Taguchi, Naoko. 2013. Instructed pragmatics at a glance: Where instructional studies were, are, and should be going. *Language Teaching* 48. 1–50.

Taguchi, Naoko. 2018. Data collection and analysis in developmental L2 pragmatics research. In Aarnes Gudmestad & Amanda Edmonds (eds.), *Critical reflections on data in second language acquisition*, 7–32. Amsterdam: John Benjamins.

Taguchi, Naoko, David Kaufer, Pia Maria Gómez-Laich, & Helen Zhao. 2017. A corpus linguistics analysis of on-line peer commentary. In Kathleen Bardovi-Harlig & J. César Félix-Brasdefer (eds.), *Pragmatics and language learning*, 357–370. Hawaii: University of Hawaii at Manoa.

Taguchi, Naoko & Julie M. Sykes (eds.). 2013. *Technology in interlanguage pragmatics research and teaching*. Amsterdam: John Benjamins.

Thorne, Steven L. 2003. Artifacts and cultures-of-use in intercultural communication. *Language Learning & Technology* 7(2). 38–67.

Thorne, Steven. L., Rebecca Black, & Julie M. Sykes. 2009. Second language use, socialization, and learning in internet interest communities and online gaming. *The Modern Language Journal* 93(1). 802–21.

Thorne, Steven L., Shannon Sauro, & Bryant Smith. 2015. Technologies, identities, and expressive activity. *Annual Review of Applied Linguistics* 35. 215–33.

Vyatkina, Nina & Julie M. Belz. 2005. Learner corpus analysis and the development of L2 pragmatic competence in networked inter-cultural language study: The case of German modal particles. *Canadian Modern Language Review/ La Revue Canadienne Des Langues Vivantes* 62(1). 17–48.

Yeh, Ellen & Nicholas Swinehart. 2020. Testing the waters: Developing interlanguage pragmatics through exploration, experimentation, and participation in online communities. *CALICO Journal* 37(1). 66–84.

Yus, Francisco. 2010. *Ciberpragmática 2.0* (2nd ed.). Barcelona: Editorial Planeta.

Zhao, Helen & David Kaufer. 2013. DocuScope for genre analysis: Potential for assessing pragmatic functions in second language writing. In Naoko Taguchi & Julie M. Sykes (eds.), *Technology in interlanguage pragmatics*, 235–259. Amsterdam: John Benjamins.

Megan DiBartolomeo
11 Pragmalinguistic variation in L2 Spanish e-mail requests: Learner strategies and instructor perceptions

Abstract: This study focuses on pragmalinguistic variation in the e-mail requests of second-year Spanish second language (L2) learners and recipients' perception of these requests. The data come from a corpus of first language (L1) English (*n*=239) and L2 Spanish (*n*=239) e-mails. Requests were analyzed regarding level of directness as well as internal mitigation strategies in both languages. Twenty-six instructors of Spanish completed a 16-item questionnaire that examined the perception of requests with varying degrees of politeness. Results indicated that participants primarily use speaker-oriented requests regardless of the language and that they tend to use direct requests regardless of degree of imposition or language of the e-mail. Participants made more high imposition requests in L1 English and used more internal modification for high imposition requests in both languages. Indirect requests were rated as more polite than direct requests, and requests with no internal modification were perceived as significantly less polite than those with modification.

Keywords: computer-mediated communication, e-mail, L2 Spanish, requests, politeness

1 Introduction

The present study investigates pragmalinguistic variation in e-mail communication between US undergraduate students and their Spanish instructors in English and Spanish. It examines institutional discourse in a computer-mediated setting in place of face-to-face communication between the instructor and the student. E-mail communication is situated within the field of Computer Mediated Discourse (CMD), which branches from the broader field of computer-mediated communication and can be defined as "... the communication produced when human beings interact with one another by transmitting messages via networked or mobile computers..." (Herring and Androutsopoulos 2015: 127). E-mails in particular are asynchronous in nature and are one of the most frequent mediums through which students and their instructors communicate. Recent research in second language (L2) pragmatics has addressed the interface between the two fields for more

https://doi.org/10.1515/9783110721775-012

advanced speakers (e.g., Félix-Brasdefer 2012a; Sykes 2013), but little is known regarding lower-proficiency Spanish learners and e-mail discourse.

Previous research has investigated the linguistic strategies used during e-mail communication between L2 learners and their instructors in a variety of L2s (e.g., Economidou-Kogetsidis 2011; Félix-Brasdefer 2012a, 2012b; Krulatz 2013; Lee 2004). Learning to construct an e-mail in an L2 is not an easy feat and requires a great deal of both pragmalinguistic knowledge (i.e., knowledge of appropriate forms and their meanings) and sociopragmatic knowledge (i.e., awareness of when those forms are contextually appropriate) (e.g., Félix-Brasdefer 2012a: 90). Previous studies on e-mails in L2 Spanish have analyzed request type and level of imposition, greetings, e-politeness, internal modification, formal and informal features of e-mail discourse, and gender differences for more advanced learners (Félix-Brasdefer 2012a, 2012b), while L1 Spanish research has concentrated on native speaker (NS) greetings and closings (Bou-Franch 2011). Research on L2 Spanish requests more generally has been focused on either the classroom (e.g., Félix-Brasdefer 2007) or study abroad contexts (e.g., Shively 2011; Shively and Cohen 2008), hence, this study adds to the small but growing body of literature on L2 Spanish requests in CMD. This study contributes to the existing knowledge base of computer-mediated L2 Spanish communication at yet another institutional level. An analysis of request strategies used by lower proficiency learners helps determine what learners know in the early stages of their development, thus advancing our understanding of L2 Spanish pragmatics. The use of certain strategies, as well as how their use is perceived by others, also sheds light on where learners might benefit from further instruction.

2 Literature review

2.1 Requests in L2 e-mail communication

The literature on the production and perception of requests in student-instructor e-mail exchanges typically focuses on the type of request being made, the level of directness and degree of imposition of the request, and the internal and external modification of the request. For L2 Spanish in particular, the request perspective is an important feature of analysis. These features are outlined in the following sections.

2.1.1 Request type

The type of request made by learners is widely cited within the L2 e-mail literature as students contact their instructors for a range of reasons. Condon and Cech (1996) classified four main types of requests: requests for action (e.g., meeting, writing recommendations), validation (e.g., "The test is tomorrow, right?"), feedback (e.g., "Can you tell me what I need to improve?"), and information (e.g., "When are your office hours?"). Recent research on L2 e-mail requests has followed this framework (e.g., Economidou-Kogetsidis 2011; Félix-Brasdefer 2012a) or has defined additional categories of request types in the data (e.g., Economidou-Kogetsidis 2018). While Félix-Brasdefer (2012a) found all four request types in his corpus of L2 Spanish learners, Economidou-Kogetsidis (2011) investigated only requests for information and action in her study of Greek Cypriot university students' L2 English e-mails to their instructors. Lee (2004) found that Chinese learners of English contacted their instructors primarily with requests for assistance (e.g., writing letters of recommendation, correcting work). Economidou-Kogetsidis (2018) added a fifth category of requests for asking for an extension on an assignment. The requests analyzed in Chen (2001) concern appointments to meet with the professor for course-related advice, recommendations, and special accommodation from the professor (e.g., extensions).

2.1.2 Directness and degree of imposition

A number of studies focusing on learners of various L2s have arrived at similar conclusions regarding the level of directness of student-faculty e-mail requests in relation to the degree of imposition of the request. The degree of imposition refers to how big a request is, and is determined by the type of request being made. On a continuum of low to high imposition, the request types can be classified as follows: (1) request for information, (2) request for validation, (3) request for feedback, and (4) request for action (Félix-Brasdefer 2012a). Requests for feedback and action are classified as higher imposition in that they require action on the part of the instructor, whether it be time spent working on something on the student's behalf, or time spent with a student in a meeting, for example.

Blum-Kulka and Olshtain (1984) operationalize three levels of directness of the head act of a request. Direct requests are the most explicit, usually involving imperatives (e.g., *Give me your book*). Conventional indirectness (CI), which is considered a more polite type of request in many languages, such as English and Spanish, can be defined as "procedures that realize the act by reference to contextual preconditions necessary for its performance, as conventionalized in a given language" (p. 201). An example of CI in English might be the use of the conditional as in "*could you* pass the salt" or "*would you* open the door." The third level of directness, nonconventional indirectness (NCI), is the use of hints when realizing a request. Requests with NCI often make reference to the object that would cause the implementation of the act, such as, "Why is the window open?" or by relying on contextual clues, as in, "Wow, it's really cold in here" (p. 201). In many varieties of L1 Spanish, CI request strategies are preferred (Félix-Brasdefer 2005; Márquez Reiter 2000; Ruzickova 2007). Social distance has also been found to influence the request strategies used; CI strategies are more commonly used when there is greater social distance between the interlocutors and direct strategies are employed when there is less (Félix-Brasdefer 2005; Márquez Reiter 2000).

Previous work analyzing directness and degree of imposition generally concludes that L2 learners most commonly use direct and CI requests regardless of the L2 under investigation. Félix-Brasdefer (2012a) found that direct requests and CI requests are frequently observed when the same group of learners requests feedback in both L2 Spanish and L1 English, while CI tends to be produced more often in high-imposition requests. That author also found that *want statements* (e.g., I want to know my grade) were more common in the L2 data than in the L1 data. Similarly, Lee (2004) found that many of the L2 English request strategies employed by Chinese learners were mostly direct requests, which are most common in Chinese. In e-mails by Greek Cypriot L2 learners of English, direct request strategies were most common, especially in the case of requests for information. However, both direct (50.58%) and CI strategies (43.6%) were found in requests for action. In a later study, Economidou-Kogetsidis (2018) reported that most e-mail requests in her corpus of L2 English e-mails were high imposition requests, and that both low and high imposition requests were most often carried out with bald on record (direct) request strategies.

Research on the pragmatics of e-mails also has also compared L1 and L2 speakers of a language. Using a natural e-mail corpus, Biesenbach-Lucas (2007) analyzed how native (NS) and non-native (NNS) English-speaking graduate students made both high and low imposition requests to faculty at a large American university over a period of a few semesters. Most requests were realized through direct strategies and hints, while CI requests were not as common for either group. While the knowledge of culturally appropriate politeness strategies in e-mail communication was still developing for learners, this study found that English NSs tended to use a wider variety of politeness resources than their NNS peers. In another study concerning American and Taiwanese graduate students' e-mail requests to professors at an American university, Taiwanese students were observed to employ discourse strategies influenced by their own culture when writing e-mails in English (Chen 2001). E-mail requests collected via a written discourse completion task revealed that Chinese L2 learners of English most frequently produced direct and CI strategies, but that English majors used significantly more indirect strategies (Zhu 2012). Baron and Ortega (2018), who investigated the effects of age difference in e-requests among Catalan/Spanish L2 learners and English NSs, found that younger L2 English students (ages 18–20) provided more direct requests (explicit and hedge performatives) than their English NS counterparts when making a high imposition request to a professor, but that there were no significant differences for the older (ages 31–40) group. These studies allow us to see how the learners' L1 might influence their L2 requests, and how NSs might have a slight advantage over their NNS peers when it comes to politeness resources.

The identity of and relationship with the e-mail recipient also seems to have an effect on how learners form a request. In a study on e-mails addressed to NS and NNS (Chinese) English teachers, Lee (2004) discovered that direct requests and hints were used, but that learners tended to use more hedges and explicit performatives in their e-mails to Chinese English teachers. Chen (2001) also noted that the students differed in their strategy use based on their familiarity with the professor and how they perceived the power relation between themselves and the professor. Factors such as power and social distance may come into play when students write e-mails to their instructors, who may have varying backgrounds with regard to perceived age and gender. These factors, in turn, may influence the directness strategies learners use when communicating with their instructors.

2.1.3 Request modification

In addition to levels of directness and request perspective, external and internal modification has been widely studied in L2 requests. Internal modification refers to the syntactic or morphological differences in the requests realized, such as the use of the conditional tense, diminutives, or politeness markers (e.g., saying "please") (Félix-Brasdefer 2007). External modification refers to various supportive moves, such as preparators, sweeteners (e.g., "you have really nice handwriting, could I borrow your notes?"), grounders (indicating a reason for a request), or promises of reward (Blum-Kulka and Olshtain 1984; Félix-Brasdefer 2007). The present analysis only focuses on internal modification.

Research investigating the use of L2 request modification yields mixed results, with some work showing its use (e.g., Alcón-Soler 2015; Lee 2004; Zhu 2012) and other studies indicating less (or a lack of) modification on the part of L2 learners (e.g., Economidou-Kogetsidis 2011; Félix-Brasdefer 2012a). For instance,

Economidou-Kogetsidis (2011) found that Greek Cypriot university students did not use many lexical/phrasal downgraders, greetings, or closings in their L2 English e-mails. In contrast, Lee (2004) found that L1 Chinese students did employ syntactic downgraders or grounders before making a direct request in L2 English. Further, Chinese English majors (EM) used more syntactic mitigation and politeness devices than non-English majors (NEM) (Zhu 2012). NEM used "please" and "I hope" more than EM, while the latter produced "I wonder" more often. However, there were very few downtowners, understaters or hedgers from either group. Instruction has also been found to have effects on request modification. Alcón-Soler (2015) investigated the instruction of request mitigation during study abroad for L1 Spanish teenagers learning English. She collected student e-mails at four times during their time abroad and compared a control group with an experimental group who received consciousness-raising instruction on the formation of English e-mail requests. Alcón-Soler found that instruction contributed to a higher frequency of use of e-mail request mitigators for the experimental group, but that this result did not hold as time abroad increased.

Research on Spanish L2 e-mail request modification in particular shows less modification overall in learners' L2 Spanish than in their L1 English. Félix-Brasdefer (2012a) reported that lexical and syntactic modifiers were more common in L1 English requests (64.4%; n = 65/101) than in L2 Spanish requests (35.6%; n = 36 /101). Lexical modifiers were not frequent for either group (n = 34 total), but were even less common in L2 Spanish (29.4%; n = 10/34). Syntactic modifiers were more frequent in L1 English data (61%; 41/67) than L2 Spanish data. With regard to lexical modifiers, "please" and understaters were most frequent in L1 English, but *por favor* ('please') was also frequent in L2 Spanish. Combinations of syntactic modifiers were more common in L1 English in both low and high imposition requests. While L2 Spanish requests demonstrate a combination of both lexical and syntactic modifiers, they lack other sociopragmatic features which are important for an academic context (e.g., use of informal *tú* vs. formal *usted*, use of imperative form with *por favor*).

2.1.4 Request perspective

Request perspective, while not analyzed in previous work on L2 Spanish e-mail communication, is a common object of analysis for L2 Spanish requests in both classroom (Félix-Brasdefer 2007) and study abroad contexts (e.g., Bataller 2010; Czerwionka and Cuza 2017a, 2017b; Halenko and Jones 2017; Hernández 2016; Hernández and Boero 2018a, 2018b; Shively 2011; Shively and Cohen 2008). Understanding what learners do in these contexts can help explain their use of certain strategies over others in the CMD context. Request perspective (Blum-Kulka & Olshtain 1984) can be divided into the following four categories: hearer-oriented (e.g., "could *you* give me a pencil?"), speaker-oriented (e.g., "could *I* have a pencil?"), joint perspective (e.g., "can *we* clean the kitchen?"), and impersonal requests, where we often see the use of passives or "people/they/one" as neutral agents (e.g., "it would be great if everything *were cleaned up* before six o'clock"). In L1 Spanish, hearer-oriented requests are preferred (Marquez Reiter 2000).

Previous research shows that English-speaking L2 Spanish learners tend to favor speaker-oriented requests (e.g., Félix-Brasdefer 2007; Hernández 2016; Shively and Cohen 2008), although they have the ability to make the shift toward hearer-oriented requests as a result of study abroad itself (e.g., Czerwionka and Cuza 2017a, 2017b) or as a result of instruction during study abroad (e.g., Hernández and Boero 2018a, 2018b; Shively 2011). However, the results are somewhat mixed. For instance, Shively and Cohen (2008) observed that learners produced hearer-oriented strategies less frequently than native speakers, used speaker-oriented and impersonal perspectives more frequently than natives, and did not change much after spending a semester abroad in a Spanish-speaking country. Similarly, Hernández (2016) analyzed L2 Spanish requests during a short-term study abroad program in Spain and found that learners still preferred speaker-oriented requests after study abroad. In contrast, Czerwionka and Cuza (2017a, 2017b) reported that learners did shift from speaker to hearer-oriented perspective as a result of short-term study abroad, and Shively (2011) found that instruction was effective in increasing learners' use of hearer-oriented strategies after a semester abroad. Studies by Hernández and Boero (2018a, 2018b) also demonstrated an increased use of hearer-oriented strategies after four-week programs in Argentina and Spain. This research shows that while English-speaking Spanish learners tend to favor speaker-oriented requests, they can shift to hearer-oriented requests after instruction and time spent abroad. While these findings do not directly apply to L2 requests in a CMD context, they are relevant in that they can help explain learners' use of requests in that setting.

2.2 Politeness perception in L2 e-mail communication

While the appropriate use of request strategies may be difficult for learners to achieve, the way in which their requests are perceived by their instructors also presents a challenge. There are many factors that influence the politeness of student e-mails, including but not limited to linguistic mitigation strategies, the form of address that is chosen, or even the greeting (or lack thereof). Notions of positive and negative politeness (Brown and Levinson 1987) come into play, as do considerations of a hierarchical system of politeness (Scollon and Scollon 2001), in which higher levels of deference and mitigation are expected of the student when communicating with their instructor.

Much research on L2 e-mail perception investigates instructor perception. Hartford and Bardovi-Harlig (1996) explored the perceptions of the faculty member recipient (and non-recipient faculty members) toward the e-mail requests made by their NS and NNS English students. The perception instrument tested whether the e-mail request positively or negatively affected the faculty recipient. The authors found that the requests that were negatively perceived often had a greater degree of obligation on the faculty member's part to fulfill the student's request. The positively perceived e-mails were often very different from the negatively perceived e-mails in terms of formality. Similarly, Economidou-Kogetsidis (2011) used a perception questionnaire (a 5-point Likert scale in terms of politeness and abruptness of the messages) in order to determine how instructors perceived certain request strategies used by Greek Cypriot learners of English. The questionnaire was administered online and was based on six e-mail messages. Results demonstrated that some direct and unmodified student e-mails were perceived to be significantly more impolite or abrupt than others. In an analysis of instructor perceptions of Korean L2 English learners' e-mail requests, Shim (2013) found that e-mails lacking politeness strategies were negatively perceived by faculty. More specifically, the author found that the format, linguistic forms, and content of the e-mails all contributed to instructors' negative perceptions. This research shows that overall formality, the imposition of the request itself, and the level of the directness all affect instructor perceptions of e-requests.

Additional research in e-mail perception focuses on the perceived personality of the sender and faculty motivation to work with students based on the politeness of their e-mails. Hendriks (2010) examined the perceived politeness of e-mail requests of Dutch learners of English based on the use (or lack thereof) of syntactic and lexical modifications. The study utilized a perception task and asked native English speakers to rate the comprehensibility and personality dimensions of the writer of the e-mail. The author found that when the sender used few request modifications (lexical and syntactic), there was a negative effect on raters' evaluation of the personality of the writer. In a similar study, Economidou-Kogetsidis (2016) analyzed direct and unmodified L2 English student e-mails to faculty and whether or not these e-mails had a negative effect on the perceived personality of the student sender. The author found that NS faculty rated the personality of the e-mail senders as significantly less favorable than a group of L2 learners did. They also rated the e-mails themselves as significantly less polite than learners did. This research sheds light on learners' lack of awareness of appropriate language use in the L2, and the necessity of this knowledge in order to have successful relationships with their instructors. In a similar vein, Bolkan and Holmgren (2012) analyzed L1 e-mail requests with constructed e-mail data and found that instructors were more motivated to work with students and felt they were more competent when their requests included politeness strategies. This research suggests that the use of politeness strategies plays a role beyond simply influencing a positive or negative perception of an e-mail in that it also has implications for perceived personality, and even the opportunities a student may be offered during their academic career.

While comparisons between NS and NNS instructor perception of pragmatics is not one that has been directly taken into consideration in previous research, it is worth exploring, as both groups may approach pragmatics differently in the classroom with regard to what is taught and how much instruction learners receive (Cohen 2018). In a survey regarding NS and NNS coverage of pragmatics in the language classroom, 21% of NNS instructors surveyed provided extensive coverage of making requests in the L2, while only 17% of NS instructors did the same. Additionally, NNS instructors felt significantly less comfortable than NS instructors regarding their knowledge about the language and sociocultural contexts. While NNSs and NSs each have unique advantages teaching pragmatics in the FL classroom (e.g., García 2005; Kidd 2016), both instructor populations draw mainly on their own experiences when it comes to knowledge of pragmatic norms and what they choose to present in their own teaching. This may also affect instructors' perception of how learners speak and what they consider to be (im)polite communication.

Overall formality of the e-mail, level of directness of the request, and the level of imposition of the request have all been found to have an effect on the perceived politeness of e-mails from students to faculty. Furthermore, these strategies may influence how the students' personalities are perceived, and even the extent to which instructors wish to work closely with these students. This research into perception shows that e-politeness may have implications for student success that extend further than the moment of the e-mail exchange itself.

The present study adds to the existing research on L2 e-mail communication in Spanish by analyzing lower proficiency learners, as previous work has focused on advanced learners of Spanish (Félix-Brasdefer 2012a). The analysis of lower level learners will allow for a more robust description of Spanish learners request forms in a computer mediated context. While most perception studies either ask students to rate e-mails (e.g., Pan 2012) or ask faculty or NSs about their perceptions of e-mails (e.g., Hartford and Bardovi-Harlig 1996; Economidou-Kogetsidis 2011; Hendriks 2010), previous studies have not considered differences in perception between NS and NNS instructors of the target language of the e-mails. The present study explores this topic and addresses the following research questions:

1. When communicating via e-mail with their instructors in English and Spanish, which request types and request perspectives are present in learners' e-mails?
    a. How do learners navigate level of directness when making e-requests?
    b. How is their use of internal modification different for requests of differing levels of imposition?
2. How do both native and non-native instructors perceive these e-requests, and how do factors such as level of directness, degree of imposition, and request modification affect perception?

3 Method

3.1 Participants

A total of 24 native and non-native Spanish-speaking graduate student instructors of L2 Spanish provided instructor-student exchanges for the e-mail corpus. There were a total of 26 participants in the perception portion of this study. All participants were graduate student instructors of L2 Spanish at the same university where the e-mail data was collected. Table 1 provides a visual description of perception task participant characteristics.

Table 1: Perception task participant characteristics.

	Gender		Age (in years)		Native Language	
Male	14 (54%)	21–29	22 (85%)	Spanish	7 (27%)
Female	12 (46%)	30–39	3 (12%)	English	19 (73%)
		40–49	1 (4%)		

Total participants: n = 26.

3.2 Data collection

3.2.1 E-mail corpus

A natural corpus of e-mail correspondences between Spanish instructors and their second-year undergraduate students[1] was collected at a large public university in the Midwestern US over the course of four semesters. The participating instructors (n=24), a group comprised of both native and non-native Spanish speakers, were contacted via e-mail and asked to share English and Spanish e-mail conversations they had recently had with their students. Not all e-mails shared contained requests; only those with requests were analyzed. Instructors were asked to send the text of the e-mail without names, e-mail addresses, or any other identifying information in order to ensure anonymity of both the students and themselves. A total of 517 e-mails containing student-initiated requests were collected. Out of 517 e-mail exchanges, only 239 requests were realized in Spanish. A total of 239 English requests were chosen at random from the corpus and were analyzed along with the 239 Spanish requests in order to ensure that the data would be comparable. In the present study, a total of 478 e-mails were analyzed.

3.2.2 Perception task

A questionnaire was used to determine how instructors of Spanish perceived the politeness of student e-mails from the corpus. This questionnaire was modeled after those employed in Economidou-Kogetsidis (2011) and Alcón-Soler (2013). The questionnaire consisted of 16 example e-mails from the Spanish portion of the corpus analyzed in the present study. Instructor participants were asked to rate each e-mail message on a 5-point Likert scale based on their perception of how polite or impolite the e-mail request was (1 being very impolite – 5 very polite). Figure 1 shows an example of one of the items in the questionnaire used in this study. The e-mail request shown in Figure 1 is taken from the L2 Spanish data and can be translated as: "Miss, when do you have time (you-informal T) to meet with me [error in Spanish] this week? I have class until 4:35 tomorrow and until 11 on Friday . . . I appreciate you!!".

---

[1] These students are second-year learners, which is considered intermediate at the institution where they study. For this reason, additional proficiency measures were not taken.

Señorita, cuando tienes tiempo para conocer conmiga esta semana? Tengo clase hasta 4:35 mañana y hasta 11 en viernes...te aprecio!!					
Esta petición es:	muy descortés	descortés	neutral	cortés	muy cortés
	1	2	3	4	5
¿Por qué la calificaste así?					

Figure 1: Example of questionnaire item.

Each of the e-mails included in the perception questionnaire was selected from the present corpus to represent a balanced distribution of varying directness levels, degrees of imposition and presence or absence of internal modification. In total, 8 of the e-mails contained direct requests and 8 contained CI or NCI requests.[2] For each level of directness, two e-mail requests with a high degree of imposition and two with a low degree of imposition were selected. Furthermore, each of these combinations included an e-mail request with internal modification and one without internal modification. The student e-mails were not altered in terms of spelling or grammar, and the participants were informed of this upon beginning the questionnaire. The request was underlined, and participants were asked to focus on the underlined portion of the e-mail when giving their rating. The entire e-mail was provided in each example in order to maintain the context of the request. Participants were also asked to write a short justification for why they rated each e-mail as they did. In addition to determining the overall frequency of politeness ratings based on the aforementioned variables, results of native vs. non-native instructors were also compared in order to see whether or not their perceptions differed.

3.3 Analysis

The data were first coded based on the level of directness of the request head act using the Cross-Cultural Speech Act Realization Project (CCSARP) segmentation and coding system proposed in Blum-Kulka and Olshtain (1984). Below is a table of the CCSARP directness levels, request strategies, and examples from the corpus.

---

[2] CI and NCI requests were combined for the purposes of the perception task data analysis due to the low frequency of indirect requests found in the present corpus.

Table 2: Request strategies used to analyze the e-mail request data.

CCSARP directness levels	Request strategies	Examples
Direct	Imperatives	Please <u>let me know</u> what I should do from here.
	Performatives	<u>I'm pretty much begging</u> you to let me take my test at either an earlier or later date or time that day.
	Want statements	<u>I want you to</u> meet with me.
	Need statements	<u>I need you to</u> tell me my grade on the exam so I can determine how to move forward.
	Direct questions	Is there another time you can meet with me?
	Like/appreciate statements	<u>I would appreciate if</u> you could forward me the information.
	Expectation statements	*<u>Espero que sea</u> possible recibir crédito* ('<u>I hope it's possible</u> to receive credit.')
Conventionally indirect	Query preparatory (ability, willingness, permission)	<u>Would I be able to</u> take my exam on Wednesday at this time instead?
Non-conventional indirectness	Hint	You told me to let you know if there was a problem. I just checked and there aren't any grades there [online]. Thanks.

The request types analyzed in the present study follow Economidou-Kogetsidis (2011) and include requests for action (e.g., meeting, writing recommendations), requests for validation (e.g., "The test is tomorrow, right?"), requests for feedback (e.g., "Can you tell me what I need to improve?"), and requests for information (e.g., "When are your office hours?"). With regard to degree of imposition, the request type determined the rating of "high" or "low" and was modeled after the continuous rating system used in Félix-Brasdefer (2012a). For the purposes of his study, the following request types were rated from low to high imposition: (1) request for information, (2) request for validation, (3) request for feedback, and (4) request for action. Instead of a continuum, the present study follows Chen (2001) and analyzes imposition as a binary factor (low: request types 1 and 2; high: request types 3 and 4).

The internal modifications analyzed in the present study were split into two categories, following Blum Kulka, House, and Kasper (1989): (1) lexical modifiers, and (2) syntactic modifiers. Table 3 shows the division of internal modification strategies with examples from the corpus.

Table 3: Internal modifications used in the analysis of e-mail requests.

Internal modifications	Strategies	Example
Lexical modifiers	Consultative devices (do you think, is there any chance, do you mind)	Is there any way I could meet with you to discuss the exam?
	Please	*Por favor* ('please')
	Downtoners (possibly, perhaps, maybe)	Could we maybe meet this Friday?
	Understaters (a bit, just, a little)	I wanted to know if it's okay if I leave class a little early tomorrow.
Syntactic modifiers	Conditional	Could we talk about it after class?
	Past tense	I was wondering . . .
	Embedded 'if' clause	I would appreciate it if . . .
	Combination (two or more syntactic modifiers)	I was wondering if I could set up an appointment.

Lastly, the data were coded for request perspective, as established in Blum Kulka and Olshtain (1984). Table 4 outlines how the data was analyzed based on the perspective of the request and shows examples of each request perspective as found in the present corpus.

Table 4: Request perspectives analyzed in e-mail requests.

Request perspective	Example
Speaker-oriented	Is there another way I can see my score?
Hearer-oriented	*¿Me puede enviar su dirección de correo?* ('Can you (formal) send me his/her e-mail address?')
Joint perspective	Can we meet during your office hours?
Impersonal	*¿Hay alguna otra manera de comentar en el sitio [web]?* ('Is there another way of commenting on the website?')

To summarize, I first conducted a quantitative analysis of the level of directness, request perspective, degree of imposition, and specific types of internal modifiers used by learners in the e-mail request. Second, I used a perception questionnaire in order to determine overall politeness perception and native and non-native instructors' perceptions of the politeness of learner request strategies in e-mail communication. The perception questionnaire was analyzed in IBM SPSS 24 using a linear regression model to determine whether there were significant differences in perception between native and non-native speaking Spanish instructors.

4 Results

4.1 Description of Spanish and English e-mail requests

Research question 1 addresses the distribution of request types, request perspective, level of directness and use of internal modification found in the e-mail corpus. Tables 5 and 6 present an overall distribution of e-mail request types and perspectives for L1 English and L2 Spanish e-mail requests.

Table 5: Overall distribution of e-mail request types by degree of imposition.

		L1 English	L2 Spanish
Type of Request	Action	91 (38%)	56 (24%)
	Information	61 (26%)	122 (51%)
	Feedback	53 (22%)	29 (12%)
	Validation	34 (14%)	32 (13%)
	Total	*239 (100%)*	*239 (100%)*

Table 6: Request perspective.

		L1 English	L2 Spanish
Request perspective	Speaker-oriented	105 (44%)	148 (62%)
	Hearer-oriented	73 (31%)	34 (14%)
	Joint perspective	20 (8%)	13 (6%)
	Impersonal	41 (17%)	44 (18%)
	Total	*239 (100%)*	*239 (100%)*

Concerning request type, the vast majority of the L1 English and L2 Spanish requests analyzed were requests for action (English: 38%, n= 91; Spanish: 24%, n= 56) or information (English: 26%, n= 61; Spanish: 51%, n= 122). Requests for action generally involved the learner asking if they could meet with the instructor (e.g., *¿Es posible quedar esta semana?* 'Is it possible to meet this week?'), and these high imposition requests were primarily carried out in L1 English. Requests for information involved asking about homework assignments or the number of days the student had missed so far that semester (e.g., *¿Sabes cuantos días he perdido?* 'Do you know how many days I've missed?') and these low imposition requests were primarily carried out in L2 Spanish. Requests for feedback (high imposition) were the next most common request type found in the corpus, albeit more common in English (22%, n= 53) than in Spanish (12%, n= 29) (e.g., *¿Puedes checar mi asignación?* 'Can you check my assignment?'). Lastly, requests for validation (low imposition) were the least frequent request type for English (14%, n= 34), and showed a similar distribution with requests for validation in Spanish (13%, n= 32) (e.g., "Our test is on Friday, right?").

With regard to request perspective, in both L1 English and L2 Spanish requests, speaker-oriented requests were the most common form in the present corpus (English: 44%, n= 105; Spanish: 62%, n= 148) (e.g. *¿Puedo tener una reunión contigo?* 'Can I have a meeting with you?'). Hearer-oriented requests were the second most common request perspective (English: 31%, n= 73; Spanish: 14%, n= 34) (e.g., *¿Me puedes decir cuándo es la prueba?* 'Can you tell me when the quiz is?') followed by impersonal requests (English: 17%, n= 41; Spanish: 18%, n= 44) (e.g., "Is there another way to access the study guide?"). Joint perspective requests were the least common request perspective used by learners in this corpus, forming 8% (n= 20) of the English e-mail requests and 6% (n= 13) of the Spanish data (e.g., *¿Podemos reunirnos pronto?* 'Can we meet soon?').

In order to explore another part of the first research question, the directness of the head act in the student e-mail requests in this corpus were analyzed. As is seen in Table 7, the majority of the requests realized by L2 Spanish students, be it in L1 English or L2 Spanish, were direct requests, specifically direct questions. In the students' L1 English, the corpus showed 46% (n= 111) direct requests, while in L2 Spanish, 72% (n= 173) of requests were direct. Following direct requests were CI requests (English: 40%, n= 96; Spanish: 21%, n= 49) and finally NCI requests (English: 14%, n= 32; Spanish: 7%, n= 17). Example 1 shows the characteristics of a direct request from the corpus, example 2 shows a CI request, and example 3 shows an NCI request:

Table 7: Directness of the head act in e-mail requests.

CCSARP directness levels	Request strategies	L1 English	L2 Spanish
Direct	Imperatives	7 (6%)	23 (13%)
	Performatives	14 (13%)	9 (5%)
	Want statements	6 (5%)	9 (5%)
	Need statements	5 (5%)	12 (7%)
	Direct questions	47 (42%)	103 (60%)
	Like/appreciate statements	25 (23%)	6 (4%)
	Expectation statements	7 (6%)	11 (6%)
	Total Direct Requests	*111 (46%)*	*173 (72%)*
Conventionally indirect	Query preparatory (ability, willingness, permission)	96 (40%)	49 (21%)
	Total CI Requests	*96 (40%)*	*49 (21%)*
Non-conventional indirectness	Hint	32 (14%)	17 (7%)
	Total NCI Requests:	*32 (14%)*	*17 (7%)*
	Total	239 (100%)	239 (100%)

(1) *¿Cuántas ausencias tengo?* 'How many absences do I have?'

(2) <u>I was wondering if I could set up an office hour appointment</u>, the office hour of 2:30–3:30 is actually during the time of one of my other classes.

(3) Hola I looked at my grades and it said my course grade was an XX and my adjusted course grade. <u>im confused as to what is my actual grade or what is actually going on</u>

The amount of NCI requests in the corpus may be attributed to the fact that the instructors of these second-year Spanish courses were all graduate students whom the learners may not have viewed as being socially distant or more powerful than themselves. However, that is outside the scope of the present study.

Lastly, the use of internal modifications based on the degree of imposition of the request was analyzed. It is worth noting that there were more high imposition requests in the L1 English data (59%, n= 141) than in the L2 Spanish data (n= 70, 29%), and more internal modification was used overall in English (75%) than in Spanish (60%). The L1 English data contained 41% (n=98) low imposition requests and the L2 Spanish data consisted of 71% (n=169) low imposition requests. Results were categorized by lexical and syntactic modifiers as well as by degree of imposition.

Table 8: Internal modifications based on degree of imposition – English e-mails.

Internal modifications	Strategies	Low Imposition	High Imposition
Lexical modifiers	Consultative devices (do you think, is there any chance, do you mind)	12 (13%)	25 (18%)
	Please	8 (8%)	7 (5%)
	Downtoners (possibly, perhaps, maybe)	6 (6%)	14 (10%)
	Understaters (a bit, just, a little)	9 (9%)	7 (5%)
Syntactic modifiers	Conditional	4 (4%)	19 (13%)
	Past tense	9 (9%)	10 (7%)
	Embedded 'if' clause	3 (3%)	11 (8%)
	Combination (two or more syntactic modifiers)	5 (5%)	30 (21%)
No internal modification		42 (43%)	18 (13%)
	Total	98 (100%)	141 (100%)
		n = 239	

As Tables 8 and 9 illustrate, these learners demonstrated more internal modification when making a high imposition request as opposed to a low imposition request. 87% of English and 66% of Spanish high imposition requests had internal modification, while only 57% of both English and Spanish low imposition requests had internal modification. One of the most common internal modification strategies seen in the data was the use of consultative devices, which were more commonly found in high imposition requests in English (18%, n= 25) than in low imposition requests in Spanish (9%, n= 16). Another common strategy seen in the corpus, particularly in the English data, was the combination of two or more syntactic modifiers (e.g., conditional and past tense) and can been seen in the following example from the English corpus:

(4)   I was hoping I could see my grade from the last exam.

There were 28 total instances of the use of the conditional tense as a syntactic modifier in high imposition requests across both the Spanish and English data, but only 16 instances in low imposition requests. The combination of request strategies was more commonly used by this group of learners when making

Table 9: Internal modifications based on degree of imposition – Spanish e-mails.

Internal modifications	Strategies	Low Imposition	High Imposition
Lexical modifiers	Consultative devices (do you think, is there any chance, do you mind)	16 (9%)	3 (4%)
	Please	21 (12%)	11 (16%)
	Downtoners (possibly, perhaps, maybe)	11 (7%)	8 (11%)
	Understaters (a bit, just, a little)	18 (11%)	7 (10%)
Syntactic modifiers	Conditional	12 (7%)	9 (13%)
	Past tense	7 (4%)	3 (4%)
	Embedded 'if' clause	5 (3%)	0 (0%)
	Combination (two or more syntactic modifiers)	7 (4%)	5 (8%)
No internal modification		72 (43%)	24 (34%)
	Total	169 (100%)	70 (100%)
		n = 239	

high imposition requests than when making low imposition requests. There were very few instances of the conditional and past tenses or embedded "if" clauses found in the Spanish data when compared with the English data, which could be due to the fact that these concepts are introduced during the second year of Spanish and students may not had been exposed to them at the time the e-mail requests were sent to their instructors.

4.2 Instructor perceptions of e-mail requests

The second research question concerned the differences in the perceptions of native and non-native instructors with regard to politeness or abruptness of the request strategies presented in the data. The average values for native and non-native speakers of Spanish were recorded based on the ratings of a 5-point

Likert scale (1: very impolite – 5: very polite). There were 16 Spanish requests included in the questionnaire, and 26 instructor participants rated these requests, thus a total of 416 items were analyzed. Table 10 shows the average ratings for all participants (regardless of their native language) based on level of directness of the head act, degree of imposition, and presence or absence of internal modification.

Table 10: Perception scores for L2 Spanish instructors (n = 26).

	Average rating (1–5 scale)
Direct requests	3.17
CI/NCI requests	3.41
High imposition requests	3.28
Low imposition requests	3.32
Requests with internal modification	3.67
Requests without internal modification	2.93

Overall mean for requests ratings for all participants: 3.29

As is seen in Table 10, on average, all participants rated CI or NCI requests as more polite (3.41) than direct requests (3.17). Low imposition requests were rated as more polite (3.32) than high imposition requests (3.28) although the average ratings are very similar for this variable. Finally, requests with internal modification were generally rated as more polite (3.67) than requests without internal modification (2.93). Table 11 shows the average ratings for the same three variables with the participants divided by native language.

As is seen in Table 11, there were some differences between native English speakers and native Spanish speakers with regard to their ratings. On average, native Spanish speakers tended to rate direct requests as more polite (3.25) than their native English-speaking counterparts (3.17). However, they also rated CI and NCI requests as being slightly more polite (3.48) than the English speakers (3.39). Results from the linear regression analysis show no significant difference in average rating for either group based on the degree of imposition of the request (English instructors: $p = .974$, Spanish instructors: $p = .792$) or level of directness of the request (English instructors: $p = .521$, Spanish instructors: $p = .435$), but both instructor groups rated requests with internal modification as significantly more polite than requests without internal modification ($p < .05$).

Participants were also required to explain why they rated each e-mail request as they did. Qualitative results show that the native English speakers

Table 11: Perception scores for native (*n* = 7) vs. non-native (*n* = 19) L2 Spanish instructors.

	Native Spanish speakers	Native English speakers
Direct requests	3.25	3.17
CI/NCI requests	3.48	3.39
High imposition requests	3.30	3.28
Low imposition requests	3.42	3.28
Requests with internal modification	3.76	3.63
Requests without internal modification	2.96	2.92

tended to be more concerned with grammar and spelling than did the native Spanish speakers. This observation may help explain why the native English speakers' overall politeness ratings were slightly lower than those of the native Spanish speakers, as many of the e-mails had a variety of spelling errors and grammatical issues. These issues can be categorized within the formality of the e-mail. The following is an example from the e-mail corpus:

(5) *Señorita, cuando tienes tiempo para conocer conmiga este semana? Tengo clase hasta 4:35 mañana y hasta 11 en viernes. . .te aprecio!!*
'Miss, when do you have time to meet with me this week? I have class until 4:35 tomorrow and until 11 on Friday. . .I appreciate it [you]'

A native English-speaking participant who gave this request a rating of 2 (impolite) stated that "there is no example of formal structure." Another participant who rated this as a 1 (very impolite) states that ". . . this reads like a text message and it seems that the student did not do a spell check before hitting 'send.'" Based on these comments, it is clear that proper spelling and grammar (i.e., formality) were important to non-native Spanish speaking instructors. This does not seem to be the case, however, for native Spanish-speaking instructors. Based on their comments for the same item, the main concerns regarding the politeness of the request seemed to be the use of the informal *tú* instead of the formal *usted*. Additionally, for a variety of items, the native Spanish-speaking instructors often commented that they felt or understood that the impoliteness of the e-mail was not intentional and that it came across that way simply because the student lacked sufficient skills in Spanish to be able to make the request in a way that would be considered polite if it were a native speaker making that request.

In sum, the majority of the comments for the less politely-rated items concerned formality of the e-mail, followed by lack of sociopragmatic knowledge (forms of address), and lack of knowledge of class structure in general. Many instructors commented that they felt the request was rude simply because it concerned something the student should be able to find out by looking at the syllabus, such as the date and time of their final exam or what the homework is for a given evening.

5 Discussion

With regard to e-request production, there was a preference of second year L2 Spanish students toward making e-mail requests primarily for information and action in both their L1 English and L2 Spanish. However, they tended to make high imposition requests in L1 English and low imposition requests in L2 Spanish. The results also showed that the majority of requests were speaker-oriented in both the L1 and the L2. In terms of the level of directness of the requests, this group of second-year Spanish students tended to use direct requests, specifically direct questions, when making e-mail requests in either language. Additionally, when making high imposition requests, CI request strategies were common. In terms of the effect of degree of imposition on the use of internal modifications in the corpus, both lexical and syntactic modifiers were preferred when making high imposition requests as opposed to low imposition requests in both L1 English and L2 Spanish. However, that modification was more frequent overall in L1 English than in L2 Spanish. It was also found that the combination of two or more syntactic modifiers was frequent when making requests with a high degree of imposition, particularly in the L1 English data.

The results of this study are consistent with those of previous studies on L2 Spanish e-mail requests. Félix-Brasdefer (2012a) found that when making requests via e-mail, direct requests are most frequent, although CI is frequently used when requesting feedback in both L2 Spanish and L1 English requests. Since a request for feedback is considered a higher imposition request, this finding is reflected in the current study in that CI requests were common for high imposition requests. It is important to note that CI requests are preferred in L1 Spanish and are more commonly used when there is greater social distance between the interlocutors

(Félix-Brasdefer 2005; Márquez Reiter 2000; Ruzickova 2007), so learners in the present study do not seem to approximate native-like norms.

The learners in the present study patterned similarly to those investigated in previous research on L2 Spanish and L2 English (Biesenbach-Lucas 2007; Economidou-Kogetsidis 2011, 2018; Lee 2004; Zhu 2012) in their preference for direct requests. In this case, their tendency toward directness may indicate that they do not recognize their instructors as interlocutors with whom they have a great degree of social distance. The instructors in this study were graduate students whose perceived age might not be much older than that of the learners themselves. Lee (2004) and Chen (2001) found that L2 English learners changed their request strategies depending on the perceived power relation with the professor, so although it is not directly addressed in the present study, differences of social power and distance could play a role in the learners' choice of request strategy. The directness and lack of CI requests in this corpus could also be related to the fact that learner sociopragmatic production is constrained by the L2 grammar (Pinto 2005), and thus learners at this level cannot produce a CI request. They may recognize that they should use a CI request when communicating with their instructors, but their Spanish grammar may not yet be sophisticated enough to form a request of that nature. Lastly, these learners preferred to make high imposition requests in the L1 and low imposition requests in the L2. This could also be related to the constraints of the L2 grammar and/or to whether the learners felt that a potential mistake in the L2 request could affect the chances of a high imposition request being fulfilled by the instructor.

Additionally, the learner participants in this study primarily produced speaker-oriented requests in both their English and Spanish e-mails. This result is corroborated by much of the previous literature on L2 Spanish requests in study abroad and face-to-face classroom settings (e.g., Félix-Brasdefer 2007; Hernández 2016; Shively and Cohen 2008). Therefore, regardless of setting or medium of communication, Spanish learners seem to prefer speaker-oriented requests in their second language. While this request perspective is more common in English, NSs of Spanish more commonly employ hearer-oriented requests (Marquez Reiter 2000), so it seems learners are transferring their English request strategies into the L2 when communicating via e-mail. The use of L1 discourse strategies in L2 e-mails has also been found for L2 English (Chen 2001).

Regarding internal modification, learners in the present study tended to employ lexical and syntactic modifiers when making high imposition requests in both L1 English and L2 Spanish, and produced more modification in L1 English than in L2 Spanish. The combination of two or more syntactic modifiers was frequent in L1 English when making high imposition requests. These results are in line with those of the learners' more advanced counterparts. Félix-Brasdefer (2012a) also found less overall modification in L2 Spanish e-requests and that the combination of syntactic modifiers was more common in L1 English requests. Learners in the present study showed a preference for using *por favor* as a syntactic modifier, as do their more advanced peers. Developmentally speaking, the learners at both institutional levels seem to perform similarly with regard to e-request making. Further, Economidou-Kogetsidis (2011) found that students did not use many lexical/phrasal downgraders in their L2 English e-mails, which is also true of the present corpus, as the majority of modification was seen in L1 English e-mails. This shows that the lack of internal modification in L2 Spanish e-requests holds true for L2 English as well, and therefore this finding may not be limited to L1 English speakers learning Spanish. Alcón-Soler (2015) highlighted that consciousness-raising instruction was beneficial for the development of request modification for L2 English speakers, so the infrequent use of modification we see in L2 Spanish e-requests could be improved with more formal instruction on the topic.

With regard to perception, all instructor participants rated CI or NCI requests as more polite than direct requests and requests with internal modification were rated as more polite than requests without it, although these results were not found to be statistically significant. There were few differences between native and non-native instructors, but both groups rated requests with internal modification as significantly more polite than requests without it. On average, native Spanish-speaking instructors rated all types of requests as more polite than non-native instructors, but this result was not found to be significant. Qualitative results demonstrated concerns with the formality of the e-mail requests and a lack of sociopragmatic knowledge.

The perception results for the current study are generally in line with those in the literature. Previous research cites formality as a factor that influences instructor perception of student e-mails in L2 English (e. g., Hartford and Bardovi-Harlig 1996; Economidou-Kogetsidis 2011, 2016; Shim 2013). Economidou-Kogetsidis (2011) found that direct and unmodified L2 English student e-mails were perceived as more impolite or abrupt than others. Similarly, the instructors in the present study rated direct requests as more impolite than other types. These results are in line with Hendriks (2010) in that when an e-mail contained few request modifications (lexical and syntactic), there was a negative effect on raters' evaluation of the e-mail for both native and non-native Spanish speakers. Trends for e-politeness perception in L2 Spanish follow those of other L2s, such as English, demonstrating that formality and the use of request modification appears to be cross-linguistically important. Instruction of these factors in a more formal setting might help learners give a better virtual impression of themselves, which may, in turn, be important for the students' academic careers (e.g., Bolkan and Holmgren 2012).

While the differences between NS and NNS instructors were generally insignificant, there were some comments made in the qualitative results that demonstrate differences between the two groups. As detailed in the previous section, many NNS instructors were concerned with spelling and grammar and overall formality of the e-mail, while NSs were more concerned with issues of sociopragmatic competence (e.g., appropriate use of forms of address). NSs were more forgiving of learners for their grammatical errors and stated that they understood that the learners might not have the grammar needed to form a more polite request in Spanish. As Cohen (2018) suggested, NNS instructors may feel less comfortable with their knowledge about the language and sociocultural contexts, so it may be that these NNS instructors were focusing on what they were comfortable with when making a judgment on the learner e-mails: spelling, grammar and formal writing as tools to aid in politeness. If most instructors focus on their own experiences when it comes to their knowledge of pragmatics, that would mean that their perceptions of learner pragmatic competence is also based on their own experience. Therefore, native Spanish-speaking instructors with arguably more experience with target cultures might focus more on sociopragmatic competence, while NNS instructors might focus more on pragmalinguistics or formality.

6 Conclusion

This study adds to the body of literature on L2 Spanish requests by addressing this speech act in e-mail communication between second year Spanish learners and their instructors. The results of the current study are in line with previous research on L2 e-mail communication (e.g., Félix-Brasdefer 2012a; Economidou-Kogetsidis 2011, 2016; Shim 2013) and add an additional institutional level to the literature on L2 Spanish e-mail communication, thus contributing to a more robust description of L2 Spanish requests in general. The qualitative portion of the perception task demonstrated that while NNS instructors are more attentive to issues of formality in learner e-mails than are NS instructors, NS instructors might be more perceptive of sociopragmatic features and allow them to influence their politeness ratings. Additionally, regardless of native language, all instructors rated e-mails with internal modification as significantly more polite than e-mails without internal modification, demonstrating that request modification plays an important role in politeness perception. Request modification could be incorporated into classroom instruction in order to assist learners in projecting a more pragmatically competent virtual image of themselves, which could help them not only in terms of interpersonal communication, but also with regard to their academic careers. Results of the present study are similar to those found for L2 Spanish requests in classroom and study abroad contexts, but they contribute to a greater understanding of the digital context in which today's language learners are immersed.

References

Alcón Soler, Eva. 2013. Mitigating e-mail requests in teenagers' first and second language academic cyber-consultation. *Multilingua* 32(6). 779–799.

Alcón-Soler, Eva. 2015. Instruction and pragmatic change during study abroad email communication. *Innovation in Language Learning and Teaching* 9(1). 34–45.

Bataller, Rebecca. 2010. Making a request for a service in Spanish: Pragmatic development in the study abroad setting. *Foreign Language Annals* 43(1). 160–175.

Barón, Júlia & Mireia Ortega. 2018. Investigating age differences in e-mail pragmatic performance. *System* 78. 148–158.

Biesenbach-Lucas, Sigrun. 2007. Students writing e-mails to faculty: An examination of e-politeness among native and non-native speakers of English. *Language Learning & Technology* 11(2). 59–81.

Blum-Kulka, Shoshana, Juliane House, & Gabriele Kasper. 1989. *Cross-cultural pragmatics: Requests and apologies* (vol. 31). New York: Ablex.

Blum-Kulka, Shoshana & Elite Olshtain. 1984. Requests and Apologies: A cross-cultural study of speech act realization patterns (CCSARP). *Applied Linguistics* 5(3). 196–213.

Bolkan, San & Jennifer L. Holmgren. 2012. "You are such a great teacher and I hate to bother you but . . .": Instructors' perceptions of students and their use of email messages with varying politeness strategies. *Communication Education* 61(3). 253–270.

Bou-Franch, Patricia. 2011. Openings and closings in Spanish e-mail conversations. *Journal of Pragmatics* 43(6). 1772–1785.

Brown, Penelope & Stephen C. Levinson. 1987. *Politeness: Some universals in language usage*. Cambridge: Cambridge University Press.

Chen, Chi-Fen Emily. 2001. Making e-mail requests to professors: Taiwanese vs. American students. Paper presented at the American Association for Applied Linguistics, St. Louis, MO, 24–27 February, 2001, 1–29.

Cohen, Andrew D. 2018. *Learning pragmatics from native and nonnative language teachers*. Bristol: Multilingual Matters.

Condon, Sherri L. & Claude G. Cech, 1996. Functional comparison of face-to-face and computer-mediated decision making interactions. In Susan Herring (ed.), *Computer-mediated communication: Linguistic, social, and cross-cultural perspectives*, 65–80. Philadelphia, PA: John Benjamins.

Czerwionka, Lori & Alejandro Cuza. 2017a. A pragmatic analysis of L2 Spanish requests: acquisition in three situational contexts during short-term study abroad. *Intercultural Pragmatics* 14(3). 391–419.

Czerwionka, Lori & Alejandro Cuza. 2017b. Second language acquisition of Spanish service industry requests in an immersion context. *Hispania* 100(2). 239–260.

Economidou-Kogetsidis, Maria. 2011. 'Please answer me as soon as possible': Pragmatic failure in non-native speakers' e-mail requests to faculty. *Journal of Pragmatics* 43(13). 3193–3215.

Economidou-Kogetsidis, Maria. 2016. Variation in evaluations of the (im) politeness of emails from L2 learners and perceptions of the personality of their senders. *Journal of Pragmatics* 106. 1–19.

Economidou-Kogetsidis, Maria. 2018. "Mr Paul, please inform me accordingly": Address forms, directness and degree of imposition in L2 emails. *Pragmatics* 28(4). 489–516.

Félix-Brasdefer, J. César. 2005. Indirectness and politeness in Mexican requests. In Paula Kempchinsky & Carlos E. Piñeros (eds.), *Theory, practice, and acquisition. Papers from the 6th Hispanic Linguistics Symposium and the 5th conference on the acquisition of Spanish and Portuguese*, 239–257. Somerville, MA: Cascadilla Press.

Félix-Brasdefer, J. César. 2007. Pragmatic development in the Spanish as a FL classroom: A cross-section study of learner requests. *Intercultural pragmatics* 4(2). 253–286.

Félix-Brasdefer, J. César. 2012a. E-mail requests to faculty. In Maria Economidou-Kogetsidis & Helen Woodfield (eds.), *Interlanguage request modification*, 87–118. Philadelphia: John Benjamins.

Félix-Brasdefer, J. César. 2012b. E-mail openings and closings: pragmalinguistic and gender variation in learner-instructor cyber consultations. *Discourse and language learning across L2 instructional settings* 24. 223–248.

García, Marta G. 2005. Topic management and interactional competence in Spanish L2 conversation. In Sara Gesuato, Franscesca Bianchi, & Winnie Chang (eds.), *Teaching, learning and investigating pragmatics: Principles, methods and practices*, 253–274. Newcastle upon Tyne: Cambridge Scholars Publishing.

Halenko, Nicola & Christian Jones. 2017. Explicit instruction of spoken requests: an examination of pre-departure instruction and the study abroad environment. *System* 68. 26–37.

Hartford, Beverly S. & Kathleen Bardovi-Harlig. 1996. "At your earliest convenience": A study of written student requests to faculty. In Lawrence F. Bouton (ed.), *Pragmatics and Language Learning* 7. 55–69.

Hendriks, Berna. 2010. An experimental study of native speaker perceptions of non-native request modification in e-mails in English. *Intercultural Pragmatics* 7(2). 221–255.

Hernández, Todd A. 2016. Acquisition of L2 Spanish requests in short-term study abroad. *Study Abroad Research in Second Language Acquisition and International Education* 1(2). 186–216.

Hernández, Todd A. & Paulo Boero. 2018a. Explicit instruction for request strategy development during short-term study abroad. *Journal of Spanish Language Teaching* 5(1). 35–49.

Hernández, Todd A. & Paulo Boero. 2018b. Explicit intervention for Spanish pragmatic development during short-term study abroad: an examination of learner request production and cognition. *Foreign Language Annals* 51(2). 389–410.

Herring, Susan. C. & Jannis Androutsopoulos. 2015. Computer-mediated discourse 2.0. *The handbook of discourse analysis* 2. 127–151.

IBM Corp. Released 2013. IBM SPSS Statistics for Windows, Version 22.0. Armonk, NY: IBM Corp.

Kidd, Joshua A. 2016. *Face and enactment of identities in the L2 classroom*. Bristol: Multilingual Matters.

Krulatz, Anna M. 2013. *Interlanguage pragmatics in Russian: The speech act of request in e-mail*. Salt Lake City, UT: University of Utah dissertation.

Lee, Cynthia F. K. 2004. Written requests in e-mails sent by adult Chinese learners of English. *Language, Culture, and Curriculum* 17(1). 58–72.

Márquez Reiter, Rosina. 2000. *Linguistic politeness in Britain and Uruguay: A contrastive analysis of requests and apologies*. Amsterdam, Netherlands: John Benjamins.

Pan, Ping Cathy. 2012. Interlanguage requests in institutional e-mail discourse. In Maria Economidou-Kogetsidis & Helen Woodfield (eds.), *Interlanguage request modification*, 119–161. Philadelphia: John Benjamins.

Pinto, Derrin. 2005. The acquisition of requests by second language learners of Spanish. *Spanish in Context* 2(1). 1–27.

Ruzickova, Elena. 2007. Strong and mild requestive hints and positive-face redress in Cuban Spanish. *Journal of Pragmatics* 39(6). 1170–1202.

Scollon, Ron & Suzanne W. Scollon. 2001. *Intercultural communication. Second edition*. Malden, MA: Blackwell.

Shim, Young-Sook. (2013). International faculty perceptions of requestive emails by Korean University students. *Multimedia-Assisted Language Learning* 16. 111–131.

Shively, Rachel & Andrew D. Cohen. 2008. Development of Spanish requests and apologies during study abroad. *Íkala: Revista de lenguaje y cultura* 13(20). 57–118.

Shively, Rachel. 2011. L2 pragmatic development in study abroad: a longitudinal study of Spanish service encounters. *Journal of Pragmatics* 43(6). 1818–1835.

Sykes, Julie M. 2013. Multiuser virtual environments: Learner apologies in Spanish. In Naoko Taguchi & Julie M. Sykes (eds.), *Technology in interlanguage pragmatics research and teaching*, 71–100. Philadelphia: John Benjamins.

Zhu, Wuhan. 2012. Polite requestive strategies in emails: An investigation of pragmatic competence of Chinese EFL learners. *RELC Journal* 43(2). 217–238.

Stephanie W.P. Knight
12 Affordances of game-enhanced learning: A classroom intervention for enhancing concept-based pragmatics instruction

Abstract: To readily access the multitude of opportunities that exist for communication, L2 learners must be able to apply their knowledge and skills across communicative contexts. Various constructivist pedagogical approaches, including concept-based pragmatics instruction (CBPI), are designed to encourage this ability within learners; these approaches situate learning in universal paradigms that promote learner authentication of classroom experiences and the realization, adaptation, and application of their knowledge and skill sets to match the diverse situations they encounter. Research that highlights the unique affordances of digital games to promote interlanguage pragmatic teaching and learning complements CBPI research by promoting learner engagement in concert with intentional language use and analysis. In this chapter, this mutuality is explored via the proposal of a classroom intervention that utilizes game-enhanced learning to fuel CBPI.

Keywords: concept-based instruction, concept-based pragmatics instruction, digital games, game-enhanced learning, authentication

1 Introduction

Successful pedagogical frameworks situate learning in universal (domain-agnostic) concepts (i.e., balance, community, and change) that promote (1) learner authentication (a "personal process of engagement" [van Lier 1996: 128]) in learning experiences and (2) learner use, adaptation, and application of knowledge and skill sets to match the multitude of real-world situations they may encounter. This reality has been explored in many transdisciplinary educational programmatic initiatives (e.g., International Baccalaureate), planning initiatives (e.g., Wiggins and McTighe's [2005] Understanding by Design), and assessment initiatives (e.g., Wiggins' [2011] Authentic Assessment). The central crux of each of these initiatives is to afford the creation of classroom experiences that are reflective of real-world relevance and engage learners in inquiry-fueled, conceptual explorations.

https://doi.org/10.1515/9783110721775-013

The purpose of this chapter is to propose the use of game-enhanced learning to complement the conceptual explorations inherent in concept-based pragmatics instruction (CBPI). To put forth this proposal, I first establish the need for learner authentication of language learning by examining the reality of attrition in world language education in the United States. Next, I explore the relationship of learner authentication and CBPI. Finally, I articulate the proposal itself by offering one example activity that showcases the approach.

2 Contemporary challenges in world language education

Currently, world language education in the United States finds itself at a precarious crossroads. As Looney and Lusin (2018) outline, language enrollments in the United States fell 9.2 percent between fall 2013 and fall 2016, the second largest decline in the history of the Modern Language Association (MLA) census. On the surface, this decline seems to indicate a prevailing disinterest in world language study; not only was there a general decline in language enrollment, but there was also an attrition rate of roughly 80 percent between introductory to advanced enrollments in even the most popular languages, like Spanish. To understand a more complete picture of language learning in the US, however, it is useful to examine the informal language learning market. In stark contrast to the MLA census, the US-based startup, Duolingo – the most downloaded language app in the world – boasted 57.8 million users in the US in 2017 (a figure that eclipsed the total number of people enrolled in language learning courses at the time). Additionally, regional language study trends indicated that most users self-selected into language study due to its perceived utility; unsurprisingly, languages studied reflected both a local prevalence of L2 speakers and local economic interests (Kron 2017). When taken in concert with the MLA census, these data seem to refute that language study is on the decline, but rather, indicate that learners are dissatisfied with opportunities to study language in formal institutions.

Still, Duolingo is not immune to the realities of attrition. For example, Lardinois (2018) writes that only 8 percent of Duolingo's users were active worldwide in 2018, an aggregate number of users that totaled less than the number of downloads in the US alone. The question then presents itself as to why learners are seeking out language learning opportunities but are failing to endure.

To propose an answer to this question, one must consider the commonality that connects Duolingo and many institutional language classrooms: a pedagogical approach that is almost exclusively dedicated to the development of grammatical competence. With respect to Duolingo, this approach is widely critiqued. For example, Munday (2016) and Teske (2017) note that the gamified platform is not communicative, nor does it focus on the development of pragmatic and cultural skills. Furthermore, a string of op-ed pieces (e.g., London 2017) highlight the app's inability to prepare users for spontaneous communication, a fact that Duolingo admits. Even the company's attempts to get users to connect interpersonally have been wildly unpopular (Adams 2019) and provide support for Rosell-Aguilar's (2017) summary of critiques that mobile apps generally are overly focused on translation and do little to take advantage of the unique affordances that mobile devices provide for the development of communicative and intercultural competences.

Anecdotally, this limited approach to language learning is characteristic of much language coursework. The presentation of content as discrete facts is perpetuated by an infrastructure of didactic tools (e.g., textbooks) that privilege the presentation of such facts over the conceptual systems at play within knowledge systems, systems that are neither transparent nor immediately evident to learners (McCoy and Ketterlin-Gellar 2004; Schill and Howell 2011; Williams, Abraham, and Negueruela-Azarola 2013). Furthermore, the narrative that learners are unable to improve their proficiency after numerous years of study is common. Perhaps, then, attrition reveals not that languages are undervalued, but rather that learners are frustrated by approaches that privilege content acquisition over content use. Practitioners must attend to this frustration by creating socially and ecologically valid conditions that intrigue and inspire ongoing study.

2.1 Learner authentication and access in SLA contexts

Undoubtedly, the reality of attrition indicates that L2 learners, as a whole, disengage and fail to authenticate their language learning experiences. Their authentication is fundamental in promoting perseverance in the study of language, proficiency development, access to target language communicative scenarios, and is an undercurrent of much contemporary literature. For example, Kern and Liddicoat (2008) emphasize the critical revisioning of learners as 'locuteur/acteur' [speaker/social actor] and Garcia et al. (2012) discuss empowering bilingual learners by expanding language study to include the genres common to the everyday experiences of learners. However, learner authentication is slippery in nature. As Sykes and Reinhardt (2013: 17–18) discuss, "Ultimately, it is the experience of the learner that creates authenticity . . . it is important to not only create tasks that are authentic and relevant, but also to give in-depth consideration to the various experiences learners have with those tasks." Indeed, while practitioners can engineer theoretically sound experiences for learners, the experience of the learners must be of equal importance to the tasks themselves. In fact, in the absence of explicit learner feedback, practitioners may be unaware of the degree to which learners have authenticated experiences. Importantly, this proposal does not endeavor to provide a false representation of this reality by promising that all learners authenticate all experiences within the proposed intervention. However, it does seek to maximize the number of learners who are genuinely engaged in language learning experiences.

2.2 Concept-based approaches to learning and SLA

Concept-based instruction (CBI) is a theoretical approach to learning that involves exposing learners to targeted, typically domain-agnostic concepts (e.g., power, balance, and community) to prime and ground the subsequent acquisition of critical content and skills and to enhance transfer of knowledge across contexts (Erikson, Lanning, and French 2017). In other words, it entails the use of overarching, global ideas to facilitate learners' organization of new knowledge, incite their inquiry, and inform the transfer of knowledge and skills. For example, in a CBI classroom, language learners working towards the objective of articulating personal descriptions may first participate in a discussion in which they examine optical illusions so that they can ground their learning of descriptor use in the concepts of appearances and self-presentation, both of which are concepts that are relevant in other domains. Or, language learners seeking to master narration in the past may explore the concepts of change and time by examining images that visually differentiate (using timelines or the like) completed events versus ongoing actions before acquiring the associated verb forms and practicing narration. Similar interventions were used by Negueruela and Lantolf (2006), Yáñez-Prieto (2010), and Harun et al. (2019) and were found to promote improved grammatical competence, language play, and experimentation with form.

Critically for CBI, the learner is agentive at the onset of the learning process. This agency is likely to promote learner authentication, not only because the learner is actively involved in the construction of knowledge (Schill and

Howell 2011), but also because the learner's experiences and intellectual faculties, regardless of his or her abilities, are explicitly valued (Erikson, Lanning, and French 2017; McCoy and Ketterlin-Geller 2004). Relatedly, learner inquiry and engagement in synergistic thinking are promoted (Erikson 2007; Erikson, Lanning, and French 2017).

2.2.1 Concept-based pragmatics instruction

CBPI builds upon the potential for CBI to promote authenticated learning and has begun to emerge as a focus in SLA over the past decade. Notably, both van Compernolle's (2011) case study of a post-secondary French learner and van Compernolle and Henery's (2014) study of a classroom of post-secondary French learners (*n*=13) revealed the potential for CBPI to positively impact learners' sociopragmatic awareness. In each case, learners were provided with diagrams and written explanations to support their understanding of targeted concepts and engaged in appropriate judgement tasks and interaction scenarios to build their understanding of the concepts at play. After this intervention, learners demonstrated a shift from a rules-of-thumb orientation (a focus on indoctrinated lists of rules related to "appropriate" language use) to a meaning-making orientation (a focus on making specific language choices to convey utterances with a desired illocutionary force). In a similar vein, van Compernolle (2013) demonstrated that learners (N=8) who enrolled in a similar CBPI tutoring intervention developed some control over and understanding of sociostylistic variation.

Taken together, these studies showcase the potential for CBPI to enhance sociopragmatic development in students. However, their Vygotskian approach (see Karpov [2003] for discussion) of utilizing explicit diagrams and written explanations to prime the awareness of scientific concepts, that is, concepts not necessarily understood through individual observation alone, is somewhat limiting; by providing instruction without first provoking inquiry or calling upon learners' previous experiences with the concepts, the capacity of the learner to construct knowledge is at least partially limited in comparison to more open-ended approaches. For some learners, this limitation may have negative implications for the authentication of learning experiences. Game-enhanced learning is thus proposed as a pedagogical tool with the potential to provide critical input for CBI while protecting learners' agency in the construction of knowledge.

3 Game-enhanced CBPI framework in practice

Importantly, the requisite cognitive engagement to ensure the success of a truly learner-driven, constructivist CBPI cannot be guaranteed by the existence of the opportunities to engage freely with concepts via gameplay (or any other medium). In this section, epistemic routines are introduced for their potential to provide the scaffolding needed to prime cognitive engagement during gameplay and, hopefully, minimize the need for teacher instruction. A classroom intervention that utilizes one such routine is also offered to provide examples of how the routines are operationalized in concert with digital games to facilitate CBPI.

3.1 Epistemic routines and their relationship to conceptual processing

As Richhart (2015: 33) states, "the chief goal of instruction . . . is the advancement of thinking." Thinking is an unavoidable requirement (and consequence of) concept-based approaches to learning. However, concepts are not immediately evident to learners and practitioners are necessarily implicated in 1) the articulation of concepts and 2) the creation of scaffolding mechanisms to promote learner conceptual development.

Epistemic routines are one such scaffolding mechanism and, in practice, are not new to CBPI. Though the term "epistemic routine" is not utilized in the research, van Compernolle (2014) identifies three critical phases of CBPI intervention (awareness building, problem-solving, and participation in communicative tasks), all of which imply a procedural approach to learner engagement in critical cognitive processes such as analysis, evaluation, and creation. However, as has already been mentioned, the instructor-centered operationalization of the awareness building phase employed by van Compernolle (2013), van Compernolle (2014), and van Compernolle and Henery (2014) via the inclusion of written explanations and diagrams may limit the potential for learner authentication.

Other epistemic routines, like the thinking routines articulated as part of Harvard's *Project Zero* (see Ritchhart et al. [2006] for examples) provide a slightly more constructivist approach to scaffolding thinking given that they often initiate by inviting learners to take inventory of what is already known/seen/heard. It is with this invitation to learners in mind that Ishihara and Cohen's (2014) constructivist approach to incorporating the study of L2 pragmatics in the classroom will be utilized for the remainder of this chapter as an epistemic routine to scaffold thinking. In this routine, learners begin by observing a language function in context to build awareness. Next, learners enhance their awareness through the analysis of the artifact(s) that they engaged with during observation, and finally, they extend work via either practice or further investigation related to the function. This progression from building awareness of targeted content, to engaging in evaluation and scrutiny of the content, to actively participating in communication is echoed in additional literature (e.g., Thorne and Reinhardt 2008; Sykes, Holden, and Knight 2019).

3.2 Classroom intervention: Game-enhanced learning and This War of Mine

The present intervention was adapted from coursework developed for secondary learners with advanced proficiency levels by the Center for Applied Second Language Studies at the University of Oregon (Knight and Pearson 2016). The intervention was developed to engage learners in meaningful reflection regarding the concept of rank of imposition, or difficulty inherent in a situation, and how the pragmatic strategies associated with speech acts in everyday interactions (e.g., greetings and requests) might differ in contexts of scarcity and danger versus contexts of provision and safety. To achieve this goal, the intervention features This War of Mine (TWoM) (https://www.thiswarofmine.com/#home), a commercial digital game in which players attempt to survive as civilians in a war-torn country. Available in 12 languages (English, French, German, Italian, Japanese, Korean, Polish, Portugues, Russian, Simplified Chinese, Spanish, and Turkish), TWoM is appropriate for a variety of L2 learners. Importantly for teachers considering implementation, however, players do not create language in the game; all discourse is scripted. Additionally, discourse at the beginning of gameplay between player-controlled characters and non-player characters (NPC) primarily features greetings and requests. Players must seek out interactions between their characters and NPCs by answering the door and by visiting as many locations as possible to scavenge for resources.

The subsequent sections are organized according to Ishihara and Cohen's (2014) approach to the learning and teaching of pragmatics, a routine involving an observation phase, analysis phase, and extension phase. At each phase, the classroom procedures associated with the operationalization of TWoM as a game-enhanced CBPI intervention are provided. Each section closes with a discussion about the specific affordances of digital games for complementing CBPI.

3.2.1 Observation phase

In the observation phase of game-enhanced CBPI, learners should examine artifacts from gameplay (e.g., screenshots that spark intrigue or are of interest) and document their observations in a recorded think-aloud, journal, or graphic organizer. In the present intervention, learners:
- Download and play TWoM for 60 minutes;
- Document the greetings and requests uttered by non-player characters;
- Record the context of each utterance as well as observations related to language choice (e.g., verb forms, vocabulary, and pragmatic strategies that seem to be at play).

An important aspect of this phase is that interactions with embedded, or in-game, discourses are goal-orienting and provide "rich and associative contexts" (Thorne and Black 2007: 6) that situate critical content for player/learners. With respect to goal orientation, the goal to survive is unavoidable from the onset (in lieu of clicking "Enter" or "Start" to begin game play, players click "Survive"). Given the reality of materials scarcity in the game, survival permeates the ongoing process of player decision making and their assessment of "abilities, risks, challenges, and rewards" (Sykes and Reinhardt 2013: 20). As a result, gameplay in this intervention affords a shared classroom community experience that has the potential to prime learners to engage in conceptual thinking related to rank of imposition as they examine the pragmatic strategies at play in a context of scarcity and danger.

Figure 1 provides an example of how the goal-orienting capacity of embedded discourse has the potential to prime players/learners to notice and to evaluate target functions. In this particular instance, the NPC issues a greeting/request in a single utterance, urging the player-controlled characters to engage in a trade.

Upon encountering this utterance, player/learners may notice a variety of characteristics: the absence of a salutation in the greeting, the use of an imperative (in lieu of more mitigated language) to deliver the request to answer the door, or the grounder (explanation) used to justify the reason that the NPC wants to talk. These characteristics all provide clues as to the pragmatic strategies one might use in the context of pervasive danger and scarcity and help cultivate player/learners understanding of the concept of rank of imposition.

Figure 1: NPC's Greeting/Request.

3.2.2 Analysis phase

In the analysis phase of game-enhanced CBPI, learners examine the artifacts they collected during gameplay to analyze and discern the language use patterns at hand. An important consideration is that if learners struggle to analyze the artifacts, teachers may have to model analysis of the artifacts during this phase. In the present intervention, learners:
- Participate in a teacher-facilitated discussion of their observations;
- Work as a class to identify the pragmatic strategies (e.g., commands) used in greetings and requests given the presence of a high rank of imposition;
- Gather additional L2 artifacts that showcase the requests and greetings in situations of little to no rank of imposition;
- Compare the artifacts collected outside of the game to the artifacts collected in the game.

Notably, the analysis of artifacts happens outside of gameplay and incorporates additional contexts for communication. However, the environmental feedback provided during gameplay supports learners in engaging in this phase; environmental feedback has the potential to provide player/learners with critical information that informs ongoing language use (Sykes and Reinhardt 2013; Thorne, Black, and Sykes 2009). For example, with this particular game, environmental feedback provides player/learners with clarifying information related to the illocutionary forces surrounding given utterances. For example, at one point during gameplay, a priest of a church (an NPC) asks the player-controlled character attempting to scavenge resources at the location to not disturb his sleeping flock. This request is actually an implied request to leave, and as soon as the player enters the basement of the church, the priest chases the player down to demand that he or she exit the building, a demand that another NPC reiterates (Figure 2).

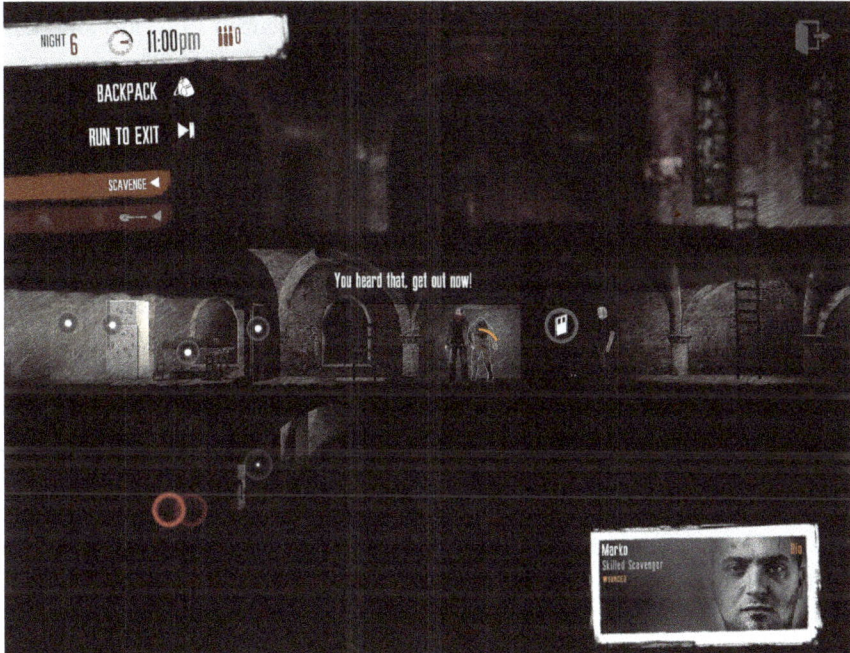

Figure 2: Confrontation at the Church.

While teachers are still encouraged to avoid direct instruction in the observation phase, the critical, clarifying role of the teacher in interpreting environmental feedback emerges here. The nuance of the implied request is one that learners might have otherwise missed if gameplay occurred via purely informal engagement (Reinhardt and Thorne 2019). In this sense, the role of a teacher in game-enhanced CBPI is somewhat dichotomous; he or she must encourage self-directed exploration while also priming learners to notice critical input.

3.2.3 Extension phase

During the final phase of the routine, the extension phase, learners may engage in a variety of activities including practicing the language functions examined with peers, practicing the functions with expert speakers, or engaging in additional, clarifying observation and analysis of artifacts. In the present intervention, player/learners:

- Use understanding from the analysis phase to plan role-play scenarios that feature learners' conceptual understanding of rank of imposition and how that concept manifests for both greetings and requests in contexts of danger and scarcity, on the one hand, and contexts of safety and access to resources, on the other;
- Perform role-play scenarios;
- Provide feedback to other learners about the pragmatic strategies they employed.

Though this phase involves no gameplay or specific examination of embedded discourse (unless player/learners choose to return to gameplay to examine additional artifacts when making decisions about language choice), it is beneficial to examine the ways in which gameplay supported its enactment. First, in the analysis phase, discourse shifted from in-game discourse to attendant discourse, or discourse about the game. This shift has the potential to engender reflective, analytic language creation (see Reinhardt and Sykes [2011] for discussion). Secondly, as is discussed by Sykes, Oskoz, and Thorne (2008: 538–539), the in-game interactions provide player/learners with an opportunity to observe high-stakes interactions without necessitating their real-life participation. This input is critical for supporting players'/learners' future interactions outside the classroom.

4 Future directions and implications

This game-enhanced CBPI intervention was included to provide practical guidance related to how and why to operationalize similar interventions. Given that the intervention capitalizes on the synergies of CBPI and game-enhanced learning, it has the potential to promote a learning environment in which learner authentication is realized.

In spite of its potential to positively impact learning, there are a myriad of considerations a teacher should take into account before choosing to use this particular game, such as cost (digital downloads can cost up to $14.99 per device) and appropriateness of content (the game includes adult language and deals with issues related to violence, hunger, and addiction). Other commercial games and their potential uses are outlined in Table 1.

Table 1: Commercial game examples.[1]

Game	Age Rating (in App Store)	Cost	Available in multiple languages?	Available Platforms	Possible classroom implementation
Sims FreePlay	12+	Freemium	Yes	App Store, Google Play, Amazon App Store	Metalinguistic intervention related to exploring the concept of social distance and solidarity-building strategies.
Plague Inc.	12+	Freemium -$14.99	Yes	App Store, Google Play, Steam, Windows Phone Store, Xbox One	Intervention related to exploring the concept of self-presentation in microblogging.
Safari Tales	4+	$2.99 -$4.99	No	App Store, Google Play, Amazon App Store	Intervention related to the concept of exploring patterns in discourse (semantic and pragmatic formulae).

---

[1] Free, downloadable classroom activities are available for TWoM, Plague Inc, and Safari Tales and other commercial games at https://games2teach.uoregon.edu/download/classroom-activities/.

Admittedly, this chapter only scratches the surface of the ways in which game-enhanced learning can complement CBPI. Engaging in deeper, comparative investigations of this potential in a variety of gaming contexts including Massively Multiplayer Online Games (MMOGs) and non-commercial games is merited; in concert, the potential for these paradigms to maximize the possibility for learner authentication of learning tasks (via the implementation of engagement of the learner as both a social and cognitive actor) is clear. Additionally, research should focus on the utility other digital tools to complement CBPI instruction (e.g., place-based mobile apps, synchronous chat, and social media platforms), all of which have been examined for their rich affordances in terms of promoting (1) the development of pragmatic competence and (2) improving learner access to communities of target language speakers (e.g., Blattner and Fiori 2011; Sykes 2018). Such an intervention can both facilitate the explicit analysis of valuable texts beyond what is typically included in classrooms (Reinhardt and Thorne 2019) and would afford learners additional opportunities to produce language themselves (Warschauer and Grimes 2007).

Additionally, replicable empirical evaluations are required to validate this framework. While it is likely that digital games will only serve to enhance and extend learner development in CBPI contexts, the magnitude of their impact cannot yet be ascertained. Future comparative analyses may reveal no discernable (or a highly context-specific) benefit to incorporating digital tools in CBPI contexts. Still, regardless of these future findings, a reality remains unchanged; learner authentication is as important as the task designs at hand (Sykes and Reinhardt 2013). Practitioners must work to promote cognitive and social engagement via their intentional use of learner-centered tools and paradigms, such as the intervention offered here.

Acknowledgements: This chapter was funded in part through public-private partnership sponsored by the National Security Education Program (NSEP). The content of the information provided does not reflect the position of the U.S. government nor imply endorsement.

References

Adams, Susan. 2019. Game of tongues: How Duolingo built a $700 million business with its addictive language-learning app. *Forbes*. https://www.forbes.com/sites/susanadams/2019/07/16/game-of-tongues-how-duolingo-built-a-700-million-business-with-its-addictive-language-learning-app/#29e88e073463 (accessed 11 November 2019).

Blattner, Geraldine & Melissa Fiori. 2011. Virtual social network communities: An investigation of language learners' development of sociopragmatic awareness and multiliteracy skills. *CALICO Journal* 29 (1). https://doi.org/10.11139/cj.29.1.24–43 (accessed 20 April 2017).

Compernolle, Remi A. van. 2011. Developing second language sociopragmatic knowledge through concept-based instruction: A microgenetic case study. *Journal of pragmatics* 43. https://doi.org/10.1016/j.pragma.2011.06.009 (accessed 15 April 2019).

Compernolle, Remi A. van. 2013. Concept appropriation and the emergence of L2 sociostylistic variation. *Language teaching research* 17 (3). https://doi.org/10.1177/1362168813482937 (accessed 15 April 2019).

Compernolle, Remi A. van 2014. Profiling second language sociolinguistic development through dynamically administered strategic action scenarios. *Language & communication* 37. 86–99.

Compernolle, Remi A. van. & Ashlie Henery. 2014. Instructed concept appropriation and L2 pragmatic development in the classroom. *Language learning* 64(3). https://doi.org/10.1111/lang.12054 (accessed 15 April 2019).

Erikson, H. Lynn. 2007. *Concept-based curriculum and instruction for the thinking classroom*. Thousand Oaks: Corwin Press.

Erikson, H. Lynn, Lois Lanning & Rachel French. 2017. *Concept-based curriculum and Instruction for the thinking classroom*. Thousand Oaks: Corwin Press.

Garcia, Ofelia, Heather H. Woodley, Nelson Flores, & Haiwen Chu. 2012. Latino emergent bilingual youth in high schools: Transcaring strategies for academic success. *Urban education* 48 (6). https://doi.org/10.1177/0042085912462708 (accessed 19 April 2016).

Harun, Haliza, Norhana Abdullah, Nursyuhada'Ab Wahab, & Nurkhamimi Zainuddin. 2019. Concept based instruction: Enhancing grammar competence in L2 learners. *RELC Journal* 50 (2). https://doi.org/10.1177/0033688217716505 (accessed 1 December 2019).

Ishihara, Noriko & Andrew D. Cohen. 2014 [2010]. *Teaching and learning pragmatics: Where language and culture meet*. New York: Routledge.

Karpov, Yuriy. 2003. Vygotsky's doctrine of scientific concepts: Its role for contemporary education. In Alex Kozulin, Boris Gindis, Vladimir S. Ageyev, & Suzanne M. Miller (eds.), *Vygotsky's educational theory in cultural context*, 65–82. Cambridge: Cambridge University Press.

Kern, Richard & Anthony J. Liddicoat. 2008. From the learner to the speaker/social actor. In Genevieve Zarate, Danielle Lévy, & Claire Kramsch (eds.), *Handbook of multilingualism and multiculturalism*. 17–23. Paris: Éditions des archives contemporaines. https://www.researchgate.net/publication/283153846_From_the_Learner_to_the_SpeakerSocial_Actor_with_Anthony_Liddicoat_in_G_Zarate_D_Levy_C_Kramsch_Eds_Handbook_of_Multilingualism_and_Multiculturalism_Paris_Editions_des_Archives_Contemporaines_2011_pp_(accessed November 30 2019).

Knight, Stephanie & Ben Pearson. 2016. Building meaningful connections for advanced secondary learners: A hybrid approach to identity and culture. *The FLT Mag*. https://fltmag.com/building-meaningful-connections-advanced-secondary-language-learners-hybrid-approach-identity-culture/ (accessed 26 July 2016).

Kron, Michaela. 2017. The United States of languages: An analysis of Duolingo usage state-by-state. | *Blog – Duolingo*. https://making.duolingo.com/the-united-states-of-languages-an-analysis-of-duolingo-usage-state-by-state (accessed 11 November 2019).

Lardinois, Frederic. 2018. Duolingo hires its first chief marketing officer as active user numbers stagnate but revenue grows. *Tech crunch*. Retrieved from https://techcrunch.

com/2018/08/01/duolingo-hires-its-first-chief-marketing-officer-as-active-user-numbers-stagnate/ (accessed 11 November 2019).

Lier, Leo. van. 1996. *Interaction in the language curriculum: Awareness, autonomy, and authenticity*. New York: Routledge.

London, Andrew. 2017. Duolingo made me 26% fluent in idiot. *Techradar*. Retrieved from https://www.techradar.com/news/duolingo-made-me-26-fluent-in-idiot (accessed 11 November 2019).

Looney, Dennis & Natalia Lusin. 2018. Enrollments in languages other than English in United States institutions of higher education, Summer 2016 and Fall 2016: Preliminary report. *Modern Language Association*. https://www.mla.org/content/download/83540/2197676/2016-Enrollments-Short-Report.pdf (accessed 28 March 2018).

McCoy, Jan D. & Leanne R. Ketterlin-Geller. 2004. Rethinking instructional delivery for diverse student populations: Serving all learners with concept-based instruction. *Intervention in School and Clinic* 40 (2). https://doi.org/10.1177/10534512040400020401 (accessed 1 November 2019).

Munday, Pilar. 2016. The case for using Duolingo as part of the language classroom experience. *Revista iberoamericana de educación a distancia* 19(1). https://digitalcommons.sacredheart.edu/cgi/viewcontent.cgi?article=1039&context=lang_fac (accessed 17 Mar 2019).

Negueruela, Eduardo & James P. Lantolf. 2006. Concept-based instruction and the acquisition of L2 Spanish. In Rafael Salaberry & Barabara A. Lafford (eds.), *The art of teaching Spanish: Second language acquisition from research to praxis*, 79–102. Washington D.C.: Georgetown University Press.

Reinhardt, Jonathan & Julie M. Sykes. 2011. Framework for game-enhanced materials development. *CERLL G2T Project white paper series*. Tucson: Center for Educational Resources in Culture, Language, and Literacy.

Reinhardt, Jonathan & Steven L. Thorne. 2019. Digital literacies as emergent multifarious repertoires. In Nike Arnold & Lara Ducate (eds.), *Engaging language learners through CALL: From theory and research to informed practice*, 208–239. Bristol: Equinox.

Ritchhart, Ron. 2015. *Creating cultures of thinking: The 8 forces we must master to truly transform our schools*. San Francisco: Jossey-Bass.

Ritchhart, Ron, Patricia Palmer, Mark Church, & Shari Tishman. 2006. Thinking routines: Establishing patterns of thinking in the classroom. Prepared for *AERA Conference*. http://www.ronritchhart.com/Papers_files/AERA06ThinkingRoutinesV3.pdf (accessed 20 Jan 2017).

Rosell-Aguilar, Fernando. 2017. State of the app: A taxonomy and framework for evaluating language learning mobile applications. *CALICO Journal* 34 (2). https://doi.org/10.1558/cj.27623 (accessed 15 March 2018).

Schill, Bethany & Linda Howell. 2011. Concept-based learning. *Science and Children* 48(6). 40–45.

Sykes, Julie M. 2018. Interlanguage pragmatics, curricular innovation, and digital technologies. *CALICO Journal* 35(2). 120–141.

Sykes, Julie M., Christopher Holden, & Stephanie Knight. 2019. Communities: Exploring digital games and social networking. In Nike Arnold & Lara Ducate (eds.), *Engaging language learners through CALL*, 353–389. Bristol: Equinox.

Sykes, Julie M. & Jonathan Reinhardt. 2013. *Language at play: Digital games in second and foreign language teaching and learning*. New Jersey: Pearson Education.

Sykes, Julie M., Ana Oskoz, & Steven L. Thorne. 2008. Web 2.0, synthetic immersive environments, and mobile resources for language education. *CALICO Journal* 25(3). 528–546.

Teske, Kaitlyn. 2017. Duolingo. *CALICO Journal* 34(3). 393–401.

Thorne, Steven L. & Rebecca Black. 2007. *New media literacies, online gaming and language education. Calper working paper series*. University Park: Center for Advanced Language Proficiency Education and Research. https://calper.la.psu.edu/content/new-media-literacies-online-gaming-and-language-education (accessed 15 March 2018).

Thorne, Steven L., Rebecca W. Black, & Julie M. Sykes. 2009. Second language use, socialization, and learning in internet communities and online games. *The Modern Language Journal* 93. https://doi.org/10.1111/j.1540-4781.2009.00974.x (accessed 1 December 2019).

Thorne, Steven L. & Jonathan Reinhardt. 2008. "Bridging activities," new media literacies and advanced foreign language proficiency. *CALICO Journal* 25(3). 558–572.

Warschauer, Mark & Douglas Grimes. 2007. Audience, authorship, and artifact: The emergent semiotics of Web 2.0. *Annual Review of Applied Linguistics*. 27. https://doi.org/10.1017/S0267190508070013 (accessed 1 November 2019).

Wiggins, Grant. 2011. Moving to modern assessments. *The phi delta kappan international*. 70 (9). 63. https://doi.org/10.1177/003172171109200713 (accessed 25 August 2016).

Wiggins, Grant & Jay McTighe. 2005. *Understanding by design*. 2nd edition. Alexandria: ASCD.

Williams, L., Lee Abraham, & Eduardo Negueruela-Azarola. 2013. Using concept-based instruction in the L2 classroom: Perspectives form current and future language teachers. *Language Teaching Research* 17(3). 363–381.

Yáñez-Prieto, María del Carmen. 2010. Authentic instruction in literary worlds: Learning the stylistics of concept-based grammar. *Language and literature* 19 (1). https://doi.org/10.1177/0963947009356723 (accessed 15 November 2019).

Part IV: **Current issues in L2 pragmatics**

Kathleen Bardovi-Harlig
13 Explicit knowledge in L2 pragmatics?

Abstract: This essay explores the concept of explicit knowledge, a theoretical construct integral to second language acquisition (SLA) theory that is largely ignored in second language (L2) pragmatics research. Although the contrast of implicit and explicit knowledge is a consideration in the design of tasks for SLA research, considerations of authenticity, consequentiality, and modality have been used to evaluate tasks employed in L2 pragmatics. Yet, explicit knowledge may play an analogous role in the investigation of L2 pragmatics. This essay considers the potential role of explicit knowledge in the collection of pragmatically relevant data. First, it considers the types of tasks used in pragmatics that might encourage the use of explicit knowledge, and second, it considers evidence of explicit knowledge from the L2 pragmatics literature. Showing that explicit knowledge may be accessed by learners, this essay argues that pragmatics research design should take explicit knowledge into account in addition to investigating it directly.

Keywords: explicit knowledge, implicit knowledge, task

1 Introduction

In this short essay, I reflect on the potential role of explicit knowledge in the acquisition and performance of second language (L2) pragmatics. Second language acquisition (SLA) research distinguishes explicit from implicit knowledge. Explicit knowledge is knowledge *about* the language, whereas implicit knowledge is knowledge *of* the language. Explicit knowledge is conscious, declarative, and learnable; it is generally accessible through controlled processing, it may be accessed during a language task that is difficult, and it may be imprecise and inaccurate (Ellis 2004). These basic characteristics of explicit knowledge should hold across all linguistic domains. Explicit knowledge of pragmatics would encompass both pragmalinguistic knowledge and sociopragmatic knowledge. Defining pragmatics as knowing how to say what to whom when, *sociopragmatics* is knowing what to say to whom when, and *pragmalinguistics* is knowing how to say it.

The point of departure for this essay is to ask what tasks might invite the use of explicit knowledge, and if there is documentation of explicit knowledge of pragmatics by learners. From there we can ask where it might come from, whether the knowledge is descriptive of the target language and culture, and perhaps whether explicit knowledge is facilitative in L2 pragmatics acquisition or use. This essay has two main sections. First, it considers the types of tasks used in pragmatics that might encourage the use of explicit knowledge, and second, it considers evidence of explicit knowledge from the L2 pragmatics literature.

2 Key issues and fundamental concepts: Task as an opportunity to use explicit knowledge

Ellis (2004: 243–244) observed that, although researchers had not investigated explicit knowledge of L2 pragmatic features, "many instruments that have been used to investigate learners' knowledge of illocutionary acts, such as the discourse completion questionnaire (see Kasper and Dahl 1991) are arguably more likely to tap explicit than implicit knowledge." *Implicit knowledge* is taken to be procedural and unconscious whereas *explicit knowledge* is thought to be analyzed knowledge which can be articulated (declarative knowledge) and may involve metalanguage (Ellis 2004; Ellis et al. 2009). Pragmatics researchers have not divided tasks into those that may promote implicit knowledge and those that may promote the use of explicit knowledge. Instead, pragmatics researchers have focused on conversation and oral simulations of conversation in data collection, underscoring the field's interest in communication – and with it, authenticity, consequentiality, and interactivity. In this way, pragmatics research seems to have privileged implicit pragmatic knowledge, with the outcome that the potential – some would say *risk* – for the use of explicit pragmatic knowledge has been largely overlooked in the development of tasks designed to elicit language samples for empirical studies as Ellis suggested (Bardovi-Harlig 2013). Nevertheless, the general absence of discussion concerning explicit knowledge in L2 pragmatics research – in contrast to its presence in SLA research more generally – makes it important to consider that tasks commonly used in pragmatics research may activate explicit knowledge.[1]

---

[1] Ellis (2004) notes that some learners may always respond by feel and others may very quickly access explicit knowledge; thus, tasks are likely to promote one type of knowledge more than another, but do not guarantee it.

In general, written production tasks provide greater opportunity for learners to draw on explicit knowledge than do oral tasks. In the realm of pragmatics, Ellis (2004) identified discourse completion tasks (DCTs) as tasks that are likely to draw on explicit knowledge. DCTs typically present a description of a situation (called a scenario) and ask the participant to respond. Most DCTs are written and are best described as "an indirect means for assessing spoken language in the form of a written production measure" (Cohen and Shively 2007: 196). There are at least two types of written DCTs, *open questionnaires* in which no conversational turns are provided (Example 1), and *dialogue completion tasks* in which an initiating turn or a rejoinder is provided (see also Ogiermann 2018 for a taxonomy of written DCTs).

(1) Open Q (Johnston, Kasper, and Ross 1998: 163)

You were in a hurry to leave on a trip, and you asked your roommate to mail an express letter for you. When you get back a few days later, the letter is still lying on the table
You:

Written DCTs invite the use of explicit knowledge by learners by virtue of their mode and their lack of time pressure (they are generally untimed tasks); both of which allow planning, further increasing the likelihood that a respondent might draw on explicit knowledge. Time pressure does not guarantee use of implicit knowledge and even lack of time pressure does not guarantee use of explicit knowledge. However, untimed tasks, especially untimed written tasks, open the door for both explicit knowledge and planning.[2]

Variations of DCTs may further enhance the potential for activating explicit knowledge. DCTs with rejoinders in which a follow-up turn is supplied allow participants to read ahead and calculate a response that fits both preceding and following turns (Blum-Kulka, House, and Kasper 1989; Johnston, Kasper, and Ross 1998). Free DCTs (FDCTs; Barron 2007; Rose and Ng 2001) in which learners compose both sides of a conversation, like script writing, may provide even more opportunity to use explicit knowledge because, as Ogiermann (2018: 240) notes, it "requires imagining several turns in advance."

---

[2] In the literature, most oral DCTs do not report limited response time, but see Bardovi-Harlig (2009), Bardovi-Harlig and Su (2018) for timed oral DCTs and Taguchi (2007) inter alia for time-pressured oral DCTs.

(2) DCT with rejoinder (Blum-Kulka, House, and Kasper 1989: 14)

At the university Ann missed a lecture yesterday and would like to borrow Judith's notes.
Ann:
Judith: Sure, but let me have them back before the lecture next week.

(3) Free DCT (Barron 2007: 160)

You are in the airport. You see a girl your own age with two huge bags. As you haven't much luggage yourself, you offer to help. She REFUSES.
You:
Girl:

Written DCTs open the door to the possibility of using explicit knowledge to an even greater extent when participants are invited to state alternatives or give interpretations. Bonikowska's (1988) combination written DCT and reflection instrument encouraged the articulation of explicit knowledge when native speakers of British English explained why they would opt out (i.e., not respond verbally) in the scenario presented. Bonikowska argued that "a serious shortcoming of such questionnaires [i.e., DCTs] is that they force the subjects to perform linguistically in situations in which, in real life, they might choose to opt out" (p. 170). Thus, her DCT items included a scenario in which one might be tempted to complain, followed by the questions, "Would you react/say anything in this situation? If not, why not? If so, what would you say?" (p. 176), as in Example (4).

(4) Complaint/Opting out scenario (Bonikowska 1988)

You're renting a room, but because the landlady's son is coming back home you'll have to move out next term. Your landlady promised to help you find new accommodation. She was to have a word with some of her friends and let you know last week. She didn't. You haven't started looking for a room on your own as you hoped to find a new place to stay through her.

The attention of the respondents was not specifically focused on what they were thinking (as in a retrospective verbal report, discussed in the next section), but rather elicited as a possible response to the main item. Participants cited four broad categories of reasons for not complaining: (a) conditions for the act of complaining (such as negating the offence, "It was a genuine mistake," or taking responsibility, "I shouldn't have left revision [reviewing] till the last day"); (b) the relationship of the act to speaker's goals ("It would be too late for anything to be done so it's not worth making an issue out of it"); (c) the relationship of the act to the social goal ("He may be offended; this could finish our relationship"); and, (d) contextual factors (power and distance; "I wouldn't feel able to tackle a person in a higher position than myself"). We see that participants articulated a range of responses that reflect explicit sociopragmatic knowledge. To my knowledge this task has not been repeated with nonnative speakers.

Further investigating opting out, Rose (1994) employed a multiple-choice DCT with speakers of Japanese. Weighing the options presented in a written multiple-choice questionnaire may encourage comparison among the alternatives, and thus explicit judgments about them. Rose's multiple-choice DCT is one of a range of written judgment tasks that have been used in interlanguage pragmatics. Ellis (2004: 249) observes that judgment tasks are "the favored method of investigating L2 explicit knowledge as conscious awareness," and further notes that, although his discussion focuses on grammaticality judgments, the main points "apply equally to pragmatic acceptability judgments" (p. 268, footnote 3). For Ellis, tasks asking learners to judge grammaticality or acceptability are more likely to tap explicit knowledge if they are untimed and encourage learners to deliberate carefully before making a judgment. Untimed tasks that may promote the use of explicit knowledge in pragmatics include card sorting (ranking of politeness levels of various expressions), identification of speech acts, judgment tasks, judgment tasks with corrections or retrospective reflections, or talking about pragmatics in groups.

Judgment tasks may be aural as well as written. One such judgment task is an audio-visual task that investigated learner judgments of pragmatic infelicities and ungrammaticality (Bardovi-Harlig and Dörnyei 1998). The basic judgment task was timed; participants viewed each scene twice, decided whether the last utterance of a short exchange was "good" or "bad," and then rated the "bad" utterances along a continuum from "not bad at all" to "very bad." The task has been replicated in different studies, showing that changing the features of a task may promote different levels of explicit pragmatic knowledge. Schauer's (2006) replication additionally interviewed learners to determine how they had classified each error; learners were told how they had responded to each item and then were asked to explain why. Niezgoda and Roever (2001) replicated the judgment task then trained participants to identify grammatical and pragmatic errors. Participants completed the task a second time, classifying each error as either pragmatic or grammatical. Thus, both studies invited the use of explicit knowledge to a greater extent than the original. The classroom activity reported by Bardovi-Harlig and Griffin (2005) used the video judgment task as the basis for classroom instruction. After completing the video judgment task, student dyads were given a written script with the pragmatically infelicitous utterances in context and asked to improve the conversations. Students performed their revised conversations in front of classmates and were video-recorded. The instructional condition is the most open to drawing on explicit knowledge through reflection, discussion, and input from others in an untimed condition.

In contrast to written DCTs and judgment tasks, which are likely to promote the use of explicit knowledge are authentic interactions, including conversations, simulated conversations, and role plays as well as timed spoken tasks (including oral DCTs in the L2; Bardovi-Harlig 2009; Taguchi 2007;) which do not. As Ellis (2004: 238) observes, "explicit knowledge may not be readily available in spontaneous language use where there is little opportunity for careful on-line planning." Thus, whether we approach the evaluation of pragmatic tasks from the perspective of pragmatic values of authenticity, consequentiality, or modality (oral-for-oral or written-for-written tasks) or from the perspective of explicit-implicit knowledge, it seems that both perspectives agree on the basic value of conversation for the study of pragmatics.

3 Current debate: Is there evidence of learner's explicit knowledge in the literature?

Now that we have considered the potential for explicit knowledge from the perspective of SLA, examining tasks that have been used in pragmatics, let us now consider whether there is evidence from learner data that learners have explicit pragmatic knowledge. This section considers evidence from verbal reports, negotiated tasks, and diary studies.

3.1 Retrospective verbal reports

In an early study of learner knowledge using retrospective verbal reports in pragmatics, Cohen and Olshtain (1993) asked learners to perform six role plays and discuss their performance after every two. Learners viewed their videotaped role plays with the researchers who asked them about words and phrases in the responses and how they were learned, language of planning, whether learners knew alternatives, whether they answered as an English speaker or Hebrew speaker, whether they thought about grammar or pronunciation, and whether they thought the response out entirely or partially before they began speaking.

In one example, a learner recounted her reasoning for replying to a scenario in which it would have been appropriate to ask, "Can I get a lift/ride," or,

"Could you give me a lift/ride?" Cohen and Olshtain (1993: 40) reported that she did not know whether she could ask, "Do you have any room in the car?" Her uncertainty led her to a less felicitous choice: "[I] decided she would understand better if I said, *I want to drive with you.*" Another learner considered both *get a ride* and *give a lift* (both felicitous), and finally asked whether she *could get a lift*. Throughout their examples we see instances of learners working through general language knowledge and arriving at decisions that impact their pragmatic production.

Later researchers used more pragmatically focused questions to promote retrospection. Félix-Brasdefer (2004) elicited retrospective verbal reports from learners immediately after refusal role plays. After each refusal situation was enacted, learners were asked to compare refusals in Spanish and American English ("In your opinion, how would a native speaker of Spanish and an American refuse in this situation?"), thus focusing learner responses on the speech act.[3]

One learner who had spent a year abroad in Mexico reported that he "would maybe beat a little more around the bush" with a Mexican, but be more direct with an American; he reflected, "directness [in Mexico] can sometimes be confused with being rude. And also, I think that as a second language speaker . . . it's necessary to even develop a little more tact, be a little more tactful, and be really careful not to offend other people" (Félix-Brasdefer 2004: 636). This same learner also showed a preference for indirectness in the refusal role plays. A second learner, noted that when declining an invitation from a boss, Americans "would be more direct: 'no, I can't, sorry.' Venezuelans in general are really hesitant to say 'no.' They would say, 'yeah, okay, I'll be there'" (Félix-Brasdefer 2004: 636).

In a second study, Félix-Brasdefer (2008) tested learners' awareness of insistence in Latin American Spanish following a refusal of an invitation. Twenty male learners who had lived in Latin America performed two role plays in which they refused an invitation and their interlocutors responded with several insistence moves. Using audio playback in retrospective verbal reports, Félix-Brasdefer asked learners about the immediately completed interactions and whether they had "noticed any cultural differences with respect to the notion of insistence between the United States and the country [they] had visited in Latin America" (2008: 200), this time focusing the learners' responses on one pragmatic strategy used in the realization of refusals. 90% (18/20) of the learners reported that they had become aware of cultural differences in insistence during their time abroad, and 85%

---

3 The repeated questioning over multiple role plays may have served to heighten the learners' awareness of the goal of the questions, thus inviting the use of the learners' explicit knowledge of refusals.

asserted that Latin Americans were more insistent than Americans, observing that "Ecuadorians would press more than Americans," and "Venezuelans would be insistent because they want you to go" (2008: 205).

This study provides some sense of how explicit knowledge and performance are related. Although 90% of the learners reported being aware of insistence patterns, when asked about whether they expected insistence to be directed at them during the role-play interaction, only 20% said that "an insistence was expected because it was a cultural expectation" (2008: 205). That means that the majority of the learners were aware of insistence from their previous experience and could articulate it, but at the same time they did not expect to encounter insistence in the role play, likely resulting from a disjunction between what they have noticed and what is integrated into their interlanguage sociopragmatics.

Kinginger (2008; Kinginger and Farrell 2004) and Villarreal (2014) employed multiple-choice questions and retrospective verbal reports to study address forms in French and Spanish, respectively. Kinginger (2008) presented study-abroad learners with six scenarios that involved speakers of different status, solidarity, and deference. Learners were asked whether they would use *tu* or *vous* in each situation, and to reflect aloud on each choice, thereby providing an immediate retrospection. Using a similar questionnaire, Villarreal's at-home learners discussed six scenarios, and selected from four preset choices, "only *usted*," "mostly *usted* but sometimes *tú*," "mostly *tú* but sometimes *usted*," and "only *tú*." Both groups had had instruction prior to the studies. The at-home learners' retrospections cited solidarity, whereas the study-abroad learners included both solidarity and awareness of L2 norms. This suggests that explicit knowledge may differentially accommodate experience, a topic for future research.

3.2 Language-related episodes

Explicit knowledge of pragmatics may also be observed in language-related episodes (LREs) in pragmatics (Eslami 2014) or pragmatic-related episodes (Taguchi and Kim 2016; Kim and Taguchi 2016). In the instructional effect studies carried out by Taguchi and Kim, students wrote "television drama" scripts involving request-making expressions. The conditions varied, but the common procedure was brief instruction on requesting in English, followed by pair work.[4] The students spoke to each other in Korean (translated in the

---

[4] Taguchi and Kim (2016) also reported individual work, but only the talk that occurred in the pair work is considered here.

original articles). These examples include only the English translations, which occur in square brackets; when the students spoke English, no brackets are used.

In Example (5) the students bring up making the request politely, selecting "I was wondering," a phrase that had been taught, and recalling from instruction that long requests are polite (Taguchi and Kim 2016: 425; all dyads are unique).

(5)   Learner 1: [Jaemyong left his Korean homework at home. He was asking whether he could go home to bring his homework during his self-study session. Then, he should make a request politely?]
Learner 2: [Yes].
------------several turns later-----------------------------
Learner 1: [We need to make a long polite request]. I was wondering
Learner 2: if I could go to?

In Examples (6) – (9), adapted from Kim and Taguchi (2016), learners relate sociopragmatic information about imposition, content, and addressee to pragmalinguistics, including length of requests and expression of head acts. Example (6) shows an LRE targeting a request head act (a student representative asks the school principal to replace old computers with new computers). This example shows two learners agreeing on the sociopragmatic evaluation of "big request" and using that to determine the pragmalinguistics; weighing the use of "I was wondering" (Learner A) against "I really want" (Learner B). Learner A argues that they "should use a long request form since it requires a big request," and Learner B seems convinced as she contributes the next word "buy."

(6)   Learner A: So I was wondering if I. . .
Learner B: I really want. [No. No. Let's write "I really want"]
Learner A: big request. [We should use a long request form since it requires a big request. This is (i.e., I really want) just to emphasize the meaning again.]
Learner B: [Then what are you going to write here?]
Learner A: I was wondering if you could. . .
Learner B: Buy. . .
Learner A: Computers.

In Example (7) different learners discuss the relation of language to the context, this time using the "I really want to" request; they insert an embedded subject "I really want *you* to," and focus on "you" to address a principal. They arrive at the correct grammar, but an overly strong request form, "I want you to buy computers," nonetheless using one of the request forms presented during instruction.

(7) Learner A: I really want to. . .
Learner B: want you to. . want you to buy computers. [Ah. Want you to. It's because the other person is doing it.]
Learner A: you. [But it sounds strange. We are using "you" to refer to a principal.]
Learner B: you. [Oh it is the same. It can also show respect too.]

Like Example (7), Example (8) shows learners considering the relationship of the speakers, this time concluding that they are friends (sociopragmatic knowledge), and therefore do not need to use respectful forms (a pragmalinguistic outcome), settling on "can I" for borrowing an umbrella.

(8) Learner A: [after school? It says it is raining. This is Taegyung and this is Chulmin.
They are friends so we do not need to use respectful forms. Then. . .]
Learner B: *can I*. . .[Yes. Since it is between friends, *can I*. . .]

In (9) the learners invoke both relationship and the request-size rule. Determining that borrowing an umbrella is a small request, not a big one, and that the speakers are classmates, they select the "can I" form as did their classmates in (8).

(9) Learner A: [Are they elementary school students?]
Learner B: [They are classmates. Junsu needs to ask. . .
Learner A: Small. Big request. [This is a small request since it is not a big request.]
Learner B: Big request [It is not a big request.]
Learner A: [Yeah, they are classmates.]
Learner B: *can you*. . .[He says *can you*. . .]

The difference between retrospection and task-based language related episodes is that in the negotiated tasks, the articulation of explicit knowledge and the outcome are both present in the same event. However, the negotiated construction of a script is an entirely explicit event and has no spontaneous production component like role plays.

3.3 Diaries

Additional documentation of explicit knowledge comes from diary studies (e.g., Siegal 1996; DuFon 2006 inter alia; Hassall 2015).[5] In a report of what learners can learn about pragmatics from each other, Hassall asked L2 learners who were studying Indonesian in Central Java to keep a diary, recording events pertaining to three pragmatic features: address terms, leaving taking, and complaints. Learners submitted a minimum of 21 journal entries divided into three periods, 2 weeks, 4 weeks, and after return (7 weeks); they met with the researcher after each submission to debrief. The three types of entries that look most like explicit knowledge include reports of discussions of pragmatic features, joint pragmatic planning, and joint pragmatic action. In Example (10), a learner reports explicitly discussing a pragmatic feature with a fellow learner.

(10) One learner to another: "I don't LIKE these terms [like bare mas] – they seem so IMPERSONAL"
To which her friend replied "just of think of MAS – as – BRO?"
First learner: "I hadn't thought of it in that WAY before and – and so when I started THINKING of it that way
it became a bit more PERSONAL?"
(Excerpted from post-return interview; Hassall 2015: 432)

Sociopragmatic knowledge seems to come to the fore when learners plan pragmatic action jointly with a fellow learner. Hassall reports that two learners jointly decided to opt out of performing a speech act after considering the potential consequences. They decided not to complain to a street vendor who was charging more for soft drinks than the advertised price, considering the vendor's right to charge foreigners more and the potential negative effect on his attitude toward foreign students if they complained. In another case, homestay partners jointly planned how to decline dishes that their homestay mother repeatedly served, but that they strongly disliked, arriving at a subtle hinting strategy which includes both a sociopragmatic plan (perform the act) and a pragmalinguistic component (a subtle hinting strategy). Performing pragmatic action jointly involved the performing of complaints, requests, and refusals, including declining food (discussed

---

5 Self-reports of pragmatic knowledge by researchers-as-L2-learners (Cohen 1997; Hassall 2006; Schmidt and Frota 1986) are not included here as one could argue that linguists are not typical learners.

above), cajoling a music-store owner to let them test a violin, refusing to pay an excessive rickshaw charge, and bargaining.

Retrospective reports, joint construction of scripts leading to pragmatic language-related episodes, and diaries show that learners have access to explicit pragmatic knowledge.

4 Future directions and conclusions

When we think of explicit knowledge, and specifically explicit knowledge about morphology and syntax, we immediately think of language instruction as the main source of explicit knowledge. However, in the case of pragmatics, we should be cautious about claiming that instruction is a source of explicit knowledge of pragmatics without further investigation. Pragmatics is rarely represented in the second/foreign language curriculum. Moreover, pragmatics is rarely represented in language textbooks, and when it is, the language is not authentic. Sources for this observation are both classic (Bardovi-Harlig et al. 1991; Boxer and Pickering 1995; Williams 1988; others followed) and recent (Bardovi-Harlig, Mossman, and Vellenga 2015; Cohen and Ishihara 2013; Ishihara and Cohen 2014). Whereas there is growing interest in instructional pragmatics, it is not yet widespread (Bardovi-Harlig 2017).

These examples have shown that some explicit knowledge comes from instruction (e.g., that big requests need long request forms; Taguchi and Kim 2016; Kim and Taguchi 2016) and some comes from observation and experience (Félix-Brasdefer 2008; Hassall 2015). When we identify explicit knowledge we might also consider whether it accurately describes the pragmatic features it addresses. In my experience, some of what learners "know" is incorrect (as Ellis 2004 observes). For example, in the instructional phase for Bardovi-Harlig and Griffin (2005), a learner pointed out to me that the felicitous *If tomorrow is good for you, I could come anytime you say* is incorrect because *could* is past and *tomorrow* is future. In other projects learners have told me that they do not use the *go*-future (*going to* verb) because *will* is more polite, a belief that I attribute directly to the labeling of *will* requests in ESL textbooks as "polite requests."

I feel confident that at least some learners know things about pragmatics in their second languages that could be helpful. Handy information about Kiswahili greetings would be "Don't stop after the first question; take many turns;" or in English after an appointment with your professor "remember to say 'thank you' but you don't have to apologize." When I lived in Hungary I was coached, "When you enter a room at a party, greet everyone individually." I imagine that sociopragmatic knowledge is easier to articulate than pragmalinguistic knowledge, but the ease of articulation could be tested in the future. I think that we are at the beginning of figuring out what learners know explicitly, how they arrive at that information, and how that might benefit their L2 pragmatics acquisition and use.

In this essay I have attempted to show that learners can access explicit knowledge during certain tasks and have argued that some tasks are more likely than others to encourage the use of explicit knowledge. In L2 pragmatics, as in other areas of SLA, we must take the availability of such knowledge into account when investigating acquisition.

References

Bardovi-Harlig, Kathleen. 2009. Conventional expressions as a pragmalinguistic resource: Recognition and production of conventional expressions in L2 pragmatics. *Language Learning* 59(4). 755–795.

Bardovi-Harlig, Kathleen. 2013. Developing L2 pragmatics. *Language Learning* 63(S1), 68–86.

Bardovi-Harlig, Kathleen. 2017. Acquisition of pragmatics. In Shawn Loewen & Masatoshi Sato (eds.), *Handbook of Instructed SLA*, 224–245. New York: Routledge.

Bardovi-Harlig, Kathleen & Zoltán Dörnyei. 1998. Do language learners recognize pragmatic violations? Pragmatic vs. grammatical awareness in instructed L2 learning. *TESOL Quarterly* 32(2). 233–259.

Bardovi-Harlig, Kathleen & Robert Griffin. 2005. L2 pragmatic awareness: Evidence from the ESL classroom. *System* 33(3). 401–415.

Bardovi-Harlig, Kathleen & Yunwen Su. 2018. The acquisition of conventional expressions as a pragmalinguistic resource in Chinese as a foreign language. *Modern Language Journal* 102(4). 732–757.

Bardovi-Harlig, Kathleen, Beverly A. S. Hartford, Rebecca Mahan-Taylor, Mary J. Morgan, & Dudley W. Reynolds. 1991. Developing pragmatic awareness: Closing the conversation. *ELT Journal* 45(1). 4–15.

Bardovi-Harlig, Kathleen, Sabrina Mossman, & Heidi E. Vellenga. 2015. Developing corpus-based materials to teach pragmatic routines. *TESOL Journal* 6(3). 499–526.

Barron, Anne. 2007. "Ah no honestly we're okay:" Learning to upgrade in a study abroad context. *Intercultural Pragmatics* 4(2). 129–166.

Blum-Kulka, Shoshana, Juliane House, & Gabriele Kasper (eds.). 1989. *Cross-cultural pragmatics: Requests and apologies*. Ablex: Norwood, NJ.

Bonikowska, Malgorzata P. 1988. The choice of opting out. *Applied Linguistics* 9(2). 169–181.

Boxer, Diana & Lucy Pickering. 1995. Problems in the presentation of speech acts in ELT materials: The case of complaints. *ELT Journal* 49(1). 44–58.

Cohen, Andrew D. 1997. Developing pragmatic ability: Insights from the accelerated study of Japanese. In Haruko M. Cook, Kyoko Hijirida, & Mildred M. Tahara (eds.), *New trends and issues in teaching Japanese language and culture* (Technical Report #15), 137–163. Honolulu: University of Hawai'i, Second Language Teaching and Curriculum Center.

Cohen, Andrew D. & Noriko Ishihara. 2013. Pragmatics. In B. Tomlinson (ed.), *Applied linguistics and materials development*, 113–126. London: Bloomsbury Academic.

Cohen, Andrew D. & Elite Olshtain. 1993. The production of speech acts by EFL Learners. *TESOL Quarterly* 27(1). 33–56.

Cohen, Andrew D. & Rachel L. Shively. 2007. Acquisition of requests and apologies in Spanish and French: Impact of study abroad and strategy-building intervention. *The Modern Language Journal* 91(2). 189–212.

DuFon, Margaret A. 2006. The socialization of taste during study abroad in Indonesia. In Margaret A. DuFon & Tim Hassall (eds.), *Language learners in study abroad contexts*, 91–119. Clevedon, UK: Multilingual Matters.

Ellis, Rod. 2004. The definition and measurement of L2 explicit knowledge. *Language Learning* 54(2). 227–275.

Ellis, Rod, Shawn Loewen, Catherine Elder, Rosemary Erlam, Jenefer Philp, & Hayo Reinders. 2009. *Implicit and explicit knowledge in second language learning, testing, and teaching*. Bristol. Multilingual Matters.

Eslami, Zohreh. 2014, October. Incidental focus on form: Linguistics vs. pragmatics related episodes in NS-NNS and NNS-NNS online text-chat. Paper presented to the 2nd international American Pragmatics (AMPRA) conference. UCLA, Los Angeles, CA.

Félix-Brasdefer, J. César. 2004. Interlanguage refusals: Linguistic politeness and length of residence in the target community. *Language Learning* 54(4). 587–653.

Félix-Brasdefer, J. César. 2008. Perceptions of refusals to invitations: Exploring the minds of foreign language learners. *Language Awareness* 17(3). 195–211.

Hassall, Tim. 2006. Learning to take leave in social conversations: A diary study. In Margaret A. Dufon & Eton Churchill (eds.), *Language learners in study abroad contexts*, 31–58. Clevedon, UK: Multilingual Matters.

Hassall, Tim. 2015. Influence of fellow L2 learners on pragmatic development during study abroad. *Intercultural Pragmatics* 12(4). 415–442.

Ishihara, Noriko & Andrew D. Cohen. 2014. *Teaching and learning pragmatics: Where language and culture meet*. New York: Routledge.

Johnston, Bill, Gabriele Kasper, & Steven Ross. 1998. Effect of rejoinders in production questionnaires. *Applied Linguistics* 19(2). 157–182.

Kasper, Gabriele & Merete Dahl. 1991. Research methods in interlanguage pragmatics. *Studies in Second Language Acquisition* 12(2). 215–247.

Kinginger, Celeste. 2008. Language learning in study abroad: Case studies of Americans in France. *The Modern Language Journal* 92(1). 1–131.

Kinginger, Celeste & Kathleen Farrell. 2004. Assessing development of meta-pragmatic awareness in study abroad. *Frontiers: The Interdisciplinary Journal of Study Abroad* 10. 19–42.

Kim, You Jin & Naoko Taguchi. 2016. Learner-learner interaction during collaborative pragmatic tasks: The role of cognitive and pragmatic task demands. *Foreign Language Annals* 49(1). 42–57.

Niezgoda, Kimberly & Carsten Roever. 2001. Pragmatic and grammatical awareness: A function of the learning environment? In Kenneth Rose & Gabriele Kasper (eds.), *Pragmatics in language teaching*, 63–79. Cambridge: Cambridge University Press.

Ogiermann, Eva. 2018. Discourse completion tasks. In Andreas H. Jucker, Klaus P. Schneider, & Wolfram Bublitz (eds.), *Methods in pragmatics*, 229–255. (Handbook of Pragmatics 10). Berlin: De Gruyter Mouton.

Rose, Kenneth R. 1994. On the validity of discourse completion tasks in non-Western contexts. *Applied Linguistics* 15(1). 1–14.

Rose, Kenneth R. & Cynthia Ng. 2001. Inductive and deductive teaching of compliments and compliment responses. In Kenneth Rose & G. Kasper (eds.), *Pragmatics in language teaching*, 145–170. Cambridge: Cambridge University Press.

Schauer, Gila A. 2006. Pragmatic awareness in ESL and EFL contexts: Contrast and development. *Language Learning* 56(2). 269–318.

Schmidt, Richard & Sylvia N. Frota. 1986. Developing basic conversational ability in a second language: A case study of a learner of Portuguese. In Richard Day (ed.), *Talking to learn*, 237–326. Rowley, MA: Newbury House.

Siegal, Meryl. 1996. The role of learner subjectivity in second language sociolinguistic competency: Western women learning Japanese. *Applied Linguistics* 17(3). 356–382.

Taguchi, Naoko. 2007. Task Difficulty in Oral Speech Act Production. *Applied Linguistics* 28(1). 113–135.

Taguchi, Naoko & Youjin Kim. 2016. Collaborative dialogue in learning pragmatics: Pragmatics-related episodes as an opportunity for learning request-making. *Applied Linguistics* 37(3). 416–437.

Villarreal, Dan. 2014. Connecting production to judgments: T/V address forms and the L2 identities of intermediate Spanish learners. *Journal of Pragmatics* 66. 1–14.

Williams, Marion. 1988. Language taught for meetings and language used in meetings: Is there anything in common? *Applied Linguistics* 9(1). 45–58.

Diana Boxer and Eleonora Rossi

14 Studying speech acts: An expanded scope and refined methodologies

Abstract: There is little danger in asserting that Andrew Cohen has been a pioneering researcher in speech act analysis. Indeed, it is clear from an overview of his work that he has contributed groundbreaking research to the theoretical and methodological underpinnings of speech act/interlanguage pragmatics analysis. In this essay we endeavor to discuss the scope of speech act research, how the scope has changed, and the various methods used to carry out such research. Thus, this chapter focuses on both theoretical and methodological issues on the progression of theory and method in pragmatics research. It addresses the questions: how did we get from there to here, and where are we headed?

Keywords: interlanguage pragmatics, Critical Discourse Analysis, Advances in methodologies, Neuroimaging approaches

1 Introduction

Andrew Cohen was one of a handful of applied linguistics scholars to take off from Hymes' (1962) theoretical work proposing that the speech act is the smallest unit of rule-governed speech. It took some 15 to 20 years for scholars to launch the widespread study of how speech acts are realized in various societies and how their inappropriate use could lead to miscommunication and misperceptions across cultures. Cohen was one of these scholars at the vanguard of speech act analysis for language learners. This work stemmed from the ample evidence that such miscommunication could have dire consequences for users of a second language. How to best acquire "communicative competence" was the focus of speech act research in the 1980s and into the 1990s. Cohen's work on bilingualism, strategies, and interlanguage pragmatics (ILP) is iconic of this important research endeavor. His publications in these areas span a lifetime of research that continues to this day and that are simply too numerous to list here.

In the past 25 years, however, we have seen a dramatic shift in two phenomena: 1) an enormous increase in international flows of people; and 2) a surge in internet communication platforms. Given these shifts, the question to address now is: "where we go from here?" Speech act analysis for ILP has taken on a new importance in the present-day world characterized by globalization and

https://doi.org/10.1515/9783110721775-015

transnationalism. We can no longer assume that second/foreign language users have the luxury of acquiring a firm basis in a language before being plunged into a foreign society as migrants and/or asylum-seekers. This is especially true of pragmatic norms. In fact, some would assert that the very concept of "pragmatic norms" is obfuscated in a shrinking planet. That is to say, as the world becomes smaller and smaller due to increased travel, trade, and immigration, the issue of how to communicate not only correctly, but more importantly, pragmatically, is crucial. The consequence is that we must now study the acquisition of pragmatics as an issue of global importance.

We outline here the progression of approaches on studying pragmatics from the early days to the present, where a Critical Discourse Analysis (CDA) perspective is paramount. Issues of inequality, voice, identity, and ideology must now be taken into account when we seek to understand second language pragmatics. In an era characterized by large flows of people across linguistic and cultural boundaries, it is increasingly critical that 1) speakers be able to present themselves as they wish and 2) that the uptake of understanding speech behavior not be obfuscated by clashing norms. From a methodological perspective, this essay undertakes to describe the progression of how we have studied speech act realization, concentrating on the earlier methods encompassing discourse completion test (DCTs), role-plays, ethnographic analysis, and think-aloud protocols. We go from here to new possibilities offered by experimental, neuro/psycholinguistic approaches that now examine bilingual acquisition employing psycholinguistic techniques. We are now at a crossroads of having the ability to assess pragmatics by actually looking into the brain to ascertain how language is processed. This essay takes a look at the cutting edge of new perspectives and techniques for the study of pragmatic acquisition.

2 Key issues: Current trends and debates

2.1 Theoretical issues

The traditional manner in which we have approached second language pragmatics has been to gather baseline information on how speech acts are realized in various linguistic/cultural groups and subsequently to determine how best to deal with contrasting formulations considered polite in one society but not in another. The thrust has been to inform second language learners regarding the possible pitfalls in assuming their L1 pragmatics can be successfully transferred to L2. In the present state of the world, however, we can no longer examine pragmatics from the view of target-like use (TLU). The current question is, in fact, what is the target?

This argument is not a new one, but harkens back to 1996 (1997 publication in *Modern Language Journal*), with Alan Firth and Johannes Wagner's colloquium at the AILA conference on problems in current trends in SLA research. Firth and Wagner advocated that we move away from the concepts of *language learner* and rather use the concept, *language user*. They also urged reconsidering our focus on the concepts of *non-native speaker* (NNS) and *interlanguage*. The fact that they did so was a direct result of recognizing what was happening in the world of English as a Lingua Franca (ELF) even so many years ago. The world since then has been rapidly undergoing enormous changes as more and more non-English speakers have started using English in all sorts of interactions in a wide range of domains. Indeed, since then there are now more users of English whose L1 is not English than those whose L1 is English. Complicating this global situation is the proliferation of modern online platforms (e.g., Facebook, Twitter, WhatsApp, online gaming) for discourse across cultural and linguistic groups. The issue of "who owns English?" (e.g., Davies 2013; Pennycook 2009) is spread to "whose pragmatic norms are relevant?"

Situations of transnationalism and globalization have been examined by sociolinguists over the past two decades at least (see Blommaert 2003; Rampton 1995 on *Crossing*). Blommaert (2004) has been especially clear in advocating a CDA approach to outlining issues of *voice* in situations of migration and asylum-seeking. We now need to examine the pragmatics of verbal interaction (oral and written) through a lens of the obfuscation of "norms." This issue is to a large extent due to the current state of "superdiversity" of western societies. In their essay on the subject, Blommaert and Rampton (2011: 4) state:

> Over a period of several decades – and often emerging in response to issues predating superdiversity – there has been ongoing revision of fundamental ideas (a) about languages, (b) about language groups and speakers, and (c) about communication. Rather than working with homogeneity, stability and boundedness as the starting assumptions, mobility, mixing, political dynamics and historical embedding are now central concerns in the study of languages, language groups and communication.

If indeed there is a loosening of "boundedness" and a proliferation of mixing, there cannot be any doubt that our prior manner of examining speech act use in bounded societal groups needs to be reconsidered. Given that groups are no longer "bounded" in the way in which they used to be, how can we reasonably view the study of ILP? Is ILP even relevant? That which must concern us now is not only the issue of specific speech act realizations across cultures but instead the ability of people in superdiversity to express themselves as they wish to be perceived by their interlocutors. In a co-edited volume (Boxer and Cohen 2004) from some fifteen years ago, Boxer (2004: 5–9) stated in the introduction:

> While it remains true that English continues to be the world's lingua franca with regard to commerce, trade and diplomacy, it is now the case that communication in the English language occurs, more often than not, among speakers none of whose first language (L1) is English (see McKay, 2002 for a good overview of this phenomenon) . . . (p. 5). Whether or not those in the position of taking on new linguistic and cultural identities choose to appropriate or reject the 'affordances' of the new language/culture may depend largely on the lived histories of the individuals, the contexts of their interactions, and the power relationships inherent in these contexts (p. 9).[1]

A major "affordance" of a new language/culture is the use of appropriate speech behavior of the L2. We need not "throw out the baby with the bathwater." Instead we need to recognize and re-work our view of ILP and intercultural pragmatics (ICP). While ILP is still a concern in some contexts of instrumental motivation, there is more fluidity needed in our theoretical underpinnings of how to go about our analyses.

This is indeed a very thorny issue. While Blommaert and Rampton appear to align with the earlier critique put forth by Firth and Wagner (1997), they take it to a new level:

> . . . Although notions like 'native speaker,' 'mother tongue' and 'ethnolinguistic group' have considerable ideological force (and as such should certainly feature as objects of analysis), they should have no place in the sociolinguistic toolkit itself. When the reassurance afforded by a priori classifications like these is abandoned, research instead has to address the ways in which people take on different linguistic forms as they align and disaffiliate with different groups at different moments and stages. It has to investigate how they (try to) opt in and opt out, how they perform or play with linguistic signs of group belonging, and how they develop particular trajectories of group identification throughout their lives.   (Blommaert and Rampton 2011: 5)

If we agree with the above assertion, then we must re-examine how we have gone about taking as given the notion that societies have differing norms of speech behavior that come into conflict in situations of contact. While this fact is certainly true, it is not as simple as previously conceived, when nation states were clearly delineated. Situations of contact are now occurring in domains not previously for-seen, and group belonging has changed dramatically in nature. Indeed, we have come far since the days of CCSARP (Cross Cultural Speech Act

---

[1] The situation described for English is not necessarily the case for other languages. With Spanish, for instance, while Spanish speakers can be found in many different non-Spanish-dominant regions, there is not yet evidence of Spanish being a lingua franca.

Realization Project) (1989), spearheaded by pioneering researchers in speech act analysis (Blum-Kulka, Kasper, and House 1989) and including other early researchers in this line of endeavor. The thrust of this body of research was to compare/contrast the realization of requests and apologies across several speech communities. The researchers employed the same DCT to come to conclusions about these two speech act sets and, by extension, afforded possible conclusions about where areas of trouble might occur.

We now have considerable diversity, even superdiversity, that offers the analyst new challenges to the goal of recognizing differences in politeness norms of speech act realizations, and the first challenge is how to reasonably move toward mutual understanding. How are we to deal with a clash of what speakers believe to be acceptable and appropriate when the slightest deviation is cause for processing difficulties leading to misinterpretation and judgment? As Blommaert and Rampton (2011: 12) note:

> For much of the time, most of the resources materialized in any communicative action are unnoticed and taken for granted, but it only takes a slight deviation from habitual and expected practice to send recipients into interpretive overdrive, wondering what's going on when a sound, a word, a grammatical pattern, a discourse move or bodily movement doesn't quite fit.

What is critical here is the fact of power dynamics in intercultural pragmatics (ICP). Cohen himself (2006, 2012 and elsewhere) has offered us a glimpse into how pragmatics can be studied with a multi-modal analysis (this will be further discussed in the next section). Given the transnationalism and globalization of the world as it presently exists, we now must always take into account the issues of identity, ideology, and power dynamics in changing societies. Methodological issues of how best to study these phenomena are paramount. We now turn to an overview of how we have studied speech acts in ILP and where we can go from here using new methods.

2.2 Methodological issues

Until recently, a large portion of studies on speech act realizations for ILP have employed DCTs to gather large amounts of data. The DCT method has the advantage of constraining the sociolinguistic variables and topics in a discourse stretch in order to ascertain how language learners (users) think they might carry out the speech act, for example, a request. The amount of imposition is therefore prearranged in the actual DCT. Traditionally, subjects would write in their response. Amassing a large quantity of DCTs would give the researcher some evidence of the canonical shape of speech act realizations and their responses. As noted by several researchers, there are at least two issues with such data. First, there is the problem of asking language users to dig into their intuitions on how they might say something. We know speaker intuition to be notoriously unreliable. Subjects want to present themselves in the best possible light, thus possibly providing answers that present them as good people; second, there is the Hawthorne effect of wanting to please the researcher. In other words, there is the possibility of the participant providing what he/she believes is the "right" answer. Notwithstanding these issues, responses provide an assessment of participants' (idealized) pragmatic knowledge.

Knowing the limitations of DCTs, ILP researchers began using oral DCTs in the form of role-plays. These improved upon the written DCT insofar as participants are at least providing oral data. Think-aloud protocols, immediately following the data provided, gave increased insight into what participants were thinking when they were speaking. Again, one can easily imagine the limitations of speaker insight.

At the same time that the above methods for acquiring ILP data were being widely employed, others (e.g., Wolfson 1986; Boxer 1993) were taking an ethnographic approach to ILP data. First and foremost, native speaker (NS) baseline information would be collected before we could say anything about language learners. Once we had a clear idea of NS norms regarding such speech acts as, for example, compliments or complaints, we could then proceed to study what members of other linguistic communities do with these speech acts. Only after amassing the two sets of data could any reasonable conclusions be reached about how to best go about teaching NS pragmatic norms to NNSs.

Clearly, such a method has inherently severe constraints. The most notable of these is the fact that one would have to wait a very long time to collect data that gives insight into how speech acts are realized in different constellations of communicative activity.

Consistent with his ongoing examination of strategies in SLA, Cohen has taken discussions with other pragmatics scholars to heart with thoughtful insights into how to best study ILP/ICP. In 2005, he published an important piece in the journal *Intercultural Pragmatics* that focused on strategies for learning and performing L2 speech acts. Subsequently, Garces Conejos-Blivitch (2006), took several of Cohen's assertions to task. In her commentary on Cohen's (2005) article, she, like others, critiques the concept of TLU. She takes into account the current issue of validity of DCTs; moreover and notably, she asks the question, what about multi-competence analysis?

Garces-Conejos-Blivitch discusses the problem that DCTs disregard multi-competence pragmatics and suggests that data derived from corpora, which are more natural, ought to complement DCTs. In his response, Cohen (2006) readily agrees and further discusses the value of data triangulation. However, he comes to the defense of elicited data (DCTs, role-plays), asserting that this kind of data is "conveniently condensed and accessible." He states:

> There is, in fact, an increase in pragmatics research that draws extensively on discourse analysis and especially conversational analysis, in an effort to better understand actual pragmatic performance. There is no doubt that such research is demonstrating that a triangulated approach to data collection is advisable. For example, a recent study comparing elicited approaches to data collection with the collection of corpus data would suggest that while there are advantages to collecting elicited data, it is valuable to complement these data with corpus data as well (e.g., Schauer and Adolphs 2006). I would firmly agree. My concern would be not to "throw the baby out with the bathwater" in our pursuit of more natural data. (Cohen 2006: 360)

In fact, Cohen's and his colleagues/students made successful efforts toward pedagogical applications of pragmatic information. For example, in 2004, Cohen and Ishihara created a website specifically for learners of Japanese. In 2006, this was followed with "the design, construction, and evaluation of a website specifically dedicated to Spanish speech acts" (http://www.carla.umn.edu/speechacts/). These sites have called for drawing from empirically based speech act sources, both natural and elicited sources. This involves efforts to reflect conversational dynamics and thus offers potential strategies for more effective speech act production.

In the introductory chapter to Boxer and Cohen's 2004 co-edited volume, *Studying Speaking to Inform Second Language Learners*, we noted the following:

> Once we have knowledge of what members of discourse communities successfully do in spontaneous spoken discourse, we can then apply these findings to situations in which novice language users are acquiring and employing an L2 in any domain and in variously configured communities and interactions. Such varied contexts include: bilingual language practices such as code alternation and switching; sensitivity to the constraints of the sociolinguistic variables (e.g., gender, social distance, and social status) in the L2; sensitivity to domains of usage (e.g., workplace, education, and social interaction); and understanding how to carry out transactional and interactional discourse (cf. Brown and Yule 1983), to take some examples. (Boxer and Cohen: 19)

While recognizing their limits, DCTs do have their place in speech act research. We can clearly see an effort in keeping the baby (DCT methods), while diversifying the bathwater. As Cohen himself states: "Although the model dialogues on the website are based on elicited interactions and not 'natural data', they are nonetheless unscripted and largely spontaneous, thus lending them some authenticity" (2006: 363).

Beyond the use of DCT methodology, Blommaert and Rampton (2011), suggest ways that we could build on the theoretical perspective of multilingual and multimodal communication in the era of "superdiversity." As we do here, Blommaert and Rampton look to engage linguistic ethnography as well as a range of other discourse-analytical approaches that have proven to be productive approaches for the study of multilingual and multimodal interaction. Among them are interactional sociolinguistics (Räisänen 2018; Vidal 2015), sociocultural linguistics (Furukawa 2014), discourse pragmatics (Félix-Brasdefer 2015), membership categorization analysis (Fukuda 2017), multimodal discourse analysis (Kim 2018), and multimodal conversation analysis (González-Lloret 2016; Hazel 2017; Mondada 2012).

3 Future directions

The great variability in defining who a bilingual and second language speaker is remains a matter of current investigation (Surrain and Luk 2019). Despite the recent reevaluation of defining bilingualism, recent research has also highlighted how interactional and social complexity (including measures of identity) might play a crucial role in explaining both linguistic and brain signatures related to second language processing and bilingualism (Gullifer et al. 2018; Gullifer and Titone 2020). If small initial steps have been taken to understand how these social variables intertwine with linguistic behavioral and brain data for variables such as contexts of language use and code switching, little to no information exists for the study of speech acts. The study of speech acts in native and in second language acquisition has grown enormously in the last 50 years. However, as described, most of the extant literature is based on off-line behavioral measures of speech processing, such as off-line DCTs or in the form of role-play. Despite the informativeness of off-line behavioral data, such as accuracy and end of the sentence response latencies, such data likely represent an aggregate measure combining different linguistic and cognitive processes that are at the bases of speech act processing. As such, the analysis of off-line behavioral data does not reveal the different linguistic and cognitive components that are involved during real-time speech act processing.

Only very recently have researchers started to utilize more sophisticated methods to investigate the linguistic and neural processes that occur during the real-time processing of speech acts. For example, scholars have begun to utilize methods such as Electroencephalography (EEG) and functional Magnetic resonance Imaging (fMRI) to study speech acts from a more immediate neurocognitive perspective, adding important information in how speech acts are processed in real time in the brain. In what follows, we will briefly describe the bases of EEG and fMRI. We will also illustrate how these methodologies are currently applied to the study of speech acts, and we will conclude the section with some ideas for future research.

3.1 EEG: Electricity in the brain

Electroencephalography (EEG) is the science that studies the spontaneous electrical activity of the brain (Luck 2014). The brain's neurons fire constantly even when at rest, and in response to cognitive stimuli, including language processing. EEG is a completely non-invasive and relatively low-cost technique that enables recording the spontaneous and/or evoked electrical activity of the brain by simply placing electrodes mounted onto an elastic cap on the participant's scalp. The discomfort is minimal, and it enables scientists to conduct a number of linguistic experiments involving comprehension and production of linguistic stimuli, from single words to sentences and discourse.

The spontaneous electrical activity of the brain is incredibly fast, with neurons firing at the rate of milliseconds. The ability to capture the change in neural signal while locked to specific linguistic experimentally-manipulated stimuli enables us to open a window into how the brain prepares for and responds to a variety of linguistic operations, including speech acts in first language and interlanguage pragmatics.

Traditionally, language researchers have analyzed the brain's EEG signal locked to specific experimental stimuli (e.g., single words or specific portions of sentences), measuring the so-called Event Related Potentials (ERPs) which result from averaging and comparing neural activation across many experimental trials of the same type and across many participants. By averaging across a number of trials for each experimental condition, and with a large enough sample, the brain signal and its course of activation can be tracked with an excellent time precision, providing researchers with "brain signatures" that have been linked to specific linguistic operations. These "brain signatures" have also been paramount to highlight similarities and differences between native and second language processing.

Decades of research using EEG for language research have revealed that there are "electrical brain components" specific to a number of linguistic operations. For example, lexico-semantic processes elicit a negative brain wave around 400 ms after a stimulus occurs, the so-called N400 (Kutas and Hillyard 1980; Kutas and Federmeier 2011). As an example, the N400 component is elicited by sentences that contain a semantic violation or anomaly such as: "*I drank coffee with a stone." This brain component has also been used to examine the very early stages of L2 learning, revealing that the brain's sensitivity to the new L2 emerges very early during L2 acquisition (McLaughlin, Osterhout and Kim 2004; Osterhout, McLaughlin, Pitkänen, Frenck-Mestre and Molinaro 2006).

Another "electrical brain component" that has been consistently recorded in response to grammatical violations is a positive brain wave visible around 600 ms after a stimulus occurs (Osterhout and Holcomb 1992; Osterhout and Nicol 1999). For example, the P600 is elicited by morpho-syntactic violations such as subject-verb violations, as for example: "*The cat eat the food" (Hagoort, Brown, and Groothusen 1993). The P600 has generally been interpreted as signaling morpho-syntactic reanalysis and repair, integration difficulties, and increased processing demands (Kaan and Swaab, 2003).

If the EEG methodology has been widely utilized to study a number of linguistic phenomena, only in recent years have neurolinguists started to apply it to study of pragmatics. In the last ten years, a growing number of neuroimaging studies have tackled the neural bases of non-conversational discourse and pragmatic inferences, and have provided evidence that shows that components of discourse are processed extremely fast (around 200 ms). However, less research has been conducted on speech act processing in a dialogue context. In an earlier study, Egorova, Shtyrov, and Pulvermuller (2013) used ERPs to study the earliest brain signatures in response to two types of speech acts, mainly *naming* and *requests*. The results revealed an early brain signal around 200 ms, with request-evoked potentials being larger for requests than naming, suggesting early pragmatic processing happening even before lexico-semantic integration. These results were interpreted by suggesting that pragmatic processes happen very early on, even preceding lexico-semantic integration. Importantly, in this study, participants observed videos of two individuals interacting in a discourse context, but they were not actively involved themselves in the speech act.

The finding that speech act recognition emerges early even while the rest of the utterance is still being processed has been supported by a number of recent EEG studies to further the understanding of speech act processing. Gisladottir, Chwilla, and Levinson (2015) recorded ERPs when participants listened to dialogues and performed an action categorization task. The speech acts that participants had to perform differed depending on the prior discourse context. Again, the results showed an early ERP modulation (around 200ms) suggesting that listeners can recognize and process speech acts very early on during discourse preparation. In a follow up study, Gisladottir, Bögels, and Levinson (2018) investigated speech act recognition during spoken dialogue that were completed by a target answer that was either an answer, a declination, or a pre-offer. This time, the authors analyzed the EEG signal in the frequency domain (i.e., they looked at frequencies in the signal, instead of the timing) and report a power reduction in the alpha and beta bands (8–30 Hz) just before declinations, suggesting a brain signature for anticipating speech acts. The authors conclude that this brain anticipation signature during speech act comprehension could be foundational to enable fluid speech and dialogue interactions.

In sum, language beyond the sentence level has begun to be studied also using EEG methodology, enabling scientists to tease apart the complex linguistic and cognitive components underlying the processing of speech acts. An important note here is that all these studies have been conducted in the native language of the participants. An open question for future research is whether these "brain anticipatory signatures" will be observed in L2 speech act processing. Advancing research in speech acts in L2 processing using neurophysiological techniques such as EEG would enable us to disentangle if L2 speakers engage different "language" neural components during speech act processing. For example, as exemplified by the few other studies conducted in the field, L2 speakers might show more of a lexical processing signature (i.e., N400) rather than a more syntactic-discourse reanalysis component (i.e., P600). Analyzing on-line neural signatures of speech act processing could also enable us to look at the development of the signature over time as a factor of changing proficiency, or changes in social interaction experiences. These are all testable future directions that the field could take to advance the understanding of speech act processing, and advance research in the context of a more naturalistic discourse setting while using brain data.

3.2 Functional magnetic resonance imaging: Tracking brain networks in speech acts

If EEG affords great temporal resolution by enabling to track the neural response in response to linguistic stimulus with millisecond precision, the spatial precision (i.e., understanding what neural network(s) are involved in specific linguistic processes) is not optimal. Without going into great detail, it is sufficient to mention here that if with EEG we capture the electrical activity of the brain on the scalp surface, the methodology does not enable us to get at the source of the neural activation without a great margin of error. Instead, the neuroimaging technique that allows us to understand what brain areas, or brain networks, are involved in a specific linguistic process or function is magnetic Resonance Imaging (fMRI).

fMRI is a non-invasive but extremely expensive technique. On an average basis, the utilization of research scanner facilities ranges from $400–600 per hour of testing. As such, the utilization of fMRI is highly reliant on the availability of external funds for research. If the EEG methodology captures the spontaneous electrical activity of the brain, MRI relies on detecting the rate of oxygenated blood that perfuses brain areas, as a proxy for brain activation. In other words, when brain areas need to be utilized for a certain cognitive function, neural activity sparks an immediate increase of blood flow to those areas, which in turn is detected by MRI. The MRI methodology has been used extensively to study language processing (for a review on the methodology, see Glover 2011). Only a handful of studies have utilized fMRI to study language processing beyond the sentence level, or pragmatics and speech act processing. One such study is by Bašnáková, Weber, Petersson, van Berkum, and Hagoort (2014), in which participants were asked to listen to utterances that were identical at the word and sentence level, but were used to express different informative intentions. Their results showed the activation of several brain regions that were previously implicated in empathy, affective and socio-communicative processing, and in discourse-level language processing, such as bilateral prefrontal cortex and right temporal regions. Another recent fMRI study suggests that the comprehension of pragmatic acts involves a number of neural regions that have been previously demonstrated to be important for theory of mind processing (Van Ackeren, Casasanto, Bekkering, Hagoort, and Rueschemeyer 2012), suggesting that pragmatic inferences and speech act processing are very complex linguistic phenomena that ought to be understood in a socio-cognitive-linguistic framework. Similar to what has been observed for the few extant EEG studies, no fMRI studies to date have looked at speech act processing in L2 learners, leaving an open field of research to be studied in future research.

In sum, the utilization of neuroimaging methodologies such as EEG and fMRI for the study of speech acts and ILP have, as any other experimental techniques, advantages and disadvantages. The advantages of moving forward to begin to apply these neuroimaging methodologies to the study of speech acts and ILP are certainly the ability to understand how speakers' brains respond during the processing of speech acts and thereby understanding what brain networks are at play in real time during speech acts and whether differences between the processing of speech acts develops during second language acquisition.

Even though it seems to be the case that dipping the toes into these new methodologies would provide considerable insights into the processing of speech acts in ILP, a number of limitations can be recognized. Both EEG and fMRI require participants to complete the task in a laboratory setting, far from a naturalistic linguistic environment, and with fMRI paradigms requiring participants to perform the task while lying in a scanner for a relatively long time. Another general characteristic of transferring a behavioral task for any type of neuroimaging techniques is the required high number of experimental items for each manipulated condition. The brain signal, an electric spike or an increase in blood flow to a specific brain area as a consequence of a linguistic act, is very small. As such, to obtain a good signal-to-noise ratio, these paradigms need a relatively large number of items and a good sample size in terms of participants. For example, according to current experimental standards for ERP studies, a signal that averages across 20–25 analyzable items per condition and collected from at least 25 participants would be the norm.

However, especially for EEG, the technical advances are making it more and more possible to utilize this methodology in a naturalistic linguistic setting, even providing the opportunity of recording the brain activity "in the wild" during a conversation in a spontaneous naturalistic environment. A growing number of studies are starting to utilize EEG during conversational interactive settings, however still in laboratory environments. A task for future research will be to adapt and utilize these novel methodologies in more naturalistic conversational settings.

4 Conclusions

We have reviewed the current state of the art for speech act research in ILP, with suggestions for how we ought to go about studying these phenomena in a world for which the hallmark is transnationalism and globalization, with continual movements of people from various places to others. These migration patterns give rise to taking a new point of view regarding just how language is used for communication across linguistic and cultural divides. Our suggestion is in line with those who, more than twenty years ago, advocated changing our traditional perspective on what it means to be a language user in such a world. Issues of power and hegemony are now paramount, and CDA is in order, at least for qualitative measures of speech act comprehension and use.

Beyond this theoretical shift, we advocate a methodological shift as well. We have described the methods by which speech act analysis for ILP has taken place over the past forty-some years. The question now is, how can we best go about measuring speech act use given new techniques that are now available to us? We have suggested new experimental techniques, employing EEG and fMRI instrumentation to look into the workings of the brain when confronted with speech act use across linguistic and cultural communities. These methods have the potential to measure processing difficulties when users of a language deal with speech act production that does not align with what is deemed acceptable or appropriate use in an L1 or L2. Here is where we might envision taking a CDA perspective in conjunction with experimental techniques. For example, a CDA paradigm could be conducted utilizing fMRI. By combining qualitative methods with these cutting-edge experimental approaches, we ought to be able to ascertain just how and when processing difficulties occur and from where these difficulties arise. These lessons have the potential to provide us, at the beginning stages at least, with fruitful information about the uptake of speech act interpretation. To the extent that processing difficulties are shown in the experimental data, we are provided with clues about how these difficulties may logically lead to misperceptions and miscommunication across groups. This kind of evidence in turn will enable us to understand and thus inform the acquisition of pragmatic norms in bilingual groups. Here is where the issues of identity, ideology, and voice may be the focus. As bilingual speakers interact, whether in the context of ILP or CCP, there are three potentially important outcomes that might very well result in more harmonious cross-cultural interactions: 1) the ability to present one's identity as one wishes to be perceived; 2) the ability to give voice to one's actions and feelings in ways that are not perceived as "weird;" and 3) the creation of a renewed ideology of understanding.

These are the ways of the future. For young, emerging scholars in the field of pragmatics and language learning, the future is here. It is up to these scholars to take up a fruitful continuation of this valuable endeavor.

References

Bašnáková, Jana, Kirsten Weber, Karl M. Petersson, Jos van Berkum, & Peter Hagoort. 2014. Beyond the language given: The neural correlates of inferring speaker meaning. *Cerebral Cortex* 24(10). 2572–2578.
Blommaert, Jan. 2003. Commentary: A sociolinguistics of globalization. *Journal of Sociolinguistics* 7(4). 607–623.
Blommaert, Jan. 2004. *Discourse*. Cambridge: Cambridge University Press.
Blommaert, Jan & Ben Rampton. 2011. *Language and Superdiversity* 13(2). 1–20.
Blum-Kulka, Shoshana, Juliane House, & Gabriele Kasper (eds). 1989. *Cross-cultural pragmatics: Requests and apologies*. Norwood, NJ: Ablex.
Boxer, Diana. 1993. Complaints as positive strategies: What the learner needs to know. *TESOL Quarterly* 27. 277–299.
Boxer, Diana. 2004. Studying speaking to inform second language learning: A conceptual overview. In Diana Boxer & Andrew D. Cohen (eds.), *Studying speaking to inform second language learning*, 3–24. Clevedon: Multilingual Matters.
Boxer, Diana & Andrew D. Cohen. 2004. *Studying speaking to inform second language learning*. Clevedon: Multilingual Matters.
Brown, Gillian & George Yule. 1983. *Discourse analysis*. Cambridge: Cambridge University Press.
Cohen, Andrew D. 2005. Strategies for learning and performing L2 speech acts. *Intercultural Pragmatics* 2(3). 275–301.
Cohen, Andrew D. 2006. Interlanguage pragmatics: A reply to Pilar Garces-Conejos Blitvich. *Intercultural Pragmatics* 3(3). 359–364.

Cohen, Andrew D. & Noriko Ishihara. 2004. A web-based approach to strategic learning of speech acts. Report to the Center for Advanced Research on Language Acquisition.

Davies, Alan. 2013. Native speaker. In Carol Chapelle (ed.), *The Encyclopedia of Applied Linguistics*. https://doi.org/10.1002/9781405198431.wbeal0855 (accessed 4 August, 2020).

Egorova, Natalia, Yuri Shtyrov, & Friedmann Pulvermuller. 2013. Early and parallel processing of pragmatic and semantic information in speech acts: neurophysiological evidence. *Frontiers in Human Neuroscience* 7. 1–13.

Félix-Brasdefer, César. 2015. *The language of service encounters: A pragmatic-discursive approach*. Cambridge: Cambridge University Press.

Firth, Alan & Johannes Wagner. 1997. On Discourse, Communication, and (Some) Fundamental Concepts in SLA Research. *The Modern Language Journal* 81(3). 285–300.

Fukuda, Chie. 2017. Gaijin performing gaijin [A foreigner performing a foreigner]: Coconstruction of foreigner stereotypes in a Japanese talk show as a multimodal phenomenon. *Journal of Pragmatics* 109. 12–28.

Furukawa, Gavin. 2014. 'Stupidest of all the primates': The role of English in Japanese television. *Journal of Asian Pacific Communication* 25(2). 196–220.

Garces-Conejos Blitvich, Pilar. 2006. Interlanguage pragmatics: A response to Andrew Cohen's "Strategies for learning and performing L2 speech acts" *Intercultural Pragmatics* 3(2). 213–223.

Gisladottir, Rosa S., Sara Bögels, & Stephen C. Levinson. 2018. Oscillatory brain responses reflect anticipation during comprehension of speech acts in spoken dialog. *Frontiers in Human Neuroscience* 12. 1–13.

Gisladottir, Rosa S., Dorothee J. Chwilla, & Stephen C. Levinson. 2015. Conversation electrified: ERP correlates of speech act recognition in underspecified utterances. *PloS One* 10(3). 1–24.

Glover, Gary H. 2011. Overview of functional magnetic resonance imaging. *Neurosurgery Clinics* 22(2). 133–139.

González-Lloret, Marta. 2016. The construction of emotion in multilingual computer-mediated interaction. In Matthew Prior & Gabriele Kasper (eds.), *Emotion in multilingual interaction*, 289–311. Amsterdam: John Benjamins.

Gullifer, Jason W. & Debra Titone. 2020. Characterizing the social diversity of bilingualism using language entropy. *Bilingualism: Language and Cognition* 23. 283–294.

Gullifer, Jason W., Xiaoquian J. Chai, Veronica Whitford, Irina Pivneva, Shari Baum, Denise Klein, & Debra Titone. 2018. Bilingual experience and resting-state brain connectivity: Impacts of L2 age of acquisition and social diversity of language use on control networks. *Neuropsychologia* 117. 123–134.

Hagoort, Peter, Colin Brown, & Jolanda Groothusen. 1993. The syntactic positive shift (SPS) as an ERP measure of syntactic processing. *Language and Cognitive Processes* 8(4). 439–483.

Hazel, Spencer. 2017. Mapping the langscape – developing multilingual norms in a transient project community. *Journal of Linguistic Anthropology* 27(3). 308–325.

Hymes, Dell. 1962. The Ethnography of Speaking. In T. Gladwin and W.C. Sturdevant (eds.), *Anthropology and Human Behavior*, 15–53. Washington, D.C.: Anthropological Society of Washington.

Kaan, Edith. & Tamara Swaab. 2003. Electrophysiological evidence for serial sentence processing: A comparison between non-preferred and ungrammatical continuations. *Cognitive Brain Research* 17(3). 621–635.

Kim, Sujin. 2018. "It was kind of a given that we were all multilingual": Transnational youth identity work in digital translanguaging. *Linguistics and Education* 43. 39–52.

Kutas, Marta & Kara. D. Federmeier. 2011. Thirty years and counting: finding meaning in the N400 component of the event-related brain potential (ERP). *Annual Review of Psychology* 62. 621–647.

Kutas, Marta & Steven A. Hillyard. 1980. Event-related brain potentials to semantically inappropriate and surprisingly large words. *Biological Psychology* 11(2). 99–116.

Luck, Steve. J. 2014. *An introduction to the event-related potential technique*. Cambridge, MA: MIT press.

McKay, Sandra. 2002. *Teaching English as an international language: Rethinking goals and approaches*. Oxford: Oxford University Press.

McLaughlin, Janet, Lee Osterhout, & Al Kim. 2004. Neural correlates of second-language word learning: Minimal instruction produces rapid change. *Nature neuroscience* 7(7). 703–704

Mondada, Lorenza. 2012. The dynamics of embodied participation and language choice in multilingual meetings. *Language in Society* 41. 213–235.

Osterhout, Lee & Philip. J. Holcomb. 1992. Event-related brain potentials elicited by syntactic anomaly. *Journal of Memory and Language* 31(6). 785–806.

Osterhout, Lee & Janet Nicol. 1999. On the distinctiveness, independence, and time course of the brain responses to syntactic and semantic anomalies. *Language and Cognitive Processes* 14(3). 283–317.

Osterhout, Lee, Judith McLaughlin, Ilona Pitkänen, Cheryl Frenck-Mestre, & Nicola Molinaro. 2006. Novice learners, longitudinal designs, and event-related potentials: A means for exploring the neurocognition of second language processing. *Language Learning* 56. 199–230.

Pennycook, Alistair. 2009. Global Englishes and transcultural flows. *Applied Linguistics* 30(2). 305–307.

Rampton, Ben. 1995. *Crossing: Language and ethnicity among adolescents*. London: Longman.

Räisänen, Tiina. 2018. Translingual practices in global business – a longitudinal study of a professional communicative repertoire. In Gerardo Mazzaferro (ed.), *Translanguaging as Everyday Practice*, 149–174. Cham: Springer.

Shauer, Gila A. & Svenja Adolphs. 2006. Expressions of gratitude in corpus and DCT data: Vocabulary, formulaic sequences, and pedagogy. *System* 34. 119–134.

Surrain, Sarah & Gigi Luk. 2019. Describing bilinguals: A systematic review of labels and descriptions used in the literature between 2005–2015. *Bilingualism: Language and Cognition* 22. 401–415.

Taguchi, Naoko (ed.). 2019. *The Routledge handbook of second language acquisition and pragmatics*. New York: Routledge.

Taguchi, Naoko & Carsten Roever. 2017. *Second language pragmatics*. Oxford: Oxford University Press.

Van Ackeren, Marcus. J., Daniel Casasanto, Harold Bekkering, Peter Hagoort, & Shirley-Ann Rueschemeyer. 2012. Pragmatics in action: indirect requests engage theory of mind areas and the cortical motor network. *Journal of Cognitive Neuroscience* 24(11). 2237–2247.

Wolfson, Nessa 1986. Research methodology and the question of validity. *TESOL Quarterly* 20(4). 689–699.

Vidal, Mónica. 2015. Talking with abuelo: Performing authenticity in a multicultural, multisited family. *Multilingua* 34(2). 187–210.

Rafael M. Salaberry
15 Converging agendas of rationalist and discursive approaches for the development of a pedagogy of L2 pragmatics

Abstract: In this chapter, I propose to integrate the significant work on concrete pedagogical/assessment applications in L2 pragmatics developed under the guidance of a rationalist approach to pragmatics (focused on individual perspectives) with central tenets of a discursive approach (focused on distributed cognition). The pedagogical integration of options is predicated on the theoretical distinction between two sub-constructs that make up the definition of interactional competence: the local and variable co-construction of knowledge during actual interactions versus the generalizable and stable discourse competence participants rely on to engage in social actions. I will argue that the pedagogical approach developed on the basis of the concept of rationalist pragmatics over several decades is eminently useful to develop at least one of the elements of a componential pedagogical infrastructure necessary to develop L2 interactional competence.

Keywords: assessment, interactional competence, discursive pragmatics, pedagogical infrastructure

1 Introduction

Over the last three decades the field of second language (L2) acquisition has witnessed two major turning points that have influenced the way we define a second language: the social turn (e.g., Block 2003; Duff 2015; Eskildsen and Majlesi 2018; Firth and Wagner 1997, 2007; Lantolf 2011) and the multilingual turn (e.g., Cook 1992; Douglas Fir 2016; García and Flores 2014; May 2014; Norton 2014; Ortega 2014). The major critique of this recent literature has been directed at the overreliance of previous L2 research on the analysis of (i) individual cognitive abilities and (ii) monologic practices of language use to the detriment of the analysis of interactional competence (IC), the latter of which is shaped by the complex environment of dynamic, co-constructed language interaction.

By its very definition, IC is inherently characterized by a dynamic and emergent understanding of the interactional event as it unfolds in real time as part of a locally co-constructed communicative act: it is "co-constructed by all participants in an interactive practice and is specific to that practice" (He and Young 1998: 7). This very simple description of the construct highlights two crucial features of IC: intersubjectivity and locally-bound knowledge. First, a critical feature of the conceptualization of IC is that all resources deployed by participants in an interaction are "contingent on what they *perceive other participants doing and thinking*" (Young 2019: 97; emphasis mine). Second, IC is not "an ability that can be deployed in other contexts with other participants, because each discursive practice is unique" (Young 2019: 97).

One problem that proposals predicated on the local and variable co-construction of knowledge face, however, is the difficult transition from theory to practical teaching/assessment applications given the daunting level of complexity that is inherent to a definition of IC shaped by the complex environment of dynamic, co-constructed language interaction. The problem prompted by the description of IC as locally bound and variable is that it entails that interlocutors cannot rely on the use of previous experiences, nor can they generalize from their current and future experiences to model and guide future interactions. Bachman (2007: 63, emphasis mine), for instance, notes that "[i]f the construct is strictly local and co-constructed by all the participants in the discursive practice, *this would imply that each interaction is unique* . . . then we have no basis for generalizing about the characteristics of [contexts or participants]."

One possible solution to this dilemma is to posit that the construct of IC is composed of two sub-constructs (i.e., a static one and a dynamic one) as it has been proposed by Young (2011, 2019) and Hall (2018), *inter alia*. Most clearly, Hall (2018: 28) advocates for theoretically demarcating these two sub-constructs, assigning the term "interactional repertoires" to the "variable, L2-specific semiotic resources comprising the objects of learning" that learners encounter in their interactions with other language users. The other sub-construct (inheriting the general label of IC), is thus restricted to the actual (generalizable) competence represented by the "basic interaction infrastructure of human sociality." In essence, Hall makes a distinction between, on the one hand, the "underlying competence" of learners to participate in social interaction and, on the other hand, the object of learning.

It is precisely this contrast in meanings (i.e., the *stability* of underlying competence versus the *variability* of the object of learning) inherent to the concept of IC that presents an opportunity to understand the apparent distinct pedagogical focus of (traditional) rationalist approaches to pragmatics on the one hand (e.g., Cohen 2008; Wyner and Cohen 2015), and discursive approaches on the other hand (e.g., Kasper 2006a, 2006b). In this chapter, I argue that the achievement of central tenets of IC (e.g., co-construction of knowledge, multimodal resources) are compatible with basic concepts of a rationalist approach to the teaching and assessment of L2 pragmatics. To this effect, I will review the relevance of the notion of a target norm (reflecting the component of underlying competence) of sociocultural practices within a given speech community, along with findings from recent studies that have started to find points of convergence between these two orientations (e.g., Hauser 2019; Youn 2015).

2 The pedagogical infrastructure of interactional competence

2.1 Rationalist pragmatics

In principle, one could argue that previous research on the development of L2 pragmatics was aligned with the claims advanced by the social turn and the multilingual turn due to its inherent focus on contextualized language use (e.g., Leech 1983). For instance, despite the fact that Leech (1983: 15) circumscribed the focus of pragmatics to a "goal-oriented speech situation, in which S [the speaker] uses language in order to produce a particular effect in the mind of H [the hearer]," he also made a distinction between pragmalinguistic and sociopragmatic competence highlighting the relevance of social factors for the overall concept of pragmatics. More specifically, whereas pragmalinguistic knowledge is focused on the linguistic resources required to perform a social action (e.g., apologies, compliments, requests), sociopragmatic knowledge is necessary for the speaker to determine the appropriate social action according to the situational and social context (i.e., social conventions) in which the action is performed.

More importantly, some researchers, whose agenda has been centrally focused on the development of L2 pragmatics, have explicitly described their work in ways that make it inherently compatible with revised conceptualizations of multilingualism with a special focus on identity formation. Ishihara and Cohen (2010: x), for instance, note that research on the development of pragmatic ability focuses on "how L2 speakers construct and negotiate their identities as they become socialized into the L2 community."

2.2 Discursive pragmatics

Despite the apparent social focus of most previous definitions of pragmatics, Kasper (2006a, 2006b), for one, proposed distinguishing the traditional notion of pragmatics centered on the speaker's intentions (e.g., Grice, Searle and Brown and Levinson), which she labeled rationalist, from the broader construct of interactional competence introduced by conversation analysis (CA), which she described as discursive pragmatics. Kasper (2006b: 307, emphasis mine) argued that CA "purchases us something that is in short supply in rationalist and convention-based speech act research, and that is *the discovery of actions that are part of members' interactional competence* but not of their metapragmatic awareness, especially when such actions are not lexicalized by illocutionary verbs." In other words, the crucial difference between rationalist and discursive pragmatics is that meaning is not in the utterance, but in the action prompted by the utterance. As a consequence, there is no need to "invoke motivations, intentions and other mental events," but rather "pay close attention to (a) where an action is placed in the sequential structure and (b) how the turn that houses the action and its immediately preceding and following turns are composed" (Kasper 2006b: 292). Crucially, the construct proposed by CA analysis is empirically grounded in the participants' own (or emic) interpretation of the co-participants' prior turns: meaning is represented "as the understandings that participants display to each other in the sequential organization of their talk" (Kasper 2006b: 296).

To be clear, Kasper (2006a: 86) defines interactional competence (IC) as the ability "to understand and produce social action in their sequential contexts," which includes not just the competence to take turns, format actions, recognize and produce boundaries, and repair problems, but also the capacity to co-construct social and discursive identities. The model also acknowledges the role of "different types of semiotic resources (linguistic, nonverbal, nonvocal), including register-specific resources" which are used for the purpose of sequencing and timing actions and turns, and constructing epistemic and affective stance. Moreover, both linguistic and non-linguistic interactional resources (e.g., embodied means of communication such as gaze, facial expressions and gestures; see Burch and Kasper 2016) enable speakers both to design their turns for a particular recipient in a particular context to accomplish social actions (e.g., invitations, requests, rejections to invitations) and, also, to react appropriately to the actions produced by other participants (Pekarek Doehler and Pochon-Berger 2015).[1] Finally, the construct of IC further expands the traditional concept of pragmatics with the analysis of the role played by identity resources (i.e., participation frameworks).

---

[1] It is important to note however that, as Young (2019) points out, not all studies focused on IC provide a comprehensive analysis of all components of the construct as described above. For instance, Young considers that the study of Pekarek Doehler and Pochon-Berger (2015) downplays the role played by identity and linguistic resources at the same time that it magnifies the effect of interactional resources.

2.3 A comprehensive pedagogical infrastructure

The relevance of the concept of IC for the appropriate conceptualization of the definition of language/language use and, consequently, L2 acquisition cannot be underestimated. For one thing, previous theoretical frameworks of communicative competence lacked an explicit focus on a realistic, contextualized definition of spoken language (e.g., Carter and McCarthy 1995; McCarthy and Carter 2002; O'Keeffe, McCarthy and Carter 2007). The new conceptualization of discursive pragmatics and IC addresses some of the flaws in the operationalization of the construct of speaking (e.g., Carter and McCarthy 1995; Golato 2003; He and Young 1998; McCarthy and Carter 2002). And, from the perspective of pedagogical design, the new construct has required a shift in focus from reliance on artificial and written-biased samples of language to natural (or realistic) samples of language interaction (e.g., Huth 2007; O'Keeffe et al. 2007). A central feature of this pedagogical framework rests on the identification of resources and their impact on the diversification of methods for talk-in-interaction (e.g. Hauser 2019; Pekarek Doehler 2019; Youn 2015). On the other hand, the effective incorporation of the theoretical framework advanced by IC for the design and implementation of pedagogical practices raises a number of significant challenges that after two decades are yet to be addressed successfully.

While expressing agreement with the expanded construct of pragmatics advanced by Kasper, Cohen (2008: 214) proposed, however, that "the more traditional speech act literature with its emphasis on isolated speech acts . . . ideally informed as much as possible by situated interaction" may be relevant for the teaching of L2 pragmatics. In effect, some incipient efforts to put the broad concept of IC into pedagogical practice have revealed that some components of the incomplete vision advanced by rationalist pragmatics – albeit placed into a distinct structural configuration – have become useful for the purpose of developing an IC pedagogical agenda. Prompted in part by the need to move from theory to application, Youn (2015), for instance, describes her extensive study on the assessment of L2 interactional competence as L2 pragmatics in interaction. More broadly, Salaberry and Kunitz (2019) point out that the limited number of publications describing and assessing viable IC pedagogical practices (e.g., Barraja-Rohan 1997 2011; Betz and Huth 2014; Félix-Brasdefer 2006; Huth 2007; Huth and Taleghani-Nikazm 2006) strategically incorporate some of the pedagogical principles that underlie the agenda of rationalist pragmatics approaches (e.g., Huth and Betz 2019; Kley 2019). The apparent advantages of focusing on the "static" definition of speech acts inherent to rationalist pragmatics (i.e., development of conventionalized linguistic resources and identification of associated benchmarks) may represent a valuable component of a comprehensive approach toward the development of pragmatic abilities and diversification of resources among L2 learners.

3 A componential view of IC

3.1 "Portable" conventional resources

The very notion that IC can be decomposed into various constituents (e.g., interactional repertoires versus interactional competence as proposed in Hall [2018]) raises an important question: what is the nature of the interaction of information across these subcomponents of the overall construct? The problem with the (possible) strict interpretation of the description of interactional competence as locally bound is that it implies that interlocutors cannot use previous experiences, nor can they generalize from the given experience to frame future interactions: "[i]f the construct is strictly local and co-constructed by all the participants . . . then we have no basis for generalizing about the characteristics of [contexts or participants]" (Bachman 2007: 63).

The solution to this theoretical conundrum is provided by Young (2009: 214), *inter alia*, who qualifies the description of IC as locally-constituted stating that "interactional competence includes the skill to mindfully and efficiently recognize contexts in which resources are employed and to use them when participating in unfamiliar practices to help them make sense of the unknown." That is, the experience developed over numerous previous (localized) interactions helps language users develop a database of language resources that can be used as a reference point during subsequent interactions. For instance, when faced with the need to turn down an invitation (i.e., a dispreferred action), competent speakers may be able to rely on previous experiences and use resources that were deployed in those interactions. In other words, interactional resources are "portable" and, as such, they can be "transported" across communication settings. Because the configuration of a discursive practice is not "sui generis . . . [t]hat configuration must then be compared with the configuration of resources employed in other contexts" (Young 2011: 439; see also Young 2019). Along the same lines, from the perspective of identity formation, Bucholtz and Hall (2005: 588) argue that the emergent property of interlocutors' roles and identities "does not exclude the possibility that resources for identity work in any given interaction may derive from resources developed in earlier interactions."

The intertwined nature of these processes is appropriately described by Kecskes (2019a, 2019b), who argues that L2 learners' limited lexical and grammatical resources in the L2 may actually be advantageous for the process of learning. As L2 learners are confronted with their limited range of conventionalized routines and formulas to participate in social interactions, they are able to identify the gaps in the "portable" resources they bring to the task of producing and negotiating different social actions. More importantly, Kecskes notes, those limited resources may prompt L2 learners to pay close attention to contextual elements of interactions for clues that would help them process necessary information to participate in social interactions, thus potentially leading to increased levels of intersubjectivity. From the perspective of intercultural communication, Kecskes (2019b: 503) observes that "actual situational experiences being standardized, conventionalized and normativized over time grow into somewhat stabilized, relatively easily recallable semantic features." More importantly, the sedimented meanings that are shared by speakers of a particular language "are presumed, *default interpretations*, arrived at by virtue of the repeated scenarios from the past" (Kecskes 2019b: 491; emphasis mine). These default interpretations represent a streamlined inventory of choices built upon numerous previous experiences.

3.2 From "benchmarks" to dynamic representation

Given the inherent value of using previous schemas for the use of language resources to carry out specific actions, Cohen (2008: 216) underlined that, despite the fact that elicited data may not reflect the complexity of natural data, their main benefit is precisely the fact that such data are not complex and, thus, inherently viable for the purpose of identifying a range of manageable options that can be used for teaching: "What has emerged from at least two decades of elicited data collection on speech acts such as requests, refusals, apologies, and complaints is that certain patterns tend to re-occur regularly enough to warrant their instruction to L2 learners." Repeating patterns represent conventionalized routines and formulas that provide a baseline, so to speak, that language users can rely on to co-construct new interactions which are, obviously, shaped and structured according to the specific conditions of the localized context.

Another important benefit of separating specific components of a broad definition of pragmatics is that it makes possible the identification of the reference point or benchmark to be used in any analysis of social action in interactions. For instance, Cohen (2018: 14) describes the practical problem about the selection of pragmatic targets prompted by contexts of interaction in Lingua Franca English (LFE): "For example, if Japanese and Korean business associates are conversing among themselves in English in Seoul, to what extent might they rely on their own respective L1 pragmatics in their interactions?" Given that new conceptualizations of multilingualism have challenged the hegemony of the native speaker as the benchmark to determine what is appropriate, Cohen (2018: 14) suggests that "the moment may be propitious for studies that look at just what elements of a given WE [World English] might be taught in the local pragmatics for that language." The same is true for other languages that are also starting to loosen their association with specific geopolitical centers of gravity (e.g., the Peninsular Spanish norm, the European French norm).

As Wyner and Cohen (2015: 521) point out, the selection of benchmarks is no simple matter, because knowledge about pragmatics "entails knowing the extent to which an utterance is acceptable and appropriate to other users of the language in conveying the speaker's intended meaning. But here is where the definitional problems start. Whose pragmatics serve as the benchmark?" The available empirical evidence seems to favor an explicit analysis of the reference or benchmark used to determine pragmatic appropriateness. Several studies have shown that in cases when L2 users want to challenge the expected norm of the target language community, they engage in the negotiation of the appropriate benchmark (e.g., Chun 2001; Siegal 1996). Chun, for instance, reported on the case of an Asian American man who disrupted naturalized associations between specific linguistic forms and social categories while appropriating forms of African American vernacular English (AAVE) (e.g., *keep it real*, *they always backstabbing*). In essence, the clear identification of precise (static) reference points is crucial for learners to make their own (dynamic) decisions about the extent to which they will conform to such norms, or whether they will select their own.

3.3 The integration of static and dynamic resources for pedagogical purposes

Kasper (2006b: 297) acknowledged that "CA recognizes conventional associations of linguistic forms and social actions and practices." Notwithstanding the relevance of separating local versus generalizable knowledge, however, she raised an important concern that the isolation of components of IC for the purpose of pedagogical design needs to explicitly address the following: the use of such *transportable* resources cannot disregard two essential features of IC: "the indexical character of situated action and especially its sequential organization" (Kasper 2006b: 298). Indexical meanings are not static, but rather dynamically defined as the interaction unfolds and interlocutors gauge emergent meanings that are discursively constructed. For instance, when faced with the need to turn down an invitation (i.e., a dispreferred action), interlocutors may choose among various relevant pragmatically sensitive options that do not convey hostility or impatience (e.g., delays, appreciations) to reject the invitation. Similarly, almost by definition, temporal features (e.g., pauses, overlaps, interruptions) constitute critical interactional resources that interlocutors use to track the sequential organization of any interaction.

In principle, the very nature of a componential approach as described by Cohen (2018) above, does not diminish or circumvent the relevance of these central features of IC. As important as indexicality and sequentiality are, they are also inherently linked to the actual interactional event. The previously built repertoire of linguistic and non-linguistic interactional resources that language users have deployed in a variety of different configurations (relevant to the localized interactional environment of previous interactions) is equivalent to the given level of experience that each language user has with various social actions. The challenge to develop both static and dynamic components of a comprehensive definition of IC is to be able to rely on a previous repertoire of linguistic resources at the same time that such repertoire is subject to change on the basis of new conversational data accessed through new interactions. Speaking from the perspective of IC, Pekarek Doehler and Pochon-Berger (2018: 557; emphasis mine) argue that pedagogical tasks need to develop "an increased capacity to *monitor* the linguistic details of co-participants' prior turns and actions and *to use grammar as a resource for interaction*". Similarly, Hauser (2019: 102, emphasis mine) points out that, as is the case for other components of language competence, there are several pedagogical options for the diversification and development of language resources across a variety of components of a comprehensive definition of interactional competence:

> This may involve explicit instruction on particular resources (e.g., instruction on formulaic expressions used to summon someone or to initiate repair), *awareness raising* (e.g., awareness of the importance of gaze and bodily position), or *reflection* on the learner's successes or difficulties in actual episodes of interaction (e.g., *reflection* on how interactional (in)competence has been constructed in particular episodes of interaction in which the L2 learner was a participant).

The previous descriptions about the teaching focus of IC highlight not just the need to consider a componential approach to the teaching of IC (backward- and forward-looking processes), but more importantly, they underline the need to use explicit pedagogical approaches that "lead to a more conscious approach to what is said, and how it is said" (Kecskes 2019a: 7).

3.4 A componential pedagogical approach to teach IC

Whether the focus is on conventional speech act resources or the "recipient design" of interactional events, the previous literature shows that the most common – and, arguably most effective – pedagogical approach has been raising learners' awareness about how to accomplish social actions. In effect, the available empirical evidence shows that the explicit identification of "portable" interactional resources and target norms in the context of natural interactions (as is the case in study abroad contexts) has proven to be crucial to increase learners' awareness about the means to diversify their overall use of resources to both recognize and accomplish social actions (e.g., Bataller 2010; Félix-Brasdefer and Hasler-Barker 2015; Taguchi, Li, and Xiao 2013). Taguchi et al., for instance, concluded that despite numerous opportunities to come across some of the formulaic expressions they studied, learners seemed more focused on getting their meaning across without making significant progress toward native-like use of form. Providing further empirical evidence, Félix-Brasdefer and Hasler-Barker (2015) analyzed data comparing study-abroad (SA) and at-home (AH) L2 Spanish learners to assess their knowledge of compliment forms in the L2. Their data were collected with a traditional non-interactive oral discourse completion task (DCT) (for disadvantages, see Golato [2003]) which they "designed to elicit explicit knowledge of L2 compliment forms" (Félix-Brasdefer and Hasler-Barker 2015: 78). Despite the obvious limitations of their data collection process, Félix-Brasdefer and Hasler-Barker discovered that, relatively speaking, learners in the SA program used a greater variety of adjectives to offer compliments when compared with the AH group of learners. Although these findings cannot be used to make any conclusions regarding the interactive, localized, and co-constructed nature of the production of social actions, the above studies are relevant to understand the affordances and limitations of learners in terms of both linguistic and interactional resources in two distinct contexts of language use.

Apart from the obvious focus on the sedimented nature of static speech acts (knowledge about pragmatics as opposed to knowledge on how to interact), the structure of interactions can also be addressed through pedagogical processes that raise learners' awareness about the types of resources used to accomplish social actions (e.g., Barraja-Rohan 2011; Betz and Huth 2014; Félix-Brasdefer 2006; Huth and Betz 2019; Tecedor 2016). Félix-Brasdefer (2006), for instance, described an elaborate (albeit logistically viable) procedure to raise conscious awareness among learners about the nature of conversational interactions. Step by step, Félix-Brasdefer showcased the procedures that can be useful to make learners aware of identifiable boundaries, the actions performed in each sequence, how each action is delivered with linguistic means, how turns are organized, and how participants construct their roles and identities. Similarly, Huth and Betz (2019: 334) highlight the potential to focus on generic practices such as the overall structuring of interactions, helping learners notice, for instance, that "conversation closings are important phases in encounters, and [that] they rely on routinized patterns." As these authors explain, this explicit focus on IC can be achieved by way of fairly traditional techniques to raise learners' awareness about language structure in general: asking them to put sequences of turns in the right order, matching interactional functions with relevant linguistic resources, unscrambling sequences of turns, completing conversations with the appropriate linguistic markers, providing an account for their selections of linguistic resources, guessing next turns, among other activities.

4 Conclusion

In general, the overreliance on the analysis of individual cognitive abilities and monologic practices of language use to the detriment of the analysis of IC compromises the validity of the construct of IC. On the other hand, some perspectives on pedagogical approaches developed under the guidance of rationalist pragmatics (Cohen 2008, 2018; Wyner and Cohen 2015) may still provide some relevant contribution to the overall agenda of discursive pragmatics.

Viewed from the perspective of a componential approach to IC (i.e., interactional repertoires versus interactional competence), the inadequate nature of rationalist pragmatics for the teaching of pragmatics in general is not so much due to the analysis of the wrong construct, but rather to the analysis – exclusively – of one sub-construct of a broad and complete definition of pragmatics. Whereas rationalist pragmatics is predicated on a static definition that is inherently backward-looking (i.e., reference to conventionalized actions as the product of previous experiences), discursive pragmatics focuses on a dynamic definition that is forward-looking (i.e., co-constructed as part of the local interaction happening in each instance). In sum, notwithstanding the limited view on interaction afforded by the traditional view of speech acts, the focus on conventional resources and associated target norms may be necessary for L2 learners to "map" both the means and trajectory of their developing IC.

References

Bachman, Lyle F. 2007. What is the construct? The dialectic of abilities and contexts in defining constructs in language assessment. In Jana Fox, Mari Wesche, & Doreen Bayliss (eds.), *Language Testing Reconsidered*, 41–71. Ottawa: University of Ottawa Press.

Barraja-Rohan, Anne-Marie. 1997. Teaching conversation and sociocultural norms with conversation analysis. *Australian Review of Applied Linguistics* 14. 71–88.

Barraja-Rohan, Anne-Marie. 2011. Using conversation analysis in the second language classroom to teach interactional competence. *Language Teaching Research* 15(4). 479–507.

Bataller, Rebeca. 2010. Making a request for a service in Spanish: Pragmatic development in the study abroad setting. *Foreign Language Annals* 43(1). 160–175.

Betz, Emma M. & Thorsten Huth. 2014. Beyond grammar: Teaching interaction in the German language classroom. *Die Unterrichtspraxis/Teaching German* 47(2). 140–163.

Block, David. 2003. *The social turn in second language acquisition*. Washington D.C.: Georgetown University Press.

Bucholtz, Mary & Kira Hall. 2005. Identity and interaction: A sociocultural linguistic approach. *Discourse studies* 7(4–5). 585–614.

Burch, Alfred. R., & Kasper, Gabriele. 2016. Like Godzilla. In Prior, M. & Kasper, G. (Eds.). *Emotion in multilingual interaction* (Vol. 266). (pp. 57–85). Philadelphia: John Benjamins Publishing Company.

Carter, Ronald & Michael McCarthy. 1995. Grammar and the spoken language. *Applied Linguistics* 16(2). 141–158.

Chun, Elaine. 2001. The construction of white, black, and Korean American identities through African American Vernacular English. *Journal of Linguistic Anthropology* 11(1). 52–64.

Cohen, Andrew. 2008. Teaching and assessing L2 pragmatics: What can we expect from learners? *Language Teaching* 41(2). 213–235.

Cohen, Andrew. 2018. Reflections on a Career in Second Language Studies: Promising Pathways for Future Research. *L2 Journal* 10(1). 1–19.

Cook, Vivian. 1992. Evidence for multicompetence. *Language Learning*, 42(4), 557–591.

Douglas Fir Group. 2016. A transdisciplinary framework for SLA in a multilingual world. *Modern Language Journal* 100(S1). 19–47.

Duff, Patricia. 2015. Transnationalism, multilingualism, and identity. *Annual Review of Applied Linguistics* 35. 57–80.

Eskildsen, Søren & Ali Majlesi. 2018. Learnables and teachables in second language talk: Advancing a social reconceptualization of central SLA tenets. Introduction to the special issue. *The Modern Language Journal* 102. 3–10.

Félix-Brasdefer, J. César. 2006. Teaching the negotiation of multi-turn speech acts. Using conversation-analytic tools to teach pragmatics in the classroom. In Kathleen Bardovi-Harlig, J. César Félix-Brasdefer, & Alwiya Omar. (eds.), *Pragmatics and language learning* (vol. 11), 165–197. Honolulu, HI: National Foreign Language Resource Center, University of Hawaii at Manoa.

Félix-Brasdefer, J. César & Maria Hasler-Barker. 2015. Complimenting in Spanish in a short-term study abroad context. *System* 48. 75–85.

Firth, Alan & Johannes Wagner. 1997. On discourse, communication, and (some) fundamental concepts in SLA research. *The Modern Language Journal* 81(3). 285–300.

Firth, Alan & Johannes Wagner. 2007. Second/foreign language learning as a social accomplishment: Elaborations on a reconceptualized SLA. *The Modern Language Journal* 91. 800–819.

García, Ofelia & Nelson Flores. 2014. Multilingualism and Common Core State Standards in the United States. In Steven May (ed.), *The multilingual turn: Implications for SLA, TESOL and Bilingual Education*, 147–166. New York: Routledge.

Golato, Andrea. 2003. Studying compliment responses: A comparison of DCTs and recordings of naturally occurring talk. *Applied Linguistics* 24(1). 90–121.

Hall, Joan Kelly. 2018. From L2 interactional competence to L2 interactional repertoires: Reconceptualising the objects of L2 learning. *Classroom Discourse* 9. 25–39.

Hauser, Eric. 2019. The construction of interactional incompetence in L2 interaction. In M. Rafael Salaberry & Silvia Kunitz (eds.), *Teaching and testing L2 interactional competence: Bridging theory and practice*, 77–105. New York: Routledge.

He, Agnes & Richard Young. 1998. Language proficiency interviews: A discourse approach. In Richard Young & Agnes He (eds.), *Talking and testing: Discourse approaches to the assessment of oral proficiency*, 1–24. Amsterdam: John Benjamins.

Huth, Thorsten. 2007. Pragmatics revisited: Teaching with natural language data. *Die Unterrichtspraxis/Teaching German* 40(1). 21–33.

Huth, Thorsten & Emma Betz. 2019. Testing Interactional Competence in Second Language Classrooms: Goals, Formats and Caveats. In M. Rafael Salaberry & Silvia Kunitz (eds.), *Teaching and testing L2 interactional competence: Bridging theory and practice*, 322–356. New York: Routledge.

Huth, Thorsten & Carmen Taleghani-Nikazm. 2006. How can insights from conversation analysis be directly applied to teaching L2 pragmatics? *Language Teaching Research* 10(1). 53–79.

Ishihara, Noriko & Andrew Cohen. 2010. *Teaching and learning pragmatics: Where language and culture meet*. Harlow, UK: Pearson.

Kasper, Gabriele. 2006a. Beyond repair: Conversation analysis as an approach to SLA. *AILA Review* 19(1). 83–99.

Kasper, Gabriele. 2006b. Speech acts in interaction: Towards discursive pragmatics. In Kathleen Bardovi-Harlig, J. César Félix-Brasdefer, & Alwiya Omar (eds.), *Pragmatics and language learning* (vol. 11), 281–314. Honolulu, HI: National Foreign Language Resource Center, University of Hawaii at Manoa.

Kecskes, Istvan. 2019a. *English as a lingua franca: The pragmatic perspective*. Cambridge: Cambridge University Press.

Kecskes, Istvan. 2019b. Impoverished pragmatics? The semantics-pragmatics interface from an intercultural perspective. *Intercultural Pragmatics* 16(5). 489–515.

Kley, Katharina. 2019. What counts as evidence for interactional competence? Developing rating criteria for a German classroom-based paired speaking test. In M. Rafael Salaberry & Silvia Kunitz (eds.), *Teaching and testing L2 interactional competence: Bridging theory and practice*, 291–321. New York: Routledge.

Lantolf, James. 2011. The sociocultural approach to second language acquisition: Sociocultural theory, second language acquisition, and artificial L2 development. In Dwight Atkinson (ed.), *Alternative approaches to second language acquisition*, 24–47. New York: Routledge.

Leech, Geoffrey. 1983. *Principles of pragmatics*. London: Longman.

May, Steven (ed.) 2014. *The multilingual turn: Implications for SLA, TESOL and bilingual education*. New York: Routledge.

McCarthy, Michael & Ronald Carter. 2002. Ten criteria for a spoken grammar. In Eli Hinkel & Sandra Fotos (eds.), *New perspectives on grammar teaching in second language classrooms*, 53–78. Lawrence Erlbaum.

Norton, Brian. 2014. Identity, literacy, and the multilingual classroom. In Steven May (ed.), *The multilingual turn: Implications for SLA, TESOL, and bilingual education*, 103–122. New York: Routledge.

O'Keeffe, Annette, Michael McCarthy, & Ronald Carter. 2007. *From corpus to classroom: language use and language teaching*. Cambridge: Cambridge University Press.

Ortega, Lourdes. 2014. Ways Forward for a Bi/Multilingual Turn in SLA. In Steven May (ed.), *The multilingual turn: Implications for SLA, TESOL and Bilingual Education*, 32–53. New York: Routledge.

Pekarek Doehler, S. 2019. On the nature and the development of L2 interactional competence: State of the art and implications for praxis. In R. M. Salaberry & S. Kunitz (Eds.), *Teaching and testing L2 interactional competence: Bridging theory and practice* (pp. 25–59). New York: Routledge.

Pekarek Doehler, Simona & Evelyn Pochon-Berger. 2015. The development of L2 interactional competence: Evidence from turn-taking organization, sequence organization, repair organization and preference organization. In Teresa Cadierno & Søren Eskildsen (eds.), *Usage-based perspectives on second language learning*, 233–268. Berlin: De Gruyter Mouton.

Pekarek Doehler, Simona & Evelyn Pochon-Berger. 2018. L2 interactional competence as increased ability for context-sensitive conduct: A longitudinal study of story-openings. *Applied Linguistics* 39(4). 555–578.

Salaberry, M. Rafael & Silvia Kunitz. 2019. *Teaching and Testing L2 Interactional Competence Bridging Theory and Practice*. New York: Routledge.

Siegal, Meryl. 1996. The role of learner subjectivity in second language sociolinguistic competency: Western women learning Japanese. *Applied Linguistics* 17. 356–382.

Taguchi, Naoko, Chuai Li, & Feng Xiao. 2013. Production of formulaic expressions in L2 Chinese: A developmental investigation in a study abroad context. *Chinese as a Second Language Research* 2(1). 23–58.

Tecedor, Marta. 2016. Beginning learners' development of interactional competence: Alignment activity. *Foreign Language Annals* 49(1). 23–41.

Wyner, Lauren & Andrew D. Cohen. 2015. Second language pragmatic ability: Individual differences according to environment. *Studies in Second Language Learning and Teaching* 5(4). 519–556.

Youn, Soo J. 2015. Validity argument for assessing L2 pragmatics in interaction using mixed methods. *Language Testing* 32(2). 199–225.

Young, Richard F. 2009. Chapter six: Contexts of teaching and testing. *Language Learning* 58. 183–226.

Young, Richard F. 2011. Interactional competence in language learning, teaching, and testing. In Eli Hinkel (ed.), *Handbook of research in second language teaching and learning* (vol. 2), 233–268. New York: Routledge.

Young, Richard F. 2019. Interactional competence and L2 pragmatics. In Naoko Taguchi (ed.), *The Routledge handbook of second language acquisition and pragmatics*, 93–110. New York: Routledge.

Noriko Ishihara

16 From a native-nonnative speaker dichotomy to a translingual framework

Abstract: This reflection essay traces the evolution of the conceptual thinking in Andrew Cohen's work as it relates to issues of native versus nonnative speakers/teachers in pragmatics research and practice. Following the assumptions in interlanguage pragmatics, Cohen's earlier work drew on a deficit view of language learning through the contrastive analysis of pragmatic language uses and discursive practices of native and nonnative speakers. In Cohen's later work, a conceptual leap can be found in acknowledging the elusiveness of the notions of native and nonnative speakers as well as in underscoring native-nonnative speaker collaboration in the teaching of pragmatics. This reflective paper concludes by discussing a translingual framework, which more judiciously reflects today's multilingualism, mobility, (super)diversity, and globalization. An alternative perspective to the native-nonnative dichotomy will be presented and illustrated.

Keywords: native vs. nonnative, translingual, bi-/multilingual, translingual practice, translanguaging

1 Introduction

1.1 Background

This reflection essay traces the evolution of the conceptual thinking in Cohen's work as it relates to issues of so-called *nativeness* and *non nativeness* in interlanguage pragmatics research and pedagogy, discusses some limitations of this dichotomy, and proposes an alternative translingual framework that more judiciously reflects today's multilingualism and global (super)diversity.[1] As can be

---

[1] To provide some background information, I had the honor of working with Andrew D. Cohen closely during my graduate studies at the University of Minnesota. After his guidance on my M.A. thesis and my research assistantship for his projects, we co-authored a book based on the materials used for a teachers' institute at the Center for Advanced Research on Language Acquisition (CARLA) focused on pragmatics instruction (2006 – currently taught by Ishihara). Over the years of our collaboration, the issues regarding *(non)nativeness* recurrently

https://doi.org/10.1515/9783110721775-017

gleaned from the primary focus of Cohen's latest book, *Learning Pragmatics from Native and Nonnative Language Teachers* (2018), this topic has been one of his utmost concerns that shapes the foundation of his view of (instructed) SLA in his extensive career over the past decades. The latter half of the chapter explores a post-normative translingual framework and draws on examples of learners' and teachers' translingual practice. It is argued that the translingual framework can serve as a more viable alternative to the dichotomy of nativeness vs. non nativeness at this time of mobility and globalization.

1.2 Empirical investigation of speech acts

Cohen's early work in second language (L2) pragmatics is best known for the investigation of the speech act of apology, often co-authored with Elite Olshtain (e.g., Cohen and Olshtain 1981; Olshtain and Cohen 1993). Their research in the early 1980s was pioneering in that the investigation of speech acts, which used to be largely impressionistic, was now implemented empirically through the use of Discourse Completion Tasks (DCTs). The DCT was prevalently used, as in the Cross-Cultural Speech Act Realization Project (CCSARP), by a team of researchers, such as Blum-Kulka, House, and Kasper (1989), in *Cross-cultural Pragmatics* to reveal different realizations of speech acts across a number of languages and language varieties. Language elicitation techniques like the DCT and role-play thrived then as methods that facilitated convenient comparison of a large volume of language data. Cohen and Olshtain, among others, applied those techniques to studies in *interlanguage pragmatics* to uncover how native and nonnative speakers used language pragmatically (e.g., Cohen and Olshtain 1981, 1993; Olshtain and Cohen 1990). In interlanguage pragmatics, a conventional practice consists of comparing and contrasting pragmatic language uses and discursive practices of native speakers with those of learners or non native speakers in order to identify details of commonalities and discrepancies.

Cohen's work, as well as others aligning with the premise of interlanguage pragmatics, was welcomed by researchers and L2 teachers interested in the traits of interlanguage, often with the intention to apply this empirical information to L2 teaching. In the late 1990s to early 2000s it was established that pragmatic competence is amenable to teaching (e.g., Kasper 1997; Jeon and Kaya 2006). A resource for teaching pragmatics was compiled online (Bardovi-Harlig and Mahan-Taylor

---

surfaced, which prompted us to develop our individual thinking. I could not have written this chapter without Andrew having challenged me repeatedly on this topic.

2003), which, to my knowledge, is the first publication with a collection of lesson plans intended to teach pragmatics on an empirical basis. Since then, quite a few practical resources have followed suit. Notably, most of these currently published resources for teaching L2 pragmatics are built upon the convention of presenting research-based native-speaker norms[2] as the basis of instruction (e.g., Houck and Tatsuki 2011; Martínez-Flor and Usó-Juan 2010; Tatsuki and Houck 2010).

2 Key issues

2.1 Interrogating premises in interlanguage pragmatics

As noted earlier, contrastive analysis of native- and nonnative-speaker language is a convention in mainstream SLA as well as in interlanguage pragmatics, a subfield of SLA. The purpose often is to pinpoint cases of *negative pragmatic transfer* or *interference* of the L1 with the L2 with a structuralist view of language, which seeks to discover rules, universals, or interrelated mechanisms that are measurable or controllable often through experimental design (e.g., Ishihara 2018, 2019; Kasper 1992, 2010; Liddicoat 2017; McConachy 2019; Morgan, 2007). Although an underlying assumption in current SLA or interlanguage pragmatics may be to descriptively identify cross-linguistic influence on the part of L2 users, the assumption is too often translated into a deficit model of L2 development and used to perpetuate die-hard stereotypes and *native-speakerism*. The latter refers to an ideology that holds that native speakers essentially offer models of correct and appropriate language use, that (idealized) native-speaker language is the optimal model for L2 learners, and that native speakers are likely to demonstrate the most effective and updated methodological approaches[3] (Swan, Aboshiha, and Holliday 2015; also see Train (2003) for interrogating native-speakerism in Spanish language education).

Cohen and Olshtain's pioneering empirical work investigating speech acts via DCT data also subscribed to this normative orientation, which reflected the

---

2 Although the term *pragmatic norms* is sometimes used almost synonymously to monolithic or static rules, in this paper it refers to socially acquired and jointly constructed practices that are viewed as preferred or acceptable in the local context, which can vary across languages and cultures or even within a single culture and can change over time.
3 The characterization of native speakers as ideal teachers is termed as *native-speaker fallacy* (e.g., Phillipson 1992; see also Canagarajah 1999).

mainstream native speaker orientation prevalent in a larger field of SLA, or at least English Language Teaching (ELT), in North America at that time. In fact, the conventionalized native- versus non native speaker dichotomy may have survived in Cohen's otherwise innovative work until the late 2000s or possibly later, including works on learner strategies for learning and using speech acts (e.g., Cohen 2005), the impact of strategies-based intervention on learners' pragmatic development during study abroad (e.g., Cohen and Shively 2007), and research methods in intercultural pragmatics (e.g., Cohen 2012b).

2.2 Conceptual evolution of the field of TESOL and applied linguistics

Meanwhile, as spacial and social mobility has surged in today's globalization, English has increasingly been used as a lingua franca in a wide range of domains. Given this, let us take English as an International Language (EIL) as an example in considering issues related to (non)nativeness. The global use and nativized varieties of English were brought to light through the conceptualization of *Inner-, Outer-,* and *Expanding-circle* countries with its visual representations in the 1980s to 1990s by Kachru (1990) and others. *Teachers of English to Speakers of Other Languages (TESOL)*, one of the largest and most active international organizations for ELT, launched the Nonnative English-Speaking Teacher (NNEST) Caucus in 1998, which promoted the legitimacy of NNESTs' expertise in ELT and advocated research on this issue. Accordingly, in EIL and wider ELT research, the native-speaker model has been interrogated and the legitimacy of qualified non native English-speaking teachers has been recognized through a burgeoning body of research literature (e.g., Braine 1999, 2005; Kamhi-Stein 2004; Liu 1999; Mahboob 2010; Motha 2014; Park 2017; Swan, Aboshiha, and Holliday 2015). The NNEST Caucus turned into an Interest Section in 2006, establishing NNEST as an area of research within TESOL and applied linguistics (Mahboob 2010). Researchers and thinkers in applied linguistics in general have also continued to question the native-speakerism in the context of globalization and linguacultural diversity (e.g., Canagarajah 1999, 2013; Holliday 2015; Kumaravadivelu 2012).

Accordingly, TESOL designated diversified English as a global language in a Position Statement (2008). TESOL also challenged the native speaker fallacy through the Statement against discrimination of nonnative speakers of English in unequal hiring practices. Regarding the ELT practice, the Position Statement on English as a Global Language has the following:

> ... With English being taught globally for very diverse purposes, a singular or monolithic approach to the modeling of English is no longer tenable ... TESOL encourages the recognition and appreciation of all varieties of English, including dialects, creoles, and world Englishes. In terms of language teaching, TESOL does not advocate one standard or variety of English over another. Rather, TESOL urges English language teachers to make informed decisions at local, regional, and/or national levels, taking into account the purposes and contexts of use that are most relevant to their learners. (TESOL 2008)

Likewise, scholars in EIL, English as a Lingua Franca (ELF), World Englishes (WEs) and other relevant fields have argued diversifying pedagogical models beyond Inner-circle Englishes, emphasizing the importance of tailoring instruction to learners' cognitive, social, cultural, and affective needs (e.g., Matsuda 2017). Meanwhile, language educators and researchers in applied linguistics and intercultural communication at large have begun to shift focus from the structuralist notion of *communicative competence* to the notions of *intercultural communicative competence* or *intercultural awareness* to underscore reflexivity, which activates learners' critical and explicit meta-awareness of cultural integration (e.g., Baker 2016; Blommaert and Rampton 2011; Byram and Fleming 1998; Díaz and Dasli 2017; also see relevant constructs of *symbolic competence*, Kramsch 2009, and interactional competence, Young 2019). Furthermore, researchers advocating a critical turn in applied linguistics emphasize the development of learners' self-reflexivity and criticality in acknowledging their interculturality, in which they exercise agency in appropriating or resisting L2 uses as well as engage in *cosmopolitan citizenship* against linguistic and social inequalities and marginalization (Ashcroft 2018; Díaz and Dasli 2017).

In this sociopolitical climate in applied linguistics, Ishihara and Cohen departed from the dichotomy of nativeness and non nativeness in the co-authored book *Teaching and Learning Pragmatics* (2010). In this volume, we viewed pragmatic use and development as not only a cognitive process but also a social phenomenon in which L2 speakers construct and negotiate their hybrid identities. That is, pragmatic competence is characterized as contextually constructed in interaction and negotiated hand-in-hand with interactants' enactment of identities and agency. For example, we noted that the demarcation between native and nonnative speakers is becoming increasingly blurred with the prevalent use of EIL. We thus aimed at language expertise and competence, rather than nativeness, for the instructional goal, characterizing *pragmatically competent* language users as learners' models (Ishihara and Cohen 2010; also in Cohen 2012a). Our primary challenges included identifying diversified pedagogical models for pragmatics that are empirically established (Taguchi and Ishihara 2018) in our efforts to narrow the gap in this area. Despite a process of trials and errors, our preliminary effort has perhaps been accepted to some degree beyond North America, as the volume was translated into Arabic in 2015 and revised and translated into Japanese in 2015, which was further translated into Korean in 2018.

3 Current trends and debates

3.1 Limitations in the dichotomy

In his most recent book, Cohen (2018) aims to contribute to teacher development in the teaching and assessment of L2 pragmatics with a stated focus on the advantages and disadvantages of native and nonnative teachers of English. His arguments are made based on an extensive review of the literature in interlanguage pragmatics and on the questionnaire he conducted online with 113 teachers of pragmatics situated in various countries. In his book, Cohen takes a major conceptual leap by identifying nativeness and non nativeness on a continuum rather than a dichotomy, although he still retains these concepts. Cohen also acknowledges the heterogeneity among native and nonnative-speaking teachers and acknowledges the complexity of multiple factors, such as the extent of exposure to the "target" culture, linguistic proficiency, professional training, and teaching experience, which influence teachers' beliefs, practice, self-confidence, and perceived sense of legitimacy. Although Cohen is rather dismissive of these important factors to focus perhaps disproportionately on the native- and nonnative distinction, he concludes by offering a constructive suggestion that both native and nonnative teachers should "take action in order to compensate for possible gaps in their knowledge in some areas" (2018: 265). Cohen's expertise in interlanguage pragmatics and SLA, along with his introduction of the issues of nativeness and non nativeness, can contribute to teacher readers' professional development in pragmatics-focused instruction.

The publication of Cohen's book, *Learning pragmatics from native and non-native language teachers*, roughly coincided with the Council of Europe's re-conceptualization of language expertise. In 2018, 17 years after the publication of the Common European Framework of References for Languages (CEFR) in 2001, the Council of Europe released its *Companion Volume*, which provides updates in alignment with advancement of the field. One of them is that although the European Council (2001) originally included 13 mentions of the term *native speaker*, each of them has been replaced by *proficient speaker* in the *Companion Volume*, reflecting the Council's plurilingual and pluricultural approach (Saito 2019). This revision aligns well with the term *pragmatically competent speakers* used in Ishihara and

Cohen (2010). One can argue that the new term is more consistent with a current understanding of language expertise, ownership, and legitimacy. Although nativeness merely regards one's arbitrary heritage or place of birth, what counts the most in L2 education is teachers' language proficiency as well as professional preparation and pedagogical expertise (Rampton 1990). Therefore, along with the understanding that nativeness or non nativeness is a highly elusive construct that defies a clear-cut definition, the focus on nativeness or non nativeness is becoming increasingly obsolete in a pluralistic approach to language learning and teaching.

The next section takes this one step further to discuss the translingual framework, which can further refine our awareness of diverse contexts of language use, as an alternative to the native-nonnative dichotomy. Using this approach, some illustrations of *negative pragmatic transfer* potentially leading to pragmatic *failure* (Cohen 2018) – especially when the divergence reflects deliberate pragmatic choice (Ishihara, 2019) – can be reconceptualized as a normal and inherent process of negotiation in intercultural interactions. The comparative and static view of native and nonnative speakers, or "[t]he extent to which native teachers and nonnative teachers are on a par when it comes to the teaching of [target-language] pragmatics" (Cohen 2018: 63), can be reconsidered from an integrative perspective, as bi- or multilingual speakers possess and capitalize on their multicompetence (Cook 1999) in a united, hybrid manner.

3.2 A translingual view of language practice and development

In the translingual framework (e.g., *translingual practice, translanguaging*), languages and language varieties are viewed as an interconnected communicative resource rather than discrete, independent, or compartmentalized systems and structures (Canagarajah 2011; García and Li 2014; Li 2018a, 2018b; Li and Ho 2018; Mazak 2017). Given the reality of today's linguistic (super)diversity, high mobility, and frequent contact, one-to-one correspondence between a language and a community (as in concepts of *nation state* or *speech community*) is no longer tenable (Blommaert and Rampton 2011; Li 2018a), or was a myth in the first place (Canagarajah 2011). The societal change in mobility and language contact has also triggered shifts in the status of individual bi-/multilingualism. One can identify him/herself as an expert speaker of multiple languages or claim ownership of several languages based on the competence and expertise without necessarily being native to them in the conventional sense. Accordingly, the notion of nativeness or non nativeness becomes unclear and less applicable. Considering dynamic linguistic diversity within a language and its diversified functions and practices in various social domains, no one knows a single language comprehensively but has partial knowledge of multiple languages or language varieties and registers (Li 2018a). "One-language-only" or "one-language-at-a-time" policies represent the narrow concept of language and are rooted in a monolingual ideology and linguistic purism, leading to fear and stigma attached to language mixing and code-switching, even though "switching and mixing between and across languages is a defining behavior of *being* bilingual" (emphasis theirs, Li and Ho 2018: 38). Instead, languages can be viewed as complementing each other rather than competing or interfering with one another, rendering the meaning-making practice creative, fluid, and open to new possibilities (Canagarajah 2013).

The translingual framework allows us to draw on an integrative understanding of the process in which language users create meaning by drawing upon a variety of social, semiotic, pragmatic, and discursive resources from more than one language or language variety. Bi-/multilingual speakers can be (re)conceptualized as *meshing* these resources (Canagarajah 2011, 2013), *performing* their multiple repertoires (García and Li 2014), or *orchestrating* those resources across multiple domains (Li 2018b) without compartmentalizing individual languages as separate systems but through holistic integration. By accessing multiple resources, interactants discursively engage in subtle and nuanced negotiations of meaning, leading to complex construction of multiple identities. Such linguistic hybridity can be seen as the potential for creative innovation, as the creativity and criticality that derive from this meaning-making transcends the meaning attainable within one language (Li 2018b). In a translingual framework, nativeness is neither an achievable nor a desirable goal.

For example, when Li's ethnic Chinese students were conversing with each other, they drew on their knowledge of Chinese and English by switching between the two languages and incorporating a bilingual pun. A Chinese equivalent of "white-collar dog" is pronounced similarly to "bilingual" and the dual meaning fits creatively into the context of future career aspirations, achieving the meaning that cannot be conveyed in either of the languages alone in an innovative and critical manner (Li 2018a: 26). This can be regarded as part of these students' pragmatic and symbolic competence as the irony negotiated by the translanguaging act does the relational work, emotionally binding the interactants together.

In a literacy autobiography, Canagarajah's (2011) graduate student weaves Arabic proverbs, verses, visual symbols as well as other semiotic resources (e.g., emoticons and idiosyncratic spelling for auditory effect) throughout her essay. Her translanguaging strategies were deliberately employed and the rhetorical implications were conveyed quite successfully even to some of her non-Arabic-speaking peers. While the monolingual ideologies privilege native speakers and frame nonnative speakers as deficient, a translingual orientation regards hybridity and multiplicity as part of the valuable expressive repertoire that enables pragmatic expressions of subtle nuances.

Another example derives from literature in heritage learner pragmatics. Although many heritage language speakers identify themselves as "native" speakers, the extent of their language expertise and socialization varies greatly. Nevertheless, their pragmatic creativity and hybridity have been documented in literature. For example, In Manosuthikit and De Costa (2016), Burmese heritage speakers (generation 1.5 adolescents) combined hierarchical and age-based address terms in Burmese with those more egalitarian in English in order to grapple with the two competing ideologies involved in the two languages. Through the uniquely crafted terms, they expressed both polite respect and casual familiarity, negotiating their multiple identities dynamically according to the ongoing individual relationship.[4]

To further illustrate, another example can be drawn from Ishihara and Menard-Warwick (2018). This narrative study of language teachers' translingual (and transcultural) identities and classroom practice revealed teachers' shifting engagement with multiple languages and language varieties. For instance, an American teacher, Derek, taught English in a junior high school in the Japan Exchange and Teaching (JET) Program. Despite the government's monolingual policy that English is to be taught (ideally exclusively) in English especially by international teachers like Derek, he drew on translingual pedagogy constructing bilingual identity and capitalizing on it in the classroom. He elected to incorporate his knowledge of Japanese and Japanese culture and humorously fueled his students' fascination with popular culture in his instruction through a translingual pun and comedy routines in Japanese. Derek's translingual pedagogy, which was built on the shared enthusiasm in contemporary culture, brought about an academic advantage as reduced anxiety enhanced their investment in learning the L2. He used multiple languages and registers as a multimodal resource across cognitive, social, semiotic, pragmatic, and affective domains in a way not possible by resorting to just one language. Notably, Derek's translingual pedagogy was part of his relational work and thus, inherently pragmatic in nature.[5]

---

[4] Also see Pinto and Raschio (2007) for the investigation of Spanish heritage learners' requests.
[5] This translingual pedagogy may be applicable in another setting, such as in instructing heritage language learners in the U.S. See also García and Li (2014); Ishihara, Carroll, Mahler, and Russo (2018); Mazak and Carroll (2017) for more examples of translingual pedagogy.

As seen in these examples, translingual practice is transformative in that speakers and writers enact their agency in a creative and innovative manner in *trans-spaces* (García and Li 2014) or a *third space* (Bhabha 1994; Kramsch and Uryu 2012).[6] That is, the knowledge of multiple languages, modalities, and pragmatic and semiotic resources are interdependent, dynamically interact with each other, and are drawn upon in the metaphorical space beyond individual languages through cohesive integration (Kramsch 2009).

4 Future directions and conclusions

This reflection paper has traced the evolution of the conceptual thinking in Cohen's work as it relates to issues of native- versus nonnative speakers and teachers in interlanguage pragmatics research and pedagogical practice. We have revisited Cohen's pioneering work on early investigation of speech acts, which was one of the first attempts to make this focus empirical through language elicitation techniques. Consistent with conventional practice in interlanguage pragmatics, Cohen's work often compared and contrasted pragmatic language uses and discursive practices of native and nonnative speakers, with an intention to identify commonalities and discrepancies as well as to provide potential evidence of pragmatic transfer.

Although the conventionalized native- versus nonnative speaker dichotomy may have lived on in Cohen's work until the late 2000s or possibly later (e.g., Cohen 2005, 2012b), some of Cohen's works (e.g., Cohen 2012a; Ishihara and Cohen 2010) challenged this dichotomy by regarding pragmatically competent bi- and multilingual speakers as effective players in intercultural communication. In his most recent book *Learning Pragmatics from Native and Nonnative Language Teachers* (2018), Cohen takes a conceptual leap by identifying nativeness and non nativeness on a continuum rather than a dichotomy. Cohen also acknowledges the heterogeneity among the native and nonnative teachers and the complexity of multiple factors in pragmatics instruction, although the dichotomous categories still remain.

Finally, this chapter has explored the post-normative translingual framework, which can serve as an alternative to the native-nonnative dichotomy in a time of

---

6 Although a spacial metaphor of *third space* or *third place* is sometimes criticized for reflecting a view of languages as static or discrete entities, it can be interpreted as a metaphoric zone where multilingual agents dynamically exercise their symbolic competence by activating hybrid perspectives and changing social reality (Kramsch 2009; Kramsch and Uryu 2012).

multilingualism, mobility, (super)diversity, and globalization. Translingual speakers and writers go beyond the confines of one language, integrate multiple linguistic, cognitive, social, semiotic, pragmatic, and affective resources and perform their hybrid identities in a third place (Bhabha 1994; Kramsch and Uryu 2012) or "sociocultural in-betweenness" (Canagarajah 2013: 3). Examples of translanguaging and translingual pedagogy have been illustrated based on data drawn from an increasing number of studies in this area. As these examples demonstrate, translingual practice can facilitate social solidarities among multilingual interactants in their relational work. Translingual practice can also activate intricate, intercultural, or more playful expression of translingual identities, thus, helping to expand their pragmatic, rhetorical, and communicative repertoires. Going beyond the deficit view of nonnative language users, the translingual framework has the potential to further advance our conceptual understanding of today's globalized contexts underlying the fields of intercultural and acquisitional pragmatics.

References

Ashcroft, Bob. 2018. An interview with Hugh Starkey. *The Language Teacher* 42(4). 23–26.
Baker, Will. 2016. Culture and language in intercultural communication, English as a lingua franca and English language teaching: Points of convergence and conflict. In Prue Holmes & Fred Dervin (eds.), *The cultural and intercultural dimensions of English as a lingua franca*, 70–89. Bristol: Multilingual Matters.
Bardovi-Harlig, Kathleen & Mahan-Taylor, Rebecca (eds.). 2003. *Teaching pragmatics*. Washington DC: Office of English Language Programs, U.S. Department of State. https://americanenglish.state.gov/resources/teaching-pragmatics (accessed 23 June 2020).
Bhabha, Homi. K. 1994. *The location of culture*. New York: Routledge.
Blommaert, Jan & Ben Rampton. 2011. Language and superdiversity. *Diversities* 13(2). 1–19.
Blum-Kulka, Shohana, Juliana House, & Gabriele Kasper. 1989. *Cross-cultural pragmatics: Requests and apologies*. Norwood, NJ: Ablex Publishing Corporation.
Braine, Gorge. 1999. *Non-native educators in English language teaching*. Mahwah, NJ: Lawrence Erlbaum.
Braine, Gorge (ed.) 2005. *Teaching English to the world: History, curriculum, and practice*. Mahwah, NJ: Lawrence Erlbaum.
Byram, Michael & Michael Fleming. 1998. *Language learning in intercultural perspective*. Cambridge: Cambridge University Press.
Canagarajah, A. Suresh. 1999. Interrogating the "native speaker fallacy": Non-linguistic roots, non-pedagogical results. In George Braine (ed.), *Non-native Educators in English Language Teaching*, 77–92. Mahwah, NJ: Lawrence Erlbaum.
Canagarajah, A. Suresh. 2011. Translanguaging in the classroom: Emerging issues for research and pedagogy. *Applied Linguistics Review* 2(1). 1–28.

Canagarajah, A. Suresh. 2013. *Translingual practice: Global Englishes and cosmopolitan relations*. New York: Routledge.

Cohen, Andrew. D. 2005. Strategies for learning and performing L2 speech acts. *Intercultural Pragmatics* 2(3). 275–301.

Cohen, Andrew D. 2012a. Comprehensible pragmatics: Where input and output come together. In Mirosław Pawlak (ed.), *New perspectives on individual differences in language learning and teaching*, 249–261. New York: Springer.

Cohen, Andrew D. 2012b. Research methods for describing variation in intercultural pragmatics for cultures in contact and conflict. In J. César Félix-Brasdefer & Dale A. Koike (eds.), *Pragmatic variation in first and second language contexts: Methodological issues*, 271–294. Amsterdam: John Benjamins.

Cohen, Andrew D. 2018. *Learning pragmatics from native and nonnative language teachers*. Bristol: Multilingual Matters.

Cohen, Andrew D. & Elite Olshtain. 1981. Developing a measure of sociocultural competence: The case of apology. *Language Learning* 31. 113–134.

Cohen, Andrew D. & Elite Olshtain. 1993. The production of speech acts by EFL learners. *TESOL Quarterly* 27(1). 33–56.

Cohen, Andrew D. & Rachel L. Shively. 2007. Acquisition of requests and apologies in Spanish and French: Impact of study abroad and strategy-building intervention. *Modern Language Journal* 91(2). 189–212.

Cook, Vivian. 1999. Going beyond the native speaker in language teaching. *TESOL Quarterly* 33(2). 185–209.

Council of Europe. 2018. *CEFL companion volume with new descriptors*. https://www.coe.int/en/web/common-european-framework-reference-languages (accessed 30 May 2020).

Díaz, Adriana Raquel & Maria Dasli. (2017). Tracing the 'Critical' trajectory of language and intercultural communication pedagogy. In Maria Dasli & Adriana Raquel Díaz (eds.), *The critical turn in language and intercultural communication pedagogy: Theory, research, and practice*, 3–21. New York: Routledge.

García, Ofelia & Wei Li. 2014. *Translanguaging: Language, bilingualism and education*. Basingstoke: Palgrave Macmillan.

Holliday, Adrian. 2015. Native-speakerism: Taking the concept forward and achieving cultural belief. In Anne Swan, Pamela Aboshiha, & Adrian Holliday (eds.), *(En)countering native-speakerism: Global perspectives*, 11–25. Basingstoke: Palgrave Macmillan.

Houck, Noël & Donna Tatsuki (eds.). 2011. *Pragmatics: Teaching natural conversation*. Alexandria, VA: TESOL.

Ishihara, Noriko. 2018. Intercultural pragmatic failure. In John Liontas, Margo DelliCarpini; TESOL International Association (eds.), *The TESOL Encyclopedia of English Language Teaching*. Hoboken, NJ: Wiley-Blackwell. https://onlinelibrary.wiley.com/action/doSearch?AllField=ishihara&ContentGroupKey=10.1002%2F9781118784235 (accessed 5 August 2020).

Ishihara, Noriko. 2019. Identity and agency in L2 pragmatics. In N. Taguchi (ed.), *The Routledge handbook of SLA and pragmatics*, 161–175. New York: Routledge.

Ishihara, Noriko & Andrew D. Cohen. 2010. *Teaching and learning pragmatics: Where language and culture meet*. Harlow, England: Pearson Education.

Ishihara, Noriko & Andrew D. Cohen. 2015. *Tabunka rikaino gogaku kyouiku: Goyoronteki shidoeno shotai*. [Language teaching for multicultural understanding: An invitation to pragmatics instruction.] Tokyo: Kenkyusha.

Ishihara, Noriko, Sherrie. K. Carroll, Dennis Mahler & Amy Russo. 2018. Finding a niche in teaching English in Japan: Translingual practice and teacher agency. *System* 79. 81–90.

Ishihara, Noriko & Julia Menard-Warwick. 2018. In "sociocultural in-betweenness": Exploring teachers' translingual identity development through narratives. *Multilingua* 37(3). 255–274.

Jeon, Eun Hee & Tadayoshi Kaya. 2006. Effects of L2 instruction on interlanguage pragmatic development: A meta-analysis. In John M. Norris & Lourtes Ortega (eds.), *Synthesizing research on language learning and teaching*, 165–211. Amsterdam: Benjamins.

Kachru, Braj B. 1990. World Englishes and applied linguistics. *World Englishes* 9(1). 3–20.

Kamhi-Stein, Lia D. (ed.) 2004. *Learning and teaching from experience: Perspectives on nonnative English-speaking professionals*. Ann Arbor: The University of Michigan Press.

Kasper, Gabriele. 1992. Pragmatic transfer. *Second Language Research* 8(3). 203–31.

Kasper, Gabriele. 1997. The role of pragmatics in language teacher education. In Kathleen Bardovi-Harlig & Beverly Hartford (eds.), *Beyond methods: Components of second language education*, 113–136. New York: McGraw Hill Company.

Kasper, Gabriele. 2010. Interlanguage pragmatics. In Mirjam Fried, Jan-Ola Östman, & Jef Verschueren (eds.), *Variation and change: Pragmatic perspectives*, 141–154. Amsterdam: John Benjamins.

Kramsch, Claire. 2009. *The multicultural subject: What foreign language learners say about their experience and why it matters*. Oxford: Oxford University Press.

Kramsch, Claire & Michiko Uryu. 2012. Intercultural contact, hybridity, and third space. In Jane Jackson (ed.), *The Routledge handbook of language and intercultural communication*, 211–225. New York: Routledge.

Kumaravadivelu, B. (2012). Individual identity, cultural globalization, and teaching English as an international language: The case for an epistemic break. In Lubna Alsagoff, Sandra Lee McKay, Guangwei Hu, & Willy A. Renandra (eds.), *Principles and practices for teaching English as an international language*, 9–27. New York: Routledge.

Li, Wei. 2018a. Linguistic (super)diversity, post-multilingualism and translanguaging moments. In Angela Creese & Adrian Blackledge (eds.), *The Routledge handbook of language and superdiversity*, 16–29. New York: Routledge.

Li, Wei. 2018b. Translanguaging as a Practical Theory of Language. *Applied Linguistics* 39(1). 9–30.

Li, Wei & Wing Yee Ho. 2018. Language Learning Sans Frontiers: A Translanguaging View. *Annual Review of Applied Linguistics* 38. 33–59.

Liddicoat, Anthony. 2017. Interpretation and critical reflection in intercultural language learning: Consequences of a critical perspective for the teaching and learning of pragmatics. In Maria Dasli & Adriana Raquel Díaz (eds.), *The critical turn in language and intercultural communication pedagogy: Theory, research, and practice*, 22–39. New York: Routledge.

Liu, Jun. 1999. Nonnative-English-speaking professionals in TESOL. *TESOL Quarterly* 33(1). 85–102.

Mahboob, Ahmar (ed.) 2010. *The NNEST lens: Nonnative English speakers in TESOL*. Newcastle upon Tyne: Cambridge Scholars Press.

Manosuthikit, Aree & Peter I. De Costa. 2016. Ideologizing age in an era of superdiversity: A heritage language learner practice perspective. *Applied Linguistics Review* 7(1). 1–25.

Martínez-Flor, Alicia & Ester Usó-Juan (eds.). 2010. *Speech act performance: Theoretical, empirical and methodological issues*. Amsterdam: John Benjamins.

Matsuda, Aya. 2017. *Preparing teachers to teach English as an international language*. Bristol: Multilingual Matters.

Mazak, Catherine M. 2017. Introduction: Theorizing translanguaging practices in higher education. In Catherine M. Mazak & Kevin S. Carroll (eds.), *Translanguaging in higher education: Beyond monolingual ideologies*, 1–10. Bristol: Multilingual Matters.

Mazak, Catherine M. & Kevin S. Carroll. 2017. *Translanguaging in higher education: Beyond monolingual ideologies*. Bristol: Multilingual Matters.

McConachy, Troy. 2019. L2 pragmatics as 'intercultural pragmatics': Probing sociopragmatic aspects of pragmatic awareness. *Journal of Pragmatics* 151. 167–176.

Morgan, Brian. 2007. Poststructuralism and applied linguistics: Complementary approaches to identity and culture in ELT. In Jim Cummins & Chris Davison (eds.), *International handbook of English language teaching, Part II*, 1033–1052. New York: Springer.

Motha, Suhanthie. 2014. *Race, empire, and English language teaching: Creating responsible and ethical antiracist practice*. New York: Teachers College.

Olshtain, Elite & Andrew. D. Cohen. 1983. Apology: A speech act set. In Nessa Wolfson & Eliot Judd (eds.), *Sociolinguistics and language acquisition*, 18–35. Rowley, MA: Newbury House.

Olshtain, Elite & Andrew D. Cohen. 1990. The learning of complex speech behavior. *The TESL Canada Journal* 7(2). 45–65.

Park, Gloria. 2017. *Narratives of East Asian women teachers of English: Where privilege meets marginalization*. Bristol: Multilingual Matters.

Phillipson, Robert. 1992. *Linguistic imperialism*. Oxford: Oxford University Press.

Pinto, Derrin & Richard Raschio. 2007. A comparative study of requests in heritage speaker Spanish, L1 Spanish, and L1 English. *International Journal of Bilingualism* 11(2). 135–155.

Rampton, M. B. H. 1990. Displacing the "native speaker": Expertise, affiliation, and inheritance. *ELT Journal* 27(2). 259–273.

Saito, Yukie. 2019. *CEFR Companion Volume no dounyuno haikeito nihonno eigo kyouikueno ouyou* [The background of the introduction of CEFR Companion Volume and its application to English language education in Japan]. Paper presented at the Gengo Kyouiku Expo 2019 [Language Education Exposition 2019], Waseda University.

Swan, Anne, Pamela Aboshiha, & Adrian Holliday (eds.). 2015. *(En)countering native-speakerism: Global perspectives*. Bashingstoke: Palgrave Macmillan.

Tatsuki, Donna & Noël Houck (eds.). 2010. *Pragmatics: Teaching speech acts*. Alexandria, VA: TESOL.

TESOL. 2008. *Position statement on English as a global language*. https://www.tesol.org/about-tesol/press-room/position-statements/social-issues-and-diversity-position-statements (accessed 30 May 2020).

Train, Robert. W. (2003). The (non)native standard in foreign language education: A critical perspective. In Carl Blyth (ed.), *The sociolinguistics of foreign language classrooms: Contributions of the native, the near-native, and the non-native speaker*, 3–39. Boston: Heinle.

Young, Richard. 2019. Interactional competence and L2 pragmatics. In Naoko Taguchi (ed.), *Routledge handbook of second language acquisition and pragmatics*, 93–110. New York: Routledge.

Bruce Fraser
17 An introduction to discourse markers

Abstract: Discourse markers are words or phrases, such as *well, but,* and *frankly,* which usually occur at the beginning of an utterance and serve as conceptual glue which binds together the material from the preceding utterance to that of the following sentence. Though they are homophonous with lexical items, they are separate linguistic entities, with distinct meanings, and are essential for making a conversation sound natural and unstilted. While the second language learner will acquire these elements late in the acquisition process, they will encounter them early on and should become familiar with them. The goal of this chapter is to provide an overview of discourse markers and to briefly discuss teaching discourse markers in a second language.

Keywords: discourse markers, order of discourse markers, lexical words, grammaticalization

1 Introduction

It has been 34 years since the publication of Deborah Schiffrin's (1987) book in which she coined the phrase *discourse markers* (DMs) for words and phrases such as *but, therefore, to the contrary, anyway, oh, well, besides,* and *after all* when they are used pragmatically, to guide interpretation, rather than be used as lexical items. For example, in response to a request for how the speaker is feeling, the reply might be the following:

(1)   **Well**, frankly I'm not feeling too **well** today.

In this example, the first *well* is a DM indicating a self-assessment by the speaker, whereas the second *well* indicates the state of their health. Following Schiffrin's (1987) lead, dozens of scholars have written on this general topic, under various labels, in hundreds of publications. The purpose of this paper is to explain what these discourse markers are, what role they play in conversation, the progress which has been made in clarifying what constitutes the classes of DMs in contrast to ordinary lexical words (LWs), and finally, to briefly discuss teaching DMs in a second language (L2). Due to constraints on length, I will be unable to discuss the written versus spoken difference in the use of

DMs, and will not be able to discuss the role that prosody plays in identifying what specific role a DM is playing in a conversation.

I shall proceed as follows. First, I will characterize DMs and distinguish them from their lexical counterparts. Then I will define the three main categories of DMs in detail, showing how these may be used alone, as well as in conjunction with one another.

2 What are discourse markers?

I will assume that a spoken interaction of sequential utterances is composed as follows:

Speaker 1: Utterance (= Pre-Sentence$_1$ + Sentence$_1$)
Speaker 2: Utterance (= Pre-Sentence$_2$ + Sentence$_2$)

Each utterance has a *potential* sequence of two elements, even though one, or both elements can be missing. In the following examples, the initial utterance has no DMs present, while the second utterance has one or more. These are examples of utterances which contain DMs (in bold), but by no means do they exhaust the possibilities:

(2) Examples of discourse markers:
    a. A: [Silence]
       B: **Well**?

    b. A: How are you?
       B: **Oh, ok, But**, I am so tired.

    c. A: I don't like you.
       B: **Ok.** That's ok with me.

    d. A: I don't like you.
       B: **So, I mean, frankly**, what should I do about it?

    e. A: [Silence]
       B: **And, anyway, look**. Stop bugging me.

    f. A: I am ready to go.
       B: **Ok. But first,** I suggest we sit down.

g. A: You're stupid.
B: **Dammit, listen here!** You can't speak to me like that.

h. A: Are you going to help?
B: **Well, yes. But, honestly** you've got to be more honest.

DMs here are only in the second speaker's (B's) reply to A, though the first speaker's utterance may contain one or more. That there may be more than a single DM in some of the examples to follow may be because there is more than one point to be considered, or because emphasis has been placed on a particular function of a DM.

Schourup (1999) suggested a basic definition for DMs, one that I will also use. DMs are (a) words which occur in the pre-sentence part of an utterance; (b) are optional and may be deleted without altering the meaning of the sentence; (c) do not affect the truth conditions of the sentence which they precede; and (d) have an interpretation, which reflect aspects of the speakers' intentions in presenting the utterance.

Simply stated, DMs are the glue that holds the meaning of the utterance together and gives it character. DMs permit the second speaker to comment briefly on what is not explicitly spoken, to reduce vagueness, and create robustness. DMs are words/phrases used as guidelines or warning signals of what has been said, or what to expect in what follows, and they are essential for making a conversation sound natural and fluid, as opposed to robotic and stilted. They are used to connect what we say, to help us organize what we say, and to manage or express our attitude, or presage how the upcoming sentence is viewed by the present speaker. However, they do not affect the truth conditions of the sentence that follows.

DMs are homophonous with specific lexical items. Thus, the DM *well* sounds like the adjective *well*, the DM *but* sounds like the conjunction *but*, and the DM *listen* sounds like the verb *listen*. However, these DMs are not LWs but rather *pragmatic units* and have pragmatic functions which orient their interpretations. These pragmatic forms are located in specific positions in an utterance – usually initially – and, as far as I can determine, do not compete with LWs for a location, as in example (3):

(3) A: How are you?
B: **Well**, I'm not very **well**.

Here, the initial *well* is a DM, the final *well* is an adverb.

3 General properties of DMs

Before examining the specific properties of DM classes, I will present some of the general properties of DMs which have a pragmatic function as opposed to the similarly-pronounced LWs. **DMs** have properties associated with them that are different from those of their homophonous LWs. The use/function of the two contrasting linguistic forms do not overlap, and their definitions differ from the grammatical functions of their corresponding homophonous forms, although in some cases they are very close, as can be seen in (4) (LW, in italics; DM, in bold):

(4) a. LW: *well*
  (N) A shaft in the ground
  (V) Rise to surface, e.g. tears
  (ADJ) Kindly, appropriate manner
  (ADV) Pleasing, cause for thanks

  b. Discourse marker: **well**
  Expression of surprise or contemplation

The DM interpretation, albeit procedural, is sometimes close to one of the semantic meanings of the LW, as in (5):

(5) a. Close: *but* (DM – *disagreement*) vs. *but* (Coordinate Conjunction – *contrast*)
  b. Less so: *look* (DM – *pay attention*) look (Verb – *observe*)
  c. Distant: *well* (DM – *contemplative*) vs. *well* (Adverb – *excellently*)

DMs are inside of the pre-sentence; LWs are inside of the sentence, as in (6, First Speaker = A; Present Speaker = B):

(6) a. A: I don't like you.
   B: [*Well, and*] [you don't lie *very well.*]
  b. A: He will come.
   B: [*However,*] [he will have to get here *however* he can.]

DMs may occur alone or with several DMs much like a string of adjectives, as in (7):

(7) a. A: I don't like you.
   B: *Ok.*

b. A: I don't like Margie.
     B: *Oh, well. Ok. But, frankly*, I wouldn't broadcast it.

DMs occur only in one DM subclass and have one (perhaps broad) interpretation, while LWs may occur in two or more LW classes (the number may reflect the different sources for the word) (e.g., *well*; see discussion below on DM classes). DMs may be deleted without changing the sentence meaning though their absence may make the utterance meaning more vague or ambiguous. With a LW this is not usually possible, as in (8):

(8) A: Can I go now?
    B: (*Ok!*) I suppose you can.

DMs do not affect the sentence's truth conditions, and can be deleted without altering the sentence meaning, though their absence may create awkwardness, as in (9):

(9) A: I didn't lie.
    B: *Well*, lying is a very bad habit.

DMs are not usually modifiable by adverbs, as in (10):

(10) A: Can I go now?
     B: (*Quite/*Awfully) well, I suppose so.

DMs are often, but not always, repeatable, but there is usually a change of interpretation, as in (11):

(11) A: We have a problem.
     B: *Oh, oh*. That's serious.

DMs can stand on their own as a complete utterance, albeit in the Pre-Sentence, so long as no second term is required, or where the second term is understood, as in (12):

(12) *Oh. Damn! Well. Ok. But. And? So? Listen!*

DMs may occur in both A and B turns, but here we will consider the B cases only, as in (13):

(13) A: *Oh*, do you have a phone?
      B: *But* why do you ask?

DMs permit the second speaker to briefly convey a message that is not the main point of the utterance, but is deemed relevant for purposes of clarification at the moment, as in (14):

(14) A: I want to go.
      B: *Well* (=I don't know about that.) we'll have to see.

DMs originate conceptually in the pre-sentence position, but in some cases they may be optionally moved by the Present Speaker to the medial/final position. This move may alter the DM's interpretation, as in (15):

(15) a. A: They asked John to stay.
          B: But *instead* John left (*instead*.)

      b. A: I don't like that
          B: Well, *frankly* you have to change it, (*frankly*.)

DMs may have several related core meanings, but "covered" a single term (e.g., *so*), as in (16):

(16) a. A: Susan is married.
          B: *So* (Significance: she is no longer single, I guess.)

      b. A: John looks tired.
          B: *So* (Reason: Why doesn't he go home?)

      c. A: I have lived here 5 years.
          B: *So* (Verification: You were here in 2015?)

      d. A: We're finally here.
          B: Yes. *So* (Request: what would you like to do now?)

Acknowledgments such as *Sorry, Ok, Alright*, when standing by themselves, qualify not only as DMs but also as complete utterances.

4 Types of DMs

This section provides a summary of DMs with examples in different categories:
a. **Retroactive Discourse Markers** (RDMs). Retroactive messages presenting Present Speaker's (PS) (B) view of the First Speaker's (FS) (A) message:
Concern RDM (*oh, hmm, damn, wow, gosh*)
Consideration RDM (*well, hold it, let's see, wait a second, sure*)
Conclusory RDM (*ok, possibly, I agree, probably, doubtful*)

b. **Linking DM** (LDM). Linking Message presenting a PS challenge toward the FS.
Primary LDM (*and, but, so*)
Semi-Primary (*however, nevertheless, still, yet*)
Secondary LDM (*on the other hand, instead, besides, moreover, thus, therefore*)

c. **Proactive DM** (PDM). Proactive Messages reflecting the view of the PS towards the FS.
Summary PDM (*anyway, by and large, in particular, continuing, to repeat*)
Attention PDM (*look, listen, in fact, look here, hear me out, mark my words*)
Epistemic PDM (*y'know, I mean, I guess, when you think about it, personally*)
Commentary PDM (usually only one CPDM)
   Assessment Markers: *fortunately, admittedly, sadly, surely, luckily*
   Manner-of-speaking Markers (*bluntly (speaking), frankly, speaking*)
   Evidential Markers: *clearly, of course, surely, after all, certainly*
   Hearsay Markers: *reportedly, allegedly*
Illustrative PDM: *for example, before I forget, namely, to clarify*
Topic Marker PDM: *first, finally, in other words, incidentally, next*

With few exceptions, if a PDM occurs, it occurs in the relative order shown above. Although seldom found, there may be "in principle," 3 RDMs, 2 LDMs, and 2–3 PDMs for a total of eight DMs strung in a row before the sentence of the utterance.

4.1 Retroactive discourse markers

Retroactive Discourse Markers (RDMs) are DMs which occur in the utterance-initial position and have the effect of "looking back at and commenting on" the previous discourse, hence the term "Retroactive DMs." There are three subtypes of RDMs. I will be discussing the primary RDMs (in bold) for each subclass and will use them for most examples, but others could be substituted.

(17) Concern RDMs: **oh**, *oh man, gosh, phooey, really, wow*
Consideration RDMs: **well**, *hold it, let's see, maybe so, well now, wait*
Conclusionary RDMs: **ok**, *yes, yup, no, nope, possibly, probably*

These RDMs occur alone (*oh*), in string of subclasses (*oh-well-ok*), in multiple tokens drawn from the members of a subtype (*oh, gosh, really*), and in various combinations of these (*oh, gosh, really, well, ok*) before the sentence in the utterance.

The RDMs form a strict order – Concern, Consideration, Conclusionary –, although there are cases where two or three members from the first class and one from the third class occur, and so on. What you do *not* find, however, is a mixing of the subclasses. Except for the first members (*oh, well, ok*), which are viewed to be the most representative member of each subclass, the members within each subclass are not ordered. There are, of course, exceptions: dialect; preference, etc. DMs occur almost exclusively at the beginning of the present speaker's (PS) turn. (There may be DM, in a preceding utterance, but that is not our concern here.) The RDM signals what information has been interpreted "retrospectively" and in doing so, the speaker sets the stage for what comes next.

These RDMs typically occur with one, two, or three members, with each individual RDM spoken by signaling a sense of how the PS has heard the former speaker's (FS's) contribution. The following examples are illustrative, as in (18):

(18) a. A: I broke the window.
B: **Oh, well.., ok**. I guess you can pay for it.

b. Oh: B's surprise/irritation at what was just uttered.
Well: B's contemplation of what to do.
Ok: B's agreement of what to do.

Each member of a subclass does the same sort of work in providing the interpretation of the situation from the speaker's viewpoint, but each of the three classes relates to a different sort of concern. The use of RDMs from successive subclasses builds up a coherent view, as illustrated above. However, depending on the intonation and stress on both the RDM as well as the following sentence, the interpretation of the utterance can be taken to be very different.

The acceptable RDM initial subclasses sequence (e.g., *oh, oh well, well ok, . . .*) are as follows, with or without punctuation. Table 1 presents spoken data from the

Corpus of Contemporary American English and shows which RDM combinations occur and with what frequency.[1]

Table 1: Description of discourse markers.

RETROACTIVE DMS	
DM(s) (Number)	Example
Oh (>100k)	**Oh,** just stop it.
Well (>100k)	**Well,** you've got an idea.
Ok (>100k)	**Ok.** Tell me about it.
Oh + well (>100)	**Oh, well.** Take another one.
Well + ok (>50)	**Well, ok.** You can stop here.
Oh + ok (>40)	**Oh, ok.** Here it is.
Oh + well + ok (4)	**Oh, well. Ok.** Don't leave..

Compound RDMs from same Sub-Class		
Oh, come on	A: I'm stuck.	B: **(Oh,) come on**. You're ok.
Oh, my God	A: I can't move.	B: **(Oh,) gosh**. But try again.
Oh, really	A: I'm not hungry.	B: **(Oh,) really**. So, I'm not surprised.
Oh, wow	A: He is here.	B: **(Oh,) wow**. That's great. And on time.
Well, wait.	A: I feel rushed.	B: **Well, wait**, but don't panic
Well, let's see	A: I am ill.	B: **Well let's see**. Where is you seat?
Well, maybe	A: I'm sick.	B: **Well, maybe** just take a seat.
Ok, yup	A: I am free now.	B: **Ok, yup**, take it away.
Ok, sure	A: Can I leave.	B: **Ok, sure**. Just take you dog with you.
Ok, probably	A: Are we here?	B: **Ok, probably**. But be careful.

---

1 The number after each combination is the number of spoken examples in the COCA Corpus, rounded off. The data is all spoken, taken from the latest version of the COCA and from observed conversation. No analysis is proposed here to explain the differing interpretations of these cases.

4.1.1 Combinations of primary-secondary RDMs from the same subtypes

Every RDM subclass has secondary members of the subclass that may occur initially or occur with another member of the subclass, thereby strengthening the interpretation (e.g., Concern: *oh gosh, hey man, gosh*). A Secondary RDM may occur with the Primary RDM from the same subcategory. The question of how the listener feels when there are one or two subclass members, as in (19), remains unanswered:

(19) a. Oh (*wow, damn, gosh, aha, Jesus*)
   A: This hurts.
   B: **Oh, gosh**. You seem ok to me.

   b. Well (*hold it, let's see, wait a second, sure*)
   A: What is this?
   B: **Well, let's see**, it looks like a joint.

   c. Ok (*yes, yup, I agree, probably, no, sure*)
   A: May I see that.
   B: **Ok, sure**. You may in fact have it.

And, the double-member from one subclass can be sequenced with another class's double-member former pair, as in (20):

(20) a. A: This hurts.
   B: **Well, let's see. Ok, yes,** it seems ok to me.

   b. A: I can't go.
   B: **Oh gosh, damn it. Well**. I was really hoping you would come.

I would say this is much like the stringing together of adjectives; some orders are fine, some are strange (Vendler 1968).

These DMs may occur by themselves to indicate one or more aspects of the speaker's understanding (in italics) of the preceding conversation, or in concert, as in (21):[2]

---

[2] Note that while "yes" and "no" are members of the third RDM category, "Conclude," they are often used by a second speaker as standing for an entire sentence. Also not discussed here is the fact that RDMs can convey very different meanings depending on the stress, intonation, and pauses of a given combination.

(21) a. **Alone**
   A: Please stop.
   B: **Oh**, if you insist.
   Concern

   A: Come here.
   B: **Well**, if you insist.
   Consider

   A: Stop.
   B: **Ok**, if you insist.
     Conclude

b. **Combinations**
   A: I want to keep that cat.
   B: **Oh my god,**   **no.**   Take it out of here.
      Concern   *Conclude*

   A: [Silence]
   B: **Well,**   **I agree.**   Your silence strongly suggests contempt.
      Consider   *Conclude*

   A: Do you want to marry me?
   B: **Oh, my**   **let's see**   **Yes**   Of course I want to.
        Concern   *Consider*   *Conclude*

c. **Multiple Combinations**
   A: May I leave.
   B: **Oh, oh my God.**   **Ok, by all mean, yes.** Go right now.
        Concern   *Conclude*

4.1.2 Linking discourse markers

The second class of DMs is Linking Discourses Markers (LDMs). They signal a major change in the PS's perspective of the topic presented in the foregoing utterance. There are four primary types, as in (22):

(22) Primary types
   a. **Contrastive:**
      A: Jack doesn't want to come with us.
      B: **But**! I don't really give a damn.

b. **Elaborative**:
   A: I made Jake angry.
   B: **And** – what the devil did you say to him to make him so mad?

c. **Inferential**:
   A: I don't like Melrose.
   B: **So**. Don't worry. We won't visit her today.

Notice that the *but, and, so, or* in the above example are not coordinate conjunctions. Rather, the *but* is a LDM providing a dissonant sense, a rejection from the Speaker of what had preceded, and this is supported by the subsequent sentence. Similarly, the *and* in the example above has the sense of challenging what A said, which is captured by uttering the following sentence. The *so* in the next-to-last sentence has the sense of B stating that A's feeling about Melrose is sufficient to not schedule a visit. The *or* suggests an excuse. When talking about the primary DMs, I do not mean the LWs referred to conjunctions *but, and, so* as in *John loves Mary but/and/so Harry loves Susan*. The words in the following examples do not represent conjunctions but rather Proactive Linking Discourse Marker (PLDMs), as in (23):

(23) a. A: John planted onions today.
        B: **But, come now**, why in the world would I stop him?

   b. A: He planted onions.
      B: **And**, I really can't believe it.

   c. A: He doesn't like onions.
      B: **So**, I imagine he won't be eating them.

   d. A: He is going to sell the onion.
      B: **Or**, is that just a guess?

As stated above, there are four types of Linking Discourse Markers: Contrastive LDMs, Elaborative LDMs Inferential LDMs and Disjunctive LDMs. Within each type, there are two subtypes: Primary and Secondary LDMs. Below I show that each of the Secondary LDM verbs, a different group associated with each of the four classes of LDM, in fact co-occur with all of the Primary LDMs.

4.1.2.1 Contrastive linking DMs
These DMs signal that the content of sentence 2 (S2) expands on the interpretation of sentence 1 (S1).

Primary CLDMs – General contrast: *but*
Secondary CLDMs – (*alternatively, in contrast, in comparison, conversely, instead, rather, on the other hand, on the contrary, in spite of*) [Only 10 of each case listed here]

(24) A: You are wrong.
B: (**But**) (**On the other hand**), I am sympathetic to your cause.

Note: Semi-Primary CLDMs (*however, nevertheless, still, yet*) – These are both general contrast DMs (like *but*), but may also follow *but* in discriminating a particular type of contrast.

(25) A: You are wrong.
B: **But, nevertheless**, I am sympathetic to your cause.

And, in addition, a Semi-Primary CLDM may occur alone with a Secondary CLDM following it, as in (26):

(26) A: You are wrong.
B: **Nevertheless**, rather than argue, I'm leaving.

4.1.2.2 Elaborative linking DMS (ELDMs)
Elaborative linking DMs signal that the content of S2 expands on the S1 meaning.

Primary ELDMs – General expansion or elaboration: *and*

(27) A: The project is finished.
B: I am delighted.

Secondary ELDMs – Indicate the specific nature of expansion of S1 (*above all, also, at any rate, furthermore, in other words, moreover, similar, in addition to, besides, likewise*)

(28) A: The project is finished.
B: (**And**) **Furthermore**, I am delighted.

4.1.2.3 Inferential linking DMs (ILDMs)

Elaborative linking DMs signal the content S2 is implied by S1.

Primary ILDMs signal a general implication of S2 that may follow from S: *so*.

Secondary ILDMs Indicate the specific nature of the implied (*therefore, thus, then, given that, as a result, as a consequence, consequently, as a conclusion, for that reason, accordingly*). See example (29):

(29) A: Henry has arrived. **So (as) a result**, we may expect confusion.

Note that each Secondary LDM may co-occur each of the four Primary LDMs, with the result that there are more than a hundred combinations (*but instead, but besides, but thus, but maybe*, etc.).

There are several other matters of note. First, the four Primary LDMs do not freely occur in PLDM-PLDM combinations (e.g., *but + and*) with normal intonation. However, if there is stress on the first PLDM and a pause thereafter, the utterance is sometimes acceptable (cf. Lohman and Koops 2016).

(30) Contrastive Primary LDM (*but*) – Inferential Primary LDM (*so*)
   A: I didn't like it there.
   B: **But. . .so** why did you stay?

(31) Primary LDM (*and*) – Contrastive Primary LDM (*but*)
   A: Mary wanted to go.
   B: **And. . .(sigh) but** I couldn't get her a ticket.

(32) Second, the PLDMs of one class may often occur with a SLDM from a different class:
   B: You are being crude.
   A: Shut up.
   B: **But moreover**, don't talk like that.

   A: I just can't learn this stuff.
   B: **And thus**, you must apply yourself.

   A: I don't drink milk.
   B: **So, instead**, you drink beer?

Third, there is generally a bleaching (weakening the force) of a Primary LDM if a Secondary LDM immediately follows, as in the examples in (33):

(33) A: He missed the meeting today.
B: **But instead**, he can go tomorrow.

A: I won't go to Mary's house
B: **And besides**, you can't go anymore..

A: We don't seem to have bus fare.
B: **So thus**, I guess we'll have to stay.

Here, the *but* in the first sentence is playing more of a connecting rather than contrasting role in the sequence. In fact, the primary linking DM is often used just to create a smoother transition of the discourse (see Oates 2000).

Fourth, for many of the Primary LDMs – Secondary LDM cases (but instead, and besides so therefore), the Secondary LDMs to be extra-posed to the middle or end of the utterance, as the examples in (34):

(34) A: He missed the meeting today.
B: **But instead**, he (**instead**) can go tomorrow (**instead**.)

A: I won't go to Mary's.
B: **And besides**, you (***besides**) can't go anymore (**besides**.)

A: We don't seem to have bus fare.
B: **So thus**, I guess we'll have to stay (***thus**.)

The interpretation of the first and third variation is mostly the same, but the second usually carries a different emphasis. The possibility of extra-position is not found for all cases, as shown.

Fifth, Secondary LDM sequences have not been studied very closely but there are several questions to ask: Do SLDMs from one class occur sequentially? There are cases of three LDMs co-occurring, usually consisting of leading PLDM followed by two SLDMs of the same class, as in the examples in (35):

(35) a. **But, rather, on the contrary**, this isn't very good. (3-CLDM)
b. **And, furthermore, in addition**, he forgot his tie. (3-ELDM)
c. **So, thus, as a result**, we lost the election. (3-ILDM)

There are also sequences, such as in (36):

(36) a. **On the other hand, in other words**, he's not very smart. (CLDM-ELDM)
b. **Consequently, instead**, we stop buying that. (ILDM-CLDM)

4.1.3 Proactive discourse markers

The third class of DMs, Proactive Discourse Markers, consist of six subclasses. Their purpose is to provide information about how the Present Speaker feels with respect to the content of the sentence about to be uttered. The swath of meaning is broad, as can be seen, and there is normally only one or two subclasses used. Proactive DMs Proactive Messages reflecting the attitude of the PS towards the FS (the following terms don't always occur in this order):[3]

4.1.3.1 Summary PDMs (*anyway, by and large, in particular, continuing, to repeat*)
(37) A: I'm ready to leave. But **that reminds me**, you are due for a bath, young man.

4.1.3.2 Attention PDMs (*look, listen, in fact, look here, hear me out, mark my words*)
(38) A: What are we going to do now that we're lost.
B: **Look,** stop bitching.

4.1.3.3 Epistemic PDMs (*y'know, I mean, I guess, when you think about it, personally*)
(39) A: Where are we now.
B: (Oh) **Y'know**. I haven't the slightest idea (y'know).

---

3 Note that some of the classes mentioned above (e.g., Epistemic PDM) might better be recognized as a different type of Marker. For my purposes here, I am treating them all as PDM, since I'm concerned with their relative position, rather than their meaning.

4.1.3.4 Commentary PDMs (There is usually only one CPDM, can be moved to the end of S) This is the name of the class which has four subclasses

a. **Assessment Markers** (*fortunately, admittedly, sadly, surely, luckily, obviously*)

(40) A: We got lost.
B: (But) **Fortunately**, a police officer happened by, fortunately

b. **Manner-of-speaking Markers** (*bluntly [speaking], frankly [speaking], candidly*)

(41) A: Mark, do something.
B: (Well) **Frankly** Harry, I don't know what to do.

c. **Evidential Markers** (*clearly, of course, surely, after all, certainly, conceivably*)

(42) A: Will he go?
B: (Yes) **Certainly**, he will go (certainly).

d. **Hearsay Markers** (*reportedly, allegedly, . . .*

(43) A: Where is he?
B: **Reportedly**, in bed.

4.1.3.5 Illustrative PDMs (*for example, before I forget, namely, to clarify*)
(44) A: What can we use for a guide?
B: (Well) **for example**, let's use this.

4.1.3.6 Topic Change Marker PDM (*first, finally, in other words, incidentally, turning, next*)
(45) A: Where do we go from here?
B. **First**, let's summarize where we are.

Most cases have at most two PDMs, and I have not found all six subclasses occurring in a single sequence. The subclasses of PDM are not as cohesive as the first two subclasses, although they seem to pattern in the order suggested above. Again, prosody permits some variation, as in the examples in (46):

(46) A single PDM (with/with another DM)

A: There isn't any more food.
B: **(So,) Anyway**, let's go home (anyway).

A: I'm hungry.
B: **(But) Listen**. I don't care.

A: Jack looks woozy.
B: **(Well) Reportedly**, he drinks too much (reportedly).

A: We have to improve our service.
B: **(So) Ok**. For example, let's use the big glasses.

(47) Two of more PDMs (with other DMs)

A: I really like Jack.
B: **In truth, honestly**, he can't be trusted.

A: Thanks a lot.
B: **But, look, first** let me thank you.

A: Is there anything more today?
B: **In fact, before I forget**, why not try these gloves.

A: What's new?
B: **Oh, but listen**. Did you know about the new bar in town.

5 Sequences of classes of discourse markers

To this point, I have dealt primarily with the three classes of DMs although some examples have involved DMs from more than one class. Now I want to discuss the ways in which they combine.

5.1 RDM + LDM + S2

Any combinations of RDMs (*oh, well, ok, oh ok, well ok, oh well ok*) may occur prior to a Primary LDM, but not usually before a PLDM + SLDM, or a SLDM alone, as in (48):

(48) A: I want to help you.
    B: **Oh, but (*instead)** you're not old enough.

    A: I wanted to help you.
    B: **Ok. So (*besides)** why didn't you do so?

5.2 PLDM + RDM + S2

This is a combination of a PLDM, only, followed by one of more RDMs, as in (49):

(49) A: You were elected.
     B: **But (*still) oh (well).** Not a surprise.

     A: You know you lied to the cops.
     B: **And (*besides) well (Ok).** I am truly sorry.

     A: Three, two, one.
     B: **(So) Ok. (*Therefore,)** time to go, Chris.

A sentence sequence such as, "I lied to the police. And oh how I paid for it later," is analyzed as a conjoined sentence, with the second sentence beginning with the DM *oh*.

5.3 RDM + PLDM + RDM + S2

There is a third possibility here, a sequence of RDMs with a LDM in between them, as in
    RDM + PLDM + RDM + S2 [keeping the same order of RDMs], as in the examples in (50):

(50) A: How dare you say that. **Oh, but well**, I'm sorry if I said anything rude.

     A: I don't want to go. **Oh but ok**. I'll see to the change.

     A: I'm really offended.
     B: **Well, but ok**. I apologize for saying that.

     A: I think John is cheating.
     B: **Oh but well ok**. He too dumb to pass anyway.

In addition, the same RDM does not occur before and after a LDM, as in (51):

(51)   *****Oh But *oh** just go ahead and do it.
     *****Well And *well** tell them that you're coming
     *****Ok. So, *Ok** why don't we stop here?

Note that any variation in their strict order (Oh, but is he smart? vs. But oh, is he smart!) may result in a change in the DM interpretation, especially when accompanied by a change in intonation.

5.4 RDM – PDM + S2

Here one or more RDMs occur before one of more PDMs, with no LDM in between, as in (52):

(52) A: Harry is a real creep.
B: **Ok. Look**, Harry is really a nice guy.

A: I'm cold and hungry.
B: **Well, listen**. We're lost.

A: Do you like my brother?
B: **Oh, well, frankly**, your brother is a creep.

5.5 LDM – PDM – S2

The case of PLDM + PDM + S2 is quite straightforward, as shown in (53).

(53) A: I washed the dishes. B: **But *(however), listen** you should have left them.
B: **So, *(therefore), that said**, why didn't you go.

5.6 RDM – LDM – PDM + S2

The following is a collection of various examples which have at least one member of each DM class used by a Present Speaker before conveying a responding utterance in (54).

(54) A: I love you.
B: **Oh, but listen, quite honestly** I really loathe you.
A: Can't we please stop now?

B: **Ok. But look**, I don't have any money.

A: Stop!

B: **Well! And** who **the devil**, do you think you're talking to?

6 Conclusion

In this chapter, I have not considered how stress and intonation come into play in the interpretation of utterances containing DMs, especially RDMs, since this is a complicated issue and would take up more space than is permitted here. Suffice it to say, there are some serious alterations in interpretation when there is a change in prosody. This makes the interpretation of RDM an interesting challenge.

However, I have attempted to make clear in this brief presentation that there is a large class of items in English called *discourse markers*, which are homophonous with lexical items, but which have different functions and interpretations. Words like *oh, well, but, so, listen, first*, and so forth are normally in utterance-initial position, before the main sentence of the utterance, and in a fixed order; they serve to reflect attention on the past speaker's utterance as well as convey the present speaker's view of the sentence about to be spoken in response. They modulate the message.

I have spoken of a number of types of DMs, the interaction of DMs, and particularly their order initially in an utterance, which they provide modulation for the main sentence. I have not addressed whether all the DMs should fall under the rubric of "DM," or even whether they all belong to the same "branch" of pragmatics. This is a subject for another time (see Traugott 2020).

I don't believe for a moment that what has appeared above is the final, correct analysis. There are sentence-final analyses (Haselow 2019), statistical analyses (Koop and Lohman 2016), historical analyses (Traugott 2020), non-English analyses (Pons Bordería and Loureda Lamas 2018), and many other analyses which are partially or fully under a different initial framework.

Finally, I want to comment on the usefulness of being aware of DMs when it comes to teaching a second language. The important thing for L2 learners to know about DMs is that they exist in all languages and that it is important to notice how they work, both in one's own language and in the new language. As DMs act as modulators/boosters of the main message of the sentence, the learner's ability to key into that messaging system will greatly improve his/her second language fluency.

Acknowledgements: I wish to thank Elizabeth Traugott, Haj Ross, and Polly Ulichny for their many constructive comments on this paper.

References

Haselow, Alexander. 2019. Discourse markers sequences: insights into the serial order of communicative tasks in real-time turn production. *Journal of Pragmatics* 146. 1–18.

Lohmann, Arne & Chris Koops. 2016. Aspects of discourse marker sequencing – empirical challenges and theoretical implications. In Evelien Keizer, Gunther Kaltenböck, & Arne Lohmann (eds.), *Outside the clause: Form and function of extra-clausal constituents*, 417–446. (Studies in Language Companion Series 178). Amsterdam: John Benjamins.

Oates, Sarah. 2000. Multiple discourse marker occurrence: Creating hierarchies for natural language generation. In *Proceeding of the 3rd CLUK Colloquium, Brighton*, 41–45.

Pons Bordería, Salvador & Óscar Loureda Lamas (eds.) 2018. *Beyond grammaticalization and discourse markers: New issues in the study of language change*. Leiden, Netherlands: Brill.

Schiffrin, Deborah. 1987. *Discourse markers*. Cambridge: Cambridge University Press.

Schourup, Lawrence. 2016 [1999]. *Discourse particles*. New York: Routledge.

Traugott, Elizabeth Closs. 2020. The development of "digressive" discourse-topic shift markers in English. In Benjamin Fagard & Michel Charolles (eds.), Special issue on topic shifters in a comparative perspective. *Journal of Pragmatics* 156. 121–135.

Vendler, Zeno. 1968. *Adjectives and nominalizations*. Berlin: De Gruyter Mouton.

Elite Olshtain
Epilogue: A personal tribute to Andrew Cohen

It is my pleasure to write a personal tribute to my friend and colleague Andrew Cohen.

I met Andrew and Sabina in Los Angeles in the early seventies of the previous century, but we really got to know each other and our families became friends when they moved to Israel and ended up living three buildings away from us. Our friendship grew out of our interests in applied linguistics, however, there was much more than that: we spent time together during holidays, local trips, and many other social events. Andrew and Sabina were always the center of the party: Andrew with his guitar and Sabina with her beautiful voice. We enjoyed their singing and we learned many songs from them, which are still cherished by our family. These were good times.

I really want to write in this brief tribute more about Andrew as a colleague and a partner in research and other academic activities. Firstly, one could not have a better colleague in the full sense of the word: I used to come home at the end of a long day at Tel Aviv University and often I would find, in my mailbox, a letter from Andrew telling me about a conference, a new publication, an article, or a book or something else that might interest me. As he used to live so close to us, on his way back from Hebrew University he would stop and put these bits of information in my mailbox, just *to share and support* a colleague and let's remember that this was before e-mail and WhatsApp and such communication was essential. *Only someone who really cares about people behaves like this.*

I was fortunate to work with Andrew on research projects. We wrote articles together and we appeared at conferences, sharing presentations, panels, and discussion groups. It was always an exhilarating experience: the collaboration, the energy, the commitment were so positive. There was always a feeling of mutual respect and appreciation and real joy in the achievements. You could not have asked for a better supporter and mentor and I remember these events as very pleasing memories.

Even after Andrew and his family left Israel we continued to work together and to meet at conferences or when visiting each other in our homes. Even if we came for a friendly visit during summer vacation or holidays there was always time for academic sharing and work and time for meeting friends and students.

I particularly cherish the memories of many conferences where in the evenings Andrew managed to arrange dinner with friends and students and my husband Zeev and I were very happy to join. It was a pleasure to see how many people liked Andrew and we were happy to spend time in his company. Such shared dinners were always multicultural, multilingual, and a very enriching gathering.

I wish Andrew and his family many more years of productive work and collaborations across the world. We sure miss him in Israel.

Elite Olshtain

Index

Acknowledgments 319
Advice-giving 16, 17, 28, 32–36, 39–41, 44, 48–52, 190
Advocates theoretically 287
Analog 198, 255
Appraisal 27, 28, 36–38, 42–50, 52
Attrition 237, 238
Awareness-raising 19, 61, 64, 81, 86, 124, 294

Backward 294, 296
Benchmark 290, 292, 293

co-construciton of knowledge 287
Collaborative practice 87, 94
Communicative and intercultural competences 238
Community 33, 59–62, 64, 65, 71, 73, 76, 103–105, 112, 114, 117, 120–122, 124, 137, 202, 236, 239, 243, 288, 293, 306
Compliment 11, 14, 16, 18, 19, 60, 63–65, 72, 81–84, 86–92, 94, 96, 97, 104–106, 108, 113, 117, 119–124, 136, 158, 275, 288, 295
Compliment responses 14, 16, 63, 64, 81–83, 86–89, 91–92, 96
Compliment strategies 87–91
Concept-based instruction (CBI) 239, 240
Concept-based pragmatics instruction (CBPI) 236, 237, 240–244, 246, 248
Context 12–21, 29–32, 51, 58–60, 62, 64, 68–70, 75–77, 81, 84, 91, 94–95, 98, 104, 105, 111, 113, 116, 117, 119–124, 132, 134, 136–138, 145, 146, 152, 158, 159, 173, 174, 179, 182, 188, 192, 198–202, 204, 209, 211, 213, 214, 216, 219, 232, 233, 238, 239, 242–244, 246, 248, 259, 260, 263, 273, 276, 277, 279, 280, 283, 287–292, 295, 302–304, 306, 307, 310
Conventional expressions 40
Conversational analysis 29, 276
Corpora 17, 18, 161, 203, 204, 275
Critical Discourse Analysis (CDA) 271, 272, 282
Cultural appropriateness 173

Digital discourse 198–204
Digital technologies 138, 199, 202
Directness 12, 32, 35, 39, 50, 59, 65, 66–68, 71, 74, 75, 133, 209–212, 215–217, 219, 220, 222–224, 227, 229, 230, 261
Discourse Completion Tasks (DCT) 17, 28–30, 63, 65, 67–73, 75, 76, 106, 132–137, 144–147, 149, 151, 156–176, 202, 204, 212, 257–260, 271, 274–277, 295, 301, 302
Discourse markers 314–335
Discursive approach 15, 16, 27, 29, 30, 134, 159, 286–296
Discursive pragmatics 29, 30, 51, 138, 150, 288–290, 296

EEG methodology 279, 280
Electroencephalography (EEG) 277–282
E-mail 208–233
E-mail perception 215
E-mail requests 208–233
English as a Lingua Franca (ELF) 272, 304
Environmental feedback 244, 245
Ethnographic 17, 59, 61, 62, 64, 73, 75–77, 83, 108–111, 120–121, 271, 275
Ethnographic analysis 271
Ethnography 58, 61, 62, 277
Event Related Potentials (ERPs) 278, 279, 282
Explicit instruction 18, 20, 21, 58, 65, 76, 84, 294
Explicit knowledge 132, 135, 142–144, 146–151, 174, 255–267, 295
Explicit pragmatic knowledge 146, 147, 152, 256, 259, 260, 266
Eye-tracking 198

Face-threat 32, 105, 107, 117, 121
Feedback 19, 58, 61, 75–77, 87, 98, 162, 210, 211, 220, 223, 229, 239, 244–246
Formulaic expressions 39, 50, 175, 294, 295
Formulas 11, 96, 105, 134, 136, 148, 149, 292
Forward-looking processes 294
Functional Magnetic resonance Imaging (fMRI) 277, 278, 280–282

https://doi.org/10.1515/9783110721775-020

Game-enhanced CBPI intervention 242
Game-enhanced learning 236–248
–game-enhanced CBPI 241–244, 246
Gender differences 103, 107, 121, 123, 124, 209
Gender variation 109–111, 119
Generic practices 296
Gesture 12, 15, 94, 120, 138, 199, 202, 289
Globalization 270, 272, 274, 282, 301, 303, 310
Grammatical competence 75, 238, 239
Grammatical functions 317

Hashtags 197, 199–202
Heterogloss 44, 49–51
Heteroglossic discourse 49
Host family 63–65, 69–73, 76, 91
Humor 138, 156–176
Humor perception 169, 171, 172
Humor production 156–176
Humor strategies 175

Identity 137, 190, 212, 271, 274, 277, 283, 288, 289, 291, 308
Identity formation 288, 291
Ideology 271, 274, 283, 302, 307
Implicit instruction 18–21
Implicit knowledge 135, 142–152, 255–257, 260
Incongruity 158
Indexical meanings 293
Informal language learning
–attrition 237
In-game discourse 246
Instruction 12, 18–21, 28, 33, 34, 58–64, 67, 69, 71, 73, 75–77, 82, 84, 89, 96, 97, 113, 123, 124, 139, 147, 151, 163, 164, 175, 209, 213, 214, 216, 231, 233, 236, 237, 239, 240, 241, 245, 248, 259, 260, 262, 263, 266, 292, 294, 300, 302, 304, 305, 308, 309
Interactional competence (IC) 13, 20, 28, 136, 145, 150, 180, 286–291, 293–296, 304
Interactional resources 16, 20, 30, 135, 289, 291, 294, 295
Interactional sociolinguistics 277

Intercultural competence 13, 61, 238
Intercultural pragmatics (ICP) 273–275, 303
Intercultural speaker 13
Interlanguage 17, 19, 58, 68, 160, 176, 236, 259, 262, 270, 272, 278, 300–302, 305, 309
Interlanguage pragmatics 19, 58, 259, 270, 278, 300–302, 305, 309
Intersubjectivity 136, 287, 292

Language Learning Strategy Instruction 82
Language play 161, 239
Language-related episodes 262, 264, 266
Learner authentication 236–239, 241, 247, 248
Lexical items 314, 316, 334
Lexical words 314
Lexico-grammatical level 28, 49
Lingua Franca 272, 273, 292, 303, 304
Linking Discourses Markers 324
L2 Spanish 58–77, 81, 85, 123, 169, 171, 208–233, 295

Magnetic resonance Imaging 280
Metapragmatic 19, 64, 65, 97, 123, 124, 147–149, 151, 160, 198, 202, 289
Metapragmatic instruction 19, 123, 124
Metapragmatic judgment 147–149, 151
Mitigation 60, 69, 70, 75, 88, 89, 92, 93, 213–215
Modality 21, 36, 44, 260
Modeling 87, 94, 97, 98, 198, 304
Mood 28, 36, 37, 42, 44, 45, 48–50, 52, 163, 184, 192
Multi-competence analysis 275
Multimodal communication 277
Multimodal discourse analysis 277
Multiple-choice DCT 145, 146, 149, 259

Native 15, 16, 29, 30, 59, 61, 63, 71, 76, 81, 83, 86–88, 91, 93–95, 97, 99, 104, 123, 137, 143, 160, 184, 209, 211, 214, 215, 217–219, 222, 226–232, 258, 261, 273, 275, 277, 278, 280, 293, 295, 300–310
Neurons 278
Nonnative 259, 300–310

Noticing 19, 76
Noticing hypothesis 19

Oral DCT 63, 65, 70, 76, 135, 146, 147, 174, 257, 260, 275
Oral proficiency interview 131, 179–182, 192
Other-directed humor 162

Pattern 17, 49, 83, 88, 97, 104–106, 111, 119, 121, 124, 149, 157, 158, 160, 175, 176, 181, 198–202, 204, 205, 230, 244, 262, 274, 282, 292, 296, 330
Pedagogical intervention 12, 18, 19, 21, 59–61, 64, 67, 68, 71, 76, 81–99, 124, 158
Perception 62, 64, 71, 75, 86, 94, 103, 104, 107, 108, 111–114, 117, 118, 121–124, 147, 158, 160, 161, 166, 168–173, 208, 209, 214–219, 222, 226, 231, 232
Piropos 103–124
Politeness 12, 13, 17, 32, 70, 71, 74, 75, 107, 133, 138, 144, 181, 209, 211–219, 222, 226, 228, 229, 231, 232, 259, 274
Pragmalinguistic 12, 17–19, 27, 30, 33, 34, 39–41, 58, 64, 85, 87, 95, 98, 103, 104, 107, 109, 111, 113, 114, 119, 124, 132, 134, 145, 150, 192, 198, 208–233, 255, 263–265, 267, 288
Pragmalinguistic competence 12
Pragmalinguistic forms 19, 30, 41, 58, 64, 95
Pragmalinguistic variation 103, 104, 107, 111, 113, 114, 119, 124, 208–233
Pragmatic competence 11–21, 27, 32, 58, 61, 62, 75, 82, 84, 98, 123, 124, 131–139, 144, 152, 180, 182, 184, 187, 190–192, 198, 232, 248, 301, 304
Pragmatic development 16, 18, 19, 58, 60, 62, 72, 73, 77, 84, 85, 201, 205, 303
Pragmatic-discursive approach 15, 16
Pragmatic functions 19, 201, 317
Pragmatic instruction 12, 18–20, 60, 62, 82, 96
Pragmatic knowledge 12, 58, 61, 85, 143, 146, 147, 151, 152, 182, 256, 259, 260, 265, 266, 275
Pragmatic units 316
Proactive Discourse Markers 329
Proactive Messages 320, 329

Rationalist approach 133, 288
Recipient design 150, 179, 295
Requests 11, 12, 14, 16–18, 30, 58–77, 85, 113, 116, 120, 133, 137, 145, 146, 147, 150, 179, 184–189, 191, 208–233, 242–246, 262–266, 274, 279, 288, 289, 292, 308, 314, 319
Retroactive Discourse Markers 320–331
Retrospective verbal reports 258, 260–262
Role play 16–18, 28–30, 64, 87, 94, 99, 133–136, 138, 145, 149–151, 158, 179–192, 246, 260–262, 264, 271, 275–277, 289, 301
Roleplay 204
Roleplay 87, 94, 99, 179, 180, 187, 188, 192, 204
Routines 11, 28, 105, 119, 120, 136, 143–145, 148–151, 173, 181, 182, 241, 242, 246, 292, 308

Second language processing 277, 278
Self-directed humor 162, 166, 169, 173
Semantic-discourse level 28
Sentence meaning 318
Service encounter 13, 16, 59, 60, 62, 67–69, 74, 76, 136, 138, 203
Socialization 61, 76, 77, 308
Sociocultural expectations 12, 13
Sociopragmatic 12, 17–19, 64, 75, 96–98, 132–134, 145, 202, 209, 213, 229–232, 240, 255, 259, 262–266, 288
Sociopragmatic competence 12, 133, 232, 288
Sociopragmatic knowledge 12, 75, 209, 229, 231, 255, 259, 264, 265, 288
Spanish requests 58–77, 209, 213, 214, 218, 223, 227, 230, 232, 233
Speech act 11–21, 27–52, 59–61, 63–65, 76, 81, 82, 84, 86, 88, 95, 96, 98, 103–106, 108, 109, 111, 113, 116, 117, 119, 120, 123, 124, 132–138, 143–146, 148–151, 156, 158, 159, 174, 179–182, 184–187, 190–192, 219, 232, 242, 259, 261, 265, 270–283, 289, 290, 292, 295, 296, 301–303, 309
Speech act sequences 15, 16
Strategic competence 138, 179–192

Study abroad 15, 19–21, 58, 85, 87, 91, 96, 97, 99, 123, 124, 209, 213, 214, 230, 233, 262, 295, 303
Superdiversity 272, 274, 277
Syntactic patterns 83, 88, 106, 121

Target-like use (TLU) 272, 275
Tasks 27, 28, 33, 34, 52, 61, 63, 65, 72, 75–77, 82, 84–86, 88, 89, 94, 95, 97–99, 106, 112, 113, 123, 132, 133, 135–138, 143–152, 156, 160, 163, 166, 173, 180–186, 188–192, 202, 204, 212, 215, 217–219, 232, 239–241, 248, 255–257, 259, 260, 264, 267, 275, 279, 281, 282, 292, 294, 295, 301

Transactions 13, 15, 59, 68, 74, 136, 182, 184–187
Translanguaging 306, 307, 310
Translingual 300–310
Truth conditions 316, 318

Voice 148, 149, 205, 271, 272, 283, 336

World-language enrollment
–attrition 237
Written DCT (WDCT) 30, 85, 87, 88, 96, 134, 135, 146, 174, 176, 257, 258, 260, 275

www.ingramcontent.com/pod-product-compliance
Lightning Source LLC
Chambersburg PA
CBHW070935180426
43192CB00039B/2199